THE U.S. CONSTITUTION

AND SECESSION

THE U.S. CONSTITUTION & SECESSION

A DOCUMENTARY ANTHOLOGY OF SLAVERY AND WHITE SUPREMACY

Edited by Dwight T. Pitcaithley

Foreword by Sanford Levinson

University Press of Kansas

Published by the University Press of Kansas (Lawrence, Kansas 66045),
which was organized by the Kansas Board of Regents and is operated
and funded by Emporia State University, Fort Hays State University,
Kansas State University, Pittsburg State University, the University of Kansas,
and Wichita State University.

Library of Congress Cataloging-in-Publication Data
Names: Pitcaithley, Dwight T., editor.
Title: The U.S. Constitution and secession : a documentary anthology of
slavery and white supremacy / Dwight T. Pitcaithley.
Description: Lawrence : University Press of Kansas, 2018. | Includes
bibliographical references and index.
Identifiers: LCCN 2018004097 | ISBN 9780700626250 (hardback) |
ISBN 9780700626267 (paperback) | ISBN 9780700626274 (ebook)
Subjects: LCSH: Constitutional history—United States—19th century—
Sources. | Secession—Southern States—History—19th century—Sources. |
Slavery—Law and legislation—History—19th century—Sources. | United
States—Politics and government—1857–1861—Sources. | United States—
History—Civil War, 1861–1865—Causes—Sources. | BISAC: HISTORY /
United States / Revolutionary Period (1775–1800). | HISTORY / United
States / Civil War Period (1850–1877). | POLITICAL SCIENCE /
History & Theory.
Classification: LCC KF4541 .P58 2018 | DDC 342.7308/7—dc23.
LC record available at https://lccn.loc.gov/2018004097.

British Library Cataloguing-in-Publication Data is available.

Printed in the United States of America

10 9 8 7 6 5 4 3 2 1

The paper used in this publication is recycled and contains 30 percent
postconsumer waste. It is acid free and meets the minimum requirements
of the American National Standard for Permanence of Paper for Printed
Library Materials Z39.48-1992.

For Sabette

~

Contents

Documents

～

Foreword

My enthusiasm for this collection of materials is almost boundless for three reasons. The first has to do with Dwight Pitcaithley's marvelous introduction. Let me simply say that I know of no comparable essay that so concisely and accessibly summarizes the constitutional issues raised by the decision of the Framers in 1787 and then afterward to make central compromises with regard to the institution of chattel slavery. There is obviously an extensive—and fine—literature on the subject, including Don E. Fehrenbacher's *The Slaveholding Republic: An Account of the United States Government's Relation to Slavery.* But for students looking for a shorter introduction to this extraordinarily important subject, they can literally do no better than to read the introduction to this volume.

Perhaps the central question of American constitutional history—and, for that matter, aspects of our constitutional present—is the extent to which William Lloyd Garrison, the notable abolitionist (who burnt the Constitution and advocated northern secession from the "slaveholders' republic") was correct in describing the Constitution as "a covenant with Death and an Agreement with Hell." This is obviously no small matter. It is tempting, for example, to view Roger Taney, the author of the Supreme Court's principal opinion in the notorious *Dred Scott* case, as exemplifying what Yale law professor Jack Balkin and I have labeled "judges on a rampage," that is, an "activist judge" who ruthlessly wrote his own political views into the Constitution. That view predominated at the time and thereafter. William Cullen Bryant at the time described it as a "perversion" of the Constitution; Charles Evans Hughes later described it as one of the three major "self-inflicted wounds" of the Supreme Court. But there is another point of view, held by scholars with no desire to defend the slave empire as such. Its most important articulation is Mark Graber's *Dred Scott and the Problem of Constitutional Evil*. For obvious reasons, it is easier to denounce purportedly renegade judges than the Constitution itself if one is upset about slavery-protecting decisions like *Dred Scott*. No one addressing this problem can be said to have spoken the "last word" on it, neither long books like Fehrenbacher's or the relatively short essay by Pitcaithley. But what I am confident in saying is that any careful reader of the latter will be fully prepared to consider the various points of view and to move on to the more extensive and detailed monographs.

The second reason for my enthusiasm is the fact that the book is laser-focused on a very short but all-important period of American history—the months between the November 1860 election of Abraham Lincoln as our first Republican president and his inauguration on March 4, 1861. It was during that time that the Union dissolved, beginning with the secession of South Carolina in December. By March 4, seven states had seceded (and four more would do so following Fort Sumter in April). Shelves of volumes have been written about whether this breakdown—and the bloody war that followed—was inevitable or whether sagacious statesmanship might have staved it off for a while longer. If it was inevitable, of course, the blame resides not so much with specific individuals as with the basic tension, what Lincoln would call the "house divided," built into the 1787 Constitution between slavery and freedom. It took time for the house to implode, but there really was no plausible alternative. William Freehling, in his magnificent book *The Road to Disunion*, refers to what most historians call "the Compromise of 1850" as more truly an "armistice" that bought ten more years of bitterly divided Union. So, from this perspective, even if there was nothing inevitable about the war breaking out in April 1861, it was destined to happen.

The alternative view, of course, is that human agency was crucial, so that the war could have been avoided, perhaps forever, by suitable negotiation. Anyone inclined to this latter view should find the documents compiled in this collection especially valuable. The central question is obviously whether there existed the basis for a negotiated settlement. Students of negotiations know that the last months—or, indeed, weeks and even days—are crucial before an irrevocable decision must be made. To be sure, it is helpful to put issues in a long-term perspective going back to their origin. But just as Samuel Johnson emphasized how the prospect of being put to death the next morning "concentrates [the] mind wonderfully," the prospect of the actual dissolution of the Union has the same impact. Between November and March, politicians had to become far less polemical and to weigh the actualities of the situation. In turn, they had to decide what was most important to them and what, perhaps, was open to genuine negotiation.

The documents make it quite clear what the central issues were. The most important, certainly, was whether Republicans would recant their insistence on preventing the further expansion into American territories. Lincoln had made it crystal clear that he would not challenge the legitimacy of slavery where it already existed. He was not in any serious sense an "abolitionist" if this meant immediately moving to end slavery in the United States. Indeed, he clung to fantasies of "compensated emancipation" that would have ended slavery only at the turn of the twentieth century. But, for whatever reasons, there was no possibility even of returning to the Missouri Compromise and its acceptance of slavery in territories south of 36° 30'. Slave owners believed that this denied them recognition as truly equal members of the polity, entitled to take to the territories their lawful property from their state of origin. Republicans, on the other hand, viewed it as an acknowledgment of the legitimacy of slavery. And, no doubt, what they really feared was not slavery in the Dakotas but slavery in areas of northern Mexico or Cuba that might well be captured by a reinvigorated Union under the sway of a slavocracy that was constantly looking for new territory to which to expand. There was no doubt that Cuba, especially, lay well south of 36° 30' and would make a welcome addition to a United States that saw no problems with chattel slavery so long as it didn't invade the North.

But there were other issues as well, as revealed in the documents. Would "free states" like Ohio or New York recognize their duty to accommodate slave owners in transit with their slaves from one slave state (say, Virginia) to another (say, Missouri or Louisiana)? It was clear that slave owners could not expect to settle in free states, but what about "sojourning" for several days or even weeks while waiting for an appropriate ship going from New York to Charleston or New Orleans? And, of course, there was also the "duty" of free states to return ostensible "fugitive slaves," themselves subject to a far more onerous law that was part of the Compromise/Armistice of 1850.

But Lincoln had also famously declared, in his "House Divided" speech, that *Dred Scott*, coupled with the *Lemmon* case before the Supreme Court in 1860, represented a conspiracy to "nationalize" slavery. No longer would the Union be composed of "slave" states and "free" ones (who had a duty, however, to return fugitives and to accept at least some measure of "sojourning"). Instead, *all* states would ultimately have to accept the legitimacy of settlement by citizens of other states and their slaves. A more "moderate" version of this argument was that states could prohibit slavery only by explicitly legislating to do so. Otherwise, the presumption would be in favor of slavery. As one might expect in such circumstances, it was antislavery forces that offered the most baleful interpretation of southern demands, while Southerners themselves attempted to appear more "reasonable." One might wonder, of course, whether the Southerners were entirely sincere. Had they achieved their demand of expansion into the territories and, along the way, demonstrated the pliability of the Republican Party, would they inevitably have escalated their demands at some future date by threatening to secede if the nationalization of slavery were not accepted? Who knows? But at least one can say that these documents are likely to present the sincere offers and counteroffers that were available during a brief period when secession had indeed become fully real and war fully thinkable.

But, as suggested above, there is a third reason I am so enthusiastic about this book. Readers are necessarily forced to wrestle with the overarching issue of compromise itself. This was obviously presented in 1787. We often see references to the "Great Compromise" by which the Philadelphia Convention acquiesced to equal state voting power in the Senate. As a matter of fact, James Madison, writing as "Publius" in *The Federalist*, denounced this as an "evil," but a "lesser evil" than would have been the case if Delaware and other small states had carried out their threat to walk out of the Convention. I suspect that most of us today are inclined to agree even if we are unhappy, as Madison definitely was, with a Constitution that gave Delaware and Rhode Island equal voting power with Virginia and New York.

But there was another compromise that rarely is described as "Great." It, of course, involved slavery, the sin that dared not speak its name but was, nonetheless, accommodated in three important ways. First, maintenance of the international slave trade was guaranteed until 1808. Then there was the 3/5 Compromise that gave slaveholding states unwarranted extra representation first in the House of Representatives and then the Electoral College (and, consequently, in the Supreme Court as well). Finally, there was the so-called fugitive slave clause that required "free states" to return poor wretches who, in the words of the Statue of Liberty, were "yearning to breathe free." What do we think of these compromises? After all, it is not as if no one at the time objected to them. Antislavery movements were already far more present than, say, movements concerned about the patriarchal subordination of women. That would come, of course, but we are entitled to say that almost all conventional wisdom of the time accepted that subordination. That was not the case with slavery, even if the opposition would surely grow in the next seventy-four years before 1861. Instead, just as with the Senate, the winning argument, as it were, was that prices had to be paid in order to get the Constitution and the ensuing United States, given the very real differences that challenged any easy picture of national unity. One price was acceptance of chattel slavery and the power of slave owners.

But then we have to confront a really terrible question: If the Compromises of 1787, including the ones involving slavery, were "worth it," according to some metric that we find satisfactory, then where does one draw the line? After all, the history of American slavery includes two subsequent "compromises," whether or not we wish to describe them as "great." The Missouri Compromise of 1820 accepted the legitimacy of slavery in that state and in all territories south of 36° 30'. And then there was the aforementioned Compromise of 1850 that included an enhanced, and even more tyrannical, fugitive slave law than the one originally passed in 1793, even as it admitted California as a free state and abolished the slave trade in the District of Columbia. So why not acquiesce to the southern demand in the winter of 1860–1861 for the largely symbolic agreement to accept slavery in any and all of the remaining territories? It should be clear from reading the documents that what defenders of slavery demanded was a full measure of respect as equal partners in the Union, and they believed, probably rightly, that adherents of the new Republican Party wished to deny them such respect. I am certainly not arguing that the slave owners were truly entitled to the respect they sought; I do not believe that is the case. But, then, I should also acknowledge my attraction to the Garrisonian understanding of the 1787 Constitution.

In our own time, we seem to be engaging in a near civil war, at least emotionally, over the respect owed the statues of Confederate "heroes" like Jefferson Davis and Robert E. Lee. I am not reluctant to see such statues removed from their places of honor, but we should recognize that not everyone agrees. It is disagreement over fundamental issues, whether slavery, abortion, or even the placement of public statuary, that elicits both the drawing of lines in the sand and the call by some to achieve some "compromise" that will allow us to live in peace with one another. There is, alas, no algorithm that dictates when lines in the sand should be honored or when concessions to one's adversaries should become the order of the day. "Compromise" does not require that one in fact change one's underlying positions about the goodness or evil of what is at issue; instead, it requires that one prefers peace to the prospect of violent contention or, as with secession, civic divorce.

So I would hope that readers of this wonderful collection would use its materials first of all to understand the very specific politics of 1860–1861 and the positions being taken by leading (and not so leading) figures of the North and South and then to move on to the far more general topic of compromise itself. *Should*, in the language of an old adage, "justice be done though the heavens fall," or should one be willing to sacrifice a certain measure of justice in order to prevent the heavens from falling?

Sanford Levinson
W. St. John Garwood and
W. St. John Garwood Jr.
Centennial Chair in Law,
University of Texas Law School,
and Professor of Government,
University of Texas at Austin

~

Preface

Although this nation has just finished commemorating the 150th anniversary of its nineteenth-century civil war, it is unclear whether that four-year effort shed increased light on the causes of the war and its long legacy. Arguments still rage over the nature of the Confederacy, the meaning of the Fourteenth Amendment, and the appropriate relationship between state and federal authority. Crucial to understanding the war is an understanding of secession. The election of the first Republican president in 1860 triggered the secession of seven southern states during the next several months. Following the Confederacy's bombardment of a federal fort in Charleston Harbor and Abraham Lincoln's call for 75,000 troops to put down the insurrection, four additional southern states seceded. Simply put, without secession there would have been no war. This book is designed to make sense of the South's need to secede after Lincoln's election.

A careful study of this period of political unrest reveals that contrary to contemporary notions that the South seceded to protect states' rights, the primary motivation driving secession was the preservation of the South's economic engine, slavery. By 1860, the slave South had convinced itself that the North was filled with abolitionists, that the Republican Party was, in fact, an abolitionist party, and that Lincoln's election meant the end of the southern way of life. The southern response to the rise of the northern antislavery party was not to demand an expansion of state authority but to argue for an expansion of federal sovereignty to protect the institution of slavery. *The U.S. Constitution and Secession* explains the centrality of slavery to the secession movement and slave states' demand for increased federal authority to protect their "peculiar institution" in the run up to the war.

Although other compilations of documents produced during Secession Winter of 1860–1861 exist, none focus on the subject of secession and the efforts at compromise to heal the sectional rift. William Freehling and Craig Simpson have provided valuable insights into the secession conventions of Georgia and Virginia through the publication of the essential speeches. See *Secession Debated: Georgia's Showdown in 1860* (1992) and *Showdown in Virginia: The 1861 Convention and the Fate of the Union* (2010). Jon Wakelyn's *Southern Pamphlets on Secession, November 1860–April 1861* (1996) reproduced twenty speeches and sermons between November 1860 and March 1861 that illuminate southern discontent. James Loewen and Edward Sebesta compiled many important nineteenth- and twentieth-century documents in *The Confederate and Neo-Confederate Reader: The "Great Truth" about the "Lost Cause"* (2010). The Library of America's *The Civil War: The First Year Told by Those Who Lived It* (2011) edited by Brooks Simpson, Stephen Sears, and Aaron Sheehan-Dean provides an extensive collection of primary sources from the first year of the war. This volume differs from these by digging deeply into the five-month period from Lincoln's election to the firing on Fort Sumter.

This examination of the secession crisis provides a detailed accounting of the methodical separation of North and South over the issue of slavery from Lincoln's election through his inauguration while providing sufficient historical context to make sense of the political debates during that period. I have attempted to slow down the action between Lincoln's election in November 1860 and the bombardment of Fort Sumter in April 1861 to reveal through speeches, proclamations, reports, and proposed solutions the essence of secession as it slowly unfolded over that fateful winter. This volume reproduces the critical documents that encourage the careful reader to understand secession from the perspective of those involved. Speeches in Congress, declarations of secession from four of the first states to secede, and the sixty-seven compromise proposals designed to prevent additional states from seceding make up the core of this book. In total, the documents included here illustrate the central role of slavery and white supremacy in the fracturing of the nation over the winter of 1860–1861.

~

Acknowledgments

My interest in the secession phenomenon began over two decades ago as a result of lengthy conversations with my friend and colleague James O. Horton. This book developed out of conversations with historian Darrell Meadows of the National Historic Publications and Records Commission. His support and advice are greatly appreciated. I am also indebted to Tony Curtis, Patrick Lewis, and Matthew Hulbert of the Kentucky Historical Society for their encouragement and careful reading of selected documents as well as an initial draft of the introduction. This project could not have been accomplished without the extraordinarily efficient team managing the Interlibrary Loan Department at New Mexico State University. Jon Hunner, Laura Feller, and Marie Tyler-McGraw offered constructive comments early in the process for which I am most grateful. Sanford Levinson provided a critical review that strengthened the manuscript immeasurably while Timothy Huebner's encouraging assessment validated my interpretation of the secession puzzle. Paul Finkelman's incredible knowledge of case law helped pin down a very vague reference. William Eamon not only assisted by translating numerous Latin phrases but also asked sharp questions which helped me clarify my own thinking about secession as we cycled the beautiful

Mesilla valley. Ann Huston, of Taos, inspired me with her art. To Sabette, my wife of almost fifty years, I owe more than I can express for her faith in me, her sense of humor, and her keen grammatical eye.

ACKNOWLEDGMENTS

Introduction

The memory of the Civil War still haunts this country. Scholars continue to churn out monographs, biographies, and analyses relating to the war. The Ken Burns documentary repeats on PBS on a regular basis. Deep-seated racist convictions continue to taint conversations about the future of the country and even infest political discourse. The long shadow of the war intrudes (or lurks in the background) every time a conversation turns to the politics of race. Even today, generations after Lee's surrender to Grant, the causes of secession and the significance of the Confederacy can prompt arguments about southern memory and identity.

Having just finished remembering the war on its 150th anniversary, the nation was again drawn into a debate over the Confederate battle flag and its links to violent racism in Charleston and Charlottesville. Defenders of the flag insist that the Confederacy should be remembered for its strong states' rights stance and not for its perpetuation of slavery. The South had to leave the Union, they rationalize, because an aggressive federal government was usurping authority constitutionally given to the states. The Confederacy was created, in other words, to protect the rights of states and not the property rights of slave owners. Attempts to separate the purpose of the Confederacy from racist ideology are based on a generations-old effort to construct an alternative history of the war that posits the Confederate States of America as an ardent defender of states' rights, a rhetorical construction wholly at odds with the historical struggles over slavery that divided the nation between 1848 and 1860.

The contention that the peculiar institution was merely a pawn in a larger contest for political power had its literary genesis in the 1866 classic, *The Lost Cause* by Edward Pollard.[1] Even more influential were the postwar writings of Alexander Stephens and Jefferson Davis. Stephens's *A Constitutional View of the Late War between the States* (1868) was the first postwar account by a high-ranking official of the Confederacy to suggest that differences over the institution of slavery were but "minor" points of disagreement between North and South. The war was, instead, "a contest between opposing principles; but not such as bore upon the policy or impolicy of African Subordination."[2] The Confederacy's vice president seemed to have forgotten that only seven years earlier he had proclaimed that slavery was "the immediate cause of our late troubles and threatened dangers."[3] Thirteen years later, Jefferson Davis published his version of the war in which he, too, sought to distance the Confederacy from the perpetuation of human bondage. Although many writers presented secession as an effort to "extend and perpetuate human slavery," Davis wrote that they were wrong. Davis claimed alternatively that "to whatever extent the question of slavery may have served as an *occasion*, it was far from being the *cause* of the conflict."[4] The Confederacy's president failed to mention that in his farewell address to the U.S. Senate, he took pains to announce that he agreed completely with Mississippi's decision to secede, which was based entirely on perceived threats to the institution of slavery.[5]

---

1. Edward A. Pollard, *The Lost Cause: A New Southern History of the War of the Confederates, Comprising a Full and Authentic Account of the Rise and Progress of the Late Southern Confederacy—the Campaigns, Battles, Incidents, and Adventures of the Most Gigantic Struggle of the World's History, Drawn from Official Sources, and Approved by the Most Distinguished Confederate Leaders* (New York: E. B. Treat, 1866).

2. Alexander H. Stephens, *A Constitutional View of the Late War between the States; Its Causes, Character, Conduct, and Results. Presented in a Series of Colloquies at Liberty Hall* (Philadelphia: National, 1868), 1:12.

3. George H. Reese, ed., *Proceedings of the Virginia State Convention of 1861: February 13–May 1, in Four Volumes* (Richmond: Virginia State Library, 1965), 4:385.

4. Jefferson Davis, *The Rise and Fall of the Confederate Government*, 2 vols. (1881; New York: Thomas Yoseloff, 1958), 1:77–78.

5. *Congressional Globe*, 36th Cong., 2nd sess., January 21, 1861, 487; *Journal of the Mississippi Secession Convention, January 1861* (1861; Jackson: Mississippi Commission on the War between the States, 1962), 86–88.

Preferring to remember the war as a noble effort instead of one focused on preserving and protecting a brutal (although inordinately profitable) institution, southern heritage groups picked up the themes presented by Stephens and Davis and, over the decades, constructed a counterhistory more palatable to white Southerners who wanted to remember the war as a glorious cause. As historian David Blight so eloquently illustrated in *Race and Reunion,* the Sons of Confederate Veterans, United Daughters of the Confederacy, and other pro-Confederate advocates devoted themselves for more than a century to the Pollard/Stephens/Davis objective of separating slavery from the causes of the war.[6]

The historical evidence of the discussions and debates this nation's elected officials conducted over the winter of 1860–1861 directly contradicts this contrived view of secession. Written history is based on evidence, evidence produced at the time of the event being studied. The evidence produced by Congress, state secession conventions, state legislatures, and other licit gatherings is extensive and detailed and provides the inquisitive student with vivid insights into the breakup of the Union.

The abridged account of Secession Winter, 1860–1861, is well known and oft-repeated. It begins with Lincoln's election in early November followed by the secession of South Carolina on December 20. Six additional states then declare their independence before Lincoln's inauguration on March 4. Five weeks later, Confederate artillery force the surrender of Fort Sumter, Lincoln responds by calling for 75,000 troops to put down the insurrection, four more states secede, and the war is on.

The retelling of those fateful five months between Lincoln's election and the firing on Fort Sumter is often compressed in order to get on with the dramatic story of the war itself. Even when the narrative is slowed down, details of the South's grievances are glossed over, and the string of events develops a pronounced sense of inevitability. The election of the first Republican president naturally led to the secession of the South, and secession naturally led to war. A greater understanding of this period can be attained when one accepts the advice of David Potter: "The supreme task of the historian is to see the past through the imperfect eyes of those who lived it and not with his own omniscient twenty-twenty vision."[7]

---

6. David W. Blight, *Race and Reunion: The Civil War in American Memory* (Cambridge: Belknap Press, 2001).

7. Quoted in Daniel W. Crofts, introduction to David M. Potter, *Lincoln and His Party in the Secession Crisis* (Baton Rouge: Louisiana State University Press, 1995), ix.

When the November to April chronology is examined day by day and week by week, as it was experienced historically, a deeper sense of clarity emerges. One discovers that beyond the hyperbole and accusations from North and South, the sectional crisis was fundamentally a constitutional crisis. By 1861, the events of the previous decade had led Northerners and Southerners to interpret the U.S. Constitution in inherently different ways over the degree to which it offered protection for the institution of slavery. As the South Carolina secession convention finalized its separation, its delegates declared that "fourteen of the States have deliberately refused, for years past, to fulfill their constitutional obligations, and we refer to their own Statutes for the proof."[8] Georgia echoed that belief by proclaiming that the northern states "have endeavored to weaken our security, to disturb our domestic peace and tranquility, and persistently refused to comply with their express constitutional obligations."[9] Texas's secession convention agreed by asserting that "the federal constitution has been violated and virtually abrogated" by the northern states.[10] Disagreements over the return of fugitive slaves, the protection of slavery in the western territories, the carrying of slaves into free states and territories, the inciting of slave rebellions, and more were all reflected in these revealing pronouncements. By November 1860, the sectional crisis had moved well beyond Congress's ability to resolve by legislative acts. For the advocates of slavery, nothing short of an amended Constitution would calm the roiling political waters.

President James Buchanan's former secretary of the treasury, Howell Cobb, clearly framed the issue in an open letter to the "People of Georgia" the month after Lincoln's election. The southern states believed, he argued, that the Constitution distinctly recognized the institution of slavery "as it exists in the fifteen Southern States," guaranteed the right of Southerners to take their slaves into the "common territories of the Union," and entitled the owner of slaves to "reclaim his property in any State to which the slave may escape."

---

8. *Journal of the Convention of the People of South Carolina, Held in 1860–'61, Together with the Reports, Resolutions, Etc.* (Charleston: Evans & Cogswell, Printers to the Convention, 1861), 328.

9. *Journal of the Public and Secret Proceedings of the Convention of the People of Georgia, Held in Milledgeville and Savannah in 1861* (Milledgeville: Boughton, Nisbet & Barnes, State Printers, 1861), 104–105.

10. *Journal of the Secession Convention of Texas 1861* (Austin: Austin Printing, 1912), 65.

By contrast, he asserted, the "Black Republican Party" claimed that slavery was not recognized in the Constitution, that the federal government was not "committed to its protection," and that property in slaves was not "entitled to the same protection at the hands of the Federal Government with other property." Republicans, he continued, believed that slavery was a moral, social, and political evil, that it was the duty of the federal government to prevent its extension, and that it was the responsibility of Congress to "prevent any Southern man from going into the common territories of the Union with his slave property." In his passionate letter designed to expose Republicans as abolitionists intent on using the power of the federal government to destroy the institution of slavery, Cobb presented the image of northern corruption. "They [Republicans] have trampled upon the Constitution of Washington and Madison, and will prove equally faithless to their own pledges. You ought not—cannot trust them. . . . Nothing now holds us together but the cold formalities of a broken and violated Constitution."[11] It was this political divide that prompted historian Michael Kammen to observe that the "presidential election of 1860 involved, as no other election before it in U.S. history, a national constitutional debate."[12]

To understand secession is to understand the degree to which interpretations of slavery's presence in the Constitution divided the country between the end of the war with Mexico in 1848 and the election of Lincoln in 1860. It was within this context of constitutional crisis that James Buchanan delivered his last address to Congress in early December 1860 and referenced the Constitution forty-three times and slavery twenty-five times. It was in that same context that Abraham Lincoln delivered his first inaugural address three months later and invoked the Constitution twenty-one times. By the time of the presidential election of 1860, the problems besetting the country did not revolve around congressional acts, but focused instead on the very nature of the Constitution and its violation (from the perspective of white Southerners) by the states north of the Mason-Dixon Line. As the historian Robert Russel noted fifty years ago, "Historians should strive to understand

---

11. Howell Cobb, "Letter . . . to the People of Georgia," in Jon L. Wakelyn, ed., *Southern Pamphlets on Secession, November 1860–April 1861* (Chapel Hill: University of North Carolina Press, 1996), 92–93, 99.

12. Michael Kammen, *A Machine That Would Go of Itself: The Constitution in American Culture* (New York: Random House, 1986), 104.

these constitutional matters . . . and treat them neither lightly nor carelessly in their general accounts of the causes of secession."[13]

Indeed, to understand the causes of secession and the constitutional crisis that occurred during the months following Lincoln's election, three areas of constitutional disagreement need to be examined: the future of slavery in the territories, the return of fugitive slaves, and the transportation of slaves by their owners through non-slave states and territories. Each of these topics deepened wedges between Northerners and Southerners, or more specifically between Republicans and Democrats, during the 1850s. The inability of the country to resolve these different perceptions of constitutional authority and rights led to the secession of the South and the onset of war in the spring of 1861.

Slavery in the Territories

Since the establishment of the Constitution, Congress had dealt with the subject of slavery in new territories in various ways. In 1787 and again in 1789, Congress asserted its right to prevent slavery from being exported into western territories. The Northwest Ordinance, which was originally authored by none other than Thomas Jefferson, prohibited slavery in the area west of Pennsylvania and north of the Ohio River by declaring that "there shall be neither slavery nor involuntary servitude in the said territory, otherwise than in the punishment of crimes."[14] A widespread belief in those immediate postrevolutionary years was that slavery was a blight on the new American political landscape and should be allowed eventually to die out.[15] Preventing its extension westward was a first step in constricting its growth. Furthermore, no one in 1787 or 1789 seemed to have any doubts about Congress's authority to prohibit slavery from a federal territory.[16] The importance of the Northwest Ordinance was not fully appreciated at the time

---

13. Robert R. Russel, "Constitutional Doctrines with Regard to Slavery in the Territories," *Journal of Southern History* 32, no. 4 (November 1966): 486.

14. Paul Finkelman, *An Imperfect Union: Slavery, Federalism, and Comity* (Chapel Hill: University of North Carolina Press, 1981), 83.

15. Joseph J. Ellis, *Founding Brothers: The Revolutionary Generation* (New York: Vintage Books, 2000), 88–90.

16. George William Van Cleve, *A Slaveholders' Union: Slavery, Politics, and the Constitution in the Early American Republic* (Chicago: University of Chicago Press, 2010), 166.

of its passing. Hindsight, however, has led at least one scholar to label it the "premier anti-slavery document in American history."[17]

Only a few years later in 1798, Congress displayed its sensitivity to regional differences on the subject of slavery by organizing the Mississippi Territory without reference to the institution because slavery already existed there. Congress again adopted a strategy of "nonintervention" when it organized the Louisiana Territory in 1805 for the same reason. With these beginnings, the federal government began a tradition of prohibiting the expansion of slavery into northwestern territories while tacitly allowing it to spread into southwestern territories.

This congressional "custom" continued until the middle portion of the Louisiana Territory—Missouri—petitioned to be admitted as a state. While it bordered, in its southern regions, the slave states of Kentucky and Tennessee, most of Missouri lay across the Mississippi River from the nonslave state of Illinois. Its existence as part of the Louisiana Territory and its location immediately north of the Arkansas Territory which had recently been organized without reference to slavery prompted many southern congressmen to presume that Missouri would be admitted to the Union as a slave state. Northern resistance, however, to the institution's expansion manifested itself in the form of a rider to the statehood bill prohibiting the introduction of any additional slaves into Missouri and providing for the emancipation of slaves born after the date of admission when they reached the age of twenty-five.[18]

White Southerners angrily reacted to this attempt to limit the westward growth of slavery and fought back using, in part, testimonials from a few of the remaining southern Founding Fathers. Both James Madison and Charles Pinckney argued that the Constitutional Convention had not provided Congress with any special authority over slavery.[19] Jefferson, the author of the exclusionary clause in the Northwest Ordinance, now decided that the expansion of slavery would have a salutary effect upon the slaves, "would make them individually happier and facilitate the accomplishment of their emancipation, by dividing the burden on a greater number of coadjutors."[20]

---

17. Don E. Fehrenbacher, *The Slaveholding Republic: An Account of the United States Government's Relations to Slavery* (New York: Oxford University Press, 2001), 255.

18. Don E. Fehrenbacher, *Slavery, Law, and Politics: The Dred Scott Case in Historical Perspective* (New York: Oxford University Press, 1981), 49.

19. Ibid., 53.

20. Merrill D. Peterson, ed., *The Portable Jefferson* (New York: Penguin Books, 1975), 568. For Jefferson's thoughts on the institution of slavery fifty years earlier, see Roger

In truth, 1820 was not 1784. The peculiar institution had grown well beyond the confines of the original thirteen states and had become increasingly profitable since Eli Whitney's invention of the cotton gin in 1793. For many white Southerners, during the early years of the nineteenth century, there existed a strong belief that their fortune and destiny lay to the west. After studying westward movement by planters during this period, historian James David Miller observed a widespread belief: "To embrace mobility was to embrace the future. To reject mobility was to cling to the past."[21] Regarding Missouri statehood, an impasse had been reached.

Smoothing the ruffled feathers of southern congressmen was not easily achieved, but taken aback by the southern reaction to the motion to abolish slavery in Missouri, the antislavery faction suggested a compromise. Missouri would be admitted as a slave state, and Maine would be admitted as a free state. Congress agreed to the deal but only after accepting an amendment offered by an Illinois representative prohibiting slavery in the remainder of the Louisiana Territory north of latitude 36° 30', the southern border of Missouri.[22] The so-called Missouri Compromise solved the immediate problem of gaining statehood for Missouri and effectively blunted antislavery rhetoric in Congress for several decades, but left white Southerners feeling wary of any form of antislavery expression from the non-slave states.

While arguments over other aspects of slavery sporadically occupied Congress during the next several decades, the territorial expansion issue did not arise again until 1846. Following his election in 1844 on a Democratic expansionist platform, James K. Polk ordered military units into the disputed boundary between Texas and Mexico in order to foment an international conflict. The subsequent clash between Mexican and U.S. forces gave Polk the excuse he needed to declare war.[23] As Congress debated an appropriations bill to fund the effort, a freshman congressman from Pennsylvania named David Wilmot rose to offer an amendment: "That, as an express and fundamental condition to the acquisition of any territory from the Republic of Mexico by the United States . . . neither slavery nor involuntary servitude

Wilkins, *Jefferson's Pillow: The Founding Fathers and the Dilemma of Black Patriotism* (Boston: Beacon Press, 2001), 46–51.

21. James David Miller, *South by Southwest: Planter Emigration and Identity in the Slave South* (Charlottesville: University of Virginia Press, 2002), 15.

22. Van Cleve, *A Slaveholders' Union*, 231–266.

23. Amy S. Greenberg, *A Wicked War: Polk, Clay, Lincoln, and the 1846 U.S. Invasion of Mexico* (New York: Vintage Books, 2012).

shall ever exist in any part of said territory."[24] With that suggestion, Wilmot reopened the "slavery and the territories" controversy that would not end until Confederate guns began their bombardment of Fort Sumter.

Many in the North supported the war (including Wilmot himself), but did not assume that territorial expansion to the Pacific implicitly meant the expansion of slavery to the Pacific. White Southerners, on the other hand, led by South Carolina senator John C. Calhoun and Mississippi senator Jefferson Davis, believed that "slavery followed the flag."[25] In short, the debate prompted by David Wilmot presaged several key constitutional questions once the 1848 Treaty of Guadalupe Hidalgo provided the transfer of most of the present-day Southwest from Mexico to the United States. Could Congress simply outlaw slavery in those lands as it had earlier with the Northwest Territory (and would in a few months with the Oregon Territory)? Did territorial legislatures have the constitutional authority to allow or prohibit slavery? Should Congress simply extend the Missouri Compromise line of 36° 30' west to the Pacific? Or, as a growing number of Southerners believed, should the right of property in slaves be protected by Congress and under the Constitution (as all other forms of property were protected under the Fifth Amendment) until a territory applied for statehood? The Constitution, as it was understood and interpreted in 1848–1849, did not provide any definitive answers.

Return of Fugitive Slaves

The other slave-related issue dividing the country at the midcentury mark had also been discussed in Philadelphia by the Founders, and provisions for the recapture of runaways had been included in the Constitution. The "Privileges and Immunities" clause (Article IV, Section 2) contained critical language for the rendition of slaves: "No Person held to Service or Labour in one State, under the Laws thereof, escaping into another, shall, in Consequence of any Law or Regulation therein, be discharged from such Service or Labour, but shall be delivered up on Claim of the Party to whom such Service or Labour may be due."

24. Bernard DeVoto, *The Year of Decision, 1846* (Boston: Little, Brown, 1943), 290.

25. Elizabeth R. Varon, *Disunion: The Coming of the American Civil War, 1789–1859* (Chapel Hill: University of North Carolina Press, 2008), 193–194; William J. Cooper, *Jefferson Davis, American* (New York: Vintage Books, 2000), 205.

The clause was deceiving in its simplicity. It was clear that the new Constitution required that the fugitive be "delivered up," but delivered up by whom? By what process? What proof of ownership would be required? Could each state develop its own regulations governing the rendition of slaves? These questions went unanswered in 1787. What was relatively clear was that the clause granted slave owners an extrajurisdictional privilege.[26] At the same time that it contained nothing that specifically indicated the federal government would or should play a role in the recapture and return of fugitive slaves, the clause did impose a restriction on the authority of free states. While the institution of slavery was officially protected and governed by state power, the Constitution, by this clause, placed limits on non-slave state authority to provide sanctuary to runaways. On this issue, slave states were more sovereign than free states as property rights trumped states' rights.

Although the return of runaway slaves during the early years of the nation did not amount to the critical problem it would become during the 1850s, the stage had been set. Under the Constitution, states could abolish slavery but still be required to accede to the legality of slavery in a neighboring state. For the time being, however, recapture remained the obligation of the owner or his/her agents. In 1793, Congress refined the clause somewhat by passing a Fugitive Slave Act in response to a dispute between Pennsylvania and Virginia over the kidnapping of a free black in Pennsylvania. The bill, signed into law by George Washington, provided only modest elaborations on the Constitution. Owners (or agents of the owner) could seize the alleged runaway and bring him or her before any judge or magistrate and present "proof" of slave status, which could simply be the word of the owner. The public official would then decide whether sufficient evidence had been presented to remand the defendant to slavery. In addition, any person who interfered with the owner or agent in pursuit of a fugitive slave could be sued by the owner.[27]

The 1793 law stipulated only vague evidentiary requirements and specifically did not provide any judicial safeguards for the accused such as a right to a lawyer, protection against self-incrimination, or a trial by jury. Nor did it include a statute of limitations or any wording that would discourage

---

26. Manisha Sinha, *The Slave's Cause: A History of Abolition* (New Haven: Yale University Press, 2016), 77.

27. Eric Foner, *Gateway to Freedom: The Hidden History of the Underground Railroad* (New York: W. W. Norton, 2015), 39–40.

INTRODUCTION

pursuers from ignoring the process altogether.[28] While the lack of clarity posed one problem, violations on both sides of the Mason-Dixon Line increasingly exacerbated sectional tensions. Some Southerners continued to reclaim their alleged property without involving judicial officials, and some northern state magistrates declined to participate in the recovery of slaves.

The continued kidnapping of northern free blacks became so commonplace that several states enacted laws aimed at the practice. New York became the first with the passage of "An Act to prevent the kidnapping of free people of color" in 1808.[29] Pennsylvania followed suit in 1820.[30] Because of Pennsylvania's shared border with slave state Maryland, friction between the two over the issue of fugitive slaves became commonplace. To prevent its free black citizens from being kidnapped, Pennsylvania enacted a "personal liberty law" in 1826 that significantly limited the reclamation process for southern owners of slaves. It repealed earlier legislation that allowed an owner or agent to seize a slave without formal judicial process, it prohibited state judges from acting solely on the slave catcher's testimony when authorizing seizure, and it made the owner's oath inadmissible in the removal hearings.[31] To no one's surprise, the legislation only intensified already strained relations between the two states.

Because recapture involved a complex set of issues including the property rights of owners, the rights of states in adjudicating rendition claims, the constitutionality of the 1793 act, and the role of the federal government (if any) in the return of fugitive slaves, Maryland and Pennsylvania agreed to a test case. The result was the U.S. Supreme Court's 1842 decision in *Prigg v. Pennsylvania.* Named for Edward Prigg, a Maryland-based slave catcher who had taken an escaped slave from Pennsylvania to Maryland without adhering to the northern state's established legal proceedings, the case complicated rather than simplified the return of fugitive slaves. Justice Joseph Story delivered a majority opinion that upheld the constitutionality of the 1793 Fugitive Slave Act and deemed Pennsylvania's 1826 law unconstitutional

---

28. Don E. Fehrenbacher, *The Dred Scott Case: Its Significance in American Law and Politics* (New York: Oxford University Press, 1978), 40–42.

29. Angela F. Murphy, *The Jerry Rescue: The Fugitive Slave Law, Northern Rights, and the American Sectional Crisis* (New York: Oxford University Press, 2016), 21.

30. Fergus M. Bordewich, *Bound for Caanan: The Underground Railroad and the War for the Soul of America* (New York: HarperCollins, 2005), 136; Sinha, *The Slave's Cause,* 382.

31. William M. Wiecek, "Slavery and Abolition before the United States Supreme Court, 1820–1860," *Journal of American History* 65, no. 1 (June 1978): 44.

because it interfered with an owner's right of recapture. Additionally, Story held that execution of the fugitive slave clause of the Constitution was exclusively a federal power, and thus the federal government could not require state officials to participate in its enforcement. The justice further allowed that states might properly prohibit their officials from participating in the return of runaway slaves. Ironically, the ruling led a number of northern states to enact more specific personal liberty laws.[32]

As a clash between those advocating for greater state authority and those arguing for greater federal authority, the *Prigg* decision continued a pattern of presumed sovereignty that would hold for the next two decades. As historian Angela Murphy observed, "In this case, Southern interests argued explicitly for the supremacy of the federal over state law, while a Northern state asserted its state's right to institute protections for its black citizens."[33] From the 1842 *Prigg* decision until the firing on Fort Sumter, the pro-slavery South consistently argued for enlarged federal authority when the subject centered on the protection of the institution of slavery. Over that period, if the choice involved expanded property rights or expanded states' rights, the South chose property rights every time.

White Southerners also favored a greatly expanded federal military over the decade of the 1850s. Between the end of the war with Mexico and the beginning of the Lincoln administration, Southerners dominated the positions of secretary of war and secretary of the navy, and over those years they significantly increased the size of the army and navy. Slave owners perceived a strong national military presence as being beneficial in the short and long run to the protection of slave owners' interests. "A powerful, well-armed American state," historian Matthew Karp recently observed, "at ease with Europe and dominant in its own hemisphere—this was the surest possible guarantee for both the South and its slave institutions."[34] It was, ironically, the U.S. military establishment constructed by Southerners that President

---

32. Ibid., 43–47; Timothy S. Huebner, *Liberty and Union: The Civil War Era and American Constitutionalism* (Lawrence: University Press of Kansas, 2016), 59–61; James M. McPherson, *Battle Cry of Freedom: The Civil War Era* (New York: Ballantine Books, 1989), 78–79. For a detailed treatment of personal liberty laws, see Thomas D. Morris, *Free Men All: The Personal Liberty Laws of the North, 1780–1861* (Baltimore: Johns Hopkins University Press, 1974).

33. Murphy, *The Jerry Rescue*, 22.

34. Matthew Karp, *This Vast Southern Empire: Slaveholders at the Helm of American Foreign Policy* (Cambridge: Harvard University Press, 2016), 218.

INTRODUCTION

Lincoln used so effectively between to 1861 and 1865 to bludgeon the Confederacy and destroy those same slave institutions.

The northern response to *Prigg* took various forms. Massachusetts and four other New England states promptly passed legislation that prohibited local and state magistrates from agreeing to take on fugitive cases and forbade state law enforcement officials from assisting in the arrest or detention of alleged fugitives.[35] New York simply left an existing law on the books that barred local magistrates from issuing arrest warrants and allowed them to provide fugitives with a jury trial.[36] Generally, northern state governments evinced widespread resistance to the recapture of slaves partly because northern free blacks were often kidnapped when the subject of the pursuit could not be located and partly because of a growing distaste for the intrusiveness of a pro-slavery ideology into free states. Indeed, because of the slave South's spirited defense of slavery following the Missouri Compromise and the introduction of David Wilmot's proposed ban on slavery in the West, Northerners were increasingly becoming convinced that an evolving and maturing "Slave Power" was intent on restricting their political liberties. Slavery, in the minds of many Northerners, symbolized the antithesis of republicanism. For many in the North, as historian William Gienapp observed, the Slave Power was "interfering with northern society, seeking to circumscribe civil liberties and subvert the Constitution."[37] Because of its growing contentiousness, the issue of fugitive slaves would play a major role in the development of the Compromise of 1850.

Compromise of 1850

In the face of growing tensions involving fugitive slaves and the organization of the land acquired from Mexico in 1848, Congress faced major challenges during the spring and summer of 1850. Of all the issues that eventually formed the Compromise of 1850, the fate of the Mexican Cession proved most thorny. White Southerners, who had enthusiastically supported the

---

35. Fehrenbacher, *The Slaveholding Republic*, 222.

36. Foner, *Gateway to Freedom*, 111.

37. William E. Gienapp, "The Republican Party and the Slave Power," in Robert H. Abzug and Stephen E. Maizlish, eds., *New Perspectives on Race and Slavery in America: Essays in Honor of Kenneth M. Stampp* (Lexington: University Press of Kentucky, 1986), 62–63.

war with Mexico and had provided the majority of troops, fully expected that the new territory west of Texas would and should be open to settlement by slave owners. During the debate over the compromise, Mississippi senator Jefferson Davis argued, "As a property recognized by the Constitution, . . . the Federal Government is bound to admit it [slavery] into all the Territories, and to give it such protection as other private property receives."[38] Historically, Congress had asserted that it could prohibit the introduction of slavery into federally controlled territories as it had demonstrated with the Northwest Territory, the northern portion of the Louisiana Territory, and, most recently, the Oregon Territory. Yet Davis and an increasing number of Southerners seeking to bypass this established congressional custom argued that under the Constitution slave property was no different from any other kind of property and was protected under the due process clause of the Fifth Amendment. Ownership of slaves, they believed, was a constitutional right that should adhere in territories as well as states.

As the debate over the western lands became progressively tempestuous, congressmen considered various solutions. At the margins, David Wilmot's proposal to ban slavery from the new territory was balanced by John C. Calhoun's belief that the Constitution required slavery to be allowed and protected there. Recognizing, however, that neither of those proposals would receive Congress's favor, many opted for compromise. The practical solution (and one that had stood the test of time) was simply to continue the Missouri Compromise line west through the Mexican Cession to the Pacific Ocean. Slavery would then be formally permitted in roughly the lower third of present-day California and most of Arizona and New Mexico, but prohibited north of that line.[39] While favored by many Southerners, the "practical solution" was not to be.

The agreed upon fix for the territorial imbroglio came in two parts. Excluding California, the remainder of the Cession would be divided into two territories: New Mexico to the south and Utah to the north. Congress would not decide the fate of slavery, but rather would leave that to the two territorial legislatures. This option, termed popular or territorial sovereignty, had become fashionable during the 1848 presidential election as a way of allowing the inhabitants of territories to decide for themselves whether they wanted to be slave or free. It also had the distinct advantage of getting

---

38. Quoted in Cooper, *Jefferson Davis, American*, 204.

39. John C. Waugh, *On the Brink of Civil War: The Compromise of 1850 and How It Changed the Course of American History* (Wilmington, Del.: SR Books, 2003), 152–161.

Congress off the hook. California would be admitted directly as a free state according to the wishes of its 92,000 inhabitants, the majority of whom were drawn to the Pacific coast by the discovery of gold in the Sacramento valley in 1848 and did not want to compete with slave labor.[40]

In addition to addressing the future of slavery in the land acquired from Mexico, the Compromise abolished the slave trade, but not slavery, in the nation's capital and settled the ongoing boundary dispute between Texas and New Mexico. Even before the war with Mexico, Texas had claimed eastern New Mexico to the Rio Grande plus a narrow strip of land north of the river's headwaters. The 1850 settlement established the boundary in its current location and, in return, Texas received $5 million from the U.S. government. The final piece of the contentious puzzle came in the form of a much strengthened Fugitive Slave Law. What the slave-owning South lost in the admission of California as a free state and in the reduction of the size of Texas, it gained in legislation governing the return of runaway slaves. Responding to southern concerns regarding escaped slaves, Congress enacted a fugitive slave law that greatly expanded federal authority at the expense of state authority. The alleged slave was specifically denied the right to a jury trial and the opportunity to testify on his or her own behalf. Furthermore, the legal process would be managed by a federal commissioner who would adjudicate each case. Additionally, the commissioner was to be paid a ten dollar fee in those cases when the alleged fugitive was returned to the claimant, but only five dollars when he or she was set free. More galling to antislavery Northerners was a clause that empowered federal marshals to enlist common citizens to aid in the enforcement of the act.[41]

With the passage of the 1850 Fugitive Slave Law, the intrusiveness of overtly pro-slavery legislation on the lives of ordinary Northerners irritated many a resident of the non-slave states and confirmed their fear of an expansive Slave Power. The poet Ralph Waldo Emerson reacted angrily and spoke for many of his fellow citizens:

---

40. Michael F. Holt, *The Fate of the Country: Politicians, Slavery Extension, and the Coming of the Civil War* (New York: Hill and Wang, 2004), 50–91; Leonard L. Richards, *The California Gold Rush and the Coming of the Civil War* (New York: Alfred A. Knopf, 2007), 91–118.

41. David M. Potter, *The Impending Crisis, 1848–1861* (New York: Harper & Row, 1976), 130–131.

I had never in my life up to this time suffered from the Slave Institution. Slavery in Virginia or Carolina was like Slavery in Africa or the Feejees, for me. There was an old fugitive law, but it had become, or was fast becoming a dead letter, and, by the genius and laws of Massachusetts, inoperative. The new Bill made it operative, required me to hunt slaves, and it found citizens in Massachusetts willing to act as judges and captors. Moreover, it discloses the secret of the new times that Slavery was no longer mendicant, but was becoming aggressive and dangerous.[42]

While antislavery forces approved of other aspects of the compromise—the admission of California as a free state, the abolition of slave markets in the nation's capital, and the settlement of the Texas–New Mexico line—the Fugitive Slave Law infuriated them.[43] As historian Michael Holt has noted, "The law forced white Northerners to become slave catchers themselves, to act at the beck and call of southern slave holders. In short, they could be symbolically reduced to the status of slaves."[44] As was regularly the case in the years between 1848 and 1861, Southerners demanded federal intervention to protect their property interests even when that intervention clearly eroded the purported southern ideal of states' rights.

Estimating Fugitive Slaves

Over the next decade, the subject of fugitive slaves continued to antagonize the South and exacerbate tensions between the two sections. In spite of the prominence the issue would play in the run-up to the war, the exact number of runaway slaves throughout the antebellum period is not known and largely unknowable. The statistics that do exist illustrate that the fugitive slave issue had several dimensions. First, slave owners presumably overstated their losses to inflate the claim that the North was "stealing" their slaves; or, conversely, they understated their runaways to reinforce the southern myth that slaves were docile and happy on the plantation. At the same time, the calculations from abolitionists tended to overestimate the

---

42. Doris Kearns Goodwin, *Team of Rivals: The Political Genius of Abraham Lincoln* (New York: Simon & Schuster, 2005), 160–161.

43. Sinha, *The Slave's Cause*, 500–501; Murphy, *The Jerry Rescue*, 75–76.

44. Holt, *The Fate of the Country*, 86.

INTRODUCTION

numbers to demonstrate a pervasive discontent among slaves.[45] Second, the majority of slaves to run away never intended to escape to a free state but rather remained away from their plantation or farm for only a few weeks or months. Historians John Hope Franklin and Loren Schweninger calculate that this number could have reached 50,000 annually.[46] Third, of those runaway slaves who left intending to reach freedom, only a small percentage were successful. For obvious reasons, those from the Upper South had a much greater chance than those from the Lower South. The 1850 U.S. census reported 1,011 fugitive slaves throughout the entire South. The state claiming the largest number of runaways, 279, was Maryland. The federal census ten years later reported only 803 successful fugitive slaves for that year, representing one-fiftieth of one percent of the South's entire slave population of 4,000,000.[47]

Estimates for the total number of slaves who managed to escape to the North throughout the antebellum period also vary. The New Orleans *Commercial Bulletin* in December 1860 placed the total between 1810 and 1860 at 1,500 annually.[48] Modern estimates for the number of escaped slaves for the period 1830 to 1860 range from 30,000 to 100,000 with the total number from 1800 to 1860 rising to between 100,000 to 150,000.[49] Historian Fergus M. Bordewich calculates the probable loss of labor to the South was closer to 100,000. In 1860, the superintendent of the federal census reported that in the decade after the passage of the Fugitive Slave Law of 1850, the number of escaped slaves was greatly reduced both numerically and proportionately. Furthermore, the census took issue with southern complaints about the "insecurity of slave property" and northern interference with the recapture of slaves, labeling those grievances an evident "misapprehension."[50]

---

45. John Hope Franklin and Loren Schweninger, *Runaway Slaves: Rebels on the Plantation* (New York: Oxford University Press, 1999), 263–294; Potter, *Impending Crisis,* 135–136; Allan Nevins, *The Emergence of Lincoln: Prologue to Civil War, 1859–1861* (New York: Charles Scribner's Sons, 1950), 489.

46. Franklin and Schweninger, *Runaway Slaves,* 282.

47. Joseph C. G. Kennedy, *Preliminary Report on the Eighth Census, 1860* (Washington: Government Printing Office, 1862), 137.

48. Quoted in *Twenty-Eighth Annual Report of the American Anti-Slavery Society, by the Executive Committee for the Year Ending May 1, 1861* (New York: American Anti-Slavery Society, 1861), 158.

49. Foner, *Gateway to Freedom,* 4; Bordewich, *Bound for Caanan,* 436–437; Sinha, *The Slave's Cause,* 382.

50. Kennedy, *Preliminary Report on the Eighth Census, 1860,* 11–12.

In an additional attempt to quantify the number of successful escapes to the North, the census analyzed the free black population in the North between 1820 and 1860. Factoring in the natural birthrate expansion, the census reported the 1820–1830 growth at 36.5 percent and the 1830–1840 expansion at just under 21 percent. For the period 1850–1860, the census calculated the rate of increase at less than 13 percent, including "slaves liberated and those who have escaped from their owners, together with the natural increase."[51] The conclusion of the census office was that the overall loss to the South in escaped slaves was not only declining but was also "small and inconsiderable."[52] As it compiled its figures during the first year of the Civil War, the federal census office estimated that the South's slave population would continue to grow and almost double by 1900.

For most of the slaveholding South, however, the issue was not one of numbers but of principle. Even though proportionately few slaves succeeded in escaping to free soil and the majority of those captured were returned to bondage, the South became increasingly alarmed over the image of fugitive slaves because, to their sensibilities, the northern states were ignoring their constitutional obligation to "deliver up" escaped slaves.[53] To be sure, between 1850 and 1860, Northerners resisted the rendition of slaves in sometimes violent fashion. In Boston, Christiana, Pennsylvania; and Syracuse, New York, antislavery crowds successfully prevented alleged slaves from being captured. In Christiana, the incident turned deadly when the slave owner was killed and his son gravely wounded. Although these and other efforts at resistance had little practical effect on the economy of slavery, each was highly publicized and each, to the white South at least, became clear evidence that Northerners while not respecting "southern rights" were also guilty of stealing slaves. As John Tyler Jr., a Virginia lawyer, railed in 1860, "Time and again have they [Northerners] not only *refused their assent* to the law of Congress, commanding the rendition of fugitive slaves, but they absolutely *nullified* that law in various modes, although passed in obedience to the solemn requirements of the Constitution as *wholesale and necessary to the public good.*"[54]

---

51. Ibid., 4, 12

52. Ibid., 12.

53. John Tyler Jr., "The Secession of the South and a New Confederation Necessary to the Preservation of Constitutional Liberty and Social Morality," *De Bow's Review* 28, no. 4 (April 1860): 369.

54. Ibid., Potter, *Impending Crisis*, 130–134; Foner, *Gateway to Freedom*, 126–150; McPherson, *Battle Cry of Freedom*, 80–88.

As far as white Southerners were concerned, the Constitution and the Fugitive Slave Law of 1850 clearly required that fugitive slaves be "delivered up" in a timely manner. The personal liberty laws while enacted by many northern states to protect free northern black citizens were often and increasingly designed to obstruct the rendition of runaways by flouting federal law. And although most Northerners respected the process, the resistance displayed in a few well publicized instances convinced the slaveholding South that Northerners in general were actively preventing their property from being returned to them.

Indeed, during the latter half of the 1850s, a number of northern states enacted legislation that provided greater legal protection for accused runaways. Wisconsin, Ohio, Michigan, and several New England states added personal liberty safeguards that included counsel for accused fugitives, jury trials, and increased penalties for kidnapping free blacks. The Wisconsin Supreme Court even formally declared the Fugitive Slave Law unconstitutional on three occasions. When it overturned the conviction of Sherman Booth, an abolitionist who had helped free a fugitive from jail, the case was appealed to the U.S. Supreme Court where Roger B. Taney wrote the decision for a unanimous court. In *Ableman v. Booth* (1859), Taney issued a ringing endorsement of federal judicial supremacy and affirmed the constitutionality of the Fugitive Slave Act of 1850.[55] Over the decade, the countermanding of federal law had become an effective northern antislavery tool. As Don Fehrenbacher has observed, "The fugitive slave issue had produced mirror images in which slaveholding Southerners invoked national authority, while antislavery Northerners pressed the doctrine of states' rights to the verge of nullification."[56]

The Georgia Platform

Southerners, like their northern counterparts, viewed the Compromise of 1850 as a mixed bag. They disliked the admission of California as a free state and the reduction of the size of Texas. They were relieved, however, that the hated Wilmot Proviso had not been enacted and that they had

---

55. Michael J. C. Taylor, "'A More Perfect Union': *Ableman v. Booth* and the Culmination of Federal Sovereignty," *Journal of Supreme Court History* 28, no. 2 (July 2003): 101–115; Finkelman, *An Imperfect Union*, 336–337.

56. Fehrenbacher, *The Slaveholding Republic*, 241.

gained a much more muscular fugitive slave law. Ultimately, but only for the time being, they were willing to abide by the compromise. It was a grudging acceptance that was represented in the language of the Georgia Platform.

Following the passage of the Compromise of 1850 in September, southern states assembled collectively and individually to formulate responses to Congress's action. The most important of these was a set of resolutions passed by Georgia in December. While Georgia did not "wholly approve" of the compromise, it would "abide by it as a permanent adjustment of this sectional controversy." The approval, however, came with a warning. Georgia would resist aggressions by the North "even (as a last resort) to a disruption of every tie which binds her to the Union," if Congress (1) abolished slavery in the District of Columbia or in any of the federal forts, shipyards, arsenals, and the like located in the slave states, (2) acted to suppress the slave trade between slave states, (3) refused to admit to the Union any territory because of the existence of slavery therein, (4) prohibited the introduction of slaves into the territories of New Mexico and Utah, or (5) repealed or modified the newly enacted Fugitive Slave Law. The final provision in this warning by the Peach State read, "That it is the deliberate opinion of this Convention that upon the faithful execution of the Fugitive Slave Bill by the proper authorities depends the preservation of our much loved Union."[57]

This moderated acceptance of the compromise effectively held southern secessionists at bay for a decade. The slave South accepted the federal administration of the Fugitive Slave Act because it worked to their advantage. Out of the 332 fugitive slave cases identified during the 1850s, 298 slaves (90 percent) were returned and only 11 (presumably kidnapping victims) released. During that same period, only 22 were rescued by antislavery Northerners.[58] Even Georgia senator Robert Toombs could praise the enforcement of the act. In an 1856 article published in De Bow's Review largely designed to defend slavery and white supremacy, Toombs claimed that "thousands of slaves have been delivered up" under the Constitution and subsequent fugitive slave acts.[59] By 1860, however, Toombs had changed his mind and

---

57. Stephens, *A Constitutional View of the Late War between the States,* 2:676–677; Potter, *Impending Crisis,* 124–130.

58. Stanley W. Campbell, *The Slave Catchers: Enforcement of the Fugitive Slave Law, 1850–1860* (Chapel Hill: University of North Carolina Press, 1968), 207.

59. Robert Toombs, "Slavery: Its Constitutional Status, and Its Influence on Society and the Colored Race," *De Bow's Review* 20, no. 5 (May 1856): 585–586. For an excellent analysis of *De Bow's Review* and its role in the sectional divide, see John F. Kvach,

demanded that, for the South to stay in the Union, Congress must pass an amendment to the Constitution guaranteeing the return of fugitive slaves without either a "writ of habeas corpus or trial by jury, or other similar obstructions of legislation by the States to which they may flee."[60]

Kansas-Nebraska Act

As the country pondered the implications of the Compromise of 1850, Washington turned, yet again, to the organization of western federal territories. Congress had organized the Oregon Territory in 1848, outlawing slavery using exactly the same language it had used in 1789 for the Northwest Territory. Likewise, slavery had been banned (in 1820) from the Louisiana Territory north of the Missouri Compromise line of 36° 30'. The only remaining territories were those of New Mexico and Utah, and the Compromise of 1850 had provided that the inhabitants of those lands (through their territorial legislatures) were authorized to accept or reject the introduction of slavery. In his address to Congress in December 1850, President Millard Fillmore hailed the compromise as "a final settlement of the dangerous and exciting subject which they embraced."[61] In truth, this "final" settlement of slavery's western march lasted less than four years.

While the Missouri Compromise had retained much of its popularity throughout the debate over the organization of the Mexican Cession, the admission of California as a free state shifted Southern Democratic votes toward the territorial sovereignty alternative.[62] In 1854, as Congress debated the organization of the Kansas and Nebraska territories north and west of Missouri, Southern Democrats demanded that the federal ban on slavery north of 36° 30' be replaced with the same territorial sovereignty option used for the Mexican Cession in 1850. The forthcoming Kansas-Nebraska Act reflected their wishes and reversed the prohibition placed by the 1820 Missouri Compromise. Not inconsequentially, it also prompted the formation of the antislavery Republican Party, which held that the Constitution

De Bow's Review: The Antebellum Vision of a New South (Lexington: University Press of Kentucky, 2013).

60. U.S. Senate, Committee of Thirteen, 36th Cong., 2nd sess., December 31, 1860, Rep. Com. No. 288, 2–3.

61. *Congressional Globe,* 31st Cong., 2nd sess., December 2, 1850 (appendix), 5.

62. Holt, *The Fate of the Country,* 79.

did not protect slavery and that the further extension of the institution must be opposed.[63]

White Supremacy

The organization of a purely sectional political party that supported freedom as the antithesis of the by now pro-slavery Democratic Party only increased sectional tensions and intensified the southern defense of slavery. Building on arguments by John C. Calhoun during the congressional debates over slavery in 1850, Georgia senator Robert Toombs penned a long defense of slavery in *De Bow's Review* six years later. Titling his article "Slavery: Its Constitutional Status, and Its Influence on Society and the Colored Race," Toombs presented the commonly held southern position that the Constitution possessed fundamental and incontrovertible protections for slavery and that the institution benefited both races. Regarding his first proposition, the senator argued that the Constitution contained no provisions that allowed the federal government "to abolish, limit, restrain, or in any other manner to impair the system of slavery in the United States." On the contrary, he wrote, every clause referencing slavery inserted into the Constitution by the Founding Fathers was "so intended, either to increase it, to strengthen it, or to protect it."[64]

The 1856 *De Bow's Review* article manifested a trend that had been developing since roughly 1830 that rationalized slave owning as a moral and religious blessing to both owner and slave. The revolutionary generation had taken the stance that slavery was evil but necessary due to the perceived social and economic complications of emancipation. Thomas Jefferson aptly captured that sentiment with his 1820 remark: "We have the wolf by the ears, and we can neither hold him, nor safely let him go. Justice is in one scale, and self-preservation in the other."[65] The rise of a very vocal and condemnatory abolitionist movement, however, pushed the South into a defensive posture.[66] Southern writers and politicians and ministers after

---

63. Ibid., 92–127; Eric Foner, *Free Soil, Free Labor, Free Men: The Ideology of the Republican Party before the Civil War* (1970; New York: Oxford University Press, 1995), 301–317.

64. Toombs, "Slavery," 584.

65. Peterson, *The Portable Jefferson,* 568.

66. For a smart reassessment of religion and proslavery arguments see John Patrick Daly, *When Slavery Was Called Freedom: Evangelicalism, Proslavery, and the Causes of the Civil War* (Lexington: University Press of Kentucky, 2002).

1832 or so intensified their defense of slavery as a positive gain for both owner and slave.

Toombs built his more general defense of slavery on "the truth that the white is the superior race, and the black the inferior." "The perfect equality of the superior race," he continued, "and legal subordination of the inferior, are the foundations on which we have erected our republican system." Believing that the North was escalating antislavery attacks, Southerners increasingly relied on a white supremacist rationale to explain their system of labor. Toombs spoke for the majority of white Southerners when he pragmatically explained that slavery was based upon "the idea of the superiority by nature of the white race over the African; that this superiority is not transient and artificial, but permanent and natural; that the same power which made his skin unchangeably black made him inferior intellectually to the white race and incapable of an equal struggle with him in the career of progress and civilization."[67]

Following the election of Lincoln in November 1860, as the deep southern states began their march toward secession, the maintenance of white supremacy became a staple element in justifying the breakup. Six weeks after the election, William L. Harris, a secession commissioner from Mississippi, urged the Georgia General Assembly to join Mississippi in leaving and based his argument on the presumed Republican Party's assault on the southern way of life. "Our fathers made this a government for the white man," he proclaimed, "rejecting the negro, as an ignorant, barbarian race, incapable of self-government, and not, therefore, entitled to be associated with the white man upon terms of civil, political, or social equality." Harris dramatically concluded his speech by hammering home his point: Mississippi "had rather see the last of her race, men, women, and children, immolated in one common funeral pile than see them subjected to the degradation of civil, political, and social equality with the negro race."[68] Commissioner Stephen F. Hale made much the same argument in his letter to the governor of Kentucky. "The Federal Government," he wrote, "has failed to protect the rights and property of the citizens of the South, and is about to pass into the hands of a party pledged for the destruction not only of their rights and their property but the equality of the States ordained by

67. Toombs, "Slavery," 581, 593.
68. Charles B. Dew, *Apostles of Disunion: Southern Secession Commissioners and the Causes of the Civil War* (Charlottesville: University Press of Virginia, 2001), 85, 89.

the Constitution and the heaven-ordained superiority of the white over the black race."[69]

While South Carolina, Georgia, and Mississippi all alluded to the threat posed by Lincoln and the Republican Party to the racial order of the South, Texas framed the danger of "abolition rule" in the clearest of terms: "We hold as undeniable truths that the governments of the various States, and of the confederacy itself, were established by the white race, for themselves and their posterity; that the African race had no agency in their establishment; that they were rightfully held and regarded as an inferior and dependent race, and in that condition only could their existence in this country be rendered beneficial or tolerable." As it wound up its justification for secession, the Texas secession convention emphasized the need to protect both slavery and the South's long-established superiority of the white race. "That in this free government *all white men are and of right ought to be entitled to equal civil and political rights* [italics in the original]; that the servitude of the African race, as existing in these States, is mutually beneficial to both bond and free; and is abundantly authorized and justified by the experience of mankind, and the revealed will of the Almighty Creator, as recognized by all Christian nations; while the destruction of the existing relations between the two races, as advocated by our sectional enemies, would bring inevitable calamities upon both and desolation upon the fifteen slave-holding States."[70]

For Presbyterian minister Benjamin M. Palmer, the inferiority of black people was not only assumed but came with a Christian obligation to perpetuate. In his Thanksgiving Day sermon in 1860, only weeks after Lincoln had won the White House, Palmer linked patriotism and religion and reminded his listeners that their "providential trust" required Southerners "to conserve and to perpetuate the institution of domestic slavery as now existing." In those troubling times, he reminded the congregation, it was incumbent upon all devout believers to defend slavery as "the cause of God and religion. The abolition spirit is undeniably atheistic."[71]

The South's elected officials understood what was at stake with a Republican and, to them, an abolitionist president. When Jefferson Buford from Barbour County, Alabama, addressed his colleagues on the day of Lincoln's inauguration, he pronounced that the responsibility of the assembled

---

69. Ibid., 100.

70. *Journal of the Secession Convention of Texas 1861*, 64.

71. Benjamin Morgan Palmer, "The South: Her Peril and Her Duty," in Wakelyn, *Southern Pamphlets*, 67, 70; see also McPherson, *Battle Cry of Freedom*, 56.

delegates was unmistakable: "We are sent to protect, not so much property, as white supremacy, and the great political right of internal self-control— but only against one specified and single danger alone, i.e., the danger of Abolition rule."[72] Likewise, when Confederate vice president Alexander Stephens addressed Virginia's secession convention on April 23, only days after the gathering had voted to secede, Stephens extolled the virtues of the new Confederate Constitution over that of the U.S. Constitution. At the core of the white South's new political charter was its protection of slavery and its overt admission that "as a race, the African is inferior to the white man. Subordination to the white man is his normal condition. He is not our equal by nature and cannot be made so by human laws or human institutions. Our system, therefore, so far as regards this inferior race, rests upon this great immutable law of nature." Stephens wanted there to be no misunderstandings about the Confederacy's fundamental doctrine: "The great truth, I repeat, upon which our system rests, is the inferiority of the African. The enemies of our institutions ignore this truth."[73] Following the election of Lincoln, the white South clearly perceived, albeit incorrectly, that both slavery and the notion of white racial superiority that undergirded the institution would, after Lincoln's inauguration on March 4, be directly and immediately threatened by the "Black Republican Party."

Dred Scott v. Sandford

The 1854 Kansas-Nebraska Act resulted, of course, in the bloody struggle for political and ideological supremacy in Kansas waged by pro- and antislavery factions.[74] The battle was conducted not only in the Kansas Territory but also in the political and judicial arenas in Washington, D.C. As congressmen continued to debate whether Congress had the authority to prohibit the peculiar institution from the territories, the Supreme Court weighed in with its *Dred Scott* decision.

---

72. William R. Smith, ed., *The History and Debates of the Convention of the People of Alabama, Begun and Held in the City of Montgomery, on the Seventh Day of January, 1861, in Which Is Preserved the Speeches of the Secret Session and Many Valuable State Papers* (Montgomery: White, Pfister, 1861), 285–286.

73. Reese, *Proceedings of the Virginia State Convention of 1861*, 4:385–386.

74. Nicole Etcheson, *Bleeding Kansas: Contested Liberty in the Civil War Era* (Lawrence: University Press of Kansas, 2004).

Dred Scott had been born into slavery in Virginia, taken to Missouri, and then sold to Dr. John Emerson, an Army surgeon. When the Army posted Emerson in Illinois and then Wisconsin Territory during the late 1830s, he took Scott and Scott's wife, Harriet, with him. After Emerson's death in 1843, Scott was loaned by Emerson's widow to another Army officer, who took him to Texas in 1845. Upon his return to St. Louis the following year, Dred and Harriet Scott filed petitions for their freedom based on their multiyear residence in the free state of Illinois and the free territory of Wisconsin. Scott's chances were quite good, as Missouri courts had long held for the plaintiffs in similar cases, and the St. Louis district court ruled in his favor. The Missouri Supreme Court, however, overturned the decision upon appeal in 1852, and the federal district court upheld Missouri's ruling two years later, paving the way to the Supreme Court.[75]

Speaking for the court on March 6, 1857, two days after he had sworn in President James Buchanan, Chief Justice Roger B. Taney attempted to settle the sectional agitation over slavery once and for all. In one of the most infamous decisions reached by the Supreme Court, Taney first determined that Dred Scott had no authority to sue in a federal court. Under Taney's reading of the Constitution, black people (not just black slaves) were ineligible to become citizens and therefore could not sue in a federal court. While Taney could have dismissed the case at that point for lack of jurisdiction, he was after larger game. He next determined that Scott had never constitutionally resided in the "free" territory of Wisconsin because Congress did not have the authority to prohibit slavery in a federal territory. The 1820 division of the upper Louisiana Territory, according to Taney, had been unconstitutional. Regarding Scott's residence in the northern state of Illinois, Taney simply ruled that the status of slaves taken by their owners into a free state and then returned to a slave state depended on the laws of the state of origin. In this case, the state of origin was Missouri, and Missouri's Supreme Court had already denied Scott his freedom. The chief justice anchored his position that Congress had no constitutional authority to ban slavery from a federal territory in the due process clause of the Fifth Amendment. Prohibiting slavery in a territory would violate the amendment's due process and just compensation clauses. In a sentence that would resonate throughout the country, Taney concluded, "The right of property in a slave is distinctly

75. Fehrenbacher, *The Dred Scott Case*, 239–250; Varon, *Disunion*, 295–296.

and expressly affirmed in the Constitution."[76] Far from settling the issue of slavery in the territories, Taney's decision exacerbated it, prompting Republicans to ignore the ruling, labeling it *obiter dictum* or not relevant to the case in question.

While Democrats and Republicans at the time divided on the constitutionality of the decision, scholars have since debated the *Dred Scott* decision with most finding, like William Cullen Bryant, that it constituted a "perversion" of the Constitution.[77] The constitutional debate revolved and revolves around interpretations of the Constitution as fundamentally a pro-slavery or an antislavery document. The abolitionist William Lloyd Garrison once famously burned a copy of the Constitution in protest of legislation favoring bondage, calling it "a covenant with death and an agreement with hell."[78] If Garrison was correct in believing that the nation's founding charter favored property rights over social justice, then Taney may have been more correct than Republicans then and many scholars today want to believe.[79]

While Kansas ultimately prohibited slavery, it was legalized by the New Mexico territorial legislature in 1859 with a slave code that one delegate to Virginia's secession convention hailed as the most "full, complete and perfect a codification of all acts necessary for the discipline, protection and safety of this population, as can be found in any one of the States of this Union."[80] (A historian recently labeled the code "a law that would make Caligula blush.")[81] The Utah territory had earlier also adopted the territorial sovereignty authority in the Compromise of 1850 and legalized slavery

---

76. Paul Finkelman, *Dred Scott v. Sandford: A Brief History with Documents* (Boston: Bedford/St. Martin's, 1997), 33–43.

77. McPherson, *Battle Cry of Freedom*, 177.

78. Henry Mayer, *All on Fire: William Lloyd Garrison and the Abolition of Slavery* (New York: St. Martin's Griffin, 1998), 445, 531.

79. For a thought-provoking analysis of this issue, see Mark A. Graber, *Dred Scott and the Problem of Constitutional Evil* (New York: Cambridge University Press, 2006).

80. Reese, *Proceedings of the Virginia State Convention of 1861*, 1:554; for the principal speeches in the Virginia Secession Convention, see William W. Freehling and Craig M. Simpson, *Showdown in Virginia: The 1861 Convention and the Fate of the Union* (Charlottesville: University of Virginia Press, 2010).

81. Mark J. Stegmaier, "A Law That Would Make Caligula Blush? New Mexico Territory's Unique Slave Code, 1859–1861," *New Mexico Historical Review* 87, no. 2 (Spring 2009): 209–242. See also John P. Hays, "The Curious Case of New Mexico's Pre-Civil War Slave Code," *New Mexico Historical Review* 92, no. 3 (Summer 2017): 251–283.

with a very mild slave code.[82] Thus, in spite of the Republican hyperbole of "no extension of slavery into the territories," the only logical territories where slavery could prosper beyond Kansas had officially become, by the end of the decade, "slave territories." By the time of the election of 1860, slavery existed in one form or another from Virginia across Texas and the territory of New Mexico to the eastern line of California. It must be acknowledged, however, that the number of African American slaves subjected to New Mexico's slave code numbered no more than two dozen, most brought in by U.S. military officers.[83]

Slavery National/Freedom Local

After the *Dred Scott* decision, with Taney's opinion that "property in a slave is distinctly and expressly affirmed in the Constitution," Southerners elaborated on the Toombs argument that slavery was not only the natural order of things but was constitutional wherever it was not specifically prohibited.[84] In early 1860, Senator James Green of Missouri observed that "the prohibition of slavery in the United States is local, and that the right to hold slave property wherever there is no prohibition is national."[85] Over Secession Winter, proponents of slavery continued to argue that slavery was (or should be) national and not local. George Wythe Randolph, Thomas Jefferson's grandson and delegate to Virginia's secession convention, argued two weeks after Lincoln's inauguration: "We maintained that like other rights of property it is not *created,* but *protected* by municipal jurisprudence; that, consequently, it [slavery] is not local, but general, and that it is especially recognized and protected by the Constitution of the United

---

82. *Acts, Resolutions, and Memorials, Passed by the First Annual, and Special Sessions, of the Legislative Assembly, of the Territory of Utah, Begun and Held at Great Salt Lake City, on the 22nd Day of September, A.D. 1851 also the Constitution of the United States, and the Act Organizing the Territory of Utah* (G. S. L. City, Utah: Brigham H. Young, Printer, 1852), 80–82.

83. Mark J. Stegmaier, ed., *Henry Adams in the Secession Crisis: Dispatches to the Boston Daily Advertiser, December 1860–March 1861* (Baton Rouge: Louisiana State University Press, 2012), 43.

84. For a detailed analysis of southern legal thought defining and regulating slavery, see Thomas D. Morris, *Southern Slavery and the Law, 1619–1860* (Chapel Hill: University of North Carolina Press, 1996).

85. *Congressional Globe,* 36th Cong., 1st sess., January 11, 1860 (appendix), 78.

States."[86] Randolph's pronouncement turned on its head his grandfather's belief that freedom was the natural state of man and that slavery could only be established by local law and custom. Northern foreboding only increased when the *Washington Union,* the official literary voice of the Democratic Party, declared that the *Dred Scott* decision unquestionably implied that northern state laws prohibiting Southerners from entering a state with their slave property were clearly unconstitutional.[87]

As tensions increased during the decade, a new subject of friction developed over the degree to which slavery was protected under the Constitution. Because the country's major financial institutions were located in the North, principally in Philadelphia and New York City, slave owners regularly visited north of the Mason-Dixon Line and, just as regularly, brought their personal slaves with them.[88] Northern legislatures that had earlier banned slavery resolved a potential problem by allowing slave owners to bring their slaves for allotted periods of time. New York law authorized a nine-month grace period. If slaves remained in the state after that period, they would automatically be freed. Pennsylvania, the first northern state to abolish slavery, albeit gradually, established a six-month grace period. It was this law that forced George Washington while president in Philadelphia to shuttle his slaves back and forth to Virginia to avoid losing them. Not all northern states were so generous. The Massachusetts Supreme Court declared in a famous 1836 ruling (*Commonwealth v. Ames*) that slaves brought into the state were automatically free when they crossed the state line. The Illinois Supreme Court, on the other hand, held in 1843 (*Willard v. The People*) that the right of slave transit was protected by the Constitution.[89]

While the case law involving fugitive slaves is extensive, the Supreme Court considered the transit of slaves with their owners on only three occasions: *Groves v. Slaughter* (1841), *Strader v. Graham* (1850), and *Dred Scott v. Sandford* (1857). Transit cases differed fundamentally from fugitive cases

---

86. Reese, *Proceedings of the Virginia State Convention of 1861,* 1:732.

87. Gienapp, "The Republican Party and the Slave Power," 68.

88. For a description of Wall Street's relationship with southerners, see Howard M. Wachtel, *Street of Dreams: Boulevard of Broken Hearts* (London: Pluto Press, 2003), 93–97; Anne Farrow, Joel Lang, and Jennifer Frank, *Complicity: How the North Promoted, Prolonged, and Profited from Slavery* (New York: Ballantine Books, 2005), 3–43; and Philip S. Foner, *Business and Slavery: The New York Merchants and the Irrepressible Conflict* (1941; New York: Russell & Russell, 1968).

89. Earl M. Maltz, *Slavery and the Supreme Court, 1825–1861* (Lawrence: University Press of Kansas, 2009), 165–166.

due to the Constitution's explicit language on the latter (Article IV, Section 2) and the lack of any language pertaining to the former. Slave owners, in arguing for the protection of their property in non-slave states, were forced to turn to the more general comity and privileges and immunities clauses (Article IV, Sections 1 and 2).

Taney's decision in *Dred Scott*, however, expanded (or attempted to expand) constitutional protections for slavery and seemed to suggest that slave owners might have more rights in free states than previously believed. In addition to pronouncing that slavery must be protected by the federal government during the territorial period and that Dred Scott's sojourn into a free state and territory did not make him free, Taney also linked protecting slave property generally under the Fifth Amendment. Late in his decision, he observed that "the right of property in a slave is distinctly and expressly affirmed in the Constitution . . . and no word can be found in the Constitution . . . which entitles property of that kind to less protection than property of any other description."[90] If Taney were correct, did slave owners have an unlimited constitutional right to take their slaves into northern states just as the *Dred Scott* decision allowed them unfettered access to the western territories?

In his remarks on the *Dred Scott* case, Justice Samuel Nelson, sensing the direction pro-slavery winds were blowing, observed, "A question has been alluded to, on the argument, namely: the right of the master with his slave of transit into or through a free State, on Business or commercial pursuits, or in the exercise of a Federal right, or the discharge of a Federal duty, being a citizen of the United States, which is not before us." He concluded, "When that question arises, we shall be prepared to decide it."[91] Nelson was acknowledging that the *Dred Scott* case established the status of slaves taken into a free state and territory and returned to a slave state, but was not the case to decide what rights owners had in non-slave states.

Nationalizing Slavery

In accepting his role as challenger to Stephen Douglas's Senate seat at the Republican State Convention in June 1858, Abraham Lincoln defined the political landscape in his now well-known "House Divided" speech.

---

90. Finkelman, *Dred Scott v. Sandford*, 75.
91. Ibid., 85.

Lincoln framed the crux of the matter—the unresolved constitutional issue of slavery's rightful role in the nation—in his opening phrases. "Either the *opponents* of slavery will arrest the further spread of it," he proclaimed, "or its *advocates* will push it forward, till it shall become alike lawful in *all* the states, *old* as well as *new—North* as well as *South*."[92] Lincoln, and many in his party, believed that the pro-slavery movement was not passive but active; that if left unchecked it would soon demand that slavery be allowed, in some form, in the non-slave states.[93]

Lincoln, like Justice Nelson, was also a keen observer of political winds and observed that the language and reasoning used by the Supreme Court in its ruling on *Dred Scott* invited a case that would test slave owners' rights in non-slave states. "Put *that* and *that* together, and we have another nice little niche, which we may, ere long, see filled with another Supreme Court decision, declaring that the Constitution of the United States does not permit a *state* to exclude slavery from its limits." A paragraph or two later, Lincoln continued, "Welcome or unwelcome, such decision *is* probably coming, and will soon be upon us, unless the power of the present political dynasty shall be met and overthrown." Dramatically he persisted: "We shall *lie down* pleasantly dreaming that the people of *Missouri* are on the verge of making their state *free;* and we shall *awake* to the *reality,* instead, that the *Supreme* Court has made *Illinois* a *slave* state."[94]

Justice Nelson and candidate Lincoln both sensed that recent developments indicated that the constitutional and political support for slavery was waxing, not waning. The prohibition of slavery in the northern portion of the Louisiana Territory guaranteed by the 1820 Missouri Compromise had been overthrown by the 1854 Kansas-Nebraska Act. The *Dred Scott* decision had declared the unconstitutionality of congressional proscription of slavery in the territories and, furthermore, that black people were not recognized by the Constitution as citizens (even in northern states which had declared them citizens). The New Mexico and Utah territories had formally adopted pro-slavery legislation. For the first time in constitutional adjudication, the chief justice of the U.S. Supreme Court had pronounced that slave property must be protected under the Constitution as all other forms of

---

92. Roy P. Basler, *The Collected Works of Abraham Lincoln*, 9 vols. (New Brunswick: Rutgers University Press, 1953), 2:461–462.

93. Varon, *Disunion,* 315–317.

94. Basler, *Collected Works,* 2:467.

property were protected.[95] The stage had been set for a case to test slavery's strength in non-slave states as *Dred Scott* had tested it in the territories. Such a case was working its way through the New York court system.

The *Lemmon* Slave Case

In 1852, Juliet and Jonathan Lemon decided to move from their home in Virginia's Shenandoah valley to Texas. As their entourage including seven children and eight slaves arrived at the port city of Richmond, the Lemons found that the quickest way to New Orleans, whence they could travel overland to Texas, was via New York City. Within hours of their arrival in New York, local antislavery activists arranged for the Lemons to be served a writ of habeas corpus and arraigned in front of a local judge who ordered their slaves detained until he could study the particulars of the case. What the Lemons had learned on their voyage northward, but had failed to appreciate, was that a decade earlier the New York legislature had revoked the nine-month law. After 1841, slaves brought into the state by their owners could not be held in bondage even temporarily. On November 13, 1852, Judge Elijah Paine of the Superior Court of the City of New York announced that the 1841 law gave him no choice but to free the eight slaves. Northern investors in southern interests on Wall Street quickly took up a collection of $5,000, which more than reimbursed the Lemons the value of their slaves.[96]

While the Lemons were somewhat mollified with their reimbursement, many in the South were angered by Judge Paine's decision. Georgia governor Howell Cobb roared, "A denial of this comity is unheard of among civilized nations, and if deliberately and wantonly persisted in, would be just cause of war." James D. B. De Bow, editor of the popular southern periodical *De Bow's Review,* labeled the manumitting of the Lemon slaves "subversive of the rights of the South in the Union." The editor of the *Richmond Daily Dispatch* objected in a way that reverberated throughout the slave-owning South: "The more we reflect upon the decision of Judge Paine,

---

95. Arthur Bestor, "State Sovereignty and Slavery: A Reinterpretation of Proslavery Constitutional Doctrine, 1846–1860," *Journal of the Illinois State Historical Society* 54, no. 2 (Summer 1961): 172.

96. Marie Tyler-McGraw and Dwight T. Pitcaithley, "The Lemmon Slave Case: Courtroom Drama, Constitutional Crisis, and the Southern Quest to Nationalize Slavery," *Common-Place* 14, no. 1 (Fall 2013). http://www.commonplace.org/vol14/no01/mcgraw/.

the more extraordinary it appears to us. If it be true that the inhabitants of one State had not the right to pass with their property through the territory of another, without forfeiting it, then the Union no longer exists."[97] Virginia governor Joseph Johnson felt especially aggrieved and sent the court's proceedings to the General Assembly requesting that Virginia appeal the decision.[98] Thus began an eight-year effort on the part of Virginia to force concessions on behalf of slave owners from a northern, non-slave state.

Lemmon v. The People (the New York court and press added the additional "m" to the Lemon name) became one of the most watched slave cases in the country and the one Abraham Lincoln referred to as the "next *Dred Scott* case." Lincoln and other Republicans who were aware of the pro-slavery leanings of the Taney Court feared the possibility that slavery would be effectively nationalized; that is, protected not only by state constitutions and legislation but also by the federal Constitution as Senator Green and others had argued it was. During his 1858 debate with Stephen A. Douglas, Lincoln rhetorically asked, "What is necessary for the nationalization of slavery? . . . It is merely for the Supreme Court to decide that no State under the Constitution can exclude it, just as they have already decided that under the Constitution neither Congress nor the Territorial Legislature can do it. When that is decided and acquiesced in, the whole thing is done."[99]

Governor Johnson and his successor, Henry A. Wise, prosecuted the case first to the New York Supreme Court and then to the New York Court of Appeals. Virginia lost in the former in the fall of 1857 (with the *Dred Scott* decision of the previous spring playing a major role) and in the latter in March 1860. Losing in the state courts was exactly what Governor Wise expected (and desired), for only by losing could the case be appealed to the U.S. Supreme Court. Historians believe that had the case been appealed to the Supreme Court, Chief Justice Taney would have decided in favor of Virginia. But Virginia failed to forward the case to Washington. John Letcher

97. Quoted in Finkelman, *An Imperfect Union*, 298–300; *De Bow's Review* 14, no. 1 (January 1853): 90.

98. New York Court of Appeals, *Report of the Lemmon Slave Case: Containing Points and Arguments of Counsel on Both Sides, and Opinions of All the Judges* (New York: Horace Greeley, 1860), 13.

99. Basler, *Collected Works*, 3:27; Eric Foner, *The Fiery Trial: Abraham Lincoln and American Slavery* (New York: W. W. Norton, 2010), 98–105. See also Gienapp, "The Republican Party and the Slave Power," 51–78.

had succeeded Henry Wise as governor in January 1860 and mysteriously declined to send the case to Taney's court.[100]

While Virginia lost in the New York courts, the argument presented by the state's attorneys reveals the expansiveness of the pro-slavery rationalization on the eve of the Civil War. As noted above, Virginia's case depended heavily on the comity and privileges and immunities clauses of the Constitution. It also, however, wove into its justification for the taking of slaves into non-slave states Howell Cobb's notion that slavery was national, not local, and that the power of the white over the black race was beneficial to the slave. New York attorney Charles O'Conor, the lead attorney for Virginia, argued that the "proposition that freedom is the general rule, and slavery the local exception, has no foundation in any just view of the law as a science." "Equally groundless," O'Conor maintained, echoing Justice Taney and Jefferson Davis and countless other southern leaders, "is the distinction taken by Judge Paine between slave property and other moveables."[101]

In his laundry list of reasons why New York should find in favor of Virginia, O'Conor invoked the white supremacist arguments then prevalent throughout the South. "Negroes," he expounded, "alone and unaided by the guardianship of another race, cannot sustain a civilized social role." In language reprehensible by today's standards yet commonplace in 1860, the northern attorney for the slave state of Virginia continued. "He is a child of the sun. In cold climates he perishes; in the territories adapted to his labors, and in which alone his race can be perpetuated, he will not toil save on compulsion, and the white man cannot; but each can perform his appointed task—the negro can labor, the white man can govern."[102]

As the *Lemmon* case worked its way through the New York Court of Appeals, a former chief justice of the Alabama Supreme Court, Arthur Francis Hopkins, expressed exasperation with northern interference with the long-established practice of slaves sojourning with their owners through free states. In an article published in *De Bow's Review* in late 1859, he observed, "The constitutional right of a slaveholder to use his slave and enjoy his services as an attendant, while he travels or sojourns in a free State, is abandoned now by nearly all [northern] men." Echoing Chief Justice Taney,

---

100. New York Court of Appeals, *Report of the Lemmon Slave Case*; see also Craig M. Simpson, *A Good Southerner: The Life of Henry A. Wise of Virginia* (Chapel Hill: University of North Carolina Press, 1985), 185–186.

101. New York Court of Appeals, *Report of the Lemmon Slave Case*, 20.

102. Ibid., 21.

Hopkins continued, "The Constitution of the United States authorizes slavery in the States, and protects it upon the ground that there is property in slaves as there is in a bale of goods."[103]

As they prepared to leave the Union, Georgia and South Carolina specifically referenced the *Lemmon* case as one of their grievances. "In several of our confederate States," Georgia complained hyperbolically, "a citizen cannot travel the highway with his servant who may voluntarily accompany him, without being declared by law a felon and being subject to infamous punishments."[104] "In the State of New York," South Carolina protested, "even the right of transit for a slave has been denied by her tribunals."[105] To rectify this problem, Governor Isham Harris of Tennessee suggested a constitutional amendment that would provide for the "protection of the owner in the peaceable possession of his slave while in transit, or temporarily sojourning in any of the States of the Confederacy."[106] In one of the rare compromise proposals to be suggested by a Deep South state, a committee of Alabama's Secession Convention encouraged a similar amendment that would guarantee the "right of transit through free states with slave property."[107] Thirty-three additional amendments proposed over Secession Winter were designed to protect, in the Constitution, slave property in non-slave states.

By 1860, the constitutional right of slave owners to take their slaves into the territories of the United States and have the institution protected there and to take their slaves into the non-slave states of the Union was assumed by most white Southerners. Chief Justice Taney's pronouncement in 1857 that "the right of property in a slave is distinctly and expressly affirmed in the Constitution" had had its desired effect. Over the course of the decade, in the minds of slave owners, the right of ownership in a slave moved steadily from being protected by state authority to being protected by the Constitution. Far from invoking states' rights to protect slavery on the eve of the 1860 presidential election, the South, as the *Lemmon* slave case illustrates, was more than willing to support an expansion of federal rights

103. *De Bow's Review* 27, no. 2 (August 1859): 152–153.

104. *Journal of the Public and Secret Proceedings of the Convention of the People of Georgia, Held in Milledgeville and Savannah in 1861*, 112.

105. *Journal of the Convention of the People of South Carolina, Held in 1860–'61, Together with the Reports, Resolutions, Etc.*, 329.

106. Robert H. White, *Messages of the Governors of Tennessee, 1857–1869* (Nashville: Tennessee Historical Commission, 1959), 263.

107. Smith, *The History and Debates of the Convention of the People of Alabama*, 79.

to protect the institution of slavery and specifically to deny northern states the right to regulate the institution within their borders. The southern need to federalize control over slavery at the expense of state control was noted by Henry Adams in 1888. "Between the slave power and states' rights," he wrote, "there was no connection. . . . Whenever a question arose of extending or protecting slavery, the slave-holders became friends of centralized power, and used that dangerous weapon with a kind of frenzy."[108]

The Election of 1860

The election of 1860 marked the final divide between those favoring the extension of slavery into the western territories and those opposing it. The vision of a Lincoln victory convinced the white South that Republican opposition to slavery in the West meant that no more slave states would be added to the Union. Slavery in the fifteen states where it then existed would be surrounded by non-slave states, and the end of slavery would be the eventual outcome. Arkansas governor Henry Rector put it most succinctly and colorfully: "The extension of slavery is the vital point of the whole controversy between the North and the South." Slavery must expand, he explained to his state's secession convention, or else it will be hemmed in "by a cordon of fire," and like a scorpion, "it will sting itself to death." A decision point had been reached, he preached, because the North believes "slavery is a sin, we do not, and there lies the trouble."[109]

The issue of slavery in the territories and Republican opposition to slavery's extension had become, in the analysis of historian Daniel Crofts, "abstract and symbolic rather than tangible."[110] Nevertheless, symbolic arguments often draw as much heat as practical arguments. The degree to which the subject had spun out of control is apparent in the Democratic response to the Republican position of no extension. Maintaining its opposition to

---

108. Henry Adams, *John Randolph* (Boston: Houghton, Mifflin, 1888), 272–273.

109. *Journal of Both Sessions of the Convention of the State of Arkansas, Which Were Begun and Held in the Capitol, in the City of Little Rock* (Little Rock: Johnson & Yerkes, State Printers, 1861), 41–49.

110. Daniel W. Crofts, *Reluctant Confederates: Upper South Unionists in the Secession Crisis* (Chapel Hill: University of North Carolina Press, 1989), 205. For a keen analysis of Republican ideology, see William J. Cooper, *We Have the War upon Us: The Onset of the Civil War, November 1860–April 1861* (New York: Vintage Books, 2012), 147–150.

the extension of slavery, the Republican platform declared, "That the normal condition of all the territory of the United States is that of freedom; . . . and we deny the authority of Congress, of a territorial legislature, or of any individuals, to give legal existence to slavery in any territory of the United States."[111]

Democrats responded by splitting their party over the meaning of the *Dred Scott* decision. The northern wing of the party clung to Stephen Douglas's "territorial sovereignty" philosophy but did so in an awkwardly worded platform plank that seemed to agree with Chief Justice Taney. "Inasmuch as a difference of opinion exists in the Democratic Party as to the nature and extent of the powers of the Territorial Legislature, and . . . Congress, . . . over the institution of slavery in the Territories, Resolved, That the Democratic party will abide by the decision of the Supreme Court of the United States upon these questions of Constitutional law." Senator Douglas, however, the northern Democratic nominee, had already gone on record arguing that even within the constitutional parameters of the *Dred Scott* decision, territories could discourage the immigration of slave owners with their slaves by simply not developing the necessary slave codes.[112]

Southern Democrats held much different and stronger views. Based on a set of resolutions pushed through the Senate by Jefferson Davis a few months earlier, the more pro-slavery faction nominated Kentucky's John C. Breckinridge (Buchanan's vice president) on a platform that overtly promoted and protected slavery in the territories.[113] During the existence of a territory, it claimed, "all citizens of the United States have an equal right to settle with their property in the Territory, without their rights, either of person or property, being destroyed or impaired by Congressional or Territorial legislation" and "it is the duty of the Federal Government, in all its departments, to protect, when necessary, the rights of persons and property in the Territories, and wherever else its constitutional authority extends." The platform adhered closely to Taney's *Dred Scott* decision and Davis's interpretation of it. The Constitution (and the federal government) should

111. William Benton, *The Annals of America*, vol. 9, *1858–1865: The Crisis of the Union* (Chicago: Encyclopædia Britannica, 1968), 188–190.

112. Benton, *Annals of America*, 9:190–191; William W. Freehling, *The Road to Disunion*, vol. 2, *Secessionists Triumphant, 1854–1861* (New York: Oxford University Press, 2007), 272; Earl M. Maltz, *Dred Scott and the Politics of Slavery* (Lawrence: University Press of Kansas, 2007), 140–154; Potter, *Impending Crisis*, 402–406.

113. William J. Cooper, ed., *Jefferson Davis: The Essential Writings* (New York: Modern Library, 2003), 172–175.

protect slavery in the territories during the territorial period as all other forms of property were so protected.[114]

On the acquisition of additional territory, however, the two Democratic platforms contained almost identical planks. Following the Compromise of 1850 and the admission of California as a non-slave state, expansionist Southerners began looking southward for areas onto which they could impose a slave-labor economy. Mexico, Central America, and Cuba were all considered likely candidates, and privately funded military adventurers attempted to expand slavery into those countries. Cuba, in particular, was singled out as an annexation that would balance the loss of California. The infamous 1854 Ostend Manifesto signed by the U.S. ministers to England, France, and Spain threateningly declared that if Spain would not sell the island, the United States would be justified in taking it by force. President Buchanan (a signatory to the Ostend Manifesto as minister to Great Britain) tried to push a bill through Congress as late as 1859 to acquire Cuba. Although it failed, Breckinridge fully supported the idea.[115] The Democratic Party platforms of 1860 contained a plank that read, "The Democratic Party are in favor of the acquisition of the island of Cuba on such terms as shall be honorable to ourselves and just to Spain." The Breckinridge platform added, ". . . at the earliest practicable moment."[116]

Thus the political storm that had been brewing since David Wilmot proposed his 1846 proviso prohibiting slavery from any land acquired from Mexico finally enveloped a presidential election. The lines were drawn over the future of slavery in the western territories where few slaves existed and the prospects of the institution flourishing were slim. No one presumed slavery could be or would be extended into the Nebraska Territory, and the issue had already been decided in Kansas, which in a few months would be admitted to the Union as a non-slave state. In the Mexican Cession, as with Nebraska, no one argued that slavery could exist north of the 36° 30' line (the Territory of Utah), and Kentucky senator John J. Crittenden had described the territory of New Mexico as "the most sterile and worthless of its extent upon this whole continent."[117] (Crittenden and his colleagues

---

114. Benton, *Annals of America*, 9:191–192.

115. Robert E. May, *The Southern Dream of a Caribbean Empire, 1854–1861* (Gainesville: University Press of Florida, 2002), 46–76, 163–189.

116. Benton, *Annals of America*, 9:191.

117. *Congressional Globe*, 36th Cong., 2nd sess., February 12, 1861, 864; Albert D. Kirwan, *John J. Crittenden: The Struggle for the Union* (Lexington: University of Kentucky Press, 1962), 417–418.

would have been shocked to learn that in 2012, Arizona ranked seventh in the nation in cotton production, ahead of South Carolina, Alabama, and Louisiana!)[118] Nevertheless, the South perceived an attack upon slavery in the territories where there were few slaves as an attack upon slavery in the states where slaves were many and the profits immense.

The subject of fugitive slaves, emphasized in the Georgia Platform of a decade earlier, continued to play a role in national politics. Over the spring and summer of 1860, both the northern and southern wings of the Democratic Party included fugitive slave planks in their platforms. While they disagreed on the future of slavery in the western territories, they crafted identical planks on the issue of fugitive slaves: "Resolved, That the enactments of State Legislatures to defeat the faithful execution of the Fugitive Slave Law are hostile in character, subversive of the Constitution, and revolutionary in their effect."[119]

Ironically, the rendition of slaves was not an issue opposed formally by the Republican Party or by Abraham Lincoln. The 1860 Republican Platform contained no language that opposed that constitutional responsibility, and the return of fugitive slaves was a statutory obligation Lincoln believed must be respected.[120] In his inaugural address on March 4, 1861, Lincoln took pains to express his support for the return of fugitive slaves while at the same time expressing the belief that the states had the constitutional right to oppose kidnapping. "Again . . . ought not all the safeguards of liberty known in civilized and humane jurisprudence to be introduced," he reasoned, "so that a free man be not . . . surrendered as a slave?"[121]

Indeed, as the policy makers in Washington attempted to find a solution to the sectional crisis over Secession Winter, Lincoln was asked what his policy would be regarding compromise. His response focused almost entirely on upholding the fugitive slave provisions of the Constitution. Just days before Christmas and presaging his inaugural comments, Lincoln suggested three resolutions which he hoped would be considered by Congress. First, that the "fugitive slave clause of the Constitution ought to be enforced by

---

118. U.S. Department of Agriculture, *Louisiana Farm Reporter* 12, no. 10 (May 17, 2012).

119. Benton, *Annals of America*, 9:190–192.

120. Richard Carwardine, *Lincoln: A Life of Purpose and Power* (New York: Vintage Books, 2007), 95–96; Henry Louis Gates Jr., ed., *Lincoln on Race and Slavery* (Princeton: Princeton University Press, 2009), 174–176; Eric Foner, ed., *Our Lincoln: New Perspectives on Lincoln and His World* (New York: W. W. Norton, 2008), 174–176.

121. Basler, *Collected Works*, 4:262–264.

a law of Congress, with efficient provisions for that object, not obliging private persons to assist in its execution, but punishing all who resist it, and that the usual safeguards to liberty, securing free men against being surrendered as slaves." Second, that "all state laws, if there be such, really, or apparently, in conflict with such law of Congress, ought to be repealed; and no opposition to the execution of such law of Congress ought to be made." Third, that the "Federal Union must be preserved."[122] While Lincoln hoped that slavery would come to an end sooner rather than later, he was also a strong constitutionalist who believed in the supremacy of the national compact. To that end, he felt strongly that the fugitive slave clause of the Constitution must be upheld, but through less offensive means than the Fugitive Slave Law of 1850.

Debating Secession

Virginia's pursuit of the *Lemmon* case is illustrative of the evolution in southern thinking at the end of the decade. The political and legal clashes over the status of slavery in the United States in the years immediately after the war with Mexico had not focused on slavery inside the southern states where the institution was unquestionably protected by state authority, but outside where slave owners hoped to extend their reach. The debates of the early 1850s specifically involved the presumed right on the part of slave owners to take their slaves into western territories and the constitutional right to have slaves that escaped to free states returned to their lawful owners. The former led to a wide range of solutions to the extension of slavery issue because the Constitution's reference to territories could be interpreted in multiple ways. Article IV, Section 3 simply states that Congress "shall have Powers to dispose of and make all needful Rules and Regulations respecting the Territory or other Property belonging to the United States; and nothing in this Constitution shall be construed as to Prejudice any Claims of the United States, or of any particular State." On the other hand, at least for Southerners, the fugitive slave clause in Article IV, Section 2 was quite clear: "No Person held to Service or Labour in one State, under the Laws thereof, escaping into another, shall, in Consequence of any Law, or regulation therein, be discharged from such Service or Labour, but shall be delivered up on Claim of the Party to whom such Service or Labour may be due."

---

122. Ibid., 156–157.

Increasingly, however, especially after Taney's 1857 decision in the *Dred Scott* case, Southerners turned to the Constitution's due process clause in the Fifth Amendment: "No person shall . . . be deprived of life, liberty, or property, without due process of law." If, as Taney believed, slaves clearly met the Constitution's definition of "property," then slave owners retained those property rights in the territories, wherever their fugitive slaves might reside, and wherever they might choose to take their slaves. This was the thinking of Virginia as it appealed the *Lemmon* case.

With the convening of the second session of the 36th Congress on December 3, 1860, the nation's elected officials began to deliberate the meaning of the election of the first Republican president. Official conversations on the future of the nation, however, also took place in more than a dozen states. Shortly after the election, eleven states called for secession conventions. South Carolina convened its gathering on December 17 and seceded three days later, Florida's deliberations began on January 3, while Mississippi and Alabama began their deliberations on January 7. Tennessee chose not to call a convention, leaving the weighty matter of secession to its general assembly, which approved an ordinance of secession on May 6. A stipulation that the voters needed to uphold the legislature's decision led to a June 8 validation making the Volunteer State the last to join the Confederacy. Missouri called a convention, but on March 19 chose, with only one dissenting vote, to remain in the Union. Kentucky, Maryland, and Delaware, being border states less influenced by secession fervor, chose not to convene secession conventions. (See appendix for convention chronology and ballots.) Additionally, during the last three weeks in February 1861, 131 delegates from twenty-one states met in the nation's capital to debate possible compromise solutions. Called by Virginia's General Assembly the month before, the Washington Peace Conference attempted to "make a final effort to restore the Union and the Constitution, in the spirit in which they were established by the fathers of the Republic."[123]

In each of these venues, the representatives of the states, North and South, debated the question raised by Georgia's Howell Cobb in his open letter of December 6, 1860: "Does the election of Lincoln to the Presidency, in the usual and constitutional role, justify the Southern States in dissolving

---

123. L. E. Chittenden, *A Report of the Debates and Proceedings in the Secret Sessions of the Conference Convention, for Proposing Amendments to the Constitution of the United States Held at Washington, D.C., in February, A.D. 1861* (New York: D. Appleton, 1864), 9.

the Union?" Seven states in the Deep South answered yes and formally left the Union before Inauguration Day, March 4, 1861. The middle and upper southern states, through their elected delegates, paused and reflected and examined the meaning of Lincoln's election to the nation, especially to the South's economic engine, slavery. Those conversations turned on the relationship of the white to the black race, constitutional protections for slavery found (or imagined) in the Constitution, and, looming over all rhetoric, the meaning of Thomas Jefferson's articulation of democratic principle: "We hold these truths to be self-evident, that all men are created equal, that they are endowed by their Creator with certain unalienable Rights, that among these are Life, Liberty, and the pursuit of Happiness."

Searching for a Solution

With momentum throughout the Deep South unrelentingly headed toward secession, the conversations in Congress, secession conventions of the middle South, and the Washington Peace Conference focused on compromise. Because those critical deliberations were occurring at the same time that seven coastal southern states were preparing to leave the Union, the stakes were high. The elected officials charged with finding a solution understood that nothing less than an amendment to the Constitution specifically protecting southern slavery would stem the tide of secessionist activity. John C. Calhoun had proposed just such an amendment in his famous Fourth of March speech a decade earlier. His recommendations for saving the Union in the face of, as he put it, "the agitation of the subject of slavery" included a recommendation "for the insertion of a provision in the Constitution, by an amendment, which will restore to the South in substance the power she possessed of protecting herself, before the equilibrium between the sections was destroyed by the action of this Government."[124] The satisfactory resolution of the slavery "agitation" by the Compromise of 1850, however, rendered the idea of amending the Constitution moot for the next decade.

In his opening address to the second session of the 36th Congress, a month after the election of Lincoln, President James Buchanan, a longtime

---

124. *Congressional Globe*, 31st Cong., 1st sess., March 4, 1850, 455. What Calhoun envisioned was a dual executive (one representing the North, one representing the South) with each possessing a veto over acts of Congress. See Richards, *California Gold Rush*, 105–106.

supporter of slaveholders' rights, placed the blame for the crisis of the Union squarely on the North. "The long-continued and intemperate interference of the northern people with the question of slavery in the southern States," he admonished, "has at length produced its natural effects." Buchanan's remarkable address on December 3, 1860, interwove the subjects of the Constitution, extension of slavery in the territories, and northern violations of the Fugitive Slave Law. Claiming that the executive branch had no authority to prevent states from seceding, he instead proposed a constitutional amendment that would "expressly" recognize (1) the right of property in slaves "in the States where it now exists or may hereafter exist," (2) the duty of protecting that right in the western territories, and (3) the right of an owner to have his escaped slave "delivered up" to him.[125] For Buchanan, like Calhoun in 1850, nothing short of an amendment to the Constitution would satisfy southern grievances.

The belief that compromise, if agreed upon, would need to take the form of a constitutional amendment quickly became the goal of the nation's elected officials. Both houses of Congress created special committees to formulate solutions to the "agitated and distracted condition of the country." On December 20, the same day that South Carolina voted to secede, the Senate established the Committee of Thirteen and appointed Senator Lazarus Powell (Democrat) of Kentucky to chair it. The Senate committee possessed many of the luminaries of the 36th Congress: Jefferson Davis, John Crittenden, William Seward, Robert Toombs, Stephen Douglas, and Jacob Collamer. Powell proposed a constitutional amendment that would give "certain, prompt, and full protection to the rights of property of the citizens of every State and Territory of the United States." In short order, Toombs, Davis, Crittenden, Douglas, and Seward all proposed their own solutions. While Crittenden's became the most viable of them all (as discussed below), the committee was not able "to agree upon any general plan of adjustment," and it officially disbanded on December 31.[126]

The Committee of Thirty-Three formed by the House of Representatives on December 4 and chaired by Republican Thomas Corwin of Ohio fared somewhat better. On January 29, 1861, it recommended to the full House (1) an assortment of nonbinding resolutions, (2) a bill providing for the

125. *Congressional Globe,* 36th Cong., 2nd sess., December 3, 1861 (appendix), 1–4; Jean H. Baker, *James Buchanan* (New York: Henry Holt, 2004), 134.

126. U.S. Senate, Committee of Thirteen, 36th Cong., 2nd sess., December 31, 1860, Rep. Com. No. 288.

admission of New Mexico as a state with or without slavery "as their constitution may provide," (3) a bill revising the 1850 Fugitive Slave Law, and (4) an awkwardly worded constitutional amendment that prevented Congress from passing any future amendment that would interfere with slavery in the states where it already existed.[127] Not all members of the committee, however, were pleased with the report. Upon publication and presentation to the House of Representatives it contained, as Henry Adams put it, "a small library of minority reports."[128] The divided committee appended a total of seven dissenting commentaries to the committee's work.

Over the next three and a half months, negotiations in those committees, the state secession conventions, the Washington Peace Conference, and several state legislatures produced no fewer than sixty-seven proposed constitutional amendments. Most came from the Upper South states of Virginia, Tennessee, and Kentucky, which proposed fifteen, nine, and six, respectively; Georgia suggested three, Mississippi one, Alabama one, and Arkansas two. Northerners suggested twenty-two amendments, with only one coming from New England. Significantly, 90 percent of the proposed amendments were designed specifically to protect the institution of slavery beyond the control of state authority.

These "solutions" to the looming constitutional crisis that had been brewing since the war with Mexico clearly present the range of problems the country could not resolve. Fifty-eight possessed articles (or subparts) that dealt with slavery in the territories, forty-nine with fugitive slaves, and thirty-five with the interstate transit of slaves. Thirty-eight addressed the issue of slavery in the District of Columbia, and thirty-three would have protected slavery in federal installations in the South. Twenty-seven were designed to guarantee slavery in the fifteen states where it already existed, and eleven of the proposed amendments would have nationalized slavery. Jefferson Davis submitted an amendment on Christmas Eve, 1860, that read: "Property in slaves, recognized as such by the local law of any of the States of the Union, shall stand on the same footing in all constitutional and Federal relations as any other species of property so recognized."[129] Two proposed redesigning the Executive Office and federal electoral process(es) in order to protect southern interests; only two articles suggested a prohibition on protective

---

127. U.S. House of Representatives, Committee of Thirty-Three, 36th Cong., 2nd sess., January 29, 1861, Report No. 31.

128. Stegmaier, *Henry Adams in the Secession Crisis,* 125.

129. *Congressional Globe,* 36th Cong., 2nd sess., December 24, 1860, 190.

tariffs. Given the impasse the nation had reached over the future of slavery, no one was surprised that the majority of the amendments mirrored exactly the demands presented in the Georgia Platform a decade earlier. What the South needed to stay in the Union, however, was something the North could not give. As historian Kenneth M. Stampp observed over fifty years ago, "What was required of the North, in fact, was not a compromise but a complete surrender."[130]

The most popular of the proposals to amend the Constitution and provide a settlement of the crisis was that suggested by Senator Crittenden. On December 18, Crittenden proposed a six-point plan to address the constitutional deadlock over slavery that would have extended the Missouri Compromise line of 36° 30' to California with slavery abolished to the north and guaranteed to the south, protected slavery in Washington D.C. and in federal installations located in slave states, safeguarded the transportation of slaves from congressional interference, and strengthened the Fugitive Slave Act. His final suggestion was that his proposed amendment could not be amended by future congresses.[131]

During the ensuing congressional debate over Crittenden's resolutions, Republican representative Rodolphus Holland Duell of New York charged that the Kentuckian's solution would "make slavery a national institution, by a constitutional recognition of the right of property in man."[132] Duell's accusation reflected a growing anxiety among Northerners that the advocates of slavery (including the aforementioned Robert Toombs, James Green, and George Wythe Randolph) were attempting to protect slavery throughout the nation except where it was prohibited by state law. A month earlier, Ohio representative Benjamin Stanton had framed the issue in even clearer terms. "The Republican party holds that slavery is a local institution, created and sustained by State laws and usages that cannot exist beyond the limits of the State, by virtue of whose laws it is established and sustained." The Democratic Party, on the other hand, "holds that African slavery is a national institution, recognized and sustained by the Constitution of the

130. Kenneth M. Stampp, *And the War Came: The North and the Secession Crisis, 1860–1861* (1950; Baton Rouge: Louisiana State University Press, 1970), 151.

131. *Congressional Globe*, 36th Cong., 2nd sess., December 18, 1860, 114 (Joint Resolution No. 50); Kirwan, *John J. Crittenden*, 374–378. For the most extensive analysis of the Seward-Adams-Corwin amendment to date, see Daniel W. Crofts, *Lincoln and the Politics of Slavery: The Other Thirteenth Amendment and the Struggle to Save the Union* (Chapel Hill: University of North Carolina Press, 2016).

132. *Congressional Globe*, 36th Cong., 2nd sess., February 16, 1861, 979.

United States throughout the entire territorial limits, where not prohibited by State constitutions and State laws."[133]

Instead of abiding by the established understanding that freedom was protected by the Constitution except where slavery was allowed by state authority, Republicans feared that Southern Democrats were attempting to reverse the equation and make slavery the norm except where prohibited. This approach to solving the nation's crisis was especially evident in the amendments proposed by Jefferson Davis, Robert Toombs, and William Goggin.[134] Others, including Trusten Polk of Missouri and Henry A. Wise of Virginia, pushed for a more comprehensive solution (and the one later adopted by the Confederacy) of nationalizing slavery by simply recognizing, as suggested in 1857 by Roger B. Taney, that slaves were property and therefore protected by the due process clause of the Fifth Amendment.[135]

In light of later actions by Congress, it is important to note that Crittenden's sixth article also contained language that would have prevented congressional interference with slavery in the states where it already existed: "No amendment will be made to the Constitution which shall authorize or give to Congress any power to abolish or interfere with slavery in any of the States by whose laws it is, or may be, allowed or permitted." The idea had been included earlier in less polished amendments proposed by Shelton Farrar Leake, an Independent Democrat from Virginia, and William H. English, a Democrat from Indiana.[136]

Protecting Slavery in the Constitution

Of all the amendments proposed over Secession Winter, Crittenden's became the most favored even above the Mason-Dixon Line. Although endorsed (for the most part) by Virginia's General Assembly and replicated (for the most part) by the Washington Peace Conference, it failed to garner the requisite number of votes in Congress. Yet as Congress and other elected bodies debated a solution to the problem, the only one they could

---

133. *Congressional Globe*, 36th Cong., 2nd sess., January 15, 1861 (appendix), 58.

134. *Congressional Globe*, 36th Cong., 2nd sess., December 24, 1860, 190; ibid., Senate Report 288, 2–3; Reese, *Proceedings of the Virginia State Convention of 1861*, 3:155–158.

135. *Congressional Globe*, 36th Cong., 2nd sess., January 14, 1861, 378; Reese, *Proceedings of the Virginia State Convention of 1861*, 2:577.

136. *Congressional Globe*, 36th Cong., 2nd sess., December 12, 1860, 77, 78.

agree on was a constitutional amendment that guaranteed the continuation of slavery in the states where it already existed. Promoted by Crittenden (as mentioned above), it had been recast by Senator William Seward (New York) for consideration by the Senate's Committee of Thirteen, proposed to the Committee of Thirty-Three by Charles Francis Adams of Massachusetts, and rephrased by Ohio's Thomas Corwin. During the early morning of March 4, only hours before Lincoln was to be inaugurated, the Senate passed an amendment to the Constitution that read simply: "No Amendment shall be made to the Constitution which will authorize or give to Congress the power to abolish or interfere, within any State, with the domestic institutions thereof, including that of persons held to labor or service by the laws of said State."[137] (It had earlier been passed by the House of Representatives on February 28.) Five states subsequently ratified the so-called Seward-Adams-Corwin amendment (the original Thirteenth Amendment) before the ratification process was nullified by the war.[138]

One important aspect of the Seward-Adams-Corwin amendment is that it passed both houses of Congress with exactly the two-thirds majorities required by the Constitution. With most of the opposition coming from Republicans, had the seven Deep South states not seceded and their senators and representatives stayed in Washington, the bill would certainly have passed with much larger margins. Moderate Republicans who did vote in the affirmative could do so without violating their party's 1860 platform because it opposed the extension of slavery in the territories but not the existence of slavery in states. The bill, as Charles Francis Adams suggested in a speech on the House floor on January 31, would give to the slaveholding states "security" against state (northern) or congressional interference with the South's peculiar institution.[139] Democrats had mixed feelings, with some favoring the amendment because it clearly eliminated the possibility of future congressional interference with slavery, while others argued it was a meaningless measure, since the Constitution gave Congress no authority over the issue of slavery in the states. As a Kentucky House resolution

---

137. *Congressional Globe*, 36th Cong., 2nd sess., February 27, 1861, 1263.

138. The five states that ratified the amendment were Kentucky, Ohio, Rhode Island, Maryland, and Illinois. David E. Kyvig, *Explicit and Authentic Acts: Amending the U.S. Constitution, 1776–1995* (Lawrence: University of Kansas Press, 1996), 151; Crofts, *Lincoln and the Politics of Slavery*, 243–254. An excellent analysis of the debates in Congress can be found in Crofts's *Lincoln and the Politics of Slavery* and *Reluctant Confederates*, 193–214.

139. *Congressional Globe*, 36th Cong., 2nd sess., January 31, 1861 (appendix), 126.

maintained, "We regard the proposed amendment as a declaration of rights we already claim to possess."[140] Most significantly, however, ratification of the amendment by three-fourths of the states would have inserted into the Constitution, for the first time, specific and unambiguous protection for the institution of slavery.

Alternatives to Secession

Just days after Lincoln's inauguration, Senator Stephen Douglas presented the choices that faced the nation. "In my opinion," Douglas intoned, "we must choose, and that promptly, between one of three lines of policy." Those three "lines" included constitutional compromise, a "peaceful dissolution" of the Union, or war.[141] As historical inquiry during the early twentieth century developed along this line, some historians concluded that compromise would have avoided the deadly war that followed had Lincoln only been willing to accept some kind of constitutional understanding regarding slavery in the New Mexico Territory. "The responsibility for the failure of compromise" wrote Clinton E. Knox in 1932, "belongs jointly to the Republican party and Abraham Lincoln."[142] In reality, accepting the possibility of slavery in the territories was the only concession the South had to have, and it was the only one Republicans could not accept, as opposition to the

---

140. *Journal of the Called Session of the House of Representatives of the Commonwealth of Kentucky, Begun and Held in the Town of Frankfort, on Thursday the Seventeenth Day of January, in the Year of Our Lord 1861, and of the Commonwealth the Sixty-Ninth* (Frankfort: John B. Major, State Printer, 1861), 427. For a detailed history of the Seward-Adams-Corwin amendment, see R. Alton Lee, "The Corwin Amendment in the Secession Crisis," *Ohio History* 70, no. 1 (January 1961): 1–26; Crofts, *Reluctant Confederates*, 234–256; and Crofts, *Lincoln and the Politics of Slavery*.

141. *Congressional Globe*, 36th Cong., 2nd sess., March 15, 1861, 1460.

142. Clinton Everett Knox, "The Possibilities of Compromise in the Senate Committee of Thirteen and the Responsibility for Failure," *Journal of Negro History* 17, no. 4 (October 1932): 465. See also George Fort Milton, *The Eve of Conflict: Stephen A. Douglas and the Needless War* (1934; New York: Octagon Books, 1969), 526–530; Stampp, *And the War Came*, 123–158; Kirwan, *John J. Crittenden*, 369–390, 423–425; Alfred H. Kelly and Winfred A. Harbison, *The American Constitution: Its Origins and Development* (New York: W. W. Norton, 1970), 404–406; Daniel Farber, *Lincoln's Constitution* (Chicago: University of Chicago Press, 2003), 93; and Graber, *Dred Scott and the Problem of Constitutional Evil*, 177, 225–226, 251.

extension of slavery had been the cornerstone of their successful campaign for the presidency in 1860.

The choice, as articulated by Douglas and Knox and other early scholars of Secession Winter, puts the burden unfairly on the North. A more productive and interesting question is, "What choices did the slaveholding South have following the election of Lincoln?" The presumption that the South had no alternative but secession is a faulty one. The Deep South had several logical options, but chose instead to rush prematurely into secession. As David Potter observed more than seventy years ago, "If Southern public men had retained enough detachment of mind to weigh the factors involved, they might well have chosen not to inaugurate the program of secession."[143] In other words, was slavery as threatened by the incoming Republican administration as fire-breathing secessionists believed?[144]

Without doubt, the slave states considered themselves beleaguered. Not only was world opinion against them, but a glance at the map of the United States told them that eventually non-slave states would greatly outnumber slave states. When Congress admitted Kansas as a non-slave state in early 1861, the slave states were already in a minority. Once the territories north of the 36° 30' line gained sufficient population to be admitted as states, they would certainly enter the Union as non-slave states. Although California had been represented in Congress by pro-Southern Democrats for the past decade, it was, nevertheless, a non-slave state. Many in the South could foresee the demise of slavery once the institution had nowhere to expand. At that point, slavery would be contained and, as Republicans hoped, put on the road to ultimate extinction. Louisiana senator Judah Benjamin envisioned that likelihood on December 31, 1860, when he confronted his northern colleagues by agreeing with them that they (Republican senators) "do not pretend to enter into our States to kill or destroy our institutions by force. Oh, no . . . you propose simply to close us in an embrace that will suffocate us." He dramatically concluded, "You do not propose to fell the tree; you promised not. You merely propose to girdle it, that it dies."[145] Yet, with only the eastern half of Texas settled by slave-owning Anglos and the New Mexico Territory sparsely settled, the death of slavery predicted by

---

143. Potter, *Lincoln and His Party in the Secession Crisis*, 41.

144. Arthur C. Cole, "Lincoln's Election an Immediate Menace to Slavery in the States?" *American Historical Review* 36, no. 4 (July 1931): 740–767.

145. *Congressional Globe*, 36th Cong., 2nd sess., December 31, 1860, 217.

Benjamin would have taken decades. Did the South, then, act prematurely in its surge for secession?

Although counterfactual theories do not often add clarity to a historical event, a thoughtful inquiry into secession might consider what options the South possessed once news of Lincoln's election became known. Many Southerners clearly agreed with Senator Alfred Nicholson of Tennessee, who insisted on Christmas Eve of 1860 that "the election of Mr. Lincoln to the Presidency . . . is tantamount to a declaration of war against an institution which, in the South, is identified with all our interests, with all our happiness, with all our prosperity, socially, politically, and materially."[146] But what would have happened had the Lower South not been in such a rush to secede?

Wait for an Act of Aggression

There were voices of reason who argued that secessionists should take a "wait and see" attitude. They made the point that the election of 1860 had resulted in only modest gains for the Republican Party. The day before South Carolina voted to leave the Union, Democratic senator Andrew Johnson of Tennessee delivered an impassioned speech on the floor of the Senate arguing not only that secession was unconstitutional but also that it amounted to treason, "and nothing but treason." He acknowledged that the South had just cause for complaint, but that secession was not the answer. Johnson urged his southern colleagues to stay and "show ourselves men, and men of courage." Reminding the Senate that Democrats had won a majority in the Senate in the recent election, he implored: "Have we not got the brakes in our hands? Have we not got the power? We have. Let South Carolina send her Senators back; let all the Senators come; and on the 4th of March next we shall have a majority of six in this body against him. This successful sectional candidate . . . cannot make his Cabinet on the 4th of March next unless this Senate will permit him."[147]

While the presidency had been lost to the Republican candidate in the recent election, Democrats had emerged with slight majorities in both the House and the Senate, and the Supreme Court remained under the domination of the pro-slavery Chief Justice Roger B. Taney. As Representative

---

146. *Congressional Globe,* 36th Cong., 2nd sess., December 24, 1860, 187.

147. *Congressional Globe,* 36th Cong., 2nd sess., December 19, 1860, 137–142.

Reese B. Brabson explained two days before Lincoln's inauguration, if the Deep South states had not seceded, "It would have been impossible for the incoming Administration, for the next two years, to ingraft upon the legislation of the country the policy of the Republican party."[148] With Democrats in charge of both houses and in control therefore of the budget and presidential appointments, Brabson argued, Lincoln could do little harm to the institution of slavery.

Others in Congress, like Thomas Corwin of Ohio and a number of like-minded northern congressmen, attempted to persuade their southern colleagues that even if Republicans wanted to abolish slavery, there were not enough free states to ratify the requisite constitutional amendment. If the fifteen slave states voted as a block, Republicans would need forty-five states to achieve the three-fourths ratification number. "Such an amendment," he lectured, "could not be ratified until we had sixty States in the Union."[149] For all the hyperbole voiced by Southerners, there was virtually no chance that slavery would have been abolished through a constitutional amendment in their lifetime or their children's or, for that matter, even today.

Early in the second session of the 36th Congress, members proposed a counterargument to the southern proposition that secession was the only path available for the protection of slavery. Tennessee senator Andrew Johnson was the first to suggest (presciently) that leaving the Union would actually hasten the demise of slavery. "If I were an Abolitionist," he lectured, "the first step that I would take would be to break the bonds of this Union, and dissolve this Government."[150] Waitman T. Willey, a delegate to Virginia's secession convention, likewise asserted on Inauguration Day that "a dissolution of the Union will be the commencement of the abolition of slavery, first in Virginia then in the Border States, and ultimately throughout the Union."[151] Most famously, Governor Sam Houston of Texas explained to John Reagan, who would soon be appointed the Confederacy's postmaster general, "Our people are going to war to perpetuate slavery, and the first

---

148. *Congressional Globe,* 36th Cong., 2nd sess., March 2, 1861 (appendix), 294.

149. *Congressional Globe,* 36th Cong., 2nd sess., January 21, 1861 (appendix), 74; see also *Congressional Globe,* 36th Cong., 2nd sess., January 18, 1861, 454; January 22, 1861, 514; February 5, 1861, 761; and February 18, 1861, 1007.

150. *Congressional Globe,* 36th Cong., 2nd sess., 36th Cong., 2nd sess., December 19, 1860, 139.

151. Reese, *Proceedings of the Virginia State Convention of 1861,* March 4, 1861, 1:366–367.

gun fired in the war will be the knell of slavery."[152] Five years later, the ratification of the Thirteenth Amendment on December 18, 1865, proved these men genuine visionaries. It is interesting to note that the requisite number of states ratified the Thirteenth Amendment five years to the day after Senator Crittenden proposed his amendment that would have protected slavery in the federal Constitution.

Ratify the Seward-Adams-Corwin Amendment

A second recourse possessed by southern discontents, had they been less eager to secede, would have been the promotion and ratification of the Seward-Adams-Corwin amendment. As outlined above, this amendment provided a constitutional guarantee against congressional interference with the institution of slavery in the fifteen states where it already existed. It should be remembered that the New Mexico territorial legislature had approved a very detailed slave code in 1859 and Utah a much less restrictive one in 1852. While slavery as a major economic or political force was certainly not guaranteed in the two territories, the ratification of the Corwin amendment would have changed the political landscape wherein the future of slavery was discussed and would have provided a baseline constitutional protection for the institution which had not previously existed.

Pursue the Lemmon Slave Case

The third option available to secessionists over Secession Winter was the possibility of nationalizing slavery through the *Lemmon* slave case. As noted above, when the New York Court of Appeals found against Virginia in March 1860, the incoming governor, John Letcher, declined to pursue the suit to the Supreme Court. Historians today believe, however, that if Virginia had continued its appeal and the case had been argued before the Supreme Court, Roger B. Taney and his fellow justices would have found against New York. Historian Paul Finkelman has reasoned that given the pro-slavery nature of the Taney court, "it is not outrageous to think the decision would have been reversed and the right of slave transit in the North

---

152. John H. Reagan, "A Conversation with Governor Houston," *Quarterly of the Texas State Historical Association* 3, no. 4 (April 1900): 279–281.

upheld."[153] Such a verdict would certainly not have gone unchallenged over the long haul. Nevertheless, the ruling would have stood as long as the Supreme Court retained its pro-slavery majority. No evidence seems to exist, however, that other slave state governors encouraged Governor Letcher to pursue the case to the Taney court.

Divide Texas

The fourth alternative to immediate secession would have been to increase the number of slave states and therefore the South's representation in Congress. As Representative Orris Ferry, a Republican from Connecticut, reminded his southern colleagues in late January, the slave states had been authorized to "add to your number four more from Texas."[154] Ferry was recalling that the annexation of Texas only fifteen years earlier included a provision that Texans retained the option of dividing their state into as many as five states, if they so desired.[155] Earlier in the session, Missouri representative John W. Noell had actually proposed that the Committee of Thirty-Three consider restoring the equilibrium between North and South in the Senate by "a voluntary division on the part of some of the slave States into two or more States."[156] Garry Wills has demonstrated in *"Negro President": Jefferson and the Slave Power* that the Constitution's three-fifths compromise created enough of a southern advantage that it swung critical votes concerning slavery to the South's benefit.[157] Representatives like Ferry and Noell understood that adding three or four more slave states would have given the South significantly more power in Congress.

The Constitution addresses the admission of new states in two sections. Article IV, Section 3 provides that "New States may be admitted by the Congress into this Union," while Article I, Section 2 requires that each state must have at least one representative and that the number of representatives "shall not exceed one for every thirty Thousand" residents. In practice, the

---

153. Finkelman, *An Imperfect Union,* 313; see also Fehrenbacher, *The Dred Scott Case,* 445; McPherson, *Battle Cry of Freedom,* 181.

154. *Congressional Globe,* 36th Cong., 2nd sess., January 24, 1861, 551.

155. Seymour V. Connor, *Texas: A History* (New York: Thomas Y. Crowell, 1971), 154.

156. *Congressional Globe,* 36th Cong., 2nd sess., December 12, 1860, 78.

157. Garry Wills, *"Negro President": Jefferson and the Slave Power* (Boston: Houghton Mifflin, 2003), 1–13.

number of settlers occupying a territory at the time of statehood varied greatly. Nevada, for example, was admitted in 1864 with a population of fewer than 42,000 while Alabama was admitted in 1819 with a population of 127,000. California became a state in 1850 with a population of 92,000. Three states gained admission at the end of the 1850s with varying populations: Minnesota (1858) with a population of 172,000, Oregon (1859) with 52,000, and Kansas (1861) with 107,000. While in 1860 only the eastern half of Texas was populated by non-Native Americans, its population totaled 604,000, easily sufficient to justify the creation of several smaller states. As the future of slavery in the New Mexico Territory remained uncertain, carving additional states from Texas would have given the South an additional hedge against northern interference and in 1860–1861 would have been less extreme than secession.

Slavery in the Confederate Constitution

Another path to understanding the 1860–1861 disruption of the Union is to explore the secessionists' treatment of slavery and states' rights in the constitution they constructed in Montgomery early in 1861. Written by delegates from the first seven states to secede and modeled closely on the U.S. Constitution, the Constitution of the Confederate States of America placed the institution of slavery well beyond the reach of state interference. Like the Seward-Adams-Corwin amendment to the U.S. Constitution, the Confederate Constitution prevented congressional tampering with slavery: "No bill of attainder, ex post facto law, or law denying or impairing the right of property in negro slaves shall be passed" (Article 1, Section 9, Part 4).

The constitution makers in Montgomery had been attentive to the debates over Secession Winter to protect slavery in the western territories and were equally aware of the proposals to change the U.S. Constitution to favor slavery in other ways. The Confederate Constitution specifically recognized and protected slavery in any future territory acquired by the Confederacy and provided that inhabitants of the Confederate states "shall have the right to take to such territory any slaves lawfully held by them in any of the States or Territories of the Confederate States" (Article IV, Section 3, Part 3).[158]

---

158. Charles Robert Lee Jr., *The Confederate Constitutions* (Chapel Hill: University of North Carolina Press, 1963), 195.

Having addressed the fundamental constitutional issue that had confounded political agreement in the United States since 1846, the Confederates then turned their attention to fugitive slaves by clarifying the fugitive slave clause to specifically include the word "slave" to define more distinctly "persons held to service of labor." They further clarified the "sojourning" issue raised by the *Lemmon* slave case by amending the "privileges and immunities" clause. The new Confederate constitution ensured that owners could travel with their slaves virtually anywhere within the Confederacy without regard to state interference. "The citizens of each State shall be entitled to all the privileges and immunities of citizens in the several States, and shall have the right of transit and sojourn in any State of this Confederacy, with their slaves and other property; and the right of property in said slaves shall not be thereby impaired" (Article IV, Section 2, Parts 1 and 3).[159]

With these "explanatory amendments," the secessionists successfully brought their constitution in line with Roger B. Taney's 1857 conviction that "property in a slave is distinctly and expressly affirmed in the Constitution." Employing precise expressions such as "property in said slaves," "property in negro slaves," and "slaves and other property," the new southern constitution effectively defined property in slaves as property covered by the Fifth Amendment which had been embedded in the body of the new Confederate charter. The protections for the peculiar institution that Southerners had been seeking throughout the preceding decade had become a reality: No person could be "deprived of life, liberty, or [slave] property without due process of law" (Article 1, Section 9, Part 16).[160] Slavery in the Confederacy was no longer protected by local authority and could not be impaired by state legislation. It had become national, defined and insulated by the new federal constitution. Safeguarding the institution of slavery in this manner was no anomaly. "From the beginning," legal scholar Mark A. Graber has observed, "proponents of slavery were nationalists whenever they thought uniform federal legislation more likely than diverse state laws to serve Southern interests."[161]

159. Ibid., 94.

160. Ibid., 182–194. See also William C. Davis, *"A Government of Our Own": The Making of the Confederacy* (Baton Rouge: Louisiana State University Press, 1994), 224–261.

161. Graber, *Dred Scott and the Problem of Constitutional Evil*, 105.

Epilogue

The election of 1860 was waged to settle the fate of slavery in the territories. "Never in any previous presidential election," declared Democratic senator Joseph Lane of Oregon (and John Breckinridge's running mate), "has the issue been so fully put, so directly made, as in the late one. The question everywhere was: shall the equality of the States be maintained; shall the people of every State have a right to go into the common territory with their property?"[162] Nevertheless, many white Southerners believed, as discussed above, that the Republican Party's ultimate goal was the abolition of slavery throughout the country. Senator Lazarus Powell of Kentucky posed the problem most clearly: "The people of the South would be stupid indeed if they did not see in all this a fixed design and purpose ultimately to overthrow and destroy their domestic institutions upon which their very existence depends."[163] Representative Albert Rust of Arkansas was equally emphatic when he observed, "We of the South believe that the leaders of the Republican party are pledged to abolish slavery wherever it exists, if they can constitutionally do it."[164] Three weeks after the election, Jabez Lamar Monroe Curry lectured a Talladega, Alabama, audience that "hostility to the South and her peculiar property" is the primary policy of the Republican Party, and the victory of Lincoln meant that "abolitionism has triumphed."[165] The evidence from Secession Winter, however, tells a different story.

While there were Republicans who were also abolitionists, the official and oft-stated policy of the Republican Party was opposition to the extension of slavery, not opposition to the continuation of slavery where it already existed. The 1860 Republican platform firmly supported "the right of each State to order and control its own domestic institutions according to its own judgement exclusively."[166] Lincoln repeatedly stated that he had no intention to "interfere with the institution of slavery in the states where it exists." He reiterated this conviction in his first inaugural address and even

---

162. *Congressional Globe*, 36th Cong., 2nd sess., December 5, 1860, 8.

163. *Congressional Globe*, 36th Cong., 2nd sess., January 22, 1861 (appendix), 95.

164. *Congressional Globe*, 36th Cong., 2nd sess., January 24, 1861 (appendix), 97.

165. Jabez Lamar Monroe Curry, "The Perils and Duty of the South," in Wakelyn, *Southern Pamphlets*, 38–39.

166. Benton, *Annals of America*, 9:189.

quoted the party's position from the Chicago Platform.[167] By the time of the election of 1860, however, passions in the South had become so vexed that Southerners could not believe that a president and a party so opposed to the extension of slavery would not turn their attention to slavery in the states. That Lincoln was an abolitionist and the North filled with abolitionists of the John Brown stripe was common, albeit erroneous, knowledge throughout the South.[168]

Secession, threatened in 1820 and again in 1850, had become by 1860 the Deep South's answer to the antislavery movement in the North. Between the opening of the second session of the 36th Congress and the inauguration of Lincoln, secession was hotly debated throughout the country. Proponents and opponents of the right of secession argued endlessly based on political preferences and emotional predispositions, but not within any constitutional framework because the U.S. Constitution was (and remains) silent on the issue of secession. Representative Edward Wade from Ohio spoke for the Union side of the argument by stating, "If a State has a right to abandon the Union, by asserting that it withdraws from the Union, then, evidently, there is no Union. Under this childish dogma the Union framed by our ever glorious fathers was, and is, a humbug and a cheat, and those who framed it FOOLS!"[169]

On the other side, Senator Louis T. Wigfall of Texas, one of the more colorful characters in the secession drama, presented the separatists' position most simply: "I say, then, a State has a right, with or without cause, to withdraw; . . . when a State has withdrawn she is out of the Union, and her citizens cease to owe obedience to the laws of this Government."[170] Alcibiades DeBlanc, a delegate from St. Martin Parish to the Louisiana secession convention, invoked not the U.S. Constitution but a higher authority in his plea for separation: "Our honor, our legitimate pride, the interests of our slaves and of mankind, command that Louisiana owes allegiance only to

---

167. Harold Holzer, *Lincoln President-Elect: Abraham Lincoln and the Great Secession Winter, 1860–1861* (New York: Simon & Schuster, 2008), 464; Crofts, *Lincoln and the Politics of Slavery,* 185–208.

168. The historian William Freehling has estimated that only 2 percent of the northern voting populace identified themselves as abolitionists. See Freehling, *The Road to Disunion,* 2:12. For an insightful assessment of the Republican position on slavery, see Crofts, *Lincoln and the Politics of Slavery,* 271–282.

169. *Congressional Globe,* 36th Cong., 2nd sess., February 19, 1861 (appendix), 230.

170. *Congressional Globe,* 36th Cong., 2nd sess., December 5, 1860, 14.

her laws and to God, and that she is compelled, by the injustice and bad faith of her sisters of the North, to abandon a Union which she has loved, still loves, and deeply regrets."[171] The arguments for and against secession raged throughout Secession Winter without resolution because the constitutional right of secession had never before been seriously considered or adjudicated. It remained an open constitutional question until 1869 when the U.S. Supreme Court (in *Texas v. White*) decided the unconstitutionality of secession.[172]

In hindsight, secession solved none of the South's three major complaints against the North: opposition to the extension of slavery into the western territories, resistance to the return of fugitive slaves, and obstruction to sojourning through non-slave states with their slaves. Once the South left the Union, New Mexico, Utah, and Nebraska were administered, as far as the Confederate South was concerned, by a foreign power—the United States. Likewise, secession made the return of fugitive slaves next to impossible because they would have escaped not to a different state but to a different country. Similarly, secession absolved the nineteen non-slave states of any obligation to allow slaves, even temporarily, to reside within their borders.

The decades-long quest to safeguard the South's economic engine had, at last, culminated in the breakup of the Union. Manifest federal meddling with the peculiar institution envisioned in the 1850 Georgia Platform, however, had failed to become a reality. During the decade between the Compromise of 1850 and the inauguration of Abraham Lincoln, Congress never implemented the dreaded Wilmot Proviso or restricted slavery in the western territories in any fashion, never modified the vigorous 1850 Fugitive Slave Act, never abolished slavery in the District of Columbia or in federal installations in the South, never acted to suppress the interstate slave trade, and never passed legislation that would have adversely affected the Supreme Court's ruling in the *Dred Scott* case.

Instead, the threat to slavery in 1860, as far as secessionists were concerned, came from the sectional Republican Party that continued to preach

---

171. *Official Journal of the Proceedings of the Convention of the State of Louisiana* (New Orleans: J. O. Nixon, Printer to the State Convention, 1861), 9. For more on the connections between slavery and religion see Paul Finkelman, *Defending Slavery: Proslavery Thought in the Old South* (Boston: Bedford/St. Martin's, 2003), 96–128; Mark A. Noll, *The Civil War as Theological Crisis* (Chapel Hill: University of North Carolina Press, 2006); and Charles Reagan Wilson, *Baptized in Blood: The Religion of the Lost Cause, 1865–1920* (Athens: University of Georgia Press, 1980), 1–17.

172. Kelly and Harbison, *American Constitution*, 448.

against the extension of slavery into the territories and disagree with Chief Justice Taney that slavery was defined as property in the Constitution, and from northern states that obstructed the return of fugitive slaves. Federal overreach was not what riled the South in 1860, but an antislavery rhetoric and a confrontational states' rights ideology of interposition and nullification adopted by some northern legislatures. Eleven southern states seceded in 1860–1861 not in defense of states' rights but in defense of property rights. The slave South's response to the election of a president and a party opposed to the extension of slavery was to rend the Union, temporarily create a separate country, prompt a war that led to 750,000 deaths, and hasten the end of slavery by decades.

As congressional debates failed to develop a solution to the constitutional crisis, Ohio's Thomas Corwin vented his frustration by lecturing his colleagues in the U.S. House of Representatives: "Some historian, writing a thousand years hence, will look back on this period of our history, and will come to the conclusion that the great experiment on this continent, which was intended to demonstrate that man was capable of self-government, was near a total failure at this time; and one of his proofs would be the very insanity—I call it nothing else—which the people of the country have exhibited touching the question of slavery."[173] Mindful that future generations would study the speeches and debates preoccupying Congress over the winter of 1860–1861, Corwin anticipated today's fascination with the war, its causes, its consequences, and with the ideology of white supremacy which continue to ripple through the social and political structure of the United States.

Sources

The long-threatened breakup of the Union over Secession Winter was remarkably well documented at both the national and state levels. Debates from the second session of the 36th Congress occupy 2,000 pages in its original typescript preserved in the Library of Congress and are easily accessed online: http://memory.loc.gov/ammem/amlaw/lwcglink.html#anchor36. Printed with ten-point type on three columns per page, the *Congressional Globe* for those three months provides a front-row seat for those attracted by the details of the sectional drama as it played out over the winter of

---

173. *Congressional Globe,* 36th Cong., 2nd sess., January 21, 1861 (appendix), 74.

1860–1861. The journal of the Washington Peace Conference contributes another 621 pages of day-by-day deliberations. Every state that seceded produced a detailed journal of its proceedings. Virginia considered secession longer than any other and left a record 3,000 pages of testimony compiled in four volumes. South Carolina published a journal totaling 420 pages and Texas one of 452 pages. When one adds the debates from the Tennessee and Kentucky general assemblies (neither state called a secession convention), the official record from Secession Winter amounts to over 8,000 pages.

With two exceptions, this official register of secession has been available to the general public since early in the war. Almost all of these sanctioned papers were published in 1861 or 1862. Lucius Chittenden published his record of the Washington Peace Conference in 1864 whereas Texas did not publish the proceedings of its convention until 1912. The documents that follow have been selected to illustrate the insurmountable differences that separated Democrats from Republicans on the eve of the Civil War. They offer an expansive and detailed window into the political debates that divided a nation in 1860–1861 and an intimate view of the economic, social, ideological, and constitutional abyss caused by this country's "peculiar institution."

[Note: Because most of the following documents include explanatory brackets in the original, the editor's emendations are included within braces, i.e., {}.]

PART ONE

James Buchanan and
John J. Crittenden

James Buchanan's Address to Congress

December 3, 1860

James Buchanan (1791–1868) was sixty-six years old when he took the oath of office on March 4, 1857, and he entered the presidency with more political experience than any president since James Madison. He had served in the Pennsylvania state legislature and in the U.S. House of Representatives and Senate. He had been appointed minister to Russia by Andrew Jackson, secretary of state by James K. Polk, and minister to Great Britain by Franklin Pierce. Although a Northerner, Buchanan's experience and friendships in Washington led him to the pro-slavery side on the issues dividing Washington and the country.

His last formal address to Congress, delivered as South Carolina was preparing to convene its secession convention, illustrates Buchanan's view of the crisis. He believed that the unrest in the country was due to the "intemperate interference of the northern people with the question of slavery in the southern States." In his analysis of the "discontent" throughout the country, he makes it clear that the problem is not with what the federal government has done but what it might do in the future. And to that end, while he declared secession unconstitutional, he believed he had no power as president to prevent southern states from leaving the Union. The careful reader will note that Buchanan does not list federal violations of state authority as one of the problems besetting the country, nor does he mention problems with tariffs except to note that they will continue to be collected in Charleston.

MESSAGE
OF THE
PRESIDENT OF THE UNITED STATES.

Fellow citizens of the Senate and House of Representatives:

Throughout the year since our last meeting, the country has been eminently prosperous in all its material interests. The general health has been excellent, our harvests have been abundant, and plenty of smiles throughout the land. Our commerce and manufactures have been prosecuted with energy and industry, and have yielded fair and ample returns. In short, no nation in the tide of time has ever presented a spectacle of greater material prosperity than we have done until within a very recent period.

Why is it, then, that discontent now so extensively prevails, and the Union of the States, which is the source of all these blessings is threatened with destruction? The long-continued and intemperate interference of the northern people with the question of slavery in the southern States has at length produced its natural effects. The different sections of the Union are now arrayed against each other, and the time has arrived, so much dreaded by the Father of his Country {George Washington}, when hostile geographical parties have been formed. I have long foreseen and often forewarned my countrymen of the now impending danger. This does not proceed solely from the claim on the part of the Congress or the Territorial Legislatures to exclude slavery from the Territories, or from the efforts of different States to defeat the execution of the fugitive slave law. All or any of these evils might have been endured by the South without danger to the Union—as others have been—in the hope that time and reflection might apply the remedy. The immediate peril arises, not so much from these causes, as from the fact that the incessant and violent agitation of the slavery question throughout the North for the last quarter of a century has at length produced its malign influence on the slaves, and inspired them with vague notions of freedom. Hence a sense of security no longer exists around the family altar. This feeling of peace at home has given place to apprehensions of servile insurrection. Many a matron throughout the South retires at night in dread of what may befall herself and her children before the morning. Should this apprehension of domestic danger, whether real or imaginary, extend and intensify itself until it shall pervade the masses of the southern people, then disunion will become inevitable. Self-preservation is the first law of nature, and has been implanted in the heart of man by his Creator for the wisest purpose; and no political union, however fraught with blessings and benefits in all other respects, can long continue, if the necessary consequence be to render the homes and firesides of nearly half the parties to it habitually and hopelessly insecure. Sooner or later the bonds of such a Union must be severed. It is my conviction that this fatal period has not yet arrived; and my prayer to God is that He would preserve the Constitution and the Union throughout all generations.

But let us take warning in time, and remove the cause of danger. It cannot be denied that, for five and twenty years, the agitation at the North against slavery in the South has been incessant. In 1835 pictorial handbills and inflammatory appeals were circulated extensively throughout the South, of a character to excite the passions of the slaves; and, in the language of General Jackson, "to stimulate them to insurrection, and produce all the horrors of a servile war." This agitation has ever since been continued by the public press, by the proceedings of State and county conventions, and by abolition sermons and lectures. The time of Congress has been occupied in violent speeches of this never-ending subject; and appeals in pamphlet and other forms, indorsed by distinguished names, have been sent forth from this central point, and spread broadcast over the Union.

How easy would it be for the American people to settle the slavery question forever, and to restore peace and harmony to this distracted country!

They, and they alone, can do it. All that is necessary to accomplish the object, and all for which the slave States have ever contended, is to be let alone, and permitted to manage their domestic institutions in their own way. As sovereign States, they, and they alone, are responsible before God and the world for slavery existing among them. For this, the people of the North are not more responsible, and have no more right to interfere, than with similar institutions in Russia or in Brazil. Upon their good sense and patriotic forbearance I confess I still greatly rely. Without their aid, it is beyond the power of any President, no matter what may be his own political proclivities, to restore peace and harmony among the States. Wisely limited and restrained as is his power, under our Constitution and laws, he alone can accomplish little, for good or for evil, on such a momentous question.

And this brings me to observe that the election of any one of our fellow-citizens to the office of President does not of itself afford just cause for dissolving the Union. This is more especially true if his election has been effected by a mere plurality, and not a majority, of the people, and has resulted from transient and temporary causes, which may probably never again occur. In order to justify a resort to revolutionary resistance, the Federal Government must be guilty of a "deliberate, palpable, and dangerous exercise" of powers not granted by the Constitution. The late presidential election, however, has been held in strict conformity with its express provisions. How, then, can the result justify a revolution to destroy this very Constitution? Reason, justice, a regard for the Constitution, all require that we shall wait for some overt and dangerous act on the part of the President elect before resorting to such a remedy.

It is said, however, that the antecedents of the President elect have been sufficient to justify the fears of the South that he will attempt to invade their constitutional rights. But are such apprehensions of contingent danger in the future sufficient to justify the immediate destruction of the noblest system of government ever devised by mortals? From the very nature of his office, and its high responsibilities, he must necessarily be conservative. The stern duty of administering the vast and complicated concerns of this Government affords in itself a guarantee that he will not attempt any violation of a clear constitutional right. After all, he is no more than the chief executive office of the Government. His province is not to make, but to execute the laws; and it is a remarkable fact in our history that, not withstanding the repeated efforts of the anti-slavery party, no single act has ever passed Congress, unless we may possibly except the Missouri compromise, impairing, in the slightest degree, the rights of the South to their property in slaves. And it may also be observed, judging from present indications, that no probability exists of the passage of such an act by a majority of both Houses, either in the present or the next Congress. Surely, under these circumstances, we ought to be restrained from present action by the precept of Him who spake as never man spake, that "sufficient unto the day is the evil thereof."[1] The day of evil may never come, unless we shall rashly bring it upon ourselves.

It is alleged as one cause for immediate secession that the southern States are denied equal rights with the other States in the common Territories. But by what authority are these denied? Not by Congress, which has never passed, and I believe never will pass, any act to exclude slavery from these

---

1. From Jesus's Sermon on the Mount, Matthew 6:34.

Territories; and certainly not by the Supreme Court, which has solemnly decided that slaves are property, and like all other property, their owners have a right to take them into the common Territories, and hold them there under the protection of the Constitution.

So far, then, as Congress is concerned, the objection is not to anything they have already done, but to what they may do hereafter. It will surely be admitted that this apprehension of future danger is no good reason for an immediate dissolution of the Union. It is true that the Territorial Legislature of Kansas, on the 23d of February, 1860, passed, in great haste, an act, over the veto of the Governor, declaring that slavery "is, and shall be, forever prohibited in this Territory." Such an act, however, plainly violating the rights of property secured by the Constitution, will surely be declared void by the judiciary whenever it shall be presented in a legal form.

Only three days after my inauguration the Supreme Court of the United States solemnly adjudged that this power did not exist in a Territorial Legislature. Yet such has been the factious temper of the times that the correctness of this decision has been extensively impugned before the people, and the question has given rise to angry political conflicts throughout the country. Those who have appealed from this judgement of our highest constitutional tribunal to popular assemblies would, if they could, invest a Territorial Legislature with power to annul the sacred rights of property. This power Congress is expressly forbidden by the Federal Constitution to exercise. Every State Legislature in the Union is forbidden by its own constitution to exercise it. It cannot be exercised in any State except by the people in their highest sovereign capacity when framing or amending their State constitutions. In like manner, it can only be exercised by the people of a Territory represented in a convention of delegates for the purpose of framing a constitution preparatory to admission as a State into the Union. Then, and not until then, are they invested with power to decide the question whether slavery shall or shall not exist within their limits. This is an act of sovereign authority, and not of subordinate territorial legislation. Were it otherwise, then indeed would the equality of the States in the Territories be destroyed, and the rights of property in slaves would depend, not upon the shifting majorities of an irresponsible Territorial Legislature. Such a doctrine, from its intrinsic unsoundness, cannot long influence any considerable portion of our people; much less can it afford a good reason for a dissolution of the Union.

The most palpable violations of constitutional duty which have yet been committed consist in the acts of different State Legislatures to defeat the execution of the fugitive slave law. It ought to be remembered, however, that for these acts, neither Congress nor any President can justly be held responsible. Having been passed in violation of the Federal Constitution, they are therefore null and void. All the courts, both State and national, before whom the question has arisen, have, from the beginning, declared the fugitive slave law to be constitutional. The single exception of that is a State court in Wisconsin; and this has not only been reversed by the proper appellate tribunal, but has met with such universal reprobation that there can be no danger from it as a precedent. The validity of this law has been established over and over again by the Supreme Court of the United States, with perfect unanimity. It is founded upon an express provision of the Constitution, requiring that fugitive slaves who escape from service in one State to another, shall be "delivered up" to their masters. Without this provision it is a well-known historical fact that the Constitution itself could never have been adopted by the convention. In one form or other under the acts of 1793 and 1850, both being substantially the same, the fugitive slave law has been the law of the land from the days of Washington until the present moment. Here, then, a clear case is presented, in which it will be the duty of the next President, as it has been my own, to act with vigor in executing this supreme law against the conflicting enactments of State Legislatures. Should he fail in the performance of this high duty, he will then have manifested a disregard of the Constitution and laws, to the great injury of the people of nearly one half of the States of the Union. But are we to presume in advance that he will thus violate his duty? This would be at war with every principle of justice and Christian charity. Let us wait for the overt act. The fugitive slave law has been carried into execution in every contested case since the commencement of the present Administration; though often, it is to be regretted, with great loss and inconvenience to the master, and with considerable expense to the Government. Let us trust that the State Legislatures will repeal their unconstitutional and obnoxious enactments. Unless this shall be done without unnecessary delay, it is impossible for any human power to save the Union.

The southern States, standing on the basis of the Constitution, have a right to demand this act of justice from the States of the North. Should it be refused, then the Constitution, to which all the States are parties, will have been willfully violated by one portion of them in a provision essential to the domestic security and happiness of the remainder. In that event, the injured States, after having first used all peaceful and constitutional means to obtain redress, would be justified in revolutionary resistance to the Government of the Union.

I have purposely confined my remarks to revolutionary resistance, because it has been claimed within the last few years, that any State, whenever this shall be its sovereign will and pleasure, may secede from the Union, in accordance with the Constitution, and without any violation of the constitutional rights of the other members of the Confederacy; that as each became parties to the Union by the vote of its own people assembled in convention, so any one of them may retire from the Union in a similar manner by the vote of such a convention.

In order to justify secession as a constitutional remedy, it must be on the principle that the Federal Government is a mere voluntary association of States, to be dissolved at pleasure by any one of the contracting parties. If this be so, the Confederacy is a rope of sand, to be penetrated and dissolved by the first adverse wave of public opinion in any of the States. In this manner our thirty-three States may resolve themselves into as many petty, jarring, and hostile republics, each one retiring from the Union, without responsibility, whenever any sudden excitement might impel them to such a course. By this process, a Union might be entirely broken into fragments in a few weeks, which cost our forefathers many years of toil, privation, and blood to establish.

Such a principle is wholly inconsistent with the history as well as the character of the Federal Constitution. After it was framed, with the greatest deliberation and care, it was submitted to conventions of the people of the several States for ratification. Its provisions were discussed at length in these bodies, composed of the first men of the country. Its opponents contended that it conferred powers upon the Federal Government dangerous to the rights of the States; while its advocates maintained that under a fair construction of the instrument there was no foundation for such apprehensions. In that mighty struggle between the first intellects of this or any other country, it never occurred to any individual, either among its opponents or advocates, to assert, or even to intimate, that their efforts were all vain labor, because the moment that any State felt herself aggrieved she might secede from the Union. What a crushing argument would this have proved against those who dreaded that the rights of the States would be endangered by the Constitution! The truth is, that it was not until many years after the origin of the Federal Government that such a proposition was first advanced. It was then met and refuted by the conclusive arguments of General Jackson {then President Andrew Jackson}, who, in his message of 16th of January, 1833, transmitting the nullifying ordinance of South Carolina to Congress, employs the following language: "The right of the people of a single State to absolve themselves at will, and without the consent of the other States, from their most solemn obligations, and hazard for liberty and happiness of the millions composing this Union, cannot be acknowledged. Such authority is believed to be utterly repugnant both to the principles upon which the General Government is constituted and to the objects which it was expressly formed to attain."[2]

It is not pretended that any clause in the Constitution gives countenance to such a theory. It is altogether founded upon inference, not from any language contained in the instrument itself, but from the sovereign character of the several States by which it was ratified. But is it beyond the power of a State, like an individual, to yield a portion of its sovereign rights to secure the remainder? In the language of Mr. {James} Madison, who has been called the father of the Constitution:

> It was formed by the States—that is, by the people in each of the States, acting in their highest sovereign capacity; and formed consequently by the same authority which formed the State constitutions.
>
> Nor is the Government of the United States created by the Constitution less a Government in the strict sense of the term, within the sphere of its powers, than the governments created by the constitutions of the States are within their several spheres. It is, like them, organized into legislative, executive, and judiciary departments. It operates, like them, directly on persons and things; and, like them, it has at command a physical force for executing the powers committed to it.

It was intended to be perpetual, and not to be annulled at the pleasure of any one of the contracting parties. The old Articles of Confederation were entitled "Articles of Confederation and Perpetual Union between the States," and by the thirteenth article it is expressly declared that "the articles of this Confederation shall be inviolably observed by every State, and the Union shall be perpetual." The preamble to the Constitution of the United States, having express reference to the Articles of Confederation, recites that it was established "in order to form a more perfect union." And yet it is contended that this "more perfect union" does not include the essential attribute of perpetuity.

---

2. In November 1832, South Carolina had passed ordinances nullifying the tariffs of 1828 and 1832. President Jackson's request of January 16 to Congress to use military force if necessary to collect tariffs led to the compromise (and lower) tariff of 1833.

But that the Union was designed to be perpetual appears conclusively from the nature and extent of the powers conferred by the Constitution on the Federal Government. These powers embrace the very highest attributes of national sovereignty. They place both the sword and the purse under its control. Congress has power to make war and to make peace; to raise and support armies and navies, and to conclude treaties with foreign Governments. It is invested with the power to coin money and to regulate the value thereof, and to regulate commerce with foreign nations and among the several States. It is not necessary to enumerate the other high powers which have been conferred upon the Federal Government. In order to carry the enumerated powers into effect, Congress possesses the exclusive right to lay and collect duties on imports, and in common with the States to lay and collect all other taxes.

But the Constitution has not only conferred these high powers upon Congress, but it has adopted effectual means to restrain the States from interfering with their exercise. For that purpose it has, in strong prohibitory language, expressly declared that "no State shall enter into any treaty, alliance, or confederation; grant letters of Marque and reprisal {commissions or warrants issued to someone to commit what would otherwise be acts of piracy}; coin money; emit bills of credit; make anything but gold and silver coin a tender in payment of debts; pass any bill of attainder, ex post facto law, or law impairing the obligation of contracts." Moreover, "without the consent of Congress, no State shall lay any imports or duties on any imports or exports, except what may be absolutely necessary for executing its inspection laws"; and, if they exceed this amount, the excess shall belong to the United States.

And "no State shall, without the consent of Congress, lay any duty of tonnage {a charge imposed on a commercial vessel for entering, remaining in, or leaving a port}; keep troops or ships-of-war in time of peace; enter into any agreement or compact with another State, or with a foreign Power; or engage in war, unless actually invaded, or in such imminent danger as will not admit of delay."

In order still further to secure the uninterrupted exercise of these high powers against State interposition, it is provided "that this Constitution and the laws of the United States which shall be made in pursuance thereof, and all treaties made, or which shall be made, under the authority of the United States, shall be the supreme law of the land; and the judges in every State shall be bound thereby, anything in the constitution or laws of any State to the contrary notwithstanding."

The solemn sanction of religion has been super-added to the obligations of official duty, and all Senators and Representatives of the United States, all members of State Legislatures, and all executive and judicial officers, "both of the United States and of the several States, shall be bound by oath or affirmation to support this Constitution."

In order to carry into effect these powers, the Constitution has established a perfect Government in all its forms, legislative, executive, and judicial; and this Government, to the extent of its powers, acts directly upon the individual citizens of every State, and executes its own decrees by the agency of its own officers. In this respect it differs entirely from the Government under the old Confederation, which was confined to making requisitions on the States in their sovereign character. This left it in the discretion of each whether to obey or to refuse, and they often declined to comply with such requisitions. It thus became necessary, for the purpose of removing this barrier, and "in order to form a more perfect Union," to establish a Government which could act directly upon the people, and execute its own laws without the intermediate agency of the States. This has been accomplished by the Constitution of the United States.

In short, the Government created by the Constitution, and deriving its authority from the sovereign people of each of the several States, has precisely the same right to exercise its power over the people of all these States, in the enumerated cases, that each one of them possesses over subjects not delegated to the United States, but "reserved to the States, respectively, or to the people."

To the extent of the delegated powers, the Constitution of the United States is as much a part of the constitution of each State, and is as binding upon its people, as though it had been textually inserted therein.

The Government, therefore, is a great and powerful Government, invested with all the attributes of sovereignty over the special subjects to which its authority extends. Its framers never intended to implant in its bosom the seeds of its own destruction, nor were they at its creation guilty of the absurdity of providing for its own dissolution. It was not intended by its framers to be the baseless fabric of a vision which, at the touch of the enchanter, would vanish into thin air; but a substantial and mighty fabric, capable of resisting the slow decay of time and of defying the storms of ages. Indeed, well may the jealous patriots of that day have indulged fears that a Government of such high powers might violate the reserved rights of the States; and wisely did they adopt the rule of a strict construction of these powers to prevent the danger! But they did not fear, nor had they any reason to imagine, that the Constitution would ever be so interpreted as to enable any State, by her own act, and without the consent of her sister States, to discharge her people from all or any of their Federal obligations.

It may be asked, then, are the people of the States without redress against the tyranny and oppression of the Federal Government? By no means. The right of resistance on the part of the governed against the oppression of their Governments cannot be denied. It exists independently of all constitutions, and has been exercised at all periods of the world's history. Under it old governments have been destroyed, and new ones have taken their place. It is embodied in strong and express language in our own Declaration of Independence. But the distinction must ever be observed, that this is revolution against an established Government, and not a voluntary secession from it by virtue of an inherent constitutional right. In short, let us look the danger fairly in the face: Secession is neither more nor less than revolution. It may or it may not be a justifiable revolution, but still it is revolution.

What, in the mean time, is the responsibility and true position of the Executive {President}? He is bound by solemn oath before God and the country "to take care that the laws be faithfully executed," and from this obligation he cannot be absolved by any human power. But what if the performance of this duty, in whole or in part, has been rendered impracticable by events over which he could have exercised no control? Such, at the present moment, is the case throughout the State of South Carolina, so far as the laws of the United States to secure the administration of justice by means of the Federal judiciary are concerned. All the Federal officers within its limits, through whose agency alone these laws can be carried into execution, have already resigned. We no longer have a district judge, a district attorney, or a marshal, in South Carolina. In fact, the whole machinery of the Federal Government, necessary for the distribution of remedial justice among the people, has been demolished; and it would be difficult, if not impossible, to replace it. The only acts of Congress on the statute-book bearing upon this subject are those of the 28th February, 1795, and 3d March, 1807. These authorize the President, after he shall have ascertained that the marshal, with his *posse comitatus* {an ad hoc deputized group of citizens}, is unable to execute civil or criminal process in any particular case, to call forth the militia and employ the Army and Navy to aid him in performing this service; having first, by proclamation, commanded the insurgents "to disperse and retire peaceably to their abodes, within a limited time." This duty cannot by possibility be performed in a State where no judicial authority exists to issue process, and where there is no marshal to execute it, and where, even if there were such an officer, the entire population would constitute one solid combination to resist him.

The bare enumeration of these provisions proves how inadequate they are without further legislation to overcome a united opposition in a single State, not to speak of other States who may place themselves in a similar attitude. Congress alone has power to decide whether the present laws can or cannot be amended so as to carry out more effectively the objects of the Constitution.

The same insuperable obstacles do not lie in the way of executing the laws for the collection of the customs. The revenue still continues to be collected, as heretofore, at the custom-house in Charleston; and should the collector unfortunately resign, a successor may be appointed to perform this duty.

Then, in regard to the property of the United States in South Carolina. This has been purchased for a fair equivalent, "by the consent of the Legislature of the State," "for the erection of forts, magazines, arsenals," &c., and over these the authority "to exercise exclusive legislation" has been expressly granted by the Constitution to Congress. It is not believed that any attempt will be made to expel the United States from this property by force; but if in this I should prove to be mistaken, the officer in command of the forts has received orders to act strictly on the defensive. In such a contingency, the responsibility for consequences would rightfully rest upon the heads of the assailants.

Apart from the execution of the laws, so far as this may be practicable, the Executive has no authority to decide what shall be the relations between the Federal Government and South Carolina. He has been invested with no such discretion. He possesses no power to change the relations heretofore existing between them, much less acknowledge the independence of that State. This would be to invest a mere Executive officer with the power of recognizing the dissolution of the Confederacy among our thirty-three sovereign States. It bears no resemblance to the recognition of a foreign de facto {existing in fact} Government, involving no such responsibility. Any attempt to do this would, on his part, be a naked act of usurpation. It is, therefore, my duty to submit to Congress the whole question in all its bearings. The course of events is so rapidly hastening forward, that the emergency may soon arise when you may be called upon to decide the momentous question whether you possess the power, by force of arms, to compel a State to remain in the Union. I should feel myself recreant to my duty were I not to express an opinion on this important subject.

The question fairly stated is: Has the Constitution delegated to Congress the power to coerce a State into submission which is attempting to withdraw or has actually withdrawn from the Confederacy? If answered in the affirmative, it must be on the principle that the power has been conferred upon Congress to declare and to make war against a State. After much serious reflection I have arrived at the conclusion that no such power has been delegated to Congress or to any other department of the Federal Government. It is manifest, upon an inspection of the Constitution, that this is not among the specific and enumerated powers granted to Congress; and it is equally apparent that its exercise is not "necessary and proper for carrying into execution" any one of these powers. So far from this power having been delegated to Congress, it was expressly refused by the convention which framed the Constitution.

It appears from the proceedings of that body, that on the 31st May, 1787, the clause "*authorizing an exertion of force of the whole against a delinquent State*" came up for consideration. Mr. Madison {James Madison, delegate from Virginia} opposed it in a brief but powerful speech, from which I shall extract but a single sentence. He observed: "The use of force against a State would look more like a declaration of war than an infliction of punishment; and would probably be considered by the party attacked as a dissolution of all previous compacts by which it might be bound." Upon his motion the clause was unanimously postponed, and was never, I believe, again presented. Soon afterwards, on the 8th June, 1787, when incidentally adverting to the subject, he said: "Any Government for the United States, formed on the supposed practicability of using force against the unconstitutional proceedings of the States, would prove as visionary and fallacious as the government of Congress," evidently meaning the then existing Congress of the old Confederation.

Without descending to particulars, it may be safely asserted that the power to make war against a State is at variance with the whole spirit and intent of the Constitution. Suppose such a war should result in the conquest of a State; how are we to govern it afterwards? Shall we hold it as a province, and govern it by despotic power? In the nature of things, we could not, by physical force, control the will of the people, and compel them to elect Senators and Representatives to Congress, and to perform all the other duties depending upon their own volition, and required from the free citizens of a free State as a constituent member of the Confederacy {the United States}.

But if we possessed this power, would it be wise to exercise it under existing circumstances? The object would doubtless be to preserve the Union. War would not only present the most effectual means of destroying it; but would banish all hope of its peaceable reconstruction. Besides, in a fraternal conflict a vast amount of blood and treasure would be expended, rendering future reconciliation between the States impossible. In the mean time, who can foretell what would be the sufferings and privations of the people during its existence?

The fact is, that our Union rests upon public opinion, and can never be cemented by the blood of its citizens shed in civil war. If it cannot live in the affections of the people, it must one day perish. Congress possess many means of preserving it by conciliation; but the sword was not placed in their hand to preserve it by force.

But may I be permitted solemnly to invoke my countrymen to pause and deliberate, before they determine to destroy this, the grandest temple which has ever been dedicated to human freedom since the world began! It has been consecrated by the blood of our fathers, by the glories of the past, and by the hopes of the future. The Union has already made us the most prosperous, and ere long will, if preserved, render us the most powerful nation on the face of the earth. In every foreign region of the globe the title of American citizen is held in the highest respect, and when pronounced in a foreign land, it causes the hearts of our countrymen to swell with honest pride. Surely when we reach the brink of the yawning abyss, we shall recoil with horror from the last fatal plunge. By such a dread catastrophe the hopes of the friends of freedom throughout the world would be destroyed, and a long night of leaden despotism would enshroud the nations. Our example for more than eighty years would not only be lost, but it would be quoted as a conclusive proof that man is unfit for self-government.

It is not every wrong—nay, it is not every grievous wrong—which can justify a resort to such a fearful alternative. This ought to be the last desperate remedy of a despairing people, after every other constitutional means of conciliation has been exhausted. We should reflect that under a free Government there is an incessant ebb and flow in public opinion. The slavery question, like everything human, will have its day. I firmly believe that it has already reached and passed the culminating point. But if, in the midst of the existing excitement, the Union shall perish, the evil may then be irreparable. Congress can contribute much to avert it by proposing and recommending to the Legislatures of the several States the remedy for existing evils, which the Constitution has itself provided for its own preservation. This has been tried at different critical periods of our history, and always with eminent success. It is to be found in the fifth article providing for its own amendment. Under this article amendments have been proposed by two-thirds of both Houses of Congress, and have been "ratified by the Legislatures of three fourths of the several States," and have consequently become parts of the Constitution. To this process the country is indebted for the clause prohibiting Congress from passing any law respecting an establishment of religion, or abridging the freedoms of speech, or the press, or of the right of petition. To this we are also indebted for the bill of rights, which secures the people against any abuse of power by the Federal Government. Such were the apprehensions justly entertained by the friends of State rights at that period as to have rendered it extremely doubtful whether the Constitution could have long survived without these amendments.

Again, the Constitution was amended by the same process after the election of President Jefferson by the House of Representatives in February, 1803. This amendment {the Twelfth Amendment} was rendered necessary to prevent a recurrence of the dangers which had seriously threatened the existence of the Government during the pendency of that election. The article for its own amendment was intended to secure the amicable adjustment of conflicting constitutional questions like the present, which might arise between the governments of the States and that of the United States. This appears from contemporaneous history. In this connection, I shall merely call attention to a few sentences in Mr. Madison's justly celebrated report, in 1799, to the Legislature of Virginia. In this he ably and conclusively defended the resolutions of the preceding Legislature against the strictures of several other State Legislatures. These were mainly founded upon the protest of the Virginia Legislature against the "alien and sedition acts," as "palpable and alarming infractions of the Constitution." In pointing out the peaceful and constitutional remedies—and he referred to none other—to which the States were authorized to resort on such occasions, he concludes by saying, "that the Legislatures of the States might have made a direct representation to Congress with a view to obtain a rescinding of the two offending acts; or they might have represented to their respective Senators in Congress their wish that two-thirds thereof would propose an explanatory amendment to the Constitution; or two-thirds of themselves, if such had been their option, might, by an application to Congress, have obtained a convention for the same object."

This is the very course which I earnestly recommend in order to obtain an "explanatory amendment" of the Constitution on the subject of slavery.

This might originate with Congress or the State Legislatures, as may be deemed most advisable to attain the object.

The explanatory amendment might be confined to the final settlement of the true construction of the Constitution on three special points:

1. An express recognition of the right of property in slaves in the States where it now exists or may hereafter exist.
2. The duty of protecting this right in all the common Territories throughout their territorial existence, and until they shall be admitted as states into the Union, with or without slavery, as their constitutions may prescribe.
3. A like recognition of the right of the master to have his slave, who has escaped from one state to another, restored and "delivered up" to him, and of the validity of the Fugitive Slave Law enacted for this purpose, together with a declaration that all State laws impairing or defeating this right are violations of the Constitution, and are consequently null and void.

It may be objected that this construction of the Constitution has already been settled by the Supreme Court of the United States, and what more ought to be required? The answer is, that a very large proportion of the people of the United States still contest the correctness of this decision, and never will cease from agitation and admit its binding force until clearly established by the people of the several States in their sovereign character. Such an explanatory amendment would, it is believed, forever terminate the existing dissensions and restore peace and harmony among the States.

It ought not to be doubted that such an appeal to the arbitrament established by the Constitution itself would be received with favor by all the States of the Confederacy. In any event it ought to be tried in a spirit of conciliation before any of these States shall separate themselves from the Union.

When I entered upon the duties of the presidential office, the aspect neither of our foreign nor domestic affairs was at all satisfactory. We were involved in dangerous complications with several nations, and two of our Territories were in a state of revolution against the Government.[3] A restoration of the African slave trade had numerous and powerful advocates.

---

3. In 1857 Buchanan had authorized a military expedition to Utah to force Brigham Young to respect federal authority; Buchanan also became deeply involved in the sectional crisis in Kansas.

Unlawful military expeditions were countenanced by many of our citizens, and were suffered, in defiance of the efforts of the Government, to escape from our shores, for the purpose of making war upon the unoffending people of neighboring Republics with whom we were at peace.[4] In addition to these and other difficulties, we experienced a revulsion in monetary affairs soon after my advent to power, of unexampled severity and of ruinous consequences to all the great interests of the country. When we take a retrospect of what was then our condition, and contrast this with its material prosperity at the time of the late presidential election, we have abundant reason to return our grateful thanks to that merciful Providence which has never forsaken us as a nation in all our past trials.

[Buchanan concluded his address on the subjects of Foreign Relations, Kansas and Utah, Finances, the African Slave Trade, the Election of Members of Congress, and the need for increased federal revenues (tariffs) through increased duties on specific materials.]

Source: *Congressional Globe*, 36th Cong., 2nd sess., December 3, 1860 (appendix), 1–4.

John J. Crittenden's Address to the U.S. Senate

December 18, 1860

John Jordan Crittenden (1786–1863) was a native Kentuckian who, like Buchanan, had served in numerous political positions. He had been elected to the state house of representatives on two occasions, served in the U.S. Senate from 1817 to 1819 and from 1835 to 1841 before being appointed U.S. attorney general by William Henry Harrison. He served a full term in the U.S. Senate between 1842 and 1848, then served one term (1848–50) as the governor of Kentucky. President Millard Fillmore appointed him U.S. attorney general, in which capacity he served from 1850 to 1853 after which he was elected as a Whig to the U.S. Senate and served there from 1855 until

---

4. Buchanan here references the numerous privately funded expeditions that attempted to seize Caribbean and Central American lands for slavery. See introduction footnotes 34 and 115.

1861. Continuing to believe he could affect national events, he thereupon served one term in the U.S. House of Representatives from 1861 to 1863.

Speaking two days before South Carolina formally declared its separation from the United States, Crittenden delivered his thoughts on the crisis of the Union and suggested what he considered a reasonable solution. Although his proposed constitutional amendment touched on a wide range of issues dealing with the rights of slave owners, his primary concern was with the territorial issue. The "present exasperation" leading to threats of disunion, he observed, was the "result of a long-continued controversy on the subject of slavery and the territory." To that end, he argued that the restoration of the Missouri Compromise line of 36° 30' and its extension through the land acquired from Mexico in 1848 to the eastern line of California constituted the fairest solution to both North and South. Throughout Secession Winter, Crittenden's resolutions became the standard around which all other proposed solutions revolved.

COMPROMISE OF THE SLAVERY QUESTION.

Mr. CRITTENDEN. I am gratified, Mr. President, to see in the various propositions which have been made, such a universal anxiety to save the country from the dangerous dissensions which now prevail; and I have, under a very serious view and without the least ambitious feeling whatever connected with it, prepared a series of constitutional amendments, which I desire to offer to the Senate, hoping that they may form, in part at least, some basis for measures that may settle the controverted questions which now so much agitate our country. Certainly, sir, I do not propose now any elaborate discussion of the subject. Before presenting these resolutions, however, to the Senate, I desire to make a few remarks explanatory of them, that the Senate may understand their general scope.

The questions of an alarming character are those which have grown out of the controversy between the northern and southern sections of our country in relation to the rights of the slaveholding States in the Territories of the United States, and in relation to the rights of the citizens of the latter in their slaves. I have endeavored by these resolutions to meet all these questions and causes of discontent, and by amendments to the Constitution of the United States, so that the settlement, if we can happily agree on any, may be permanent, and leave no cause for future controversy. These resolutions propose, then, in the first place, in substance, the restoration of the Missouri compromise, extending the line throughout the Territories of the United States to the eastern border of California, recognizing slavery in all the territory south of that line, and prohibiting slavery in all the territory north of it; with a provision, however, that when any of those Territories, north or south, are formed into States, they shall then be at liberty to exclude or admit slavery as they please; and that, in the one case or the other, it shall be no objection to their admission into the Union. In this way, sir, I propose to settle the question, both as to territory and slavery, so far as it regards the Territories of the United States.

I propose, sir, also, that the Constitution shall be so amended as to declare that Congress shall have no power to abolish slavery in the District of Columbia so long as slavery exists in the States of Maryland and Virginia; and that they shall have no power to abolish slavery in any of the places under their special jurisdiction within the southern States.

These are the constitutional amendments which I propose, and embrace the whole of them in regard to the questions of territory and slavery. There are other propositions in relation to grievances and in relation to controversies, which I suppose are within the jurisdiction of Congress, and may be removed by the action of Congress. I propose, in regard to legislative action, that the fugitive slave law, as it is commonly called, shall be declared by the Senate to be a constitutional act, in strict pursuance of the Constitution. I propose to declare, that it has been decided by the Supreme Court of the United States to be constitutional, and that the southern States are entitled to a faithful and complete execution of that law, and that no amendment shall be made hereafter to it which will impair its efficiency. But, thinking that it would not impair its efficiency, I have proposed amendments to it in two particulars. I have understood from gentlemen of the North that there is objection to the provision giving a different fee where the commissioner decides to deliver the slave to the claimant, from that which is given where he decides to discharge the alleged slave; the law declares that in the latter case he shall have but five dollars, while in the other he shall have ten dollars—twice the amount in one case than in the other. The reason for this is very obvious. In case he delivers the servant to his claimant, he is required to draw out a lengthy certificate, stating the principal and substantial grounds on which his decision rests, and to return him either to the marshal or to the claimant to remove him to the State from which he escaped. It was for that reason that a larger fee was given to the commissioner, where he had the largest service to perform. But, sir, the act being viewed unfavorably and with great prejudice, in a certain portion of our country, this was regarded as very obnoxious, because it seemed to give an inducement to the commissioner to return the slave to the master, as he thereby obtained the larger fee of ten dollars instead of the smaller one of five dollars. I have said, let the fee be the same in both cases.

I have understood, furthermore, sir, that inasmuch as the fifth section of that law was worded somewhat vaguely, its general terms had admitted of the construction in the northern States that all the citizens were required, upon the summons of the marshal, to go with him to hunt up, as they express it, and arrest the slave; and this is regarded as obnoxious. They have said, "in the southern States you make no such requisition on the citizen"; nor do we, sir. The section, construed according to the intentions of the framers of it, I suppose, only intended that the marshal should have the same right in the execution of process for the arrest of a slave that he has in all other cases of process that he is required to execute—to call on the *posse comitatus* {an ad hoc deputized group of citizens} for assistance where he is resisted in the execution of his duty, or where, having executed his duty by the arrest, an attempt is made to rescue the slave. I propose such an amendment as will obviate this difficulty and limit the right of the master and the duty of the citizen to cases where, as in regard to all other process, persons may be called upon to assist in resisting opposition to the execution of the laws.

I have provided further, sir, that the amendments to the Constitution which I here propose, and certain other provisions of the Constitution itself, shall be unalterable, thereby forming a permanent and unchangeable basis for peace and tranquillity among the people. Among the provisions in the present Constitution, which I have by amendment proposed to render unalterable, is that provision in the first article of the Constitution which provides the rule for representation, including in the computation three-fifths of the slaves. That is to be rendered unchangeable. Another is the provision for the delivery of fugitive slaves. That is to be rendered unchangeable.

And with these provisions, Mr. President, it seems to me we have a solid foundation upon which we may rest our hopes for the restoration of peace and good-will among all the States of this Union, and all the people. I propose, sir, to enter into no particular discussion. I have explained the general scope and object of my proposition. I have provided further, which I ought to mention, that, there having been some difficulties experienced in the courts of the United States in the South in carrying into execution the laws prohibiting the African slave trade, all additions and amendments which may be necessary to those laws to render them effectual should be immediately

adopted by Congress, and especially the provisions of those laws which prohibit the importation of African slaves into the United States. I have further
provided it as a recommendation to all the States of this Union, that whereas
laws have been passed of an unconstitutional character (and all laws are of
that character which either conflict with the constitutional acts of Congress,
or which in their operation hinder or delay the proper execution of the acts
of Congress), which laws are null and void, and yet, though null and void,
they have been the source of mischief and discontent in the country, under
the extraordinary circumstances in which we are placed; I have supposed
that it would not be improper or unbecoming in Congress to recommend
to the States, both North and South, the repeal of all such acts of theirs as
were intended to control, or intended to obstruct the operation of the acts
of Congress, or which in their operation and in their application have been
made use of for the purpose of such hindrance and opposition, and that they
will repeal these laws or make such explanations or corrections of them as
to prevent their being used for any such mischievous purpose.

I have endeavored to look with impartiality from one end of our country
to the other; I have endeavored to search up what appeared to me to be the
causes of discontent pervading the land; and, as far as I am capable of doing
so, I have endeavored to propose a remedy for them. I am far from believing
that, in the shape in which I present these measures, they will meet with
the acceptance of the Senate. It will be sufficiently gratifying if, with all the
amendments that the superior knowledge of the Senate may make to them,
they shall, to any effectual extent, quiet the country.

Mr. President, great dangers surround us. The Union of these States is
dear to the people of the United States. The long experience of its blessings, the mighty hopes of the future, have made it dear to the hearts of
the American people. Whatever politicians may say; whatever of dissension may, in the heat of party politics, be created among our people, when
you come down to the question of the existence of the Constitution, that
is a question beyond all party politics; that is a question of life and death.
The Constitution and the Union are the life of this great people—yes, sir,
the life of life. We all desire to preserve them, North and South; that is the
universal desire. But some of the southern States, smarting under what they
conceive to be aggressions of their northern brethren and of the northern
States, are not contented to continue this Union, and are taking steps, formidable steps, towards a dissolution of the Union, and towards the anarchy
and the bloodshed, I fear, that are to follow. I say, sir, we are in the presence
of great events. We must elevate ourselves to the level of the great occasion.

No party warfare about mere party questions or party measures ought now to engage our attention. They are left behind; they are as dust in the balance. The life, the existence of our country, of our Union, is the mighty question; and we must elevate ourselves to all those considerations which belong to this high subject.

I hope, therefore, gentlemen will be disposed to bring the sincerest spirit of conciliation, the sincerest spirit and desire to adjust all these difficulties, and to think nothing of any little concessions of opinions that they may make, if thereby the Constitution and the country can be preserved.

The great difficulty here, sir—I know it; I recognize it as the difficult question, particularly with the gentlemen from the North—is the admission of this line of division for the territory, and the recognition of slavery on the one side, and the prohibition of it on the other. The recognition of slavery on the southern side of that line is the great difficulty, the great question with them. Now, I beseech them to think, and you, Mr. President, and all, to think whether, for such a comparative trifle as that, the Union of this country is to be sacrificed. Have we realized to ourselves the momentous consequences of such an event? When has the world seen such an event? This is a mighty empire. Its existence spreads its influence throughout the civilized world. Its overthrow will be the greatest shock that civilization and free government have received; more extensive in its consequences; more fatal to mankind and to the great principles upon which the liberty of mankind depends, than the French revolution with all its blood, and with all its war and violence. And all for what? Upon questions concerning this line of division between slavery and freedom? Why, Mr. President, suppose this day all the southern States, being refused this right; being refused this partition; being denied this privilege, were to separate from the northern States, and do it peacefully, and then were to come to you peacefully and say, "let there be no war between us; let us divide fairly the Territories of the United States": could the northern section of the country refuse so just a demand? What would you then give them? What would be the fair proportion? If you allowed them their fair relative proportion, would you not give them as much as is now proposed to be assigned on the southern side of that line, and would they not be at liberty to carry their slaves there, if they pleased? You would give them the whole of that; and then what would be its fate?

Is it upon the general principle of humanity, then, that you [addressing Republican Senators] wish to put an end to slavery, or is it to be urged by you as a mere topic and point of party controversy to sustain party power? Surely I give you credit for looking at it upon broader and more generous principles. Then, in the worst event, after you have encountered disunion, that greatest of all political calamities to the people of this country, and the disunionists come, the separating States come, and demand or take their portion of the Territories, they can take, and will be entitled to take, all that will now lie on the southern side of the line which I have proposed. Then they will have a right to permit slavery to exist in it; and what do you gain for the cause of anti-slavery? Nothing whatever. Suppose you should refuse their demand, and claim the whole for yourselves: that would be a flagrant injustice which you would not be willing that I should suppose would occur. But if you did, what would be the consequence? A State north and a State south, and all the States, north and south, would be attempting to grasp at and seize this territory, and to get all of it that they could. That would be the struggle, and you would have war; and not only disunion, but all these fatal consequences would follow from your refusal now to permit slavery to exist, to recognize it as existing, on the southern side of the proposed line, while you give to the people there the right to exclude it when they come to form a State government, if such should be their will and pleasure.

Now, gentlemen, in view of this subject, in view of the mighty consequences, in view of the great events which are present before you, and of the mighty consequences which are just now to take effect, is it not better to settle the question by a division upon the line of the Missouri compromise? For thirty years we lived quietly and peacefully under it. Our people, North and South, were accustomed to look at it as a proper and just line. Can we not do so again? We did it then to preserve the peace of the country. Now you see this Union in the most imminent danger. I declare to you that it is my solemn conviction that unless something be done, and something equivalent to this proposition, we shall be a separated and divided people in six months from this time. That is my firm conviction. There is no man here who deplores it more than I do; but it is my sad and melancholy conviction that that will be the consequence. I wish you to realize fully the danger. I wish you to realize fully the consequences which are to follow. You can give increased stability to this Union; you can give it an existence, a glorious existence, for great and glorious centuries to come, by now setting it upon a permanent basis, recognizing what the South considers as its rights; and this is the greatest of them all: it is that you should divide the territory by this line and allow the people south of it to have slavery when they are admitted into the Union as States, and to have it during the existence of the territorial government. That is all. Is it not the cheapest price at which such a blessing as this Union was ever purchased? You think, perhaps, or some of you, that there is no danger, that it will but thunder and pass away. Do not entertain such a fatal delusion. I tell you it is not so. I tell you that as sure as we stand here disunion will progress. I fear it may swallow up even old Kentucky in its vortex—as true a State to the Union as yet exists in the whole Confederacy—unless something be done; but that you will have disunion, that anarchy and war will follow it, that all this will take place in six months, I believe as confidently as I believe in your presence. I want to satisfy you of the fact.

Mr. President, I rise to suggest another consideration. I have been surprised to find, upon a little examination, that when the peace of 1783 was made, which recognized the independence of this country by Great Britain {marking the end of the American Revolution}, the States north of Mason and Dixon's line had but a territory of one hundred and sixty-four thousand square miles, while the States south of Mason and Dixon's line had more than six hundred thousand square miles.[5] It was so divided. Virginia shortly afterwards ceded to the United States all that noble territory northwest of the Ohio river, and excluded slavery from it. That changed the relative proportion of territory. After that, the North had four hundred and twenty-five thousand square miles, and the South three hundred and eighty-five thousand. Thus, at once, by the concession of Virginia, the North, from one hundred and sixty-four thousand, rose to four hundred and twenty-five thousand square miles, and the South fell from six hundred thousand to three hundred and eighty-five thousand square miles. By that cession the South became smaller in extent than the North. Well, let us look beyond. I intend to take up as little time as possible, and to avoid details; but take all your subsequent acquisitions of Florida, of Louisiana, of Oregon, of Texas, and the acquisitions made from Mexico. They have been so divided and so disposed of that the North has now two millions, two hundred thousand square miles of territory, and the South has less than one million.

Under these circumstances, when you have been so greatly magnified—I do not complain of it, I am stating facts—when your section has been made so mighty by these great acquisitions, and to a great extent with the perfect consent of the South, ought you to hesitate now upon adopting this line which will leave to you on the north side of it nine hundred and odd thousand square miles, and leave to the South only two hundred and eighty-five

---

5. Between 1763 and 1767, Charles Mason and Jeremiah Dixon surveyed the boundaries between the states of Pennsylvania, Maryland, and Delaware.

thousand? It will give you three times as much as it will give her. There is three times as much land in your portion as in hers. The South has already occupied some of it, and it is in States; but altogether the South gets by this division two hundred and eighty-five thousand square miles, and the North nine hundred thousand. The result of the whole of it is that the North has two million two hundred thousand square miles and the South only one million.

I mention this as no reproach, as no upbraiding, as no complaint—none at all. I do not speak in that spirit; I do not address you in that temper. But these are the facts, and they ought, it seems to me, to have some weight; and when we come to make a peace-offering, are we to count it, are we to measure it nicely in golden scales? You get a price, and the dearest price, for all the concession asked to be made—you have the firmer establishment of your Union; you have the restoration of peace and tranquillity, and the hopes of a mighty future, all secured by this concession. How dearly must one individual, or two individuals, or many individuals, value their private opinions if they think them more important to the world than this mighty interest of the Union and Government of the United States!

Sir, it is a cheap sacrifice. It is a glorious sacrifice. This Union cost a great deal to establish it; it cost the yielding of much of public opinion and much of policy, besides the direct or indirect cost of it in all the war to establish the independence of this country. When it was done, General Washington himself said, Providence has helped us, or we could not have accomplished this thing. And this gift of our wisest men; this great work of their hands; this work in the foundation and the structure of which Providence himself, with his benignant hand, helped—are we to give it all up for such small considerations? The present exasperation; the present feeling of disunion, is the result of a long-continued controversy on the subject of slavery and of territory. I shall not attempt to trace that controversy; it is unnecessary to the occasion, and might be harmful. In relation to such controversies, I will say, though, that all the wrong is never on one side, or all the right on the other. Right and wrong, in this world, and in all such controversies, are mingled together. I forbear now any discussion or any reference to the right or wrong of the controversy, the mere party controversy; but in the progress of party, we now come to a point where party ceases to deserve consideration, and the preservation of the Union demands our highest and our greatest exertions. To preserve the Constitution of the country is the highest duty of the Senate, the highest duty of Congress—to preserve it and to perpetuate it, that we may hand down the glories which we have received to our children and to our posterity, and to generations far beyond us. We are, Senators, in positions where history is to take notice of the course we pursue.

History is to record us. Is it to record that when the destruction of the Union was imminent; when we saw it tottering to its fall; when we saw brothers arming their hands for hostility with one another, we stood quarreling about points of party politics; about questions which we attempted to sanctify and to consecrate by appealing to our conscience as the source of them? Are we to allow such fearful catastrophes to occur while we stand trifling away our time? While we stand thus, showing our inferiority to the great and mighty dead, showing our inferiority to the high positions which we occupy, the country may be destroyed and ruined; and to the amazement of all the world, the great Republic may fall prostrate and in ruins, carrying with it the very hope of that liberty which we have heretofore enjoyed; carrying with it, in place of the peace we have enjoyed, nothing but revolution and havoc and anarchy. Shall it be said that we have allowed all these evils to come upon our country, while we were engaged in the petty and small disputes and debates to which I have referred? Can it be that our name is to rest in history with this everlasting stigma and blot upon it?

Sir, I wish to God it was in my power to preserve this Union by renouncing or agreeing to give up every conscientious and other opinion. I might not be able to discard it from my mind; I am under no obligation to do that. I may retain the opinion, but if I can do so great a good as to preserve my country and give it peace, and its institutions and its Union stability, I will forego any action upon my opinions. Well now my friends [addressing the Republican Senators], that is all that is asked of you. Consider it well, and I do not distrust the result. As to the rest of this body, the gentlemen from the South, I would say to them, can you ask more than this? Are you bent on revolution, bent on disunion? God forbid it. I cannot believe that such madness possesses the American people. This gives reasonable satisfaction. I can speak with confidence only of my own State. Old Kentucky will be satisfied with it, and she will stand by the Union and die by the Union if this satisfaction be given. Nothing shall seduce her. The clamor of no revolution, the seductions and temptations of no revolution, will tempt her to move one step. She has stood always by the side of the Constitution; she has always been devoted to it, and is this day. Give her this satisfaction, and I believe all the States of the South that are not desirous of disunion as a better thing than the Union and the Constitution will be satisfied and will adhere to the

Union, and we shall go on again in our great career of national prosperity and national glory.

But, sir, it is not necessary for me to speak to you of the consequences that will follow disunion. Who of us is not proud of the greatness we have achieved? Disunion and separation destroy that greatness. Once disunited, we are no longer great. The nations of the earth who have looked upon you as a formidable Power, a mighty Power, and rising to untold and immeasurable greatness in the future will scoff at you. Your flag that now claims the respect of the world, that protects American property in every port and harbor of the world, that protects the rights of your citizens everywhere, what will become of it? What becomes of its glorious influence? It is gone; and with it the protection of American citizens and property. To say nothing of the national honor which it displayed to all the world, the protection of your rights, the protection of your property abroad is gone with that national flag, and we are hereafter to conjure and contrive different flags for our different republics according to the feverish fancies of revolutionary patriots and disturbers of the peace of the world. No, sir; I want to follow no such flag. I want to preserve the union of my country. We have it in our power to do so, and we are responsible if we do not do it.

I do not despair of the Republic. When I see before me Senators of so much intelligence and so much patriotism, who have been so honored by their country, sent here as the guardians of that very union which is now in question, sent here as the guardians of our national rights and as guardians of that national flag, I cannot despair; I cannot despond. I cannot but believe that they will find some means of reconciling and adjusting the rights of all parties, by concessions, if necessary, so as to preserve and give more stability to the country and to its institutions.

Mr. President, I have occupied more time than I intended. My remarks were designed and contemplated only to reach to an explanation of this resolution.

The PRESIDING OFFICER (Mr. FITZPATRICK {Benjamin Fitzpatrick, Alabama} in the chair). Does the Senator desire the resolution to be read?

Mr. CRITTENDEN. Yes, sir; I ask that it be read to the Senate.

Mr. GREEN {James S. Green, Missouri}. The hour has arrived for the consideration of the special order.

Mr. CRITTENDEN. I desire to present this resolution now to the Senate; and I ask that it may be read and printed.

The PRESIDING OFFICER. The Secretary will report the resolution.

The Secretary read it, as follows:

A joint resolution (S. No. 50) proposing certain amendments
to the Constitution of the United States.

Whereas serious and alarming dissensions have arisen between the northern and southern States, concerning the rights and security of the rights of the slaveholding States, and especially their rights in the common territory of the United States; and whereas it is eminently desirable and proper that these dissensions, which now threaten the very existence of this Union, should be permanently quieted and settled by constitutional provisions, which shall do equal justice to all sections, and thereby restore to the people that peace and good-will which ought to prevail between all the citizens of the United States: Therefore,

Resolved by the Senate and House of Representatives of the United States of America in Congress assembled (two-thirds of both Houses concurring), That the following articles be, and are hereby, proposed and submitted as amendments to the Constitution of the United States, which shall be valid to all intents and purposes, as part of said Constitution, when ratified by conventions of three-fourths of the several States:

ARTICLE 1. In all the territory of the United States now held, or hereafter acquired, situate north of 36° 30', slavery or involuntary servitude, except as a punishment for crime, is prohibited while such territory shall remain under territorial government. In all the territory south of said line of latitude, slavery of the African race is hereby recognized as existing, and shall not be interfered with by Congress, but shall be protected as property by all the departments of the territorial government during its continuance. And when any Territory, north or south of said line, within such boundaries as Congress may prescribe, shall contain the population requisite for a member of Congress according to the then Federal ratio of representation of the people of the United States, it shall, if its form of government be republican, be admitted into the Union, on an equal footing with the original States, with or without slavery, as the constitution of such new State may provide.

ART. 2. Congress shall have no power to abolish slavery in places under its exclusive jurisdiction, and situate within the limits of States that permit the holding of slaves.

ART. 3. Congress shall have no power to abolish slavery within the District of Columbia, so long as it exists in the adjoining States of Virginia and Maryland, or either, nor without the consent of the inhabitants, nor without just compensation first made to such owners of slaves as do not consent to such abolishment. Nor shall Congress at any time prohibit officers of the Federal Government, or members of Congress, whose duties require them to be in said District, from bringing with them their slaves, and holding them as such during the time their duties may require them to remain there, and afterwards taking them from the District.

ART. 4. Congress shall have no power to prohibit or hinder the transportation of slaves from one State to another, or to a Territory in which slaves are by law permitted to be held, whether that transportation be by land, navigable rivers, or by the sea.

ART. 5. That in addition to the provisions of the third paragraph of the second section of the fourth article of the Constitution of the United States, Congress shall have power to provide by law, and it shall be its duty so to provide, that the United States shall pay to the owner who shall apply for it, the full value of his fugitive slave in all cases when the marshal or other officer whose duty it was to arrest said fugitive was prevented from so doing by violence or intimidation, or when, after arrest, said fugitive was rescued by force, and the owner thereby prevented and obstructed in the pursuit of his remedy for the recovery of his fugitive slave under the said clause of the Constitution and the laws made in pursuance thereof. And in all such cases, when the United States shall pay for such fugitive, they shall have the right, in their own name, to sue the county in which said violence, intimidation, or rescue was committed, and to recover from it, with interest and damages, the amount paid by them for said fugitive slave. And the said county, after it has paid said amount to the United States, may, for its indemnity, sue and recover from the wrong doers or rescuers by whom the owner was prevented from the recovery of his fugitive slave, in like manner as the owner himself might have sued and recovered.

ART. 6. No future amendment of the Constitution shall affect the five preceding articles; nor the third paragraph of the second section of the first article of the Constitution; nor the third paragraph of the second section of the fourth article of said Constitution; and no amendment shall be made to the Constitution which shall authorize or give to Congress any power to abolish or interfere with slavery in any of the States by whose laws it is, or may be, allowed or permitted.

And whereas, also, besides those causes of dissension embraced in the foregoing amendments proposed to the Constitution of the United States, there are others which come within the jurisdiction of Congress, and may be remedied by its legislative power; and whereas it is the desire of Congress, as far as its power will extend, to remove all just cause for the popular discontent and agitation which now disturb the peace of the country, and threaten the stability of its institutions: Therefore,

1. *Resolved by the Senate and House of Representatives of the United States of America in Congress assembled,* That the laws now in force for the recovery of fugitive slaves are in strict pursuance of the plain and mandatory provisions of the Constitution, and have been sanctioned as valid and constitutional by the judgment of the Supreme Court of the United States; that the slaveholding States are entitled to the faithful observance and execution of those laws, and that they ought not to be repealed, or so modified or changed as to impair their efficiency; and that laws ought to be made for the punishment of those who attempt by rescue of the slave, or other illegal means, to hinder or defeat the due execution of said laws.

2. That all State laws which conflict with the fugitive slave acts of Congress, or any other constitutional acts of Congress, or which, in their operation, impede, hinder, or delay the free course and due execution of any of said acts, are null and void by the plain provisions of the Constitution of the United States; yet those State laws, void as they are, have given color to practices, and led to consequences, which have obstructed the due administration and execution of acts of Congress, and especially the acts for the delivery of fugitive slaves, and have thereby contributed much to the discord and commotion now prevailing. Congress, therefore, in the present perilous juncture, does not deem it improper, respectfully and earnestly to recommend the repeal of those laws to the several States which have enacted them, or such legislative corrections or explanations of them as may prevent their being used or perverted to such mischievous purposes.

3. That the act of the 18th of September, 1850, commonly called the fugitive slave law, ought to be so amended as to make the fee of the commissioner, mentioned in the eighth section of the act, equal in amount in the cases decided by him, whether his decision be in favor of or against the claimant. And to avoid misconstruction, the last clause of the fifth section of said act, which authorizes the person holding a warrant for the arrest or detention of a fugitive slave, to summon to his aid the *posse comitatus,* and which declares it to be the duty of all good citizens to assist him in its execution, ought to be so amended as to expressly limit the authority and duty to cases in which there shall be resistance or danger of resistance or rescue.

4. That the laws for the suppression of the African slave trade, and especially those prohibiting the importation of slaves in the United States, ought

to be made effectual, and ought to be thoroughly executed; and all further enactments necessary to those ends ought to be properly made.

[Note: The Senate ultimately rejected Crittenden's amendment by a vote of 20–19 on March 4, 1861; *Congressional Globe,* 36th Cong., 2nd sess., 1405.]

Source: *Congressional Globe,* 36th Cong., 2nd sess., 112–114 (Joint Resolution No. 50).

Also submitted to the Senate's Committee of Thirteen on December 22, 1860; 36th Cong., 2nd sess., Senate Report 288, 3–4.

PART TWO

Declarations of Secession

Among the official documents produced over Secession Winter, none convey the justification for secession better than the formal declarations authorized by the secession conventions of South Carolina, Mississippi, Georgia, and Texas. Each of these states established a committee to draft an official statement explaining and justifying the convention's reasons for voting in favor of secession, and each convention formally approved the language. These proclamations represent the collective thinking of the assembled delegates.

Unlike the ordinances of secession which formally (and briefly) severed the various states from their obligations to the United States, these declarations carefully articulate the grievances against the North that necessitated immediate secession. The attention each of these states devoted to listing northern abuses illustrates the centrality of slavery to the sectional crisis. Mississippi communicated its apprehension most clearly: "Our position is thoroughly identified with the institution of slavery—the greatest material interest in the world. . . . A blow at slavery is a blow at commerce and civilization. . . . There was no choice left us but submission to the mandates of abolition, or a dissolution of the Union." Concern for the future of slavery was woven throughout each of these official statements as they variously reflected the slave South's anxiety over the expansion of slavery into the western territories, the return of fugitive slaves, and the sojourning of owners with their slaves into northern states, among other issues. Significantly, the declarations directed their protestations not against the federal government but against the "anti-slavery sentiment of the North," the "disloyalty of the Northern States," and to "an increasing hostility of the non-slaveholding States to the institution of slavery." The general complaint was not that the government had overreached, but that it had done too little to protect southern interests.

SOUTH CAROLINA

DECLARATION OF THE IMMEDIATE CAUSES
WHICH INDUCE AND JUSTIFY
THE SECESSION OF SOUTH CAROLINA
FROM THE FEDERAL UNION.

The People of the State of South Carolina, in Convention assembled, on the 26th day of April, A.D., 1852, declared that the frequent violations of the Constitution of the United States, by the Federal Government, and its encroachments upon the reserved rights of the States, fully justified this State in then withdrawing from the Federal Union; but in deference to the opinions and wishes of the other slaveholding States, she forbore at that time to exercise this right. Since that time, these encroachments have continued to increase, and further forbearance ceases to be a virtue.

And now the State of South Carolina having resumed her separate and equal place among nations, deems it due to herself, to the remaining United States of America, and to the nations of the world, that she should declare the immediate causes which have led to this act.

In the year 1765, that portion of the British Empire embracing Great Britain, undertook to make laws for the government of that portion composed of the thirteen American Colonies. A struggle for the right of selfgovernment ensued, which resulted, on the 4th of July, 1776, in a Declaration, by the Colonies, "that they are, and of right ought to be, FREE AND INDEPENDENT STATES; and that, as free and independent States, they have full power to levy war, conclude peace, contract alliances, establish commerce, and to do all other acts and things which independent States may of right do."

They further solemnly declared that whenever any "form of government becomes destructive of the ends for which it was established, it is the right of the people to alter or abolish it, and to institute a new government."

Deeming the Government of Great Britain to have become destructive of these ends, they declared that the Colonies "are absolved from all allegiance to the British Crown, and that all political connection between them and the State of Great Britain is, and ought to be, totally dissolved."

In pursuance of this Declaration of Independence, each of the thirteen States proceeded to exercise its separate sovereignty; adopted for itself a Constitution, and appointed officers for the administration of government in all its departments—Legislative, Executive and Judicial. For purposes of defense, they united their arms and their counsels; and, in 1778, they entered into a League known as the Articles of Confederation, whereby they agreed to entrust the administration of their external relations to a common agent, known as the Congress of the United States, expressly declaring in the first article "that each State retains its sovereignty, freedom and independence, and every power, jurisdiction and right which is not, by this Confederation, expressly delegated to the United States in Congress assembled."

Under this Confederation the War of the Revolution was carried on, and on the 3d September, 1783, the contest ended, and a definite Treaty was signed by Great Britain, in which she acknowledged the Independence of the Colonies in the following terms;

"*Article* 1.—His Britannic Majesty acknowledges the said United States, viz: New Hampshire, Massachusetts Bay, Rhode Island and Providence Plantations, Connecticut, New York, New Jersey, Pennsylvania, Delaware, Maryland, Virginia, North Carolina, South Carolina and Georgia, to be FREE, SOVEREIGN AND INDEPENDENT STATES: that he treats with them as such; and for himself, his heirs and successors, relinquishes all claims to the government, propriety and territorial rights of the same and every part thereof."

Thus were established the two great principles asserted by the Colonies, namely: the right of a State to govern itself; and the right of a people to abolish a Government when it becomes destructive of the ends for which it was instituted. And concurrent with the establishment of these principles was the fact that each Colony became and was recognized by the mother Country as a FREE, SOVEREIGN, AND INDEPENDENT STATE.

In 1787, Deputies were appointed by the States to revise the Articles of Confederation, and on 17th September, 1787, these Deputies recommended for the adoption of the States, the Articles of Union, known as the Constitution of the United States.

The parties to whom this Constitution was submitted were the several sovereign States; they were to agree or disagree, and when nine of them agreed, the compact was to take effect among those concurring; and the General Government, as the common agent, was then to be invested with their authority.

If only nine of the thirteen States had concurred, the other four would have remained as they then were—separate, sovereign States, independent of any of the provisions of the Constitution. In fact, two of the States {North Carolina and Rhode Island} did not accede to the Constitution until long after it had gone into operation among the other eleven; and during that interval, they each exercised the functions of an independent nation.

By this Constitution, certain duties were imposed upon the several States, and the exercise of certain of their powers was restrained, which necessarily implied their continued existence as sovereign States. But to remove all doubt, an amendment was added, which declared that the powers not delegated to the United States by the Constitution, nor prohibited by it to the States, are reserved to the States, respectively, or to the people. On 23d May, 1788, South Carolina, by a Convention of her people, passed an Ordinance assenting to this Constitution, and afterwards altered her own Constitution, to conform herself to the obligations she had undertaken.

Thus was established, by compact between the States, a Government, with defined objects and powers, limited to the express words of the grant. This limitation left the whole remaining mass of power subject to the clause reserving it to the States or to the people, and rendered unnecessary any specification of reserved rights.

We hold that the Government thus established is subject to the two great principles asserted in the Declaration of Independence; and we hold further, that the mode of its formation subjects it to a third fundamental principle, namely: the law of compact. We maintain that in every compact between two or more parties, the obligation is mutual; that the failure of one of the contracting parties to perform a material part of the agreement entirely releases the obligation of the other; and that where no arbiter is provided, each party is remitted to his own judgment to determine the fact of failure, with all its consequences.

In the present case, that fact is established with certainty. We assert that fourteen of the States have deliberately refused, for years past, to fulfill their constitutional obligations, and we refer to their own Statutes for the proof.

The Constitution of the United States, in its Fourth Article, provides as follows:

"No person held to service or labor in one State, under the laws thereof, escaping into another, shall, in consequence of any law or regulation therein, be discharged from such service or labor, but shall be delivered up, on claim of the party to whom such service or labor may be due."

This stipulation was so material to the compact that without it that compact would not have been made. The greater number of the contracting parties held slaves, and they had previously evinced their estimate of the value of such a stipulation by making it a condition in the Ordinance for the government of the territory ceded by Virginia, which now composes the States north of the Ohio river.

The same article of the Constitution stipulates also for rendition by the several States of fugitives from justice from the other States.

The General Government, as the common agent, passed laws to carry into effect these stipulations of the States. For many years these laws were executed. But an increasing hostility on the part of the nonslaveholding States to the Institution of Slavery, has led to a disregard of their obligations, and the laws of the General Government have ceased to effect the objects of the Constitution. The States of Maine, New Hampshire, Vermont, Massachusetts, Connecticut, Rhode Island, New York, Pennsylvania, Illinois, Indiana, Michigan, Wisconsin and Iowa, have enacted laws which either nullify the Acts of Congress or render useless any attempt to execute them. In many of these States the fugitive is discharged from the service or labor claimed, and in none of them has the State Government complied with the stipulation made in the Constitution. The State of New Jersey, at an early day, passed a law in conformity with her constitutional obligation; but the current of anti-slavery feeling has led her more recently to enact laws which render inoperative the remedies provided by her own law and by the laws of Congress. In the State of New York even the right of transit for a slave has been denied by her tribunals; and the States of Ohio and Iowa have refused to surrender to justice fugitives charged with murder and with inciting servile insurrection in the State of Virginia. Thus the constituted compact has been deliberately broken and disregarded by the nonslaveholding States, and the consequence follows that South Carolina is released from her obligation.

The ends for which this Constitution was framed are declared by itself to be "to form a more perfect union, establish justice, insure domestic tranquility, provide for the common defence, promote the general welfare, and secure the blessings of liberty to ourselves and our posterity."

These ends it endeavored to accomplish by a Federal Government, in which each State was recognized as an equal, and had separate control over its own institutions. The right of property in slaves was recognized by giving to free persons distinct political rights, by giving them the right to represent, and burthening them with direct taxes for threefifths of their slaves; by authorizing the importation of slaves for twenty years; and by stipulating for the rendition of fugitives from labor.

We affirm that these ends for which this Government was instituted have been defeated, and the Government itself has been made destructive of them by the action of the nonslaveholding States. Those States have assumed the right of deciding upon the propriety of our domestic institutions; and have denied the rights of property established in fifteen of the States and recognized by the Constitution; they have denounced as sinful the institution of Slavery; they have permitted the open establishment among them of societies, whose avowed object is to disturb the peace and to eloign {remove or carry away} the property of the citizens of other States. They have encouraged and assisted thousands of our slaves to leave their homes; and those who remain have been incited by emissaries, books, and pictures to servile insurrection.

For twentyfive years this agitation has been steadily increasing, until it has now secured to its aid the power of the Common Government. Observing the *forms* of the Constitution, a sectional party has found within that Article establishing the Executive Department, the means of subverting the Constitution itself. A geographical line has been drawn across the Union, and all the States north of that line have united in the election of a man to the high office of President of the United States, whose opinions and purposes are hostile to slavery. He is to be entrusted with the administration of the Common Government, because he has declared that that "Government cannot endure permanently half slave, half free," and that the public mind must rest in the belief that Slavery is in the course of ultimate extinction.

This sectional combination for the submersion of the Constitution, has been aided in some of the States by elevating to citizenship, persons, who, by the Supreme Law of the land, are incapable of becoming citizens; and their votes have been used to inaugurate a new policy, hostile to the South, and destructive of its peace and safety.

On the 4th March next, this party will take possession of the Government. It has announced that the South shall be excluded from the common Territory; that the Judicial Tribunals shall be made sectional, and that a war must be waged against slavery until it shall cease throughout the United States.

The guaranties of the Constitution will then no longer exist; the equal rights of the States will be lost. The slaveholding States will no longer have the power of selfgovernment, or selfprotection, and the Federal Government will have become their enemy.

Sectional interest and animosity will deepen the irritation, and all hope of remedy is rendered vain by the fact that public opinion at the North has invested a great political error with the sanctions of a more erroneous religious belief.

We, therefore, the people of South Carolina, by our delegates, in Convention assembled, appealing to the Supreme Judge of the world for the rectitude of our intentions, have solemnly declared that the Union heretofore existing between this State and the other States of North America is dissolved and that the State of South Carolina has resumed her position among the nations of the world as a separate and independent State; with full power to levy war, conclude peace, contract alliances, establish commerce, and to do all other acts and things which independent States may of right do.

Adopted December 24, 1860

Source: *Journal of the Convention of the People of South Carolina, Held in 1860–'61* (Charleston: Evans & Cogswell, Printers to the Convention, 1861), 325–331.

MISSISSIPPI

Mr. {Alexander Mosby} Clayton of Marshall, from the committee to whom was referred the subject of preparing an address, setting forth the causes which induce and justify the secession of Mississippi from the Federal Union, submitted the following report:

A DECLARATION OF THE IMMEDIATE CAUSES WHICH INDUCE AND JUSTIFY THE SECESSION OF THE STATE OF MISSISSIPPI FROM THE FEDERAL UNION.

In the momentous step which our State has taken of dissolving its connection with the government of which we so long formed a part, it is but just that we should declare the prominent reasons which have induced our course.

Our position is thoroughly identified with the institution of slavery—the greatest material interest of the world. Its labor supplies the product which constitutes by far the largest and most important portions of the commerce of the earth. These products are peculiar to the climate verging on the tropical regions, and by an imperious law of nature, none but the black race can bear exposure to the tropical sun. These products have become necessities of the world, and a blow at slavery is a blow at commerce and civilization. That blow has been long aimed at the institution, and was at the point of reaching its consummation. There was no choice left us but submission to the mandates of abolition, or a dissolution of the Union, whose principles had been subverted to work out our ruin.

That we do not overstate the dangers to our institution, a reference to a few unquestionable facts will sufficiently prove.

The hostility to this institution commenced before the adoption of the Constitution, and was manifested in the wellknown Ordinance of 1787, in regard to the Northwestern Territory.

The feeling increased, until, in 1819–20, it deprived the South of more than half the vast territory acquired from France.

The same hostility dismembered Texas and seized upon all the territory acquired from Mexico.

It has grown until it denies the right of property in slaves, and refuses protection to that right on the high seas, in the Territories, and wherever the government of the United States had jurisdiction.

It refuses the admission of new slave States into the Union, and seeks to extinguish it by confining it within its present limits, denying the power of expansion.

It tramples the original equality of the South under foot.

It has nullified the Fugitive Slave Law in almost every free State in the Union, and has utterly broken the compact which our fathers pledged their faith to maintain.

It advocates negro equality, socially and politically, and promotes insurrection and incendiarism in our midst.

It has enlisted its press, its pulpit and its schools against us, until the whole popular mind of the North is excited and inflamed with prejudice.

It has made combinations and formed associations to carry out its schemes of emancipation in the States and wherever else slavery exists.

It seeks not to elevate or to support the slave, but to destroy his present condition without providing a better.

It has invaded a State, and invested with the honors of martyrdom the wretch whose purpose was to apply flames to our dwellings and the weapons of destruction to our lives.

It has broken every compact into which it has entered for our security.

It has given indubitable evidence of its design to ruin our agriculture, to prostrate our industrial pursuits, and to destroy our social system.

It knows no relenting or hesitation in its purposes; it stops not in its march of aggression, and leaves us no room to hope for cessation or for pause.

It has recently obtained control of the Government, by the prosecution of its unhallowed schemes, and destroyed the last expectation of living together in friendship and brotherhood.

Utter subjugation awaits us in the Union, if we should consent longer to remain in it. It is not a matter of choice but of necessity. We must either submit to degradation, and to the loss of property worth four billions of money, or we must secede from the Union framed by our fathers, to secure this as well as every other species of property. For far less cause than this, our fathers separated from the Crown of England.

Our decision is made. We follow in their footsteps. We embrace the alternative of separation; and for the reasons here stated, we resolve to maintain our rights with the full consciousness of the justice of our course, and the undoubting belief of our ability to maintain it.

On motion of Mr. Clayton of Marshall, the report was received and agreed to.

Adopted January 26, 1861

Source: *Journal of the Mississippi Secession Convention, January 1861* (1861; Jackson: Mississippi Commission on the War between the States, 1962), 86–88.

GEORGIA

Mr. {E. A.} Nisbet {Bibb County}, from the committee of seventeen, to report the Ordinance of Secession, after stating that it was written by Mr. {Robert} Toombs {Wilkes County}, made the following

REPORT,

which was taken up, read, and adopted.

"The people of Georgia having dissolved their political connection with the Government of the United States of America, present to their confederates, and the world, the causes which have led to the separation. For the last ten years we have had numerous and serious causes of complaint against our non-slaveholding confederate States, with reference to the subject of

African slavery. They have endeavored to weaken our security, to disturb our domestic peace and tranquility, and persistently refused to comply with their express constitutional obligations to us in reference to that property, and by the use of their power in the Federal Government, have striven to deprive us of an equal enjoyment of the common Territories of the Republic. This hostile policy of our confederates has been pursued with every circumstance of aggravation which could arouse the passions and excite the hatred of our people, and has placed the two sections of the Union for many years past, in the condition of virtual civil war. Our people, still attached to the Union, from habit and National traditions, and averse to change, hoped that time, reason, and argument would bring, if not redress, at least exemption from further insults, injuries, and dangers. Recent events have fully dissipated all such hopes, and demonstrated the necessity of separation. Our Northern confederates, after a full and calm hearing of all the facts, after a fair warning of our purpose not to submit to the rule of the authors of all these wrongs and injuries, have, by a large majority, committed the Government of the United States into their hands. The people of Georgia, after an equally full and fair and deliberate hearing of the case, have declared with equal firmness, that they shall not rule over them. A brief history of the rise, progress and policy of anti-slavery, and of the political organization into whose hands the administration of the Federal Government has been committed, will fully justify the pronounced verdict of the people of Georgia. The party of Lincoln, called the Republican party, under its present name and organization is of recent origin. It is admitted to be an anti-slavery party, while it attracts to itself by its creed, the scattered advocates of exploded political heresies, of condemned theories in political economy, the advocates of commercial restrictions, of protection, of special privileges, of waste and corruption in the administration of Government; anti-slavery is its mission and its purpose. By anti-slavery it is made a power in the State. The question of slavery was the great difficulty in the way of the formation of the Constitution. While the subordination and the political and social inequality of the African race were fully conceded by all, it was plainly apparent that slavery would soon disappear from what are now the non-slaveholding States of the original thirteen; the opposition to slavery was then, as now, general in those States, and the Constitution was made with direct reference to that fact. But a distinct abolition party was not formed in the United States for more than half a century after the Government went into operation. The main reason was that the North, even if united, could not control both branches of the Legislature during any portion of that time.

Therefore, such an organization must have resulted, either in utter failure, or in the total overthrow of the Government. The material prosperity of the North was greatly dependent on the Federal Government; that of the South not at all. In the first years of the Republic, the navigating, commercial and manufacturing interests of the North began to seek profit and aggrandizement at the expense of the agricultural interests. Even the owners of fishing smacks sought and obtained bounties for pursuing their own business, which yet continue—and half a million dollars are now paid them annually out of the Treasury. The navigating interests begged for protection against foreign ship builders and against competition in the coasting trade; Congress granted both requests, and by prohibitory acts, gave an absolute monopoly of this business to each of their interests, which they enjoy without diminution to this day. Not content with these great and unjust advantages, they have sought to throw the legitimate burthens of their business as much as possible upon the public; they have succeeded in throwing the cost of light-houses, buoys, and the maintenance of their seamen upon the Treasury, and the Government now pays above two millions annually for the support of these objects. These interests in connection with the commercial and manufacturing classes have also succeeded, by means of subventions to mail steamers and the reduction of postage, in relieving their business from the payment of about seven millions of dollars annually, throwing it upon the public Treasury, under the name of postal deficiency. The manufacturing interest entered into the same struggle early, and has clamored steadily for Government bounties and special favors. This interest was confined mainly to the Eastern and Middle non-slaveholding States. Wielding these great States, it held great power and influence, and its demands were in full proportion to its power. The manufacturers and miners *wisely* based their demands upon special facts and reasons, rather than upon general principles, and thereby mollified much of the opposition of the opposing interest. They pleaded in their favor, the infancy of their business in this country, the scarcity of labor and capital, the hostile legislation of other countries towards them, the great necessity of their fabrics in the time of war, and the necessity of high duties to pay the debt incurred in our war for independence; these reasons prevailed, and they received for many years enormous bounties by the general acquiescence of the whole country.

But when these reasons ceased, they were no less clamorous for government protection; but their clamors were less heeded,—the country had put the principle of protection upon trial and condemned it. After having enjoyed protection to the extent of from fifteen to two hundred per cent upon their entire business for above thirty years, the Act of 1846 was passed.[1] It avoided sudden change, but the principle was settled, and free-trade, low duties, and economy in public expenditures was the verdict of the American people. The South and the Northwestern States sustained this policy. There was but small hope of its reversal,—upon the direct issue, none at all. All these classes saw this, and felt it, and cast about for new allies. The anti-slavery sentiment of the North offered the best chance for success. An anti-slavery party must necessarily look to the North alone for support; but a united North was now strong enough to control the Government in all of its departments, and a sectional party was therefore determined upon. Time and issues upon slavery were necessary to its completion and final triumph. The feeling of anti-slavery, which it was well known was very general among the people of the North, had been long dormant or passive,—it needed only a question to arouse it into aggressive activity. This question was before us: we had acquired a large territory by successful war with Mexico; Congress had to govern it, how—in relation to slavery—was the question then demanding solution. This state of facts gave form and shape to the anti-slavery sentiment throughout the North, and the conflict began. Northern anti-slavery men of all parties asserted the right to exclude slavery from the territory by Congressional legislation, and demanded the prompt and efficient exercise of this power to that end. This insulting and unconstitutional demand was met with great moderation and firmness by the South. We had shed our blood and paid our money for its acquisition; we demanded a division of it, on the line of the Missouri restriction, or an equal participation in the whole of it. These propositions were refused, the agitation became general, and the public danger great. The case of the South was impregnable. The price of the acquisition was the blood and treasure of both sections—of all; and therefore it belonged to all, upon the principles of equity and justice. The Constitution delegated no power to Congress to exclude either party from its free enjoyment; therefore, our right was *good*, under the Constitution. Our rights were further fortified by the practice of the Government from the beginning. Slavery was forbidden in the country Northwest of the Ohio river, by what is called the Ordinance of 1787.[2] That

---

1. The so-called Walker Tariff of 1846 greatly lowered rates and led to a marked increase in foreign trade, especially with Great Britain.

2. The Ordinance of 1787 organized the land north of the Ohio River and west of Pennsylvania, territory that had been ceded to the United States by the state of Virginia.

PART TWO

ordinance was adopted under the old confederation and by the assent of Virginia, who owned and ceded the country; and, therefore, this case must stand on its own special circumstances. The government of the United States claimed territory by virtue of the treaty of 1783 with Great Britain [ending the American Revolution]; acquired territory by cession from Georgia and North Carolina; by treaty from France, and by treaty from Spain. These acquisitions largely exceeded the original limits of the Republic. In all of these acquisitions the policy of the government was uniform. It opened them to the settlement of all the citizens of all the States of the Union. They emigrated thither with their property of every kind (including slaves),—all were equally protected by public authority in their persons and property, until the inhabitants became sufficiently numerous, and otherwise capable of bearing the burthens and performing the duties of self-government, when they were admitted into the Union upon equal terms with the other States, with whatever republican constitution they might adopt for themselves.

Under this equally just and beneficent policy, law and order, stability and progress, peace and prosperity marked every step of the progress of these new communities, until they entered as great and prosperous commonwealths into the sisterhood of American States. In 1820, the North endeavored to overturn this wise and successful policy, and demanded that the State of Missouri should not be admitted into the Union, unless she first prohibited slavery within her limits, by her Constitution. After a bitter and protracted struggle, the North was defeated in her special object; but her policy and position led to the adoption of a section in the law, for the admission of Missouri, prohibiting slavery in all that portion of the territory acquired from France, lying North of 36 deg. 30 min. North latitude and outside of Missouri. The venerable {James} Madison, at the time of its adoption, declared it unconstitutional; Mr. {Thomas} Jefferson condemned the restriction, and foresaw its consequences, and predicted that it would result in the dissolution of the Union. His prediction is now history. The North demanded the application of the principle of prohibition of slavery to all of the territory acquired from Mexico, and all other parts of the public domain, then and in all future time. It was the announcement of her purpose to appropriate to herself all the public domain then owned and thereafter to be acquired by the United States. The claim itself was less arrogant and insulting than the reason with which she supported it. That reason was her fixed purpose to limit, restrain, and finally to abolish slavery in the States where it exists. The South, with great unanimity, declared her purpose to resist the principle of prohibition to the last extremity. This particular question, in connection with a series of questions affecting the same subject, was finally disposed of by the defeat of prohibitory legislation.

The Presidential election of 1852 resulted in the total overthrow of the advocates of restriction and their party friends.[3] Immediately after this result, the anti-slavery portion of the defeated party resolved to unite all the elements in the North opposed to slavery and to stake their future political fortunes upon their hostility to slavery everywhere. This is the party to whom the people of the North have committed the government. They raised their standard in 1856 and were barely defeated; they entered the Presidential contest again, in 1860 and succeeded.

The prohibition of slavery in the territories, hostility to it everywhere, the equality of the black and white races, disregard of all constitutional guarantees in its favor, were boldly proclaimed by its leaders and applauded by its followers.

With these principles on their banners and these utterances on their lips, the majority of the people of the North demand that we shall receive them as our rulers.

The prohibition of slavery in the territories is the cardinal principle of this organization.

For forty years this question has been considered and debated in the halls of Congress, before the people, by the press, and before the tribunals of justice. The majority of the people of the North in 1860 decided it in their own favor. We refuse to submit to that judgment, and in vindication of our refusal, we offer the constitution of our country, and point to the total absence of any express power to exclude us; we offer the practice of our government, for the first thirty years of its existence, in complete refutation of the position that any such power is either necessary or proper to the execution of any other power in relation to the territories. We offer the judgment of a large minority of the people of the North, amounting to more than one-third who united with the unanimous voice of the South against this usurpation; and finally, we offer the judgment of the Supreme Court of the United States, the highest judicial tribunal of our country in our favor. This evidence ought to be conclusive, that we have never surrendered this right;

---

3. Democrats Franklin Pierce and William R. King routed the Whig Party candidates of Winfield Scott and William C. Graham by carrying all but four states and the Electoral College, 254–42.

the conduct of our adversaries admonishes us that if we had surrendered it, it is time to resume it.

The faithless conduct of our adversaries is not confined to such acts as might aggrandize themselves or their section of the Union; they are content, if they can only injure us. The constitution declares that persons charged with crimes in one State and fleeing to another shall be delivered up on the demand of the Executive authority of the State from which they may flee, to be tried in the jurisdiction where the crime was committed. It would appear difficult to employ language freer from ambiguity; yet for above twenty years the non-slaveholding States, generally, have wholly refused to deliver up to us persons charged with crimes affecting slave property; our confederates, with punic faith, shield and give sanctuary to all criminals, who seek to deprive us of this property, or who use it to destroy us. This clause of the constitution has no other sanction than their good faith; *that* is withheld from us; we are remediless in the Union; out of it, we are remitted to the laws of nations.

A similar provision of the Constitution requires them to surrender fugitives from labor. This provision and the one last referred to were our main inducements for confederating with the Northern States; without them, it is historically true, that we would have rejected the Constitution. In the fourth year of the Republic, Congress passed a law to give full vigor and efficiency to this important provision. This act depended to a considerable degree upon the local magistrates in the several States for its efficiency; the non-slaveholding States generally repealed all laws intended to aid the execution of that act, and imposed penalties upon those citizens whose loyalty to the Constitution, and their oaths, might induce them to discharge their duty. Congress then passed the act of 1850, providing for the complete execution of this duty by Federal Officers.[4] This law, which their own bad faith rendered absolutely indispensable for the protection of constitutional rights, was instantly met with ferocious revilings and all conceivable modes of hostility. The Supreme Court unanimously, and their own local Courts, with equal unanimity, (with the single and temporary exception of the Supreme Court of Wisconsin,) sustained its constitutionality in all of its provisions. Yet it stands to-day a dead letter, for all practicable purposes, in every non-slaveholding State in the Union. We have their covenants, we have their oaths, to keep and observe it, but the unfortunate claimant, even

---

4. The Fugitive Slave Law of 1850 amended the earlier law of 1793 and placed fugitive slave cases under the jurisdiction of federal magistrates.

accompanied by a Federal Officer, with the mandate of the highest judicial authority in his hands, is everywhere met with fraud, with force, and with legislative enactments, to elude, to resist and defeat him; claimants are murdered with impunity; Officers of the law are beaten by frantic mobs, instigated by inflammatory appeals from persons holding the highest public employment in these States, and supported by legislation in conflict with the clearest provisions of the Constitution, and even the ordinary principles of humanity. In several of our confederate States, a citizen can not travel the high-way with his servant, who may voluntarily accompany him, without being declared by law a felon, and being subjected to infamous punishments. It is difficult to perceive how we could suffer more by the hostility than by the fraternity of such brethren.

The public law of civilized nations requires every State to restrain its citizens or subjects from committing acts injurious to the peace and security of any other State, and from attempting to excite insurrection, or to lessen the security, or to disturb the tranquility of their neighbors, and our Constitution wisely gives Congress the power to punish all offenses against the laws of nations.

These are sound and just principles which have received the approbation of just men in all countries, and all centuries. But they are wholly disregarded by the people of the Northern States, and the Federal Government is impotent to maintain them. For twenty years past, the Abolitionists and their allies in the Northern States have been engaged in constant efforts to subvert our institutions and to excite insurrection and servile war amongst us. They have sent emissaries among us for the accomplishment of these purposes. Some of these efforts have received the public sanction of a majority of the leading men of the Republican party in the National Councils, the same men who are now proposed as our rulers. These efforts have in one instance led to the actual invasion of one of the slave-holding States, and those of the murderers and incendiaries, who escaped public justice by flight, have found fraternal protection among our Northern Confederates.

These are the men who say the *Union shall be preserved.*

Such are the opinions and such are the practices of the Republican Party, who have been called by their own votes to administer the Federal Government under the Constitution of the United States; we know their treachery, we know the shallow pretenses under which they daily disregard its plainest obligations; if we submit to them, it will be our fault and not theirs. The people of Georgia have ever been willing to stand by this bargain, this contract; they have never sought to evade any of its obligations; they have never hitherto sought to establish any new government; they have struggled to maintain the ancient right of themselves and the human race, through and by that Constitution. But they know the value of parchment rights, in treacherous hands, and therefore, they refuse to commit their own to the rulers whom the North offer us.[5] Why? Because by their declared principles and policy, they have outlawed three thousand millions of our property in the common territories of the Union, put it under the ban of the Republic in the States where it exists, and out of the protection of Federal law everywhere; because they give sanctuary to thieves and incendiaries who assail it to the whole extent of their power, in spite of their most solemn obligations and covenants; because their avowed purpose is to subvert our society, and subject us, not only to the loss of our property but the destruction of ourselves, our wives and our children, and the desolation of our homes, our altars, and our firesides. To avoid these evils, we resume the powers which our Fathers delegated to the Government of the United States, and henceforth will seek new safeguards for our liberty, equality, security and tranquillity."

On motion of Mr. Nisbet, 10,000 copies of the report were ordered to be printed in pamphlet form, for the use of the Convention.

Adopted January 29, 1861

Source: *Journal of the Public and Secret Proceedings of the Convention of the People of Georgia, Held in Milledgeville and Savannah in 1861* (Milledgeville: Boughton, Nisbet & Barnes, State Printers, 1861), 104–113.

TEXAS

Mr. {John Henry} Brown {Bell and Lampasas Counties}, from the committee to prepare an address to the people of Texas, made the following report.

The undersigned committee appointed to prepare and report an address for the consideration of the Convention, setting forth the causes which induced the State of Texas to secede from the Federal Union, herewith report a 'declaration' of such causes and recommend its adoption.

---

5. "Parchment rights" is a reference to the written obligations and requirements of the Constitution, which would be worthless in the hands of unscrupulous politicians.

John Henry Brown,
George Flournoy,
Jno. A. Wilcox,
M. D. Graham and
A. P. Wiley, committee

A declaration of the causes which impel the State of Texas to secede from the Federal Union.

The government of the United States, by certain joint resolutions, bearing date the 1st day of March, in the year A.D. 1845, proposed to the Republic of Texas, then *a free, sovereign and independent nation,* the annexation of the latter to the former, as one of the coequal States thereof,

The people of Texas, by deputies in convention assembled, on the fourth day of July of the same year, assented to and accepted said proposals and formed a constitution for the proposed State, upon which on the 29th day of December in the same year, said State was formally admitted into the Confederated Union.

Texas abandoned her separate national existence and consented to become one of the Confederated States to promote her welfare, insure domestic tranquility and secure more substantially the blessings of peace and liberty to her people. She was received into the confederacy with her own constitution, under the guarantee of the federal constitution and the compact of annexation, that she should enjoy these blessings. She was received as a commonwealth holding, maintaining, and protecting the institution known as negro slavery—the servitude of the African to the white race within her limits—a relation that had existed from the first settlement of her wilderness by the white race, and which her people intended should exist in all future time. Her institutions and geographical position established the strongest ties between her and other slaveholding States of the confederacy. Those ties have been strengthened by association. But what has been the course of the government of the United States, and of the people and authorities of the nonslaveholding States, since our connection with them?

The controlling majority of the Federal Government, under various pretences and disguises, has so administered the same as to exclude the citizens of the Southern States, unless under odious and unconstitutional restrictions, from all the immense territory owned in common by all the States on the Pacific Ocean, for the avowed purpose of acquiring sufficient power in the common government to use it as a means of destroying the institutions of Texas and her sister slave-holding States. By the disloyalty of the

Northern States and their citizens and the imbecility of the Federal Government, infamous combinations of incendiaries and outlaws have been permitted in those States and the common territory of Kansas to trample upon the federal laws, to war upon the lives and property of Southern citizens in that territory, and finally, by violence and mob law, to usurp the possession of the same as exclusively the property of the Northern States.

The Federal Government, while but partially under the control of these our unnatural and sectional enemies, has for years almost entirely failed to protect the lives and property of the people of Texas against the Indian savages on our border, and more recently against the murderous forays of banditti from the neighboring territory of Mexico; and when our State government has expended large amounts for such purpose, the Federal Government has refused reimbursement therefor, thus rendering our condition more insecure and harrassing than it was during the existence of the Republic of Texas.

These and other wrongs we have patiently borne in the vain hope that a returning sense of justice and humanity would induce a different course of administration.

When we advert to the course of individual nonslaveholding States and that a majority of their citizens, our grievances assume far greater magnitude. The States of Maine, Vermont, New Hampshire, Connecticut, Rhode Island, Massachusetts, New York, Pennsylvania, Ohio, Wisconsin, Michigan and Iowa, by solemn legislative enactments, have deliberately, directly or indirectly violated the 3rd clause of the 2nd section of the 4th article of the federal constitution, and laws passed in pursuance thereof; thereby annulling a material provision of the compact, designed by its framers to perpetuate amity between the members of the confederacy and to secure the rights of the slaveholding States in their domestic institutions—a provision founded in justice and wisdom, and without the enforcement of which the compact fails to accomplish the object of its creation. Some of those States have imposed high fines and degrading penalties upon any of their citizens or officers who may carry out in good faith that provision of the compact, or the federal laws enacted in accordance therewith.

In all the nonslaveholding States, in violation of that good faith and comity which should exist between entirely distinct nations, the people have formed themselves into a great sectional party, now strong enough in numbers to control the affairs of each of those States, based upon the unnatural feeling of hostility to these Southern States and their beneficent and patriarchal system of African slavery, proclaiming the debasing doctrine of the equality of all men, irrespective of race or color—a doctrine at war with nature, in opposition to the experience of mankind, and in violation of the plainest revelations of the Divine Law. They demand the abolition of negro slavery throughout the confederacy, the recognition of political equality between the white and the negro races, and avow their determination to press on their crusade against us, so long as a negro slave remains in these States.

For years past this abolition organization has been actively sowing the seeds of discord through the Union, and has rendered the federal congress the arena for spreading firebrands and hatred between the slaveholding and nonslaveholding States.

By consolidating their strength, they have placed the slaveholding States in a hopeless minority in the federal congress, and rendered representation of no avail in protecting Southern rights against their exactions and encroachments.

They have proclaimed, and at the ballot box sustained, the revolutionary doctrine that there is a "higher law" than the constitution and laws of our Federal Union, and virtually that they will disregard their oaths and trample upon our rights. They have for years past encouraged and sustained lawless organizations to steal our slaves and prevent their recapture, and have repeatedly murdered Southern citizens while lawfully seeking their rendition.

They have invaded Southern soil and murdered unoffending citizens, and through the press their leading men and a fanatical pulpit have bestowed praise upon the actors and assassins in these crimes, while the governors of several of their States have refused to deliver parties implicated and indicted for participation in such offences, upon the legal demands of the States aggrieved.

They have, through the mails and hired emissaries, sent seditious pamphlets and papers among us to stir up servile insurrection and bring blood and carnage to our firesides.

They have sent hired emissaries among us to burn our towns and distribute arms and poison to our slaves for the same purpose.

They have impoverished the slaveholding States by unequal and partial legislation, thereby enriching themselves by draining our substance.

They have refused to vote appropriations for protecting Texas against ruthless savages, for the sole reason that she is a slaveholding State.

And, finally, by the combined sectional vote of the seventeen nonslaveholding States, they have elected as president and vicepresident of the whole confederacy two men whose chief claims to such high positions are their approval of these long continued wrongs, and their pledges to continue them to the final consummation of these schemes for the ruin of the slaveholding States.

In view of these and many other facts, it is meet that our own views should be distinctly proclaimed.

We hold as undeniable truths that the governments of the various States, and of the confederacy itself, were established exclusively by the white race, for themselves and their posterity; that the African race had no agency in their establishment; that they were rightfully held and regarded as an inferior and dependent race, and in that condition only could their existence in this country be rendered beneficial or tolerable.

That in this free government *all white men are and of right ought to be entitled to equal civil and political rights*; that the servitude of the African race, as existing in these States, is mutually beneficial to both bond and free, and is abundantly authorized and justified by the experience of mankind, and the revealed will of the Almighty Creator, as recognized by all Christian nations; while the destruction of the existing relations between the two races, as advocated by our sectional enemies, would bring inevitable calamities upon both and desolation upon the fifteen slaveholding States.

By the secession of six of the slaveholding States, and the certainty that others will speedily do likewise, Texas has no alternative but to remain in an isolated connection with the North, or unite her destinies with the South.

For these and other reasons, solemnly asserting that the federal constitution has been violated and virtually abrogated by the several States named, seeing that the federal government is now passing under the control of our enemies to be diverted from the exalted objects of its creation to those of oppression and wrong, and realizing that our own State can no longer look for protection, but to God and her own sons—We the delegates of the people of Texas, in Convention assembled, have passed an ordinance dissolving all political connection with the government of thc United States of America and the people thereof and confidently appeal to the intelligence and patriotism of the freemen of Texas to ratify the same at the ballot box, on the 23rd day of the present month.

Adapted in Convention on the 2nd day of Feby, in the year of our Lord one thousand eight hundred and sixty-one and of the independence of Texas the twenty-fifth.

Source: E. W. Winkler, ed., *Journal of the Secession Convention of Texas, 1861* (Austin: Austin Printing, 1912), 61–65.

PART THREE

U.S. House of Representatives, Journal of the Committee of Thirty-Three

In its deliberations from December 4, 1860, until January 14, 1861, the Committee of Thirty-Three considered a wide range of resolutions and constitutional amendments designed to address the "existing discontent among the southern people." The bulk of its deliberations dealt with slavery in the western territories, fugitive slaves, northern obstruction of the Fugitive Slave Act, the acquisition of additional territory, New Mexico statehood, and slavery in the District of Columbia and in federal installations in the South. Representative Miles Taylor of Louisiana even proposed a constitutional amendment that would have, in part, restricted the elective franchise to those "of the Caucasian race, and of pure, unmixed blood." Ultimately, the committee approved a new fugitive slave bill, a bill providing for the admission of New Mexico into the Union, a constitutional amendment that prohibited Congress from interfering with slavery in the states, and five resolutions designed to encourage the maintenance of order and respect for slave property. Only the constitutional amendment received the approval of the full House.

REPORT OF SPECIAL COMMITTEE OF THIRTY-THREE, JANUARY 11, 1861

January 7, 1861

On the question to agree to the passage of the bill as amended,

It was determined in the affirmative—yeas 13, nays 11.

Those who voted in the affirmative are—Messrs. Bristow {Francis M. Bristow—Opposition, Kentucky}, Campbell {James H. Campbell—R, Pennsylvania}, Corwin {Thomas Corwin—R, Ohio}, Curtis {Samuel R. Curtis—R, Iowa}, H. Winter Davis {American, Maryland}, Dunn {W. McKee Dunn—R, Indiana}, Ferry {Orris S. Ferry—R, Connecticut}, Howard {William A. Howard—R, Michigan}, Humphrey {James Humphrey—R, New York}, Kellogg {Francis W. Kellogg—R, Michigan}, Morse {Freeman H. Morse—R, Maine}, Robinson {Christopher Robinson—R, Rhode Island}, Stratton {John L. N. Stratton—R, New Jersey}.

Those who voted in the negative are—

Messrs. Adams {Charles F. Adams—R, Massachusetts}, Burch {John C. Burch—D, California}, Millson {John S. Millson—D, Virginia}, Morrill {Justin S. Morrill—R, Vermont}, Nelson {Thomas A. R. Nelson—Opposition, Tennessee}, Phelps {John S. Phelps—D, Missouri}, Stout {Lansing Stout—D, Oregon}, Tappan {Mason W. Tappan—R, New Hampshire}, Washburn {Cadwallader Washburn—R, Wisconsin}, Whiteley {William G. Whiteley—D, Delaware}, and Windom {William Windom—R, Minnesota}.

The bill as amended and passed is as follows:

Be it enacted by the Senate and House of Representatives of the United States of America in Congress assembled, That every person arrested under the laws of Congress for the delivery up of fugitives from labor shall be produced before a court, judge, or commissioner, mentioned in the law approved the eighteenth of September, eighteen hundred and fifty, for the State or Territory, wherein the arrest may be made; and upon such production of the person, together with the proofs, mentioned in the sixth or the tenth section of said act, such court, judge, or commissioner shall proceed to hear and consider the same publicly; and if such court, judge, or commissioner is of the opinion that the person arrested owes labor or service to the claimant according to the laws of any other State, Territory, or the District of Columbia, and escaped therefrom, the court, judge, or commissioner shall make out and deliver to the claimant, or his agent, a certificate stating those facts;

and if the said claimant shall, upon the decision of the court, judge, or commissioner being made known to him, aver that he is free, and does not owe service or labor according to the law of the State or Territory to which he is to be returned, such averment shall be entered on the certificate, and the fugitive shall be delivered by the court, judge, or commissioner to the marshal, to be by him taken and delivered to the marshal of the United States for the State or District from which the fugitive is ascertained to have fled, who shall produce said fugitive before one of the judges of the circuit court of the United States for the last-mentioned State or District, whose duty it shall be, if said alleged fugitive shall persist in his averment, forthwith, or at the next term of the circuit court, to cause a jury to be impanelled and sworn to try the issue whether such fugitive owes labor or service to the person by or on behalf of whom he is claimed, and a true verdict to give according to the evidence, on which trial the fugitive shall be entitled to the aid of counsel, and to process for procuring evidence, at the cost of the United States; and upon such finding, the judge shall render judgement, and cause said fugitive to be delivered to the claimant, or returned to the place where he was arrested, at the expense of the United States, according to the finding of the jury; and if the judge or court be not satisfied with the verdict, he may cause another jury to be impanelled forthwith, whose verdict shall be final. And it shall be the duty of said marshal so delivering said alleged fugitive to take from the marshal of the State from which said fugitive is alleged to have escaped a certificate acknowledging that said alleged fugitive had been delivered to him, giving a minute description of said alleged fugitive, which certificate shall be authenticated by the United States district judge, or a commissioner of a United States court for said State from which said fugitive was alleged to have escaped, which certificate shall be filed in the office of the clerk of the United States district court for the State or district in which said alleged fugitive was seized, within sixty days from the date of the arrest of said fugitive; and should said marshal fail to comply with the provisions of this act, he shall be deemed guilty of a misdemeanor, and shall be punished by a fine of one thousand dollars and imprisoned for six months, and until his said fine is paid.

Sec. 2. *And be it further enacted,* That no citizen of any State shall be compelled to aid the marshal or owner of any fugitive in the capture or detention of such fugitive, unless where force is employed or reasonably apprehended to prevent such capture or detention, too powerful to be resisted by the marshal or owner; and the fees of the commissioners under the act of eighteenth September, eighteen hundred and fifty, shall be ten dollars for every case of a fugitive from labor heard and determined by such commissioner.

On motion, at 5 o'clock p.m., the committee adjourned to meet tomorrow at 12 m.

January 11, 1861

Mr. Dunn {W. McKee Dunn—R, Indiana}, from the special committee of three, submitted the following report:

The special committee to whom was referred certain measures, have instructed their chairman to report the accompanying joint resolution to amend the Constitution of the United States, a bill for the admission of New Mexico as a State into the Union, and certain resolutions.

The committee proceeded to consider the joint resolution amendatory of the Constitution of the United States.

Be it resolved by the Senate and House of Representatives of the United States of America in Congress assembled, two-thirds of both houses concurring, That the following article be proposed to the legislatures of the several States as an amendment to the Constitution of the United States, which, when ratified by three-fourths of said legislatures, shall be valid, to all intents and purposes, as part of the said Constitution, viz:

ARTICLE XII. No amendment of this Constitution having for its object any interference within the States with the relation between their citizens and those described in section second of the first article of the Constitution as "all other persons" shall originate with any State that does not recognize that relation within its own limits, or shall be valid without the assent of every one of the States composing the Union.

On the question to agree,

It was determined in the affirmative—yeas 20, nays 5.

Those who voted in the affirmative are—

Messrs. Bristow {Francis M. Bristow—Opposition, Kentucky}, Burch {John C. Burch—D, California}, Campbell {James H. Campbell—R, Pennsylvania}, Corwin {Thomas Corwin—R, Ohio}, Curtis {Samuel R. Curtis—R, Iowa}, H. Winter Davis {American, Maryland}, Dunn {W. McKee Dunn—R, Indiana}, Houston {George S. Houston—D, Alabama}, Howard {William A. Howard—R, Michigan}, Humphrey {James Humphrey—R, New York}, Love {Peter E. Love—D, Georgia}, Millson {John S. Millson—D, Virginia}, Morrill {Justin S. Morrill—R, Vermont}, Nelson {Thomas A. R.

Nelson—Opposition, Tennessee}, Phelps {John S. Phelps—D, Missouri}, Robinson {James C. Robinson—R, Illinois}, Rust {Albert Rust—D, Arkansas}, Taylor {Miles Taylor—D, Louisiana}, Whiteley {William G. Whiteley—D, Delaware}, and Windom {William Windom—R, Minnesota}.

Those who voted in the negative are—

Messrs. Adams {Charles F. Adams—R, Massachusetts}, Ferry {Orris S. Ferry—R, Connecticut}, Kellogg {Francis W. Kellogg—R, Michigan}, Tappan {Mason W. Tappan—R, New Hampshire}, and Washburn {Cadwallader Washburn—R, Wisconsin}.

The committee then proceeded to consider the following act for the admission of New Mexico into the United States of America:

Whereas by the act of Congress approved on the 9th of September, in the year 1850, it was provided that the people of New Mexico, when admitted as a State, shall be received into the Union with or without slavery, as their constitution may provide at the time of their admission:

And whereas the population of said Territory is now sufficient to constitute a State government: Therefore—

Be it enacted by the Senate and House of Representatives of the United States of America in Congress assembled, That the inhabitants of the Territory of New Mexico, including therein the region called Arizona, be, and they are hereby, authorized to form for themselves a constitution of State government, by the name of the State of New Mexico; and the said State, when formed, shall be admitted into the Union upon the same footing with the original States in all respects whatever. And said constitution shall be formed by a convention of the people of New Mexico, which shall consist of twice the number of members now by law constituting the house of representatives of the Territory. Each representative district shall elect two members to said convention for every member now by law elected in such district to the territorial house of representatives; and in such election only those persons shall vote for such delegates as are, by the laws of said Territory now in force, entitled to vote for members of the territorial house of representatives. The election for the convention shall be held on the 5th day of August, 1861, by the same officers who would hold an election for members of the said house of representatives; and those officers shall conform to the law now in force in said Territory for election for members of said house of representatives in all respects, in holding the election, receiving and rejecting votes, and making the returns of the election for the convention. The convention shall assemble at the city of Santa Fé, on the 2d day of September, 1861, and continue its sessions at that place until its deliberations shall be closed. The constitution agreed on by the convention shall be submitted to the people of the Territory for their approval or rejection as a whole; at such election on the constitution, all those and others shall be entitled to vote who are now entitled to vote for members of the house of representatives of said Territory; and such election shall be held by the same officers who conduct, by the present laws, the election for members of the house of representatives of the Territory, at the same place for voting, and in the same manner in all respects; and such election shall be held on the 4th day of November, 1861, and the returns thereof made to the governor of the Territory, who shall forthwith sum up and declare the result, and shall send a certificate thereof, together with a copy of the constitution, to the President of the United States.

The said State shall be entitled to one member of the House of Representatives of the United States of America, held until the apportionment under the next census.

On the question to agree,

It was determined in the affirmative—yeas 14, nays 9.

Those who voted in the affirmative are—

Messrs. Bristow {Francis M. Bristow—Opposition, Kentucky}, Burch {John C. Burch—D, California}, Campbell {James H. Campbell—R, Pennsylvania}, Corwin {Thomas Corwin—R, Ohio}, H. Winter Davis {American, Maryland}, Dunn {W. McKee Dunn—R, Indiana}, Houston {George S. Houston—D, Alabama}, Howard {William A. Howard—R, Michigan}, Humphrey {James Humphrey—R, New York}, Love {Peter E. Love—D, Georgia}, Millson {John S. Millson—D, Virginia}, Nelson {Thomas A. R. Nelson—Opposition, Tennessee}, Stout {Lansing Stout—D, Oregon}, and Stratton {John L. N. Stratton—R, New Jersey}.

Those who voted in the negative are—

Messrs. Adams {Charles F. Adams—R, Massachusetts}, Curtis {Samuel R. Curtis—R, Iowa}, Kellogg {William Kellogg—R, Illinois}, Morrill {Justin S. Morrill—R, Vermont}, Morse {Freeman H. Morse—R, Maine}, Robinson {Christopher Robinson—R, Rhode Island}, Tappan {Mason W. Tappan—R, New Hampshire}, Washburn {Cadwallader C. Washburn—R, Wisconsin}, and Windom {William Windom—R, Minnesota}.

The committee next proceeded to consider the following resolutions reported from the select committee of three:

Resolved, That the faithful observance, on the part of all the States, of all their constitutional obligations to each other and to the federal government is essential to the peace of the country.

Resolved, That it is the duty of the federal government to enforce the federal laws, protect the federal property, and preserve the union of these States.

Resolved, That each State be requested to revise its statutes, and, if necessary, so to amend the same as to secure, without legislation by Congress, to citizens of other States travelling therein the same protection as citizens of such State enjoy; and also to protect the citizens of other States travelling or sojourning therein against popular violence or illegal summary punishment, without trial in due form of law, for imputed crimes.

Resolved, That each State be also respectfully requested to enact such laws as will prevent and punish any attempt whatever in such State to organize or set on foot the lawless invasion of any other State or Territory.

Resolved, That the President be requested to transmit copies of the foregoing resolutions to the governors of the several States, with a request that they be communicated to their respective legislatures.

On the question to agree to the same,

It was determined in the affirmative without a division.

Mr. Curtis asked and obtained leave to enter the following on the record:

I voted against the proposition for admitting New Mexico—

1st. Because the mover, Mr. Adams, himself, votes against it, and I had formerly expressed my deference for his preference in this respect.

2d. I think adjoining sections, especially Kansas, Nebraska, Pike's Peak, and Nevada, should be brought in at the same time.

When, on motion, the committee adjourned to meet on Monday at 10 o'clock a. m.

Source: U.S. Congress, House, Journal of the Committee of Thirty-Three, 36th Cong., 2nd sess., Report No. 31, January 29, 1861, 31–32, 35–37.

COMMITTEE OF THIRTY-THREE:
MINORITY REPORT NO. 1

Although it accomplished much more than its Senate counterpart, the Committee of Thirty-Three was far from united on its recommendations. The committee's printed proceedings contained no fewer than seven dissenting reports, the first two of which are reproduced below. John Burch of California and Lansing Stout of Oregon, both first-term congressmen, penned the third minority report. Burch and Stout generally favored the committee's conclusions, but believed a general constitutional convention would be a better (although not shorter) path to sectional accommodation. While they approved of the Seward-Adams-Corwin amendment, they did not believe it could pass both houses of Congress. Representative Thomas Nelson of eastern Tennessee also dissented, believing that only the constitutional amendment proposed by John Crittenden could bring a "final settlement of the slavery question." While he could not support either New Mexico statehood or the proposed revision of the Fugitive Slave Law, Nelson supported the Seward-Adams-Corwin amendment.

Charles Francis Adams of Massachusetts was also a first-term congressman who had just been elected to a second term. He resigned his seat in Congress shortly after Lincoln's inauguration to become the new president's minister to England, where he served throughout the war. Adams penned the fifth minority report, believing that the majority report was inadequate to its task. Listing the three causes of sectional discontent as the existence of the northern personal liberty laws, slavery in the territories, and the "apprehension" among southerners that slavery in the states will become the target of future constitutional amendments, Adams believed that only a constitutional obligation to "protect and extend slavery" would satisfy the South. Orris Ferry of Connecticut, also a Republican, protested the majority report, objecting that some of the committee's recommendations "ought not receive the sanction of Congress." Ferry failed, however, to specify the objectionable sections. Peter Early Love of Georgia and Andrew Jackson Hamilton of Texas objected to the committee's report "because it may delude and mislead the public." Believing that the recommendations of the majority would not effectively constitute a solution to the crisis, they, like Tennessee's Thomas Nelson, supported Crittenden's proposals as "the only settlement which can relieve us from existing and impending troubles."

The first two minority reports are both the longest of the seven and, as a result, the most detailed. Written after the secession of South Carolina, Mis-

sissippi, Florida, and Alabama, they provide very clear windows into the po-
larized nature of the country and furnish explicit examples of the rancor and
resentment that, on the eve of Lincoln's inauguration, had developed North
and South. Republicans Cadwallader Colden Washburn (1818–1882) from
Wisconsin and Mason Weare Tappan (1817–1886) from New Hampshire
were the first to object to the committee's majority report. Representing
the opinion of many Republicans that the country should not negotiate the
results of the recent election, Washburn and Tappan express the belief that
compromise is inappropriate and would be totally ineffective. South Caro-
lina, they wrote, is a "sick man," suffering from "acute mania" that cannot
be restored to health by any of the committee's presumed solutions. They
conclude by quoting New Hampshire senator Daniel Clark that "the provi-
sions of the Constitution are ample for the preservation of the Union."

DISTURBED CONDITION OF THE COUNTRY.

JANUARY 14, 1861.—Ordered to be printed, and made the special order
for Monday the 21st instant, at 1 o'clock, and continued from day to day
thereafter until disposed of

Mr. C. C. WASHBURN and Mr. TAPPAN, from the select committee of thirty-
three, made the following

MINORITY REPORT.

The undersigned, comprising a part of the minority of the committee of one
from each State, to whom was referred so much of the President's message
as related to the present disturbed condition of the country, respectfully
submit the following report:

On the 6th day of November last the people of the United States were in
a condition of tranquility and peace. They were at peace with other nations,
and at peace among themselves. The excitement of a general election was
then at its height, but as such excitements necessarily result from our republican system of government, and had always before passed away with the
announcement of the general result, the people always before having grace-
fully yielded their submission to the popular verdict, and shown their loyalty
to the Constitution and laws, it was believed and hoped by all good men and
patriots that the excitement then existing would pass away with the election.

It was not supposed that there were any considerable number of people in the Union who would turn traitors to the country in the event of a party defeat. The leading idea in a republican government is that the majority under the Constitution shall rule, and when the people of the several States join in a general election of a Chief Magistrate, it has always been with this recognized tacit understanding. To abide by the result was the paramount duty of every one who took part in the election, and to refuse acquiescence was such manifest bad faith as no one could be guilty of without a palpable repudiation of an implied contract. But the result of this last election had scarcely been announced when the people of one of the southern States proclaimed that they would not submit to the verdict of the majority. They declared that though a minority, they would rule the country or else destroy it. Certain it is that those who now propose to destroy the Union have for many years had the control of the government. Legislation has invariably been passed to suit them. The Supreme Court has been constituted expressly with the view to uphold their interests, and has not only given decisions to favor them, but has travelled out of its way to announce opinions upon subjects not before it. They cannot, therefore, complain of any wrongs received from the general government, for they have had that entirely in their own way. But on that 6th day of November the people of the United States, at an election conducted with perfect order, and in strict accordance with the requirements of the Constitution, elected as Chief Magistrate one of her citizens, of most unblemished character, and whose principles we believe were in strict conformity with those of the founders of the republic. No sooner was the fact of his election known than the fires of sectional hate and long meditated treason, which had been smouldering for nearly thirty years in South Carolina, broke out in devastating fury, and great was the rejoicing among those misguided people, who hailed that event as the harbinger of their deliverance from a union that they had long regarded as a thing accursed.

A State convention was promptly called to adopt measures for secession. Other States that had lent a too willing ear to her syren song were induced to initiate measures in imitation of that deluded State.[1] Such was the position of affairs when Congress assembled, on the 3d day of December. At this crisis the President of the United States, in his annual message, was guilty of the criminal folly of adding fuel to the flame by the most gross misrepresentation of the feelings, principles, and purposes of the people of the north,

---

1. In Greek mythology, sirens lured mariners to their doom with their bewitching songs.

and while he palliated the course of the secessionists he declared his inability to stay the tide of treason and rebellion. On the delivery of that message, contrary to the usual practice, it was referred to a select committee, consisting of one from each State.

From this unusual proceeding, we, composing a part of the minority of the committee, could anticipate no good result, and voted against the formation of said committee. But having been appointed members of it, we entered upon the discharge of our duties ready and eager to co-operate with the other members of the committee in any measures promising peace to the country, and requiring no sacrifice of principle or humiliating concession on the part of those people who had ever been loyal to the Constitution.

The first resolution that passed this committee confirmed us in our previous impressions. It was as follows:

"*Resolved,* That, in the opinion of this committee, the existing discontents among the southern people, and the growing hostility among them to the federal government, are greatly to be regretted; and that, whether such discontents and hostility are without just cause or not, any reasonable, proper, and constitutional remedies, and additional and more specific and effectual guarantees of their peculiar rights and interests as recognized by the Constitution, necessary to preserve the peace of the country and the perpetuation of the Union, should be promptly and cheerfully granted."

The above resolution laid down a basis of action which to our minds was entirely inadmissible, declaring, as it did, that a groundless complaint was entitled to receive the same measure of redress as a complaint founded on just cause. Establish that principle, and there will be no end to the frivolous complaints and absurd exactions that will arise from disaffected States. Acting on this principle, and not inquiring into the right or justice of alleged grievances, the majority of the committee have adopted several propositions from which we are obliged to dissent. It is understood that the design of these various propositions is to restore harmony and concord between the two sections of the country. Will they do it? We say no, for the reason that they do not, in our judgement, touch any real ground of complaint. Their adoption will not appease the south, while it will only incense the north. The successful party in the last election did not elect their candidates to have their principles sacrificed.

The first of these measures, from which we are compelled to dissent, is embraced in the following resolution:

"*Resolved by the Senate and House of Representatives,* That the several States be respectfully requested to cause their statutes to be revised, with a view to ascertain if any of them are in conflict with or tend to embarrass or hinder the execution of the laws of the United States, made in pursuance of the second section of the fourth article of the Constitution of the United States for the delivery up of persons held to labor by the laws of any State, and escaping therefrom; and the Senate and the House of Representatives earnestly request that all enactments having such tendency be forthwith repealed, as required by a just sense of constitutional obligations and by a due regard for the peace of the republic; and the President of the United States is requested to communicate these resolutions to the governors of the several States, with a request that they will lay the same before the legislatures thereof respectively."

The presumption is, that each and every State knows what is due to herself and her own citizens as well as what is due to her sister States, and that they will make their legislation conform to what is right, just, and proper, without any outside interference.

If any of the States have passed unconstitutional laws, the Constitution has provided a tribunal by which that fact is to be determined, and that tribunal is not the Congress of the United States. If any unconstitutional laws have been passed, when that fact shall be determined in a proper way, they will no doubt be promptly repealed, or amended so as to conform to the Constitution. The courts of the north are always open, and history records no instance where the constitutionality of any law in a northern State was sought to be tested, that it was prevented by an armed mob. Had it been otherwise, there would be some excuse for the present interference of Congress; and here we deem it not impertinent to inquire of gentlemen, and particularly of northern gentlemen, who are now so anxious to convey their advice to sovereign States, how it is that they have so long delayed an expression of opinion, and withheld their advice in regard to well known unconstitutional laws, long in existence, which deprive the citizens of some of the northern States of the confederacy of the "rights and immunities of the citizens of the several States." This last class of laws are practically oppressive; the former have never in a single instance been the means of depriving a southern man of a single right. The resolution goes further than to request the repeal of all unconstitutional laws, but also asks them to repeal all such as "delay" the operation of the fugitive slave laws. States are justly sensitive in regard to their reserved rights, and look with just concern upon all attempts to usurp them on the part of the general government. Concede the point that Congress has the right to advise or indicate the character of their legislation, or pronounce, even indirectly, upon the constitutionality of their laws, will only lead to additional usurpations. We prefer to meet all such attempts on the part of the central government at the threshold. While we would not recommend to any State to pass or maintain unconstitutional laws upon any subject, we are still to leave all such questions to the sense of justice of each State to determine; and when the present excitement shall have passed away, and the public mind, especially at the south, shall become more calm and reasonable, if any northern State, being appealed to in the spirit of kindness and conciliation to revise any laws that may be deemed unconstitutional, and which bear unjustly upon any of her sister States, we have no doubt such appeal would be effective.

Some of these personal liberty laws were passed nearly twenty years ago, and before the passage of the present fugitive slave law. Their object and design was the prevention of the crime of kidnapping. Their constitutionality in a few of the States has been disputed by men of equal legal ability. The clamor now against them is a mere excuse for long meditated treason. The rights of no men have ever been prejudiced by them. If such laws are wrong now, they were so when they were enacted. They have been amply discussed and considered heretofore by the States in which they have been passed, both before and since their enactment. If wrong or unconstitutional, they never should have been enacted, or, having been enacted, should be repealed. This proposition is too plain to require us to communicate it to a State. While the country was at peace, and the public mind in a condition to fairly and justly consider such laws, the States that have passed them have considered them right, just, and proper. Shall they now be required, while a portion of the country is in arms, and threatening dissolution and civil war, to review their legislation? Is this the time when they can fairly review it? Would their repeal pacify the malcontents? Would it not rather be justly regarded as an acknowledgment of a disposition to do injustice heretofore which nothing but an open rebellion could induce them to rectify? It will be in vain for the States to say that they repeal these laws because they are wrong, and not because they are threatened with evil consequences should they fail to do so. While upon this subject we desire to notice another and kindred proposition of the committee which is embodied in the following resolution:

"*Resolved,* That each State be requested to revise its statutes, and if necessary, so to amend the same as to secure, without legislation by Congress, to citizens of other States travelling therein the same protection as citizens of such State enjoy; and also to protect the citizens of other States travelling or sojourning therein against popular violence or illegal summary punishment, without trial in due form of law, for imputed crimes."

It will readily be seen that the objection which we have before interposed to the resolution in regard to personal liberty bills will apply to this resolution. We will do no southern State the injustice to suppose that they have not now laws to protect recognized citizens of the north who travel or sojourn among them. The outrages that have been perpetuated on northern men do not result from the want of proper laws on their statute-books, but from the public sentiment of those States.

But not to dwell longer on this subject, we pass to consider the proposed amendment to the Constitution. The substance of it is embodied in the following resolution adopted by the committee:

"*Resolved,* That it is expedient to propose an amendment to the Constitution of the United States, providing that no amendment having for its object any interference within the States with the relation between their citizens and those described in the section second of the first article of the Constitution as 'all other persons' shall originate with any State that does not recognize that relation within its own limits, or shall be valid without the assent of every one of the States composing the Union."

Let us give this proposed amendment a moment's examination. While no party in the Union proposes to interfere in any way with slavery in the States, and the present dominant party expressly disclaim any such right or intention, we are asked to say, not only in our own behalf, but in behalf of millions yet unborn, that no matter what may be the change of circumstances of the people, no matter what may be the wishes of vast majorities north and south, no measures shall be adopted that any way interfere with the relation between the citizens of any State and those described in the second section of the first article in the Constitution as "all other persons," that does not receive the sanction of all the States in the Union. This we regard as a constitutional decree of perpetual bondage in the United States.

To any such amendment of the Constitution we are opposed, and at the present time to any amendment.

The Constitution, as our fathers made it, in our judgement, if maintained, sufficiently guarantees the rights of all parties living under it. Distinguished men who have lately spoken, and who are deeply involved in the revolutionary designs of the southern section of the confederacy, have declared that all they asked was that the existing Constitution should be lived up to and fairly interpreted. If the present Constitution is violated, what reason have we for believing that any new one will be better observed. The present Constitution gives no right to any party to interfere with slavery in the States, and no party desires so to interfere—certainly we desire no such interference, and protest against the possession of any such power.

The platform of the republican party adopted at Chicago declares "That the maintenance inviolate of the rights of the States, and especially the right of each State to order and control its own domestic institutions, according to its own judgement exclusively, is essential to that balance of power on which the perfection and endurance of our political fabric depends; and we denounce the lawless invasion by armed force of the soil of any State or Territory, no matter under what pretext, as among the gravest of crimes."

By the above declaration the people of the north will faithfully abide; and in our judgement, they will not assent to any greater guarantees of good faith than the present Constitution gives. What good is likely to result from the submission of the proposed amendment? Will it be adopted? In our judgement, it will not. It will be rejected, not because the people of the north desire or intend to interfere with slavery, but because they will regard it as a humiliating requirement, proposing, as it does, that they shall enter into bonds for their good behaviour when they have neither committed nor meditated wrong. The submission of such an amendment is a virtual acknowledgment by Congress that there is danger of such interference, and the voting of it down will be claimed by the south as such a declaration of intention to interfere as will greatly add to the present hostile feeling; and as we can see that no good is likely to arise from the submission of this amendment, but only evil, we feel constrained to oppose it.

The majority of the committee, as a further remedy for existing ills, propose to admit New Mexico and Arizona into the Union as a State "as soon as may be," with or without slavery, as her constitution may determine. To this proposition we also feel bound to interpose our protest. The people of New Mexico have not asked to be admitted into the Union, and there was no evidence before the committee that they had any such desire, or that they possess the population or ability to maintain a State government. On the contrary, it was satisfactorily shown before the committee that the entire population of the country sought to be brought in as a State did not exceed 75,000, scattered over a vast extent of territory. Of this number all but about seven hundred are natives of that country, who do not speak our language, and the great mass of whom are sunk in the lowest ignorance. Over one-half of the entire population are peons, or persons held as slaves for a limited period. The number of persons of pure Caucasian blood is very small, but the great majority are a mixture of Mexicans and Indians. They are a pastoral people, generally poor, unused to paying taxes, and unable and unwilling to do so. Small as is the population, it is believed to be quite as large as can be sustained there from the products of the soil of that country. As an inducement to create New Mexico and Arizona into a State, it will, no doubt, be claimed by some that the moment it is admitted the free people of the north will go there and control its destinies. How far they will be likely to do so we will presently inquire. We express the opinion that it will come into the Union as a slave State, and it cannot be supported as a measure of adjustment upon any other assumption. In saying that it will come in as a slave State, we do not mean to say that it is a country where it will ever be profitable to take slaves in any considerable numbers; but that it is a country where the sentiment is not adverse to holding slaves is proven by the fact that the Territory, which was free when it was acquired, has established slavery, and adopted a slave code of the most barbarous character. If a State is admitted, the laws now existing establishing slavery will remain in force; and the same power that established it in the Territory will maintain it in the State. But were we certain that it would come in without slavery, our objections to its admission would still remain. The lack of population, the inability to support a State government, and the mongrel character of its inhabitants, all interpose obstacles of the gravest character.

To give such a State the same weight and influence in controlling the legislation of the country as is possessed by the old States would be a serious objection under any circumstances; but it might be overcome was there a prospect that within a reasonable time they would have a population entitling them to any such control or influence. If it comes in as a free State, it will only further add to the excitement of the south, and they will maintain that it was the object and intention in bringing it in to still further destroy the balance between the two sections of the country, and that it discloses a determination on the part of the north to create States for the purpose of overwhelming them, regardless of their want of population or other fitting reasons to entitle them to admission.

To those who intend to vote for her admission on the ground that it will be a free State, and in the expectation that free white laboring men will seek that country as a place of settlement, and control its institutions, we beg to submit a few facts. It is now over twelve years since the most of that country was acquired, and yet to-day it is believed that it contains less population than at the time of its acquisition. Why is this? It is certainly not because that country has not been sufficiently puffed into notice, for it is well known that persons interested in imaginary gold and silver mines there have been indefatigable in their efforts to commend that country to the favorable notice of the public.

To gentlemen who see in this measure a new State opened out to the world, which is to invite the free men of Massachusetts, Ohio, and other States to take possession of it, we beg to commend some description of that country.

In 1846, Major {William Hemsley} Emory passed, with General {Stephen Watts} Kearney and his military force, across this portion of the continent {on their way to invade New Mexico at the beginning of the war with Mexico}. He says, speaking of the country where the San Pedro joins the Gila—

"In one spot only we found a few bunches of grass. More than four-fifths of the plain was destitute of vegetation. The soil, a light brown, loose, sandy earth, I supposed contained something deleterious to vegetation."

Passing along that region, he says of it:

"We travelled till long after dark, and dropped down into a dust hole. There was not a sprig of grass or a drop of water, and during the whole night the mules kept up a piteous cry for both."

He says further:

"From information collected from the Indians and others, it appears that we shall meet with no more grass from this spot to the settlement, estimated to be three hundred miles distant."

In speaking of the long route over which he had passed, he says:

"In no part of this vast tract can the rains from heaven be relied on (to any extent) for the cultivation of the soil. The earth is destitute of trees, and in a great part also of any vegetation whatever."

Lieutenant {Nathaniel} Michler, who was attached to the boundary survey, speaking of this country, says: "The climate of this region is in accordance with everything else relating to it."

"Having returned the following August to Fort Yuma, the thermometer, in the shade at the post, was found to be 116° Fahrenheit, and over 120° in the shade along the river."

One hundred and twenty degrees! Mr. {Lorin} Blodgett says, in his work on Climatology {*Climatology of the United States and of the Temperate Latitudes of the North American Continent* (1857)}, (page 191) that—

"At Fort Yuma the mean for the year is 73°5', and that for the warmest month 93°—measures only equalled in the lowest basins and valleys of Arabia."

Giving an account of his travels from Sonoyta to Fort Yuma and back, in the middle of August, 1855, Lieutenant Michler says:

"It was the most dreary and tiresome I have ever experienced. Imagination cannot picture a more dreary, sterile country, and we named it 'Mal Pais.'[2] The burnt, limelike appearance of the soil is ever before you; the very stones look like the scoriæ of a furnace. There is no grass, and but a sickly vegetation, more unpleasant to the sight than the barren earth itself; scarce an animal to be seen, not even the wolf or the hare, to attract the attention; and save the lizard and the horned frog, naught to give life and animation to this region.

"The eye may watch in vain for the flight of a bird; to add to all this, is the knowledge that there is not one drop of water to be depended upon from the Sonoyta to the Colorado or Gila. All traces of the road are sometimes erased by the high winds sweeping the unstable soil before them, but death has strewn a continuous line of bleached bones and withered carcasses of horses and cattle, as monuments to mark the way."

We could add numerous other testimonials in regard to this delightful region, which, in the estimation of some, is to become the future abode of freemen, but we think that we have given enough.

The majority have also reported an amendment to the fugitive slave law. The design of this amendment is understood to be to make the law more efficient and at the same time render it less offensive to the people of the north. That they have succeeded in the former there is no doubt, but that it will in its practical operation be of any benefit to the alleged fugitive or satisfy the north that is in any improvement on the old law is very questionable. It provides for the conducting of all the operations of slave catching at the expense of the United States, and affords no indemnity or just protection to persons who may be wrongfully seized, and transported for trial to a distant State. Under it a free man may be seized in the State of Maine and transported to Texas, and there held in custody until the next term of the circuit court, which may not be for months, and if he should finally be adjudged a free man, the only satisfaction he can obtain for his loss of time and restraint of his liberty is in being transported back again at the expense of the United States. The last section of the bill is designed to remove an offensive provision in the existing law, that authorized the marshal to summon to his aid any person or persons he saw proper; the amendment only authorizes it in case the marshal reasonably apprehends that he shall need their aid. Practically, there is very little difference between the existing law and the proposed amendment, and the whole of the amendment is so doubtful an

2. Literally, "badlands"; in this case probably lava fields.

improvement on the present law that we feel justified in withholding from it our support.

The majority of the committee also recommend an amendment of the law of 1793 in regard to fugitives from justice, making it the duty of the United States judges to surrender fugitives instead of the executive of the State to which the fugitive had fled. The people are justly jealous of the power of the United States courts, and, as we have before said, are particularly sensitive in regard to measures that propose to abridge the rights of the States, and enlarge the power of the general government. The disposition of the United States courts to enlarge their power has been so manifest heretofore, that we feel unwilling to assent to any proposal that will enable them to do so.

Having thus expressed our views on all the propositions of the committee that contemplate any action, we feel compelled to say that in our judgement they are, one and all, powerless for permanent good. The present dissatisfaction and discontent does not arise from the fact that the north has passed personal liberty bills or that the fugitive slave law is not faithfully executed; neither does it arise from an apprehension that the north proposes to interfere with slavery in the States where it exists.

The treasonable purposes of South Carolina are not of recent origin. In the recent convention of that State leading members made use of the following language in the debate on the passage of the ordinances of secession:

"Mr. {Francis S.} Parker—Mr. President, it appears to me, with great deference to the opinions that have been expressed, that the public mind is fully made up to the great occasion that now awaits us. *It is no spasmodic effort that has come suddenly upon us, but it has been gradually culminating for a long series of years, until at last it has come to that point when we may say the matter is entirely right.*

"Mr. {John A.} Ingliss—Mr. President, if there is any gentleman present who wishes to debate this matter, of course this body will hear him; but as to delay for the purpose of discussion, I for one am opposed to it. As my friend (Mr. Parker) has said, *most of us have had this matter under consideration for the last twenty years, and I presume we have by this time arrived at a decision upon the subject.*

"Mr. {Lawrence M.} Keitt—Sir, we are performing a great act, which involves not only the stirring present, but embraces the whole great future of ages to come. *I have been engaged in this movement ever since I entered political life.* I am content with what has been done to-day, and content with what will take place to-morrow. We have carried the body of this Union to its last resting place, and now we will drop the flag over its grave. After that is done I am ready to adjourn and leave the remaining ceremonies for to-morrow.

"*Mr. {R. Barnwell} Rhett—The secession of South Carolina is not an event of a day. It is not anything produced by Mr. Lincoln's election, or by non-execution of the fugitive slave law. It has been a matter which has been gathering head for thirty years.* The election of Lincoln and Hamlin was the last straw on the back of the camel. But it was not the only one. The back was nearly broken before. The point upon which I differ from my friend is this: He says he thought it expedient for us to put this great question before the world upon this simple matter of wrongs on the question of slavery, and that question turned upon the fugitive slave law. Now, in regard to the fugitive slave law, I myself doubt its constitutionality, and I doubted it on the floor of the Senate, when I was a member of that body. The States, acting in their sovereign capacity, should be responsible for the rendition of fugitive slaves. That was our best security."

Such sentiments, expressing the opinions of leading representative men in the South Carolina movement, ought to satisfy, it seems to us, any reasonable man that the proposed measures of the majority of the committee will be powerless for good.

South Carolina is our "sick man" that is laboring under the influence of the most distressing of maladies. A morbid disease which has been preying upon that State for a long series of years has at last assumed the character of acute mania, and has extended to other members of the confederacy, and to think of restoring the patient to health by the nostrums proposed is, in our judgement, perfectly idle.

But we hear it said that "something must be done or the Union will be dissolved." We do not care to go into a nice calculation of the benefits and disadvantages to the several States arising from the Union, with a view of striking a balance between them. Should we do so, we are convinced that that balance would largely favor the southern section of the confederacy. The north has never felt inclined to calculate the value of the Union. It may not be improper to inquire, in this connexion, whether the State of South Carolina and the other ultra secession States have been so oppressed by our government as to render their continuance in the Union intolerable to their citizens.

It is not pretended that they ever lose fugitive slaves, or that any escaping from these States have not been delivered up when demanded; nor is it pretended that the personal liberty laws of any State have practically affected any of their citizens; neither do they complain that they cannot now go with their slaves into any territory of the United States. The Supreme Court has decided that they have that right.

Is it then complained that their citizens, under the operation of the federal laws, are compelled to contribute an undue proportion of the means to maintain the government? If so, and the complaint is well founded, it is deserving of notice.

But it is not true in point of fact. We could easily demonstrate, by official figures, that the government of the United States annually expends for the exclusive use and benefit of South Carolina a much larger sum than that State contributes for the support of the government. This same will hold true in regard to most of the States that are now so anxious to dissolve their connexion with the Union. Florida, a State that contains less than one five hundredth part of the white population of the Union, and a State which has cost us, directly and indirectly, not less than $40,000,000, and upon which the general government annually expends sums of money for her benefit more than four times in excess of her contributions to the support of the government, has raised her arm against the power which has so liberally sustained her.

But we will not pursue this subject further. The union of these States is a necessity, and will be preserved long after the misguided men who seek its overthrow are dead and forgotten, or, if not forgotten, only remembered as the attempted destroyers of the fairest fabric erected for the preservation of human liberty that the world ever saw.

It is not to be preserved by compromises or sacrifices of principle. South Carolina, it is believed, is fast learning the value of the Union, and the experience she is now acquiring, will be of immeasurable value to her and her sister States when she shall return to her allegiance. If other States insist upon the purchase of that knowledge in the school of experience at the price paid by South Carolina, while we may deprecate their folly, we cannot doubt its lasting value to them.

Regarding the present discontent and hostility in the south as wholly without just cause, we submit the following resolution, which is the same as that recently offered in the United States Senate by Mr. {Daniel} Clark, of New Hampshire.

Resolved, That the provisions of the Constitution are ample for the preservation of the Union, and the protection of all the material interests of the country; that it needs to be obeyed rather than amended; and our extrication from present difficulties is to be looked for in efforts to preserve and protect the public property and enforce the laws, rather than in new guarantees for particular interests, or compromise or concessions to unreasonable demands.

C. C. WASHBURN. {*Wisconsin*}
MASON W. TAPPAN. {*New Hampshire*}

Source: U.S. Congress, House, Journal of the Committee of Thirty-Three, Report No. 31, Minority Report No. 1, 36th Cong., 2nd sess., January 29, 1861.

COMMITTEE OF THIRTY-THREE: MINORITY REPORT NO. 2

The second, and by far the longest, dissent from the majority report was compiled by representatives from five slave states: Miles Taylor (1805–1873) from Louisiana, John Smith Phelps (1814–1886) from Missouri, Albert Rust (1818–1870) from Arkansas, William Gustavus Whiteley (1819–1886) from Delaware, and Warren Winslow (1810–1862) from North Carolina. Their comprehensive objection to the work of the committee is as revealing of southern sentiments after Lincoln's election as the Washburn-Tappan report was of northern sentiments. This protest is illustrative of the grievances the South long held toward the North and exemplifies the slave states' defense of slaves as property and of the right of secession. It covers all of the major sources of discontent—return of fugitive slaves, exclusion of slaves from the territories, the right of sojourning into non-slave states, as well as the earlier tension created by the protective tariff issue.

DISTURBED CONDITION OF THE COUNTRY.

JANUARY 14, 1861.—Ordered to be printed, and made the special order for Monday the 21st instant, at 1 o'clock, and continued from day to day until disposed of.

Mr. TAYLOR, from the select committee of thirty-three, made the following

MINORITY REPORT.

The undersigned, a minority of the special committee of thirty-three, to whom was referred "so much of the President's annual message as relates to the present perilous condition of the country," having dissented from the action of the majority, now submit their views on the subject referred to the committee, together with the accompanying propositions for the consideration of the House.

The President, in his message, told us that "the different sections of the Union" were arrayed against each other, and that the time had "arrived, so much dreaded by the Father of his Country," when hostile geographical parties had "been formed," and that the "Union of the States," through which we had grown, under the protection of Heaven, to be a great people, "is threatened with destruction."

Since that message was referred to the committee, "the discontents," of which the President spoke as extensively prevailing, and which he states grew out of "the long-continued and intemperate interference of the northern people with the question of slavery in the southern States," have caused the people of four of the States of the confederacy to withdraw from it and to declare themselves to be free and independent States, clothed with all the rights of sovereignty as separate nations: and we know, too, from information of the most reliable character, that before three weeks have passed two other States will have taken the same step; and that there is imminent danger that before the session of this Congress is closed, by constitutional limitation, every State, in which African slavery is recognized and established as a domestic institution, will have followed their example. Whilst we have been sitting here the dismemberment of this mighty nation, to which the President only looked forward, has been actually begun; and it is as certain as that time rolls on, that whilst we are still sitting here, its destruction will have been completed, leaving a continent encumbered with its ruins, if something conceived in wisdom, and matured in the spirit of harmony and conciliation has not been done by Congress towards the removal of the causes which are impelling the entire people of fifteen States to the breaking of the bands of brotherhood and good-fellowship which had hitherto held us together under the authority of a federal Constitution.

Never since the world began was there a more momentous crisis in the affairs of any people. The question whether we shall hereafter be united under one government is not the only one now dependent on the action of the two houses of Congress and of the people of the different States. That action may determine whether the peaceful relations, which have hitherto subsisted between the various sections of this widely extended confederacy, are to be replaced by conflicts of force; and whether those who have heretofore striven with each other only in the opposing fields of gainful industry are

_____ "to meet in the intestine shock
And furious close of civil butchery"[3]

There are many, we are fully aware, who maintain that the Union of States formed by the adoption of the federal Constitution cannot be dissolved by the withdrawal of any of its members without the consent of the others, and who also assert that it is the duty of the government established by that Constitution, to maintain the Union, as it was formed, by force of arms, and to enforce its laws by the exercise of all the military means at its disposal, within the limits of the withdrawing States, in despite of the opposition of their people, acting, not as individuals, but as members of political sovereignties, and exercising their power through all the departments of regularly created and actually subsisting, separate, and independent governments. In our view, the doctrine of the indissolubility of the general government has no foundation in the public law of the world or in reason; and we are certain that no power was conferred upon the general government, by the Constitution, to retain States in the Union by the employment of the "armies" it was authorized "to raise and support" or of the "navy" it was "to provide and maintain." But if this were otherwise, it would be altogether inexpedient and impolitic to attempt to carry out such pretensions with a view to the preservation of the Union. A union of States for the common good, formed between them with the consent of all, cannot be perpetuated, with advantage to any, by the exercise of the physical strength of a portion of its members, in opposition to the will of the rest. If this be true with respect to any union of States founded on the right of self-government, no matter how small or feeble were the States refusing to continue in it, it would be clearly absurd and preposterous to countenance the making of any attempt of that kind in the present instance.

The American Union, when the unhappy differences to which the President has directed our attention reached their height, was composed of thirty-

---

3. William Shakespeare, *Henry IV, Part I*, act 1, scene 1. For more on Shakespeare during Secession Winter, see John Andrews and Dwight T. Pitcaithley, "Cry Havoc," *New York Times*, February 19, 2011, https://opinionator.blogs.nytimes.com/2011/02/19/cry-havoc/

three States, having a distinct and independent existence as separate sovereignties. That union of States was formed, among other things, to provide for their "common defence," promote their "general welfare," and to insure their "domestic tranquility." Fifteen of these States, with a population of 12,000,000, now believe that the majority of the people of the other States have become hostile to them and to their institutions, and that the union into which they entered with friendly States has become a union with enemies. It is useless to inquire whether the belief is well or ill-founded. It is now the belief of a majority of their people. They have become convinced, from the occurrences of the few past years, that by changes which have taken place in the condition, the feelings, and the temper of the people of the other States, the Union, of which they became members, has ceased to answer the ends it was designed to accomplish; and that, by a violent and most unjust perversion of the powers vested in the general government, the Union itself threatens to become an instrument, through the mere force of superior numbers, for the overthrow of their domestic institutions and the subversion of a large portion of their most important rights of property. Thus believing, the people of most, if not all, of those States, in a few short weeks or months, will have withdrawn from the existing Union, and the question then presents itself, what is to be done by the States remaining in the Union?

It is idle to talk of the maintenance of a government of consent by the exercise of force. A whole people cannot be guilty of treason. You cannot coerce fifteen sovereign States. What, then, is to be done, it may be asked? But one answer to this question, in our view, is possible. Justice, sound policy, and the public interest all alike demand that the causes which impel so many States to go out of the Union should be inquired into and that when these causes have been ascertained, an honest effort should be made by all to determine if they cannot be removed by the application of proper and adequate remedies, with the assent of the people of all the other States. If this cannot be done, it is well for us to know it at once, for it will then become the duty of the whole American people to look to it and see that a separation, which has become inevitable, shall be bloodless. If we are to descend from our high position among the nations of the earth by breaking to pieces, we owe it to our fathers to vindicate the principle which they asserted, that "man was capable of self-government," by making that separation peaceful, and by arranging its terms, after full and mature deliberation between delegates representing the different States, in such a manner as will be likely to advance the separate interests of all, when the separation is once complete.

With the intent of contributing, in some degree, to the attainment of one or the other of these objects, the undersigned will now proceed to speak of the causes which, in their opinion, have led to the present disorder of our national affairs and to present for consideration the remedies, which they believe would be effectual for their entire and permanent removal, if they are applied at once.

When the colonies took up arms in the struggle for independence with Great Britain, African slavery was a subsisting institution in all of them, and the right of property in persons held to service or labor, under the authority of that institution, was recognized and established by their laws, and was protected, like any other right of property, through the action of their courts, and by the direct agency of the public officers in all the departments of their respective governments. Offences against that species of property were regarded and punished as crimes. A slave, in all of the colonies, was then, like any other property, the subject of larceny or theft, and those who deprived their masters of their possessions or hindered them illegally in their enjoyment of their labor, were held to be responsible for their pecuniary value in actions at law. When the Constitution of the United States was framed, and at the time it was adopted by the action of the several States, African slavery was a subsisting institution in all of the States entering into the federal Union but one. In that State it had ceased to exist, it is true, as an established institution, prior to the formation of the federal Union; but it is also true that the right of property in slaves was still recognized in that State at the time and after the adoption of the national Constitution, both in their legislative proceedings and in the action of their courts.

Thus it will at once be seen that at the time of the adoption of the Constitution of the United States there was no question in the minds of the American people as to the existence of the right of property in persons held to service or labor under the laws of the different States. That was a fact universally acknowledged. In the estimation of the whole American people, at that time, to use the language of a distinguished chief justice of the supreme court of Massachusetts, in a case decided in that State in 1808, "The slave was the property of his master, subject to his orders and to reasonable correction for misbehavior; was transferable, like a chattel by gift or sale; and was assets in the hands of his executor or administrator."[4] Under the

---

4. From Massachusetts Chief Justice Theophilus Parsons's decision in *Winchendon v. Hatfield*, a case that determined the township responsible for the welfare of Edom London, a former slave and pauper. (Thanks to Paul Finkelman for unearthing the citation.)

circumstances then existing there could have been no distinct mention of such a right of property in the Constitution, because it was not called for by anything within the contemplated scope of its provisions, and would certainly have been considered as superfluous if it had been proposed. The relation of master and slave could not have properly come into view with the framers of that instrument, whilst engaged in their work, in the then state of the public mind with respect to it, had it not been for the necessity of agreeing upon a basis for the apportionment of representation and direct taxes between the several States, and for making some provision against the loss of property in slaves by their escaping from one State into another. In both of these instances the words made use of are such only as were requisite to effect the object aimed at; but in each instance they import, undeniably, a clear recognition of African slavery as an established institution in the several States, and of the possession, by their citizens, of a valuable right of property in the slaves themselves.

The union of the States, under a federal government, was formed, among other things, for our protection against foreign countries and to insure domestic tranquility among the States at home. The military resources of all were placed under the control of a federal head, not only to provide for the common defence in time of war but also to secure redress for injuries done to our citizens, as individuals, in their intercourse with other nations. And the provisions contained in the two paragraphs of section two, in article four, for the delivery of fugitives from justice, or from service or labor, were designed to prevent the contests likely to grow up between neighboring States, when one was made an asylum for offenders against the laws of the other or became a receptacle for the lost property of her people.

The obligation of the national government, in its relations with foreign powers, to protect the rights of our citizens to their property in slaves was regarded as perfect, under the Constitution, at the time of its adoption, as it was with respect to any other species of property. That obligation was recognized by the general government under the old articles of confederation, when it stipulated, in the treaty of peace with Great Britain in 1783, that the British armies should be withdrawn, "without causing any destruction, or carrying away any negroes or other property of the American inhabitants." And it was again recognized by the general government, after the adoption of the Constitution, in the first article of the treaty of peace made with Great Britain in 1814, which provided for the evacuation of all territories taken by either party from the other, without carrying away any public property or "any slaves or other private property."

This action of the general government was a necessary consequence of the fact that the right of property in slaves under the laws of the different States was universally acknowledged by the American people in all the earlier days of the republic. It is true that in the course of the first thirty years after the adoption of the federal Constitution, a number of the States in which African slavery then existed had altogether abolished it, and that provision had been made in others for its gradual extinction. This action on the part of a portion of the States, however, neither did or could change, in any degree, the character of the federal government, or of the rights and obligations of the States, and of the citizens of the States, with respect to each other, which had been established, or were imposed by the Constitution. For this reason, though seven of the thirteen States which had originally adopted the Constitution had abolished slavery for themselves, or provided for its extinction, in the first thirty years of our national existence, the rendition of fugitive slaves and of fugitives from justice, even when charged with offences committed against the right of property in slaves, still went on under the authority of the provisions embodied in the Constitution. No one in those days ever dreamed that States by acting for themselves, in their own limits, upon subjects within their own peculiar jurisdiction, could in any way affect the relations before existing between them and the other States, as established and determined at the time of the formation of the Union.

It is a fact well known to every citizen at all acquainted with the history of the country that for the first half century of our national existence no opposition was ever made in any State to the rendition of fugitives from labor, or to the delivery of fugitives from justice who had committed offences against the right of property in slaves, when claimed by the State or by the citizens of the State from which they had escaped, under the provisions of the Constitution of the United States. No one then denied the right of property in slaves as recognized in different States of the Union, and all were perfectly satisfied that the constitutional provisions in relation to those two classes of fugitives should be carried out in the spirit in which they were made. This state of things, however, was to be broken up by the arts of designing and ambitious men in the pursuit of political power.

The extraordinary tide of emigration which the disturbed state of Europe threw upon our shores, soon after we became a nation, had given to the northern States, in which slavery had been abolished, a considerable preponderance in numbers over those of the south at a very early day, and the idea soon presented itself that a certain and apparently a very easy way to obtain the full control of the affairs of the federal government would be to array the citizens of the non-slaveholding States together in opposition to those in which the institution of slavery existed. The first opportunity which seemed available for such an attempt was found when Missouri, a slaveholding Territory, presented herself in 1819 for admission into the Union as a new State.

Up to that time the formation of the parties in the United States had, in a great degree, depended upon the clashing between the agricultural and the commercial and manufacturing interests of our people. The commercial and manufacturing interests of the country were nearly all concentrated in the northern and eastern States, whilst a portion of the people of those States, and the almost entire population of the south, were engaged in the pursuits of agriculture. In countries situated as the United States then were, and as they will long continue to be, the agricultural masses necessarily constitute a great majority of the people. This fact always gave a decided predominance to the political party reflecting the wishes and feelings of those of our citizens who were interested in the support of an agricultural policy and, unhappily for the best interests of the nation, laid the foundation for a feeling of hostility in the minds of the northern leaders of the party in the minority against the south, because the strength of the party which had always defeated them was found in that section of the confederacy. To break down the majority opposed to them, and thus obtain for themselves the supreme control of the national councils, these leaders saw that it was necessary to introduce some new question into politics, which would have the certain effect of dividing the members of the dominant party in such a way as would prevent them again {from} acting together in the same organization. The southern States, to whose votes they had hitherto owed their defeat in national contests, maintained the institution of African slavery. The northern States had abolished it. It was thus clear that there was a wide difference of opinion between the two sections of country on the subject of slavery, and they therefore determined, in entire disregard of the rights of their southern brethren, and in violation of the great principle of self-government which our whole republican system reposes, to make that the great question for the overthrow of their political opponents, and therefore raised the cry, when the application of Missouri was brought forward, of "no more slave States."

The greatest of our then living statesmen {Thomas Jefferson}, who was passing the evening of his days in repose, at a distance from the turmoils of public life, declared that that cry broke upon his ear "like a fire bell in the night," and "filled him with terror." "I considered it at once," he said, "the knell of the Union." And if the position then taken by those men upon that question had been maintained, is there any one who does not know that the Union would then have been broken up? But the times were not yet ripe for a dissolution of the Union. The evils which had afflicted our people before its formation were still fresh in their memories, and the benefits conferred by it were estimated by our citizens in all sections of the country at their true value. The circumstances, too, under which the Union had been entered into were familiar to the minds of all. Every one knew that slavery existed in all of the States but one when it was formed, and that its exclusion from a new State as a condition precedent to its admission deprived that State of a right, enjoyed by all the others, of deciding for itself whether it would or would not maintain that institution. This was apparent to all; and as the spirit of fanaticism had not yet been abroad to fire the minds of men and make them unwilling that others should retain and exercise their own rights in their own way, the movement to force the slavery question into national politics failed at that time, and the contest between the agricultural and commercial and manufacturing interests went on as before from 1820–1832.

In this contest the commercial and manufacturing classes at last obtained a complete victory and fastened upon the country, among other measures connected with their schemes of policy, the high, protective tariff of 1828. Assault after assault was made upon this tariff in Congress, by those opposed to it, from all sections of the Union. But these assaults, though made with consummate ability, session after session, by the most distinguished statesmen of the day, were entirely fruitless and unsuccessful, until the State of South Carolina arrayed herself against it, in her capacity of a sovereign State, and passed her ordinance, in 1832, declaring it to have been made in violation of the Constitution, and therefore null and void. It is not necessary to speak of the occurrences of that day further than to say that the attitude then taken by South Carolina had the effect of preparing the way for the overthrow of the high tariff policy advocated by the commercial and manufacturing classes of the country; and that it seems to the undersigned, from a careful consideration of the history of the times, that the overthrow of that policy was the immediate cause of the renewal of the attempt to force the slavery question into the politics of the country, and that it mainly contributed to making that attempt successful.

The position of South Carolina at that time would not have been productive of so decisive a result if it had not been that she had the sympathy of the agricultural portion of the whole nation. All of them, north as well as south, were as much opposed to the protective features of the tariff of 1828 as South Carolina; but, as the people of the agricultural south, in which

African slavery existed as a permanent domestic institution, constituted, in point of fact, the bulk of the party opposed to that tariff, its overthrow was imputed directly to them; and from that time a settled hostility to the south, as a section, and to her citizens, as a people, seems to have taken full possession of the minds of those men in the northern and eastern States who had had a direct pecuniary interest in the maintenance of the protective policy.

The passion for gain is one of the most unscrupulous, as well as untiring, which operates upon mankind. Whatever stands in the way of its gratification it never hesitates to remove, when it is in its power, without regard to the means it may be called on to employ. The separation of the northern members of the party opposed to a high protective tariff from the southern members of that party was a political necessity to these men. The experience of upwards of forty years had shown them that the tendency in all governments to the formation of sectional parties, growing out of differences in geographical position, was altogether unequal to the formation of sectional parties in the United States, in consequence of the universal and almost equal diffusion of the agricultural element among the different States. The only thing left to them to bring this about was the introduction of a marked moral principle into national politics which should be coincident with a geographical line. They knew that, as the great statesman to whom we before alluded had said, in the letter from which we then quoted, such a line "once conceived and held up to the angry passions of men" would "never be obliterated" and that "every new irritation" would "sink it deeper and deeper."

Such an element of division, in the then existing condition of the country, was to be found in the slavery question alone. It was true that an unsuccessful attempt had been made, but a few years before, to bring this very question into national politics. But this was not sufficient to deter them. That attempt was made by mere politicians, filled only with an appetite for office. This was to be made by men moved by the passion of gain, and who, like Shylock {a Jewish money lender}, would be avenged on those who had "hindered" them of "half a million" and had railed

"On them, their bargains, and their well-won thrift."[5]

And the times, too, were now favorable to such an undertaking. That Power which has always desired to arrest us in our progress in the path of

---

5. William Shakespeare, *The Merchant of Venice*, act 1, scene 3.

greatness, by sowing the seeds of dissension among our people, had then abolished slavery in their own West India colonies, in order to enable them to strike a fatal blow at our national existence, and at that very time had their emissaries among us engaged in the work of stirring up our northern brethren to begin a war on slavery in the south.

Previous to the overthrow of the protective policy, through the agency of southern votes in Congress, anti-slavery societies, it is true, had been gotten up in New England and in some of the middle States, by numbers of our citizens acting in concert with these foreign agitators; but they had excited no public attention, and the sentiment of hostility to the south, which they sought to inculcate, had taken no root in the northern mind until the tariff act of 1828 had been superseded by the "compromise tariff act" of March 2, 1833. That event, however, brought new allies into the field to strengthen and carry on the movement begun by our transatlantic enemies. Great numbers of the commercial and manufacturing classes in the north and east came forward to give it aid and comfort. The "New York City Anti-Slavery Society" was established in October of the same year, under the auspices of some of her most prominent citizens, "to take," to use the language of the second article of its constitution, "all lawful, moral, and religious means to effect a total and immediate abolition of slavery in the United States." Societies, with the same avowed object, were formed very soon after this in all quarters of the north and east; and thus, in an incredibly short space of time, under the stimulus of "material aid" furnished by those who had been "hindered of their profits" under the protective system, a great organization was formed in the northern States, with the declared purpose of interfering with their fellow-citizens in the southern States, and overturning one of the institutions which they had seen fit to maintain!

It is unnecessary to enter into any further details on this subject. It is sufficient for our purpose to state that through the influence of these societies petitions to Congress were everywhere gotten up in the north, asking for the prohibition of the slave trade among the southern slaveholding States and in the District of Columbia and, at last, for the entire and absolute abolition of slavery in the District of Columbia, and in the slaveholding States themselves. The presentation of these petitions to Congress, by thousands, day after day, during successive sessions of that body, led to the most excited, violent, and inflammatory discussions in relation to slavery, until that subject was forced upon the attention of the public mind of the north, and a separate and distinct political organization was created there which aimed directly at the overthrow of southern institutions, in opposition to the will of the southern people, through the perversion of the powers of the federal government, delegated to it for certain specified national purposes.

This new party {the Republican Party}, though weak in numbers, was strong in wealth and determination. It entered into the field of political contention by the nomination of candidates, from time to time, until it became known that in many neighborhoods, and even States, it had strength enough to determine the victory in favor of one or the other of the two great parties into which the nation was then divided, although they were unable to secure it for themselves. From that moment the abolitionists became "a balance of power party" in nearly every non-slaveholding State; and under the management of bold, unscrupulous, and skilful leaders, they began the work of demoralizing the two other parties in those States by lending their support to the politicians in either, who, without espousing their cause, were willing to go farthest in aiding them in the propagation of their own peculiar sentiments.

From this time their progress was rapid. The countenance given to them by subservient politicians, belonging to the other two great parties, enabled them to penetrate into the seats of learning, to take possession of the pulpit, and to gain control of the public press. In the schools, in the churches, and in the newspapers of the day at the north, African slavery was asserted to be a crime; the right of southern men to property in persons held to labor under it by the law of their respective States was denied; and direct action for the overthrow of that peculiar and most important institution of the south, and for the deprivation of their citizens of their rights under it, was inculcated as a moral and religious duty. The existence of a higher law than the Constitution was then, for the first time, proclaimed, and under its pretended authority, the provision of the Constitution designed to secure the return of fugitive slaves, when they escaped from one State to another, was made inoperative in many of the northern States from the opposition of mobs of lawless persons excited to violence by the exhortations and example of misguided fanatics.

But the evil did not stop here. High public functionaries began to pander to the newly created sentiment of hostility to the peculiar rights of the citizens of the southern States. The chief magistrates of northern States lent themselves, and prostituted their offices, to the promotion of the seditious and mischievous designs of these men, who aimed directly at the disturbance of the public peace of the nation. To bring them to their support and to the support of their party friends in popular elections, they refused to deliver up the fugitives from the justice of southern States, whenever the crimes they were charged with grew out of offences against the right of property in slaves, upon the pretence that the violations of that right of property were no longer regarded by them as crimes, because slavery had ceased to exist in their respective States. This pretence was first set up by one who was placed in the executive chair of the "Empire" State, by the votes of one of the former great political parties of the country—and who has since become the mouth-piece and exponent of that new party whose rise to power has already dismembered the government, and whose continued existence now threatens it with complete destruction—at the very time when laws still existed upon the statute book of that State recognizing the right of property in slaves, and giving to southern men, visiting the State temporarily, the right to bring their slaves with them and to hold them "In slavery," if the time of their sojourn there did not exceed nine months.[6]

This open violation both of the letter and spirit of a provision of the Constitution of the United States by the governor of a State for the advancement of party interests was soon followed by action of the legislature of his State in the same direction. The law giving to southern men the right to sojourn in the State with their slaves for a limited time was repealed, and laws were passed, under the guise of personal liberty bills, which were intended to hinder or prevent the recovery of fugitive slaves, coming into the State, by their masters. The examples of the governor and of the legislature of the State of New York were soon followed by the governors and legislatures of other States, and we then saw, for the first time, a large number of States, in one section of the Union, openly arrayed, through the action of all the departments of their respective governments, against the rights of the States and of the citizens of the States of another section of the Union, which had been secured to them by separate, distinct, and unmistakable provisions embodied in the very instrument which had created that Union.

This action of governors and of the legislatures of States had the effect of stimulating the anti-slavery societies and the propagandists of the anti-slavery sentiment in the north to still greater activity. Incendiary publications, calculated and designed to sow discontent among the servile population; to excite them against their masters; and to stir them up to insurrection and bloodshed, were busily disseminated in the south, whilst in the north the character of African slavery, as it exists in the southern States, was studiously misrepresented and perseveringly painted in the most repulsive

---

6. William Seward was elected to the governorship of New York in 1838 and again in 1840.

colors, and the people were continually urged by professors in schools and colleges, by ministers of religion in churches, and by travelling lecturers in every neighborhood, to engage in the work of its extirpation. This agitation was kept up for years; and whilst it was still at its height, the acquisition of territory from Mexico in 1848 gave an opportunity to those engaged in it to connect the slavery question with the political questions which grew out of the necessity imposed on Congress of providing for the temporary government of the newly acquired territory.

When the attempt was made to bring the slavery question into national politics by imposing an anti-slavery restriction upon Missouri as a condition precedent to her admission into the Union as a State, the contest which grew up in relation to it was terminated in 1820 by substituting a prohibition of slavery in the remainder of the Territories of the United States acquired from France, lying west of the Mississippi river and north of the parallel of 36° 30' north latitude, by way of compromise, in place of one upon the new State, and admitting her upon a footing of equality with the other States. The agitation excited by the attempt to impose that restriction upon Missouri was so full of menace to the continued union of the States, that all men grasped at anything which was likely to bring it to a peaceful close; and for that reason the substitution of a restriction of that character upon a territory not yet peopled, in place of one upon the population of a State then in existence, was accepted at once and without any general consideration as to whether it was proper in itself or if it was within the constitutional power of Congress to impose it on the citizens of the United States who might establish themselves in a Territory. The power of Congress to impose any such restriction, even upon a Territory, was then doubted by many of our most eminent statesmen, and subsequently, after much discussion on the subject, public men in the south settled down into the belief, with scarcely an exception, that no such power could be rightfully exerted by the national legislature. But as the anti-slavery restriction thus imposed by Congress only extended to a part of the unpeopled territories of the United States, and the remainder was left open to the peculiar institution of the southern States, the south continued to acquiesce in it as a settlement of the territorial question by a division of the common territories of the United States between the two sections and without reference to constitutional principle.

This mode of settlement of the territorial question was broken up, however, by the north, through the force of numbers, when we were called on to take action with reference to the disposition of the territories acquired by us in 1848 from Mexico. One of the great parties in the north then asserted the existence in Congress of an absolute right to legislate for the territories upon all subjects whatsoever, and manifested a fixed determination, under the influence of the anti-slavery element which had been infused into it through the practices of its leaders, to exert itself to unite the north, upon the slavery issue alone, for the purpose of excluding the institutions of one-half of the States of the confederacy altogether from the common territories of the United States, which had just been acquired by their united efforts, and at the expense of the blood and treasure of both sections of the country. The south protested against such an exercise of power as without warrant in the Constitution, and denounced the proposed anti-slavery restriction upon all of the newly acquired territory as an attempt, by a usurpation of power on the part of Congress, through the action of a sectional majority of its members, to deprive the southern States of their rights in the newly acquired territories and to destroy the equality of those States, and of the citizens of those States, with the other States and their citizens, in the Union under the federal Constitution.

The federal Constitution contains no provision for the government of Territories, and it is more than probable that the framers of that instrument did not look forward to any future territorial acquisitions. But the absence of such a provision does not leave Congress free to govern or dispose of such Territories, when acquired, at the mere will and pleasure of a numerical majority of the two houses. After the transfer of a country has been made from one power to another, the new sovereign, by the usage of nations, has a perfect right to remodel its institutions as it may see fit. But whilst this is true, as a general proposition, under the public law of the world, the exercise of the right of the new sovereign is necessarily controlled by the constitutional principles of the government through which the right of sovereignty is exercised. The general government of the United States is one of delegated, not inherent powers; and if any one thing of a political nature is more certain than another, in the eye of reason, it is that Congress can no more legislate to exclude slavery from a Territory than it can from a State. The want of legislative power in Congress over the whole subject, in the Territories as well as the States, is absolute, because it is one of local or municipal concern, and no legislative power whatever, of that character, has been given to Congress by the Constitution.

Although slavery does not exist in all of the States, it is recognized as a rightful institution under our governmental system, wherever citizens of the United States, forming distinct political communities, may see fit to maintain it. Slaves, as persons, enter as an element into the apportionment of the representation of the States in Congress and in the apportionment of direct taxes among the States; and, as property, those holding them are protected in their rights to them by a provision for their being delivered up to their owners when they escape into another State, and by a prohibition on such State from discharging them from service or labor, by any law or regulation of its own. Our situation as a people is, in one respect, peculiar. We have no law of property common to the whole United States. Each State makes that law for itself, within its own limits, and as the States are equals under the Constitution, the rights of property, resulting from these laws of the several States, must be of equal validity and effect wherever the sovereignty of the United States alone exists and gives protection. To exclude the slaves which citizens of the southern States might wish to take with them into the newly acquired Territories of the United States, or to destroy their citizens' right of property in their slaves after they had carried them there, by the action of the general government, through an act of Congress, would not only be a usurpation of power, but would be such a violation of the principle of the equality of the States under the Constitution as must inevitably lead to the immediate breaking up of the confederacy.

The movements set on foot in the south in consequence of this flagrant attempt to reduce the slaveholding States and their citizens to a position of inferiority in the Union made that fact apparent to the people of the north, and their representatives paused in their work. With a view to conciliation, the southern people then expressed their willingness to waive a decision upon their constitutional rights in the Territories in question and to settle the contest which had sprung up in relation to them upon the principle of "a division" of the Territories between the two sections, which was involved in the establishment of the Missouri compromise line; and propositions for the prolongation of that line to the Pacific ocean were again and again brought before Congress in the hope that it might at last be adopted, but this hope was not realized. The anti-slavery sentiment operated to such an extent upon the northern mind that every attempt at settlement in that manner was defeated by those who yielded to its influence, and the sectional agitation went on, augmenting, until the conservative elements of the nation became alarmed for the continuance of the Union and demanded that it should be terminated by a new compromise—and it was so terminated in 1850.

The new compromise repudiated all interference by Congress with the subject of slavery in the Territories, and contemplated the delegation of all the legislative power, which could be rightfully exercised in subordination to the Constitution of the United States, to the people of the Territories themselves, through the legislatures to be created for them, and provided for the submission of all questions growing up in the Territories, with respect to property in slaves, to the tribunals of the United States for their final adjudication. This settlement of the territorial question was believed to be right in principle by a great majority of the people of the United States, and it was hoped that it was final. This belief, however, was soon discovered to be unfounded. When another occasion arose for the establishment of temporary governments in other Territories, it so happened that the territory over which they were to operate constituted a part of the territory acquired from France, lying north of the parallel of 36° 30' of north latitude, which had been subjected to the prohibition of slavery contained in the eighth section of the Missouri act. From 1848 to 1850 the anti-slavery element of the north had constantly refused to consent to any adjustment of the territorial question upon the principle of division, upon which that prohibition was based. In 1850 the contest then going on was settled by the introduction of the new principle into our territorial policy of which we just spoke. That new principle was very naturally introduced into the new territorial bills, and what was the result? Why the recital of the fact that the clause in the eighth section of the Missouri act was "inconsistent with the principle of non-intervention by Congress with slavery in the States and Territories, as recognized by the legislation of 1850," and was therefore "inoperative and void," (which was contained in the act,) was laid hold of by the politicians who wished to avail themselves of the sectional strength of the north in pursuit of place, and the anti-slavery agitation was again revived, under their lead, with greater violence than ever.

It is not necessary at this time to speak of the progress and varying fortunes of that agitation. All are aware that Kansas, one of the Territories thus newly organized, became at once a scene of contention, from the intrusion into its limits of bands of armed men, sent there and supported by emigrant aid societies and other combinations of individuals formed at a distance, not for the purposes of peaceful and permanent settlement in the Territory as residents, but with a view to determine the character of the institutions which should be finally established there; and that all the enginery of evil was put in motion to invent and give circulation to tales of blood and horror as to what was passing in that distracted Territory, in order to inflame the public mind of the north against the citizens of the slaveholding States, who were always represented as the authors of all these reported atrocities, and at last secure a complete union of the northern States in the war against African slavery as it exists in the south.

This new state of things led at once to a reconstruction of parties in our political world. One of the former great national parties of the day {Whig Party} disappeared altogether from the north, and for the first time in our history a purely sectional party {Republican Party} arose upon its ruins, which asserted a determination to take possession of the government, and to control its policy upon all subjects, and in all the States, and in all parts of our vast territory, through the agency of a physical majority composed of the inhabitants of the non-slaveholding States alone, who were united together by the single sentiment of hostility to slavery. If the result aimed at was fully achieved, it was obvious to all that our system of republican government would be at an end. The republican forms of the Constitution might, indeed, be preserved, but it was certain that the spirit of republicanism, which it was designed should operate through it, would have been lost forever. Such a party could never, by any possibility, exist in one of the slaveholding States in their present condition. To become national, it was a necessity to such a party that slavery should be abandoned by the other States. And if the people of those States were unwilling to abandon the institution, what then? Why they would be deprived of their character of citizens, and be reduced to the condition of subjects. They would no longer have any voice in the management of the national affairs in which they had a common interest with their northern brethren; and it would be an abuse of terms to call them any longer "citizens of the United States." From citizens of the United States they would have sunk to bear the same relation to the people of the north that the oppressed and down-trodden ryots of unhappy India do to imperial Britain.

When such a party was organized it needed no prophet to foretell that it could never administer the affairs of the then existing United States of America. It was plain to all that the complete success of its leaders, in securing such a sectional majority as they looked forward to, would at once break up the national government. Warning after warning was given to those citizens of the north who valued the union of the States, that such would be the inevitable result of carrying into effect the schemes of these men for the sectionalization of one of the great parties of the country. But these warnings were not heeded. The new party, from year to year, obtained majorities in State after State, in the northern portion of the confederacy, until in November last the electoral votes of the northern States alone were concentrated on the candidates of that party, and elected them to the offices of President and Vice-President of the United States, under the Constitution. To the apprehension of a large portion of the people of the southern States, the work of sectionalism was thus completed; and the popular movements which have since taken place in all of them indicate, beyond the shadow of a doubt, that the days of the republic are numbered unless that apprehension is speedily removed.

We are aware that much has been said in relation to the right of a State to secede from the Union, and as to the existence of a right on the part of the general government to employ the military power conferred upon it by the Constitution to coerce a seceding State into submission as a member of the confederacy created by it; but we shall engage in no discussion upon those questions, because, in our view, the questions—interesting as they are in themselves—have no importance whatever at this crisis. The people of the United States are now to deal with facts, not theories; with stern realities, not fine-spun abstractions. Whether any State has or has not the right to secede under the Constitution, it is a fact that four States have already seceded; and that in a few short months—perhaps weeks—all of the other slaveholding States will have in like manner seceded, with the purpose of maintaining their new position, by force of arms, if no adjustment is made of the differences between them and the non-slaveholding States. Whether the general government has or has not the right to employ the military power conferred upon it by the Constitution, to coerce a seceding State into remaining in the Union, it can employ it to carry on war against seceding States as foreign States, when they have ceased to be members of the Union. Two great practical questions, then, are now pressing upon Congress and the country for solution. Shall the revolution which is now in progress, and which is about to end in the final separation of the slave-holding States from the other members of the confederacy, be arrested by an amicable and fair adjustment of the differences between them? And if this cannot be brought about, then shall this separation, which has become inevitable, be made peacefully? or shall it be followed by war between the two sections of a once united confederacy? These questions must be met now; and it is worse than useless to attempt to evade them by indulging in groundless hopes, or proposing to pass resolutions which lead to no action, or to adopt measures which can produce no results.

The common interest of the whole American people and the separate interests of all the States require that the differences which now unhappily divide us should be terminated by an amicable and fair adjustment. The committee of thirty-three was created in the hope that it might do something which would prepare the way in that direction, and by the order of a majority of its members it has directed its chairman to submit a number of propositions to the House for that very purpose. The undersigned, however, dissented from the majority directing that report, because they could not bring themselves to believe that any good could come out of the propositions reported if every one of them were now adopted by a unanimous vote of both houses of Congress. The only one of the propositions made which, in their view, is of any present importance is that for an amendment of the Constitution in such a manner that it cannot be in the future so amended as to give Congress any power to interfere with the subject of slavery in the States without the consent of every State. Such an amendment of the Constitution would certainly afford a complete guarantee against invasions upon the rights of property in slaves in the States, hereafter, by Congress. If other measures were agreed upon which were calculated to remove the existing grounds of discontent in the southern mind, this proposed measure would be of the very highest value, as it would interpose an impassable barrier against any subsequent difficulties from such an attempt. But standing alone as it does, we cannot regard it as likely to contribute in any material degree to the settlement of the existing troubles.

With respect to the other propositions reported, the undersigned are constrained to say that, in their view, none of them will be likely to promote the object had in view by the committee, whilst some of them would certainly be prejudicial to the public interest if they should be carried into effect. This is particularly true with respect to the enabling act for the admission of the Territory of New Mexico as a State. The admission of New Mexico into the Union as a State, though she has established slavery within her limits by the action of her territorial legislature, would in no way tend to the settlement of the principle involved in the territorial question, which has become, of late years, such a fruitful source of agitation in both sections of the Union. An evasion of that settlement by erecting Territories into States decides nothing as to the rights of the southern people in the Territories of the United States. But the admission of New Mexico as a State, whilst it can avail nothing as a measure of peace with reference to the territorial question, would be a bad precedent for the future. The population of the Territory is far too small to entitle it to a representative in Congress; and it would be clearly unjust to the other States, and wrong in principle, to admit her into the Union, and thus give her two senators in Congress, in addition to a representative, to which her people would not have a shadow of a claim if they formed a distinct community within the limits of another State.

The amendments proposed to the fugitive slave laws are not acceptable to us, and can have no effect towards remedying the grievance of the south in relation to the failure on the part of the northern States to return their fugitive slaves. That grievance is the result of the non-execution of laws already in force; and it seems certain that it cannot be removed unless a mean is supplied which will insure the execution of those laws. That, in the opinion of the undersigned, can only be supplied by a new constitutional provision which will make it to the interest of the States and of their people to have the fugitives delivered.

With respect to the other propositions ordered to be reported by the chairman, they are all, so far as the undersigned remember, contained in resolutions giving expression to abstract truths or to opinions as to what are the duties of our people under particular circumstances. However excellent and valuable they may be as enunciations of proper views and correct principles of human action, they look forward to no congressional or constitutional action; and as they, in consequence, require no further notice from us at this time, we will now proceed to give our own views as to what, in our opinion, ought to be done at this extraordinary conjuncture.

From the rapid sketch we have already given of the condition of things among our people when the Constitution was adopted, and of the changes which have taken place since that time in their situation and sentiments and in the character and composition of parties, it is clear that the Constitution has been perverted from its original purpose and that through misconstructions of some of its provisions and the introduction of new principles for the guidance of party action which are in direct antagonism with the practice and usages and the common understanding of the inhabitants of all of the original States when it went into effect, it has now ceased to answer some of the most important ends for which it was established.

It was intended to provide for the common defence, and for the protection of the rights of all of our citizens, of whatever nature, and wherever situated. The employment of the national power for the protection of the slave property of our citizens upon the ocean, and when illegally interfered with by foreign states, is now so violently opposed by a large body of our people in one section of the Union that this has become impossible.

It was intended to prevent neighboring States from becoming an asylum for the offenders against the laws of the other States. By the action of the chief magistrates of a portion of the States the most of the non-slaveholding States have been converted into cities of refuge for offenders against an important portion of the laws of property in the slaveholding States, upon the pretence that those States now recognize no right of property in slaves by their laws.

It was intended to provide a secure way for the return of persons held to service or labor by the laws of the States in which African slavery was maintained when they escaped into another State. But the provision to that effect is continually nullified in the States in which slavery is now prohibited by law, because many of their people see fit to denounce slavery as a crime and to assert, through lawless assemblages, that there can be no right of property in man.

It was intended that the people of the different States should be equal in the support of the burdens of the national government and that they should share equally in all of the benefits to be derived from it. But it is now declared by a majority of the States that this is to be no longer the case; for while the slaveholding States are still to be required to contribute their money to the federal treasury, and to yield up their sons to recruit the federal armies, they are to be hereafter excluded from the federal Territories unless they will consent to emigrate without taking with them their domestic servants held to labor.

And, finally, it was intended that the people of each State should have had a voice in the ordering of their common affairs in obedience to the principles of the republicanism of our revolutionary fathers. But we find at last that this is to be denied to one entire portion of the confederacy, by the formation of a sectional party, under the auspices of Garrisonian republicanism, which is to concentrate the whole national power in the hands of those residing in the northern States alone.[7]

Under these circumstances, it must be clear to every right-minded man that the American people can no longer go on as they are. The Constitution must be changed, by amendment, so as to make its existing provisions restrain the action of parties within the boundaries which were set to them when it was framed, by the common understanding of those who were to live under it, and by the universal sentiment of the times, or the union between the slaveholding and the non-slaveholding States will be broken up.

The differences which exist between the slaveholding and the non-slaveholding States, if they are to be settled at all, can only be settled, in the opinion of the undersigned, by the adoption of amendments to the Constitution. Nothing else can accomplish it. The interests of both sections of the country imperiously demand that the slavery agitation should be removed now and

---

7. William Lloyd Garrison was the leading abolitionist in the North, editor of *The Liberator*, and an advocate of the immediate end of slavery. His political influence in the Republican Party was greatly exaggerated by secessionists.

forever from the halls of Congress. From the nature of the subject, and the relative positions of the parties to it, that agitation necessarily begets feelings and passions in politics which are akin to those engendered by fanaticism in the disputes of religion. When the spirit of fanaticism has taken full possession of a people, it is known to all that the bands of morality are loosened, and that every species of vice, misconduct, and disorder are tolerated by devotees, in their spiritual teachers, if they only continue to give a violent and unyielding support to their favorite dogmas of faith. And the same thing has taken place in politics under the influence of the party fanaticism—if we may be allowed so to call it—which has grown out of the contest on the subject of slavery. Under its influence the public mind will scarcely tolerate any illusion to the qualifications of candidates for office or inquiries into the conduct of public officials. Men may be shown to be unfit to fill the places for which they are candidates, and yet they are elected by the people if they are believed to be true on the slavery question. Public officers may be known to have been guilty of abusing their trusts, and yet they are maintained, year after year, in their places, because they have been decided and unyielding on the slavery question. It is to the political fanaticism engendered by the slavery question, and to this cause alone, that the growing demoralization in the public mind is to be attributed, which has, within the few past years, been signalized by the notorious robbery of so many State treasuries in the north; by the published accounts of the corruptions displayed in the action of the legislature of the Empire State during the last winter; and by the unchecked rumors as to the existence of monstrous abuses in some branches even of the different departments of the national government. Every consideration of public policy, then, seems to require that the slavery agitation should be gotten rid of in the interest of good government in the several States, as well as for the preservation of our greatness as a nation. And we are thus led to the inquiry, can nothing be done, by which this can be brought about, which will be right in itself, and which will be fair and just towards all sections of the country?

The answer to this is plain. The object aimed at can be accomplished by the adoption of the series of amendments to the Constitution rejected by the committee and now reported to the House, and which are in substance the same brought to the notice of the Senate recently by Mr. Crittenden, of Kentucky, and which are familiarly known as the "Crittenden resolutions."[8]

---

8. Senator John J. Crittenden of Kentucky introduced a constitutional amendment on December 18, 1860, that would have protected slavery in different ways throughout the nation.

Though these proposed amendments do not embrace all that some of the undersigned would desire to see embodied in the Constitution, they yet afford such a basis for an adjustment as they would all cheerfully accept, with a strong conviction that, if the proposed amendments were adopted by the northern States, harmony and peace would be restored to our people, and our Union would soon again be reconstructed without the loss of a member, and upon such a foundation that it could never again be shaken.

And why should not these amendments be acceptable to the people of the northern States? They would, in point of fact, operate no real change in the Constitution; they would only bring it back to what it was on the day of its adoption. These amendments involve, it is true, a distinct recognition of the right of property in southern men in persons held to labor under the laws of their respective States; but that right of property was admitted by the whole American people when the Constitution was framed, and was specially recognized in it, when there was any necessity for it, at the time. They will put an end, too, to the possibility of getting up any sectional agitation on the subject of slavery in relation to its continuance in places under the exclusive jurisdiction of the United States, and with respect to the inter-State slave trade; but this was just as impossible when the Constitution was formed, because slavery then existed in the north as well as the south, and because it was also repugnant to the public sentiment of the day. And they recognize, for all time to come, the equal right of the southern people in the Territories of the United States, by dividing those Territories between the two sections; but that right has always been recognized under the Constitution ever since its formation.

Why, then, we would ask, cannot the people of the northern States consent to the adoption of these constitutional amendments? They will, in point of fact, operate no real change in that instrument. Their adoption, now, would only have the effect of making it, in the estimation of men of our day and generation, what it was in the minds of its framers and of those great fathers of the republic who put it in operation and administered our affairs under it in the early days of our national existence. It would, in truth, be a restoration of the Constitution as it stood, amid the circumstances which surrounded it, when it went into operation, and not a change. Cannot these amendments, then, be adopted? If there is not virtue enough in our brethren of the north to do this and make the Constitution what it was—if they have not patriotism enough to enable them to put aside the prejudices which have been created in their minds by the arts of the unscrupulous and designing, so as to put an end to the civil discords which have destroyed the harmony of the States, then, indeed, have we reached the term of our existence as a nation; and it is full time that we should be broken into pieces, in order that the disjointed fragments of a once great and noble structure may sink into obscurity and insignificance—the certain doom pronounced, as ever shown by history, upon all divided nationalities.

The undersigned therefore respectfully recommend the adoption by the House of the "Crittenden resolutions," now reported, in order that the amendments to the Constitution proposed in them may be immediately submitted to conventions of the different States for their decision upon them.

If, however, these resolutions do not receive the assent of the constitutional majority of the House required to give them effect, then the undersigned would respectfully recommend the adoption of the resolution proposed by Mr. {John Chilton} Burch, of California, looking to the convocation of a convention of all the States, in accordance with article five of the Constitution. If, unhappily, no adjustment of the differences between the States can be effected, it is the duty of the American people to provide the way for a dignified, peaceful, and fair separation, upon equitable terms and conditions. In the event of a final separation there must be a partition of the common property. There must be a settlement of the terms on which the divided States are to have social and commercial intercourse with each other. There must be a definite and precise arrangement with respect to the navigation of the Mississippi river through its whole extent from its headwaters to the Gulf of Mexico. All of these various matters will be best provided for in a convention of the States. They must be settled at once if we mean to remain at peace among ourselves after a separation. If provision be not made looking forward to all this, we shall be soon engaged in a fratricidal war; and he who shall refuse to do what he can, to prevent such a war, will not be guiltless of the blood that will then be shed.

MILES TAYLOR, *Louisiana.*
JOHN S. PHELPS, *Missouri.*
A. RUST, *Arkansas.*
WILLIAM G. WHITELEY, *Delaware.*
WARREN WINSLOW, {*North Carolina.*}

Source: U.S. Congress, House, Journal of the Committee of Thirty-Three, Report No. 31, Minority Report No. 2, 36th Cong., 2nd sess., January 29, 1861.

Proposals to Amend the U.S. Constitution

Between the opening of the second session of the 36th Congress on December 3, 1860, and the firing on Fort Sumter on April 12, 1861, those elected to find a solution to the nation's problems suggested sixty-seven amendments to the Constitution. The proposals came from governors, members of Congress, state legislatures, and delegates to state secession conventions and the Washington Peace Conference.

Designed as compromise measures—efforts to placate both Democrats and Republicans—the proposed amendments offer penetrating insights into the nature of the secession crisis. The overwhelming majority of the amendments (sixty-three out of sixty-seven) focused on slavery in the territories, the return of fugitive slaves, preserving slavery in the District of Columbia and in federal installations in the slave states, and guaranteeing the transit of slaves through non-slave states and territories. Eleven proposed nationalizing slavery while five suggested a framework for considering the orderly withdrawal of a state from the union. Arkansan Hugh French Thomason proposed a major reorganization of the executive branch, and Ohio representative Clement Vallandigham proposed reorienting the entire governmental electoral system. Of the more than three hundred articles (or subparts) represented in the sixty-seven amendments, only two suggested regulations on the collection of tariffs.

In their quest to build protections for the institution of slavery into the Constitution, some of those who favored compromise also attempted to prohibit free blacks from voting. Twelve of the proposed constitutional amendments contained clauses that limited voters to those "of the Caucasian race, and of pure, unmixed blood." (See Stephen Douglas's amendment below.) While the greater number of these came from below the Mason-Dixon Line, twenty-three were proposed by Northerners, but only eight by Republicans. It is interesting to note that Virginia's secession convention continued to craft compromise amendments until it received word that Fort Sumter was under bombardment.

In many ways, these proposals illuminate the essence of the secession movement, for they embody formal solutions to the crisis facing the nation and clearly reveal the depth to which the institution of slavery was the fundamental issue being debated over Secession Winter. Three amendments (those by James Buchanan, John J. Crittenden, and the House of Representatives Committee of Thirty-Three) are presented elsewhere in this volume.

Kentucky Senator Lazarus Whitehead Powell (Democrat)

December 6, 1860

Resolved, That so much of the President's message as relates to the present agitated and distracted condition of the country, and the grievances between the slaveholding and the non-slaveholding States, be referred to a special committee of thirteen members; and that said committee be instructed to inquire whether any additional legislation within the sphere of Federal authority be necessary for the protection and security of property in the States and Territories of the United States; and if so, that they report by bill. And that said committee be also instructed to consider and report upon the expediency or proposing such an amendment or amendments to the Constitution of the United States as may be necessary to give certain, prompt, and full protection to the rights of property of the citizens of every State and Territory of the United States, and ensure the equality of the States, and the equal rights of all the citizens aforesaid, under the Federal Constitution.

Source: *Congressional Globe,* 36th Cong., 2nd sess., 19.

Kentucky Governor Beriah Magoffin (Democrat)

December 9, 1860

To his Excellency, the Governor of the State of _____ [1]

Entertaining the opinion that some movement should be instituted at the earliest possible moment, to arrest the progress of events which seem to be rapidly hurrying the Government of the Union to dismemberment, as an initiatory step, I have, with great diffidence, concluded to submit to the Governors of the slave States a series of propositions, and ask their counsel and co-operation in bringing about a settlement upon them as a basis. Should the propositions be approved, they can be submitted to the assembling Legislatures and Conventions of the slave States, and a Convention of all of said States, or of those only approving, be called to pass upon them, and ask a general Convention of all the States of the Union that may be disposed to meet us on this basis for a full conference. The present good to be accomplished would be to arrest the secession movement until the question as to whether the Union can be preserved upon fair and honorable terms, can be fully tested. If there be a basis for the adjustment of our difficulties within the Union, nothing should be left undone in order to its development. To this end, it seems to me there should be a conference of the States in some form, and it appears to me the form above suggested would be the most effective. I, therefore, as the Governor of a State having as deep a stake in the perpetuity of the Union, and at the same time as much solicitude for the maintenance of the institution of slavery as any other, would respectfully beg leave to submit for your consideration the following outline of propositions:

1st. Repeal, by an amendment of the Constitution of the United States, all laws in the free States in any degree nullifying or obstructing the execution of the fugitive slave law.

2d. Amendments to said law to enforce its thorough execution in all the free States, providing compensation to the owner of the slave from the State which fails to deliver him up under the requirements of the law, or throws obstructions in the way of his recovery.

---

1. The letter was a draft that was going to be sent to the governors of each of the other slave-owning states. The names of the individual governors were to be added later.

3d. The passage of a law by Congress, compelling the Governors of the free States to return fugitives from justice, indicted by a grand jury in another State, for stealing or enticing away a slave.

4th. To amend the Constitution so as to divide all the Territories now belonging to the United States, or hereafter to be acquired, between the free and the slave States, say upon the line of the 37th degree of north latitude—all north of that line to come into the Union with requisite population as free States, and all south of the same to come in as slave States.

5th. To amend the Constitution so as to guarantee forever to all the States the free navigation of the Mississippi river.

6th. To alter the Constitution so as to give the South the power, say in the United States Senate, to protect itself from unconstitutional and oppressive legislation upon the subject of slavery.

Source: *Journal of the Called Session of the House of Representatives of the Commonwealth of Kentucky, Begun and Held in the Town of Frankfort, on Thursday, the Seventeenth Day of January, in the Year of Our Lord 1861, and of the Commonwealth the Sixty-Ninth* (Frankfort: Printed at the Kentucky Yeoman Office, John B. Major, State Printer, 1861), 19.

New York Representative John Cochrane (Democrat)

December 12, 1860

Whereas a conflict of opinion dangerous to the peace and permanence of the Union has arisen concerning the true intent and meaning of the Constitution of the United States, in relation to the subject of African slavery: Therefore,

Resolved by the Senate and House of Representatives, &c., (two thirds of both Houses concurring,) That the following articles be proposed as amendments to the Constitution of the United States; which, when ratified by conventions in three fourths of the several States, shall be valid as parts of said Constitution, viz:

ART.—. In all territory of the United States lying north of 36° 30' north latitude, and not included within the limits of any of the existing States, slavery and involuntary servitude, except in punishment of crime, shall be, and are hereby, prohibited: *Provided,* That the said territory, or any portion of the same, when admitted as a State, shall be received into the Union with or without slavery, as its constitution may prescribe at the time of its admission.

ART.—. In all territory of the United States lying south of 36° 30' north latitude, not included within the limits of any existing State, neither Congress nor any territorial government shall pass any law prohibiting or impairing the establishment of slavery: *Provided always,* That the said Territory, or any part of the same, when admitted as a State, shall be received into the Union with or without slavery, as its constitution may prescribe at the time of its admission.

ART.—. Congress shall pass no law prohibiting or interfering with the trade in slaves between the several slaveholding States and Territories.

ART.—. The migration or importation of slaves into the United States or any of the Territories thereof, from any foreign country, is hereby prohibited.

ART.—. No person held to service or labor in any State or in any Territory of the United States, under the laws thereof, escaping into any other State or Territory of the United States, shall, in consequence of any law or regulation therein, be discharged from such service or labor, but shall be delivered up on claim of the party to whom such service or labor may be due.

ART.—. The right of transit through and temporary sojourn in the several States and Territories of the United States, is hereby guaranteed to all the citizens of the several States and Territories; and their right to the possession and control of their slaves during such transit and sojourn shall not be infringed.

ART.—. No law enacted by Congress for the rendition of fugitive slaves shall be in any degree impaired or infringed by anything contained in the laws or constitution of any State or Territory; but all such State and territorial laws and all such provisions in any State or other constitution shall be wholly null and void.

Source: *Congressional Globe,* 36th Cong., 2nd sess., 77.

VIRGINIA REPRESENTATIVE SHELTON FARRAR LEAKE
(INDEPENDENT DEMOCRAT)

December 12, 1860

Resolved, That the Constitution of the United States ought to be amended, so as to provide:

1. That Congress shall have no power or jurisdiction over the subject of domestic slavery, either in the States, the Territories of the United States, or the District of Columbia, or over the trade in slaves in or between them, except so far as hereinafter provided.

2. That where domestic slavery may exist in any Territory or district of the United States, it shall be the duty of Congress to protect it by adequate and efficient legislation.

3. That no Territorial Legislation, or other territorial authority, shall have power or jurisdiction over such subject.

4. That the rights of masters or owners to their slaves, while sojourning in, or *in transitu* through, any State or Territory of the United States, shall be guaranteed and protected; and,

5. That fugitive slaves shall be given up on demand of their owners or masters, and that all such fugitives as may be lost by reason of the legislation of any State, or the act of its constituted authorities, shall be paid for by such State.

[Note: Leake's amendment was the first of twenty-seven that would have protected slavery in the states from congressional interference.]

Source: *Congressional Globe,* 36th Cong., 2nd sess., 77.

VIRGINIA REPRESENTATIVE ALBERT GALLATIN JENKINS
(DEMOCRAT)

December 12, 1860

Resolved, That the committee of one from each State, recently appointed by this House, be instructed to inquire into the expediency of so amending the fugitive slave law as best to promote the rendition of fugitives under the operation of the same, the more adequate punishment of its infraction, and the affording *proper* compensation to the owners of those who are not returned; also, to inquire into the propriety of providing, either by constitutional amendment or legislative enactment, for the better security of the rights of slaveholders in the common Territories of the United States; also, to inquire what further constitutional checks are demanded by a sense of self-preservation on the part of the slaveholding States against the operation of the Federal Government, when about to be administered by those who have avowedly come into power on the ground of hostility to their institutions, and to consider whether this fact does not of itself so isolate and antagonize the slaveholding interest as to make it necessary to its own security that its concurrent voice, separately and distinctly given, should be required to sanction each and every operation of the Federal Government; and to consider whether a dual Executive, or the division of the Senate into two bodies, or the making a majority of Senators from both the slaveholding and non-slaveholding States necessary to all action on the part of that body, or the creation of another advisory body or council, or what other amendments to the Federal Constitution would best promote that result, and to report thereon.

Source: *Congressional Globe,* 36th Cong., 2nd sess., 77.

Kentucky Representative Robert Mallory (Opposition/Unionist)

December 12, 1860

Resolved, That the special committee of thirty-three be instructed to report amendments to the Constitution of the United States, so that in all the Territories of the United States north of the line 36° 30' north latitude, slavery or involuntary servitude, except for crime, be prohibited; that in all territory south of that line, the institution of African slavery, as it exists at this time in the slave States of this Union, may exist, and shall be protected by the Government of the United States. That when any Territory shall have attained a population sufficient to entitle it to at least one Representative in Congress, and not until then, it shall be authorized to form a State government, and, provided its form of government be republican, be admitted into the Union on a perfect equality with the several States, with or without slavery, as its constitution may provide; that Congress shall be prohibited from abolishing or interfering with the inter-State slave trade; from abolishing slavery in the District of Columbia, in the arsenals and dock-yards of the United States, and wherever it may have the power of exclusive legislation.

Source: *Congressional Globe,* 36th Cong., 2nd sess., 78.

INDIANA REPRESENTATIVE WILLIAM HAYDEN ENGLISH (DEMOCRAT)

December 12, 1860

By Mr. ENGLISH:

Resolved, That for the purpose of doing justice, and securing peace and prosperity, the committee of thirty-three be instructed to inquire into the expediency of providing for the settlement of the present unfortunate and dangerous sectional controversy upon the following basis: 1. The Territories of the United States to be equitably divided between the slaveholding and non-slaveholding sections, slavery to be prohibited in that portion set apart for the non-slaveholding, and to be recognized in that portion set apart for the slaveholding section, the status of each upon the subject of slavery to remain unchanged during the territorial condition; but when the population in any portion of the territory set apart to either section shall equal or exceed the ratio required for a Representative in Congress, and the people shall have formed and ratified a constitution, and asked admission into the Union as a State, such State shall be admitted with or without slavery, as such constitution may prescribe. 2. The rights of property in slaves in the slaveholding States, and in the portion of the territories set apart for the slaveholding section, shall not be destroyed or impaired by legislation in Congress, in the Territories, or in the non-slaveholding States; and whenever a fugitive slave shall be rescued from his master, or from the proper United States officers, by reason of mob violence or State legislation in conflict with the Constitution or laws of the United States, or whenever a slave shall, in like manner, be rescued from his master while *in transitu* through any non-slaveholding State, the city, county, or township in which such rescue is made shall be liable to the master in double the value of the slave, recoverable in the United States courts.

Source: *Congressional Globe,* 36th Cong., 2nd sess., 78.

Illinois Representative John Alexander McClernand (Democrat)

December 12, 1860

Resolved, That the committee of thirty-three be instructed to inquire and report whether Congress has constitutional power to make the people of any particular State, or municipal corporation therein, liable to indemnify any owner of any slave escaping into such State and who has been rescued from rightful custody by force or otherwise; and also, whether it is expedient to establish a *special* Federal police for the purpose of executing the laws of the United States, and promptly suppressing any unlawful resistance thereof; and also, whether any further legislation is requisite to secure a prompt, certain, and full enforcement of the guarantees of the Constitution, or whether an amendment of the Constitution is necessary for that purpose.

Source: *Congressional Globe,* 36th Cong., 2nd sess., 78.

Missouri Representative John William Noell (Democrat)

December 12, 1860

By Mr. NOELL:

Whereas there now exists, on the part of the people of the southern States of this Union, a well-founded apprehension that they no longer hold the power in the Federal Government necessary to secure their peace and the safety of their property against the aggressions of the Federal Government, should it become the will of the people of the northern States to assail them through the Federal Administration or by hostile legislation; and whereas security and peace, held by one section at the mere will of another, cannot be safely relied on; and whereas the great material interests of the country, in every section, are involved in the safety of the Union and the perpetuity of the Constitution on such terms as will give to every section the means of protection against the aggressions of other sections: Therefore,

Be it resolved, That the select committee of thirty-three be instructed to take into consideration the propriety and necessity of abolishing, by amendments to the Constitution, the office of the President of the United States, and of establishing, in lieu thereof, an executive council, to consist of three members to be elected by districts composed of contiguous States as near as practicable; each member of said council to be armed with a veto power, such as is now vested in the President of the United States; and if such plan be deemed practicable by said committee, that they report to this House such details thereof as may be necessary to accommodate the same to the existing Constitution of the United States.

Be it further resolved, That said committee be also requested to take into consideration the means necessary (if any can be devised) to restore the equilibrium between the free and the slave States in the Senate of the United States; and particularly whether this end can be accomplished by a voluntary division on the part of some of the slave States into two or more States.

Source: *Congressional Globe,* 36th Cong., 2nd sess., 78.

ARKANSAS REPRESENTATIVE THOMAS CARMICHAEL HINDMAN (DEMOCRAT)

December 12, 1860

By Mr. HINDMAN:

Resolved, That amendments of the Constitution of the United States ought to be made as follows, to wit: 1. An express recognition of the right of property in slaves in the States where it now exists or may hereafter exist, and an express denial to the Federal Government of all right or power to prohibit or restrict the trade in slaves between the States. 2. An express requirement that the Federal Government shall protect the right of property in slaves in the District of Columbia, in all the Territories of the United

States while the territorial condition exists, wherever else the Federal jurisdiction extends. 3. A provision that every Territory authorized by act of Congress to hold a convention, and whose convention shall adopt a constitution republican in form, shall be admitted into the Union as a State, with or without slavery, as its constitution may prescribe. 4. A provision that citizens of any State or Territory, who may be the owners of slaves, shall be permitted to hold their slave property while passing through or temporarily residing within the jurisdiction of States whose constitutions do not recognize the institution of slavery. 5. A provision that any State whose Legislature has enacted, or may hereafter enact, laws defeating or impairing the right of the master to have his escaped slave delivered up to him, according to the provisions of the fugitive slave law of 1850, shall not be entitled to representation in either House of Congress until the repeal of such nullifying statutes. 6. Such further provisions as will secure to the slaveholding States, through their representation in Congress, an absolute negative upon all action of Congress relating to the subject of slavery. 7. A provision for the appointment, by State authority, of all Federal officers exercising their functions within the limits of the States. 8. A provision that all of the above amendments, together with the existing provisions for slave representation upon the three-fifths basis, shall forever be irrepealable and unamendable.

Source: *Congressional Globe,* 36th Cong., 2nd sess., 78–79.

Tennessee Representative Thomas Amos Rogers Nelson (Opposition Party)

December 12, 1860

Joint Resolution to Amend the Constitution of the United States

Be it resolved by the Senate and the House of Representatives of the United States of America in Congress assembled, two-thirds of both houses concurring, That the following articles be proposed to the legislatures of the several States as amendments to the Constitution of the United States; all or any of which articles, when ratified by three-fourths of said legislatures, shall be valid to all intents and purposes as part of the said Constitution, viz:

Article XIII. In all that territory ceded by France to the United States, under the name of Louisiana, and in all the territory ceded by Mexico to the United States, which lies north of thirty-six degrees and thirty minutes north latitude, which is not included within the limits of any State, slavery and involuntary servitude, otherwise than in the punishment of crimes, whereof the parties shall have been duly convicted, shall be, and is hereby, forever prohibited.

In all territories, or parts of territories, south of said line of thirty-six degrees and thirty minutes, slavery may exist, and shall be protected by such rules and regulations as Congress may prescribe. When such Territories form constitutions with a view to their admission into the Union as States, or when new States may be formed, as now provided for, out of any State or States, any part of which is situate south of a line thirty-six degrees and thirty minutes of north latitude, extending from the Atlantic to the Pacific ocean, such Territory or new State, applying for admission into the Union, may continue or abolish slavery, and shall be admitted on the same footing as other States.

No law shall be passed by Congress interfering with or prohibiting the slave trade in the slaveholding States, or in the Territories, or new States, now existing, or which may be created south of said line.

Congress shall not abolish slavery in the District of Columbia.

The importation of persons from Africa, or any foreign State or country, to be held as slaves or in involuntary servitude, shall not be allowed.

Article XIV. Congress shall provide by law for the arrest of fugitive slaves and servants escaping from one State or Territory into another and for their return to their owners or masters.

If such fugitives cannot be arrested, Congress may enact laws providing for indemnity from the persons, counties, or towns, by whom or in which the escape may have been aided.

All laws or customs interfering with these provisions shall be null and void.

Congress may enact such statutes as may be deemed proper to enforce these amendments.

Article XV. The electors shall meet in their respective States and vote by ballot for President and Vice-President; one of whom shall be an inhabitant north of said line of thirty-six degrees and thirty minutes of north latitude, extending from the Atlantic to the Pacific ocean; the other, an inhabitant south of said line; and both of whom shall not be inhabitants of the same State.

Source: *Congressional Globe*, 36th Cong., 2nd sess., House of Representatives Report No. 31, 3–4.
(Journal of the Committee of Thirty-Three)

LOUISIANA REPRESENTATIVE MILES TAYLOR (DEMOCRAT)

December 12, 1860

Mr. Taylor offered the following resolutions, viz:

Amendments to the Constitution of the United States which ought to be proposed by a vote of two-thirds of both houses of Congress:

First.—With respect to the action of the general government in its foreign relations.

The rights of property, whether in persons held to labor or to things, as recognized by the laws of the different States, or of the Territories of the United States, shall be vindicated and enforced in favor of our citizens by the power of the general government when cases arise involving them in our relations with foreign States.

Second.—With respect to the rights of the citizens of the different States in the Territories of the United States.

The common Territories of the United States shall be open to the citizens of the several States, who shall be free to enter them, taking with them their families and property, and shall be protected in the enjoyment of their rights of property, whether in persons held to labor or to things, as vested in them by the laws of the States from which they may have gone, respectively, and to the maintenance of the relations existing between them and those held to labor under the laws of those States so long as the Territories remain the common possessions of the United States, and are governed temporarily as Territories.

When a Territory passes from the territorial condition and is admitted into the Union as a State, the persons held to labor therein may be removed by those holding them therefrom, and no law shall be passed by such State impairing such right of removal.

Third.—In relation to the admission of new States.

No Territory shall be erected into a State and admitted into the Union unless it shall have a permanent population equal or exceeding in number that fixed upon in the last apportionment of representation among the States as giving a right to a representative.

Upon the admission of a State into the Union no question shall be made with regard to the subject of African slavery, but the State admitted with or without slavery, as the people thereof may have determined; and they shall be afterwards left at all times free to settle that question for themselves as they may deem fit, without any interference with them by the general government or the people of other States.

Fourth.—As to the delivery of fugitive slaves.

The value of fugitives from labor, as assessed by a jury of the neighborhood from which they escaped, with twenty-five per centum in addition, shall be paid to their owners by the State in which they take refuge, unless delivered up in ___ days after the fact of their escape is established and made known to the executive of the State in which they take refuge.

Fifth.—The right of suffrage under the Constitution and in the Territories.

No person shall vote in any election in any State, under the Constitution of the United States, or in any Territory of the United States, unless he is of the Caucasian race and of pure, unmixed blood.

Sixth.—The power of Congress in relation to slavery.

The Congress of the United States is interdicted from legislating on the subject of slavery in the District of Columbia, or in any other district, Territory, or place in which it may exercise authority or jurisdiction.

[Note: Taylor's amendment was the first of twelve that would have prevented those "of the African race" from voting or holding elective office.]

Source: *Congressional Globe,* 36th Cong., 2nd sess., House of Representatives Report No. 31, 4–5.

(Journal of the Committee of Thirty-Three)

Tennessee Senator Andrew Johnson (Democrat)

December 13, 1860

Mr. JOHNSON, of Tennessee. I introduce the following resolution, with a view of referring it at the proper time:

Resolved, That the select committee of thirteen be instructed to inquire into the expediency of establishing, by constitutional provision: 1. A line running through the territory of the United States, not included within the States, making an equitable and just division of said territory, south of which line slavery shall be recognized and protected as property, by ample and full constitutional guarantees, and north of which line it shall be prohibited. 2. The repeal of all acts of Congress in regard to the restoration of fugitives from labor, and an explicit declaration in the Constitution, that it is the duty of each State for itself to return fugitive slaves when demanded by the proper authority, or pay double their cash value out of the treasury of the State. 3. An amendment of the Constitution, declaring that slavery shall exist in navy-yards, arsenals, &c., or not, as it may be admitted or prohibited by the States in which such navy-yards, arsenals, &c., may be situated. 4. Congress shall never interfere with slavery in the District of Columbia, so long as it shall exist in the State of Maryland, nor even then, without the consent of the inhabitants and compensation to the owners. 5. Congress shall not touch the representation of three-fifths of the slaves, nor the inter-State trade, coastwise or inland. 6. These provisions to be unamendable, like that which relates to the equality of the States in the Senate.

Source: *Congressional Globe,* 36th Cong., 2nd sess., 83.

Pennsylvania Representative Thomas Birch Florence (Democrat)

December 17, 1860

Resolved, That the following amendments be proposed to the Constitution of the United States: The right of property in slaves is recognized; and no law shall be passed, and nothing shall be done, to impair, obstruct, or prevent the full and free enjoyment and use of such right in any Territory or other property of the United States. No new State shall be admitted into the Union without the consent of two thirds of all the members of both branches of Congress, and the vote shall be taken by yeas and nays, which shall be entered on the Journal; and every bill for such purpose shall be subject to the approval or rejection of the President of the United States, as in other cases, except that, when returned with his objections, it shall require the votes of three-fourths of all the members of Congress to pass it notwithstanding.

Source: *Congressional Globe*, 36th Cong., 2nd sess., 106.

NEW YORK REPRESENTATIVE JOHN COCHRANE (DEMOCRAT)

December 17, 1860

Whereas a conflict of opinion, dangerous to the peace and permanence of the Union, has arisen concerning the true intent and meaning of the Constitution of the United States in relation to African slavery within the Territories of the United States; and whereas the opinion of the majority of the court pronounced in the Supreme Court of the United States, in the Dred Scott case, determines that the citizens of the United States have an equal right to take with them into the Territories of the United States any article of property which the Constitution of the United States recognizes as property, and that said Constitution recognizes slaves as property; and further, that the right neither of persons nor of property can be destroyed or impaired by either congressional or territorial legislation; and whereas such determination, while it has been accepted by some as a judicial exposition of the Constitution aforesaid by the supreme judicial tribunal, has by others been rejected as destitute of the force of a judicial precedent; yet, in view of the probability that such opinion will hereafter become the reason of decisions of a similar character by the same tribunal, and in the hope of averting the immeasurable calamities which national dissolution threatens:

Therefore,

Resolved, That the opinion of the majority of the Supreme Court of the United States, delivered by Chief Justice Taney, in the Dred Scott case, should be received as the settlement of the questions, under the Constitution of the United States, therein discussed and decided.

Resolved further, (two thirds of both Houses concurring,) That the following articles be proposed as an amendment to the Constitution of the United States, which, when ratified by conventions in three fourths of the several States, shall be valid as part of such Constitution, namely: Congress may establish governments for the Territories of the United States; but any Territory having a population equal to the constituency of one member of Congress and having adopted, by a vote of the citizens of the United States resident therein, a constitution republican in form may be admitted by Congress into this Union as a State; and neither Congress nor the people of a Territory, during the territorial condition, shall, by legislation or otherwise, annul or impair the rights of property recognized by the laws of any of the States.

Source: *Congressional Globe,* 36th Cong., 2nd sess., 107.

New York Representative Daniel Edgar Sickles (Democrat)

December 17, 1860

Mr. SICKLES offered the following preamble and resolutions; which were read, considered, and referred to the select committee of thirty-three:

Whereas it is represented that one or more of the States have declared, through their executive and legislative authorities, the desire of such States to reconsider and annul their ratification of the Constitution establishing the Government of the United States; and whereas conflicting opinions prevail as to the right of any State to secede from the Union; and whereas it is expedient to prescribe the mode in which a State may resume its sovereignty with the consent of the other States, thereby removing all occasion for the employment of forcible means, of constraint, or resistance, and, at the same time, providing additional guarantees against injustice by ordaining an effectual, prompt, and peaceful remedy for grievances:

Be it therefore resolved, That the Congress propose to the several States the following amendment to the Constitution:

ART. 8. Whenever a convention of delegates, chosen in any State by the people thereof, under the recommendation of its Legislature, shall rescind and annul its ratification of this Constitution, the President shall nominate, and by and with the advice and consent of the Senate shall appoint, commissioners, not exceeding three, to confer with the duly appointed agents of such State, and agree upon the disposition of the public property and territory belonging to the United States lying within such State, and upon the proportion of the public debt to be assumed and paid by such State; and if the President shall approve the settlement agreed upon by the commissioners, he shall thereupon transmit the same to the Senate, and upon the ratification thereof by two thirds of the Senators present, he shall forthwith issue his proclamation declaring the assent of the United States to the withdrawal of such State from the Union.

[Note: Sickles's amendment was the first of five that proposed a constitutional process for secession.]

Source: *Congressional Globe*, 36th Cong., 2nd sess., 107.

Georgia Senator Robert Toombs (Democrat)

December 22, 1860

Mr. Toombs submitted the following propositions:

Resolved, That declaratory clauses to the Constitution of the United States, amply securing the following propositions, be recommended for adoption:

1. That the people of the United States shall have an equal right to emigrate to and settle in the present or any future acquired territories, with whatever property they may possess, (including slaves,) and be securely protected in its peaceful enjoyment, until such Territory may be admitted as a State in the Union, with or without slavery, as she may determine, on an equality with all existing States.

2. That property in slaves shall be entitled to the same protection from the government of the United States in all of its departments, everywhere, which the Constitution confers the power upon it to extend to any other property; provided nothing herein contained shall be construed to limit or restrain the right now belonging to every State to prohibit, abolish, or establish and protect slavery within its limits.

3. That persons committing crimes against slave property in one State and fleeing to another shall be delivered up in the same manner as persons committing other crimes, and that the laws of the State from which such persons flee shall be the test of criminality.

4. That Congress shall pass efficient laws for the punishment of all persons in any of the States who shall in any manner aid and abet invasion or insurrection in any other State, or commit any other act against the laws of nations, tending to disturb the tranquility of the people or government of any other State.

5. That fugitive slaves shall be surrendered under the provisions of the fugitive slave act of 1850, without being entitled to either a writ of habeas corpus or trial by jury, or other similar obstructions of legislation by the States to which they may flee.

6. That no law shall ever be passed by Congress in relation to the institution of African slavery in the States or Territories, or elsewhere in the United States, without the consent of a majority of the senators and representatives of the slaveholding States.

7. That none of these provisions, nor any other provisions of the Constitution in relation to slavery, (except the African slave trade,) shall ever be altered except by the consent of each and all of the States in which slavery exists.

Source: *Congressional Globe,* 36th Cong., 2nd sess., Senate Report 288, 2–3.
(Report of the Senate Committee of Thirteen)

Mississippi Senator Jefferson Davis (Democrat)

December 22, 1860

Mr. Davis submitted the following proposition:

Resolved, That it shall be declared, by amendment of the Constitution, that property in slaves, recognized as such by the local law of any of the States of the Union, shall stand on the same footing in all constitutional and federal relations as any other species of property so recognized; and, like other property, shall not be subject to be divested or impaired by the local law of any other State, either in escape thereto, or of transit or sojourn of the owner therein; and in no case whatever shall such property be subject to be divested or impaired by any legislative act of the United States, or of any of the Territories thereof.

Source: *Congressional Globe,* 36th Cong., 2nd sess., Senate Report 288, 3.
   (Report of the Senate Committee of Thirteen)

Illinois Senator Stephen Arnold Douglas (Democrat)

December 24, 1860

Mr. Douglas submitted the following joint resolution:

> JOINT RESOLUTION proposing certain amendments to the
> Constitution of the United States.

Resolved by the Senate and House of Representatives of the United States of America in Congress assembled, (two thirds of both houses concurring,) That the following articles be, and are hereby, proposed and submitted as amendments to the Constitution of the United States, which shall be valid, to all intents and purposes, as part of said Constitution, when ratified by conventions of three fourths of the several States:

ARTICLE 13.

SECTION 1. Congress shall make no law in respect to slavery or servitude in any Territory of the United States, and the *status* of each Territory in respect to servitude, as the same now exists by law, shall remain unchanged until the Territory, with such boundaries as Congress may prescribe, shall have a population of fifty thousand white inhabitants, when the white male citizens thereof over the age of twenty-one years may proceed to form a constitution and government for themselves and exercise all the rights of self government consistent with the Constitution of the United States; and when such new States shall contain the requisite population for a member of Congress, according to the then federal ratio of representation, it shall be admitted into the Union on an equal footing with the original States, with or without slavery, as the constitution of such new State shall provide at the time of admission; and in the meantime such new States shall be entitled to one delegate in the Senate, to be chosen by the legislature, and one delegate in the House of Representatives, to be chosen by the people having qualifications requisite for electors of the most numerous branch of the legislature; and said delegates shall have all the rights and privileges of senators and representatives respectively, except that of voting.

SEC. 2. No more territory shall be acquired by the United States, except by treaty, or by the concurrent vote of two thirds of each house of Congress; and, when so acquired, the status thereof in respect to servitude, as it existed at the time of acquisition, shall remain unchanged until it shall contain the population aforesaid for the formation of new States, when it shall be subject to the terms, conditions, and privileges herein provided for the existing Territories.

SEC. 3. The area of all new States shall be as nearly uniform in size as may be practicable, having due regard to convenient boundaries and natural capacities, and shall not be less than sixty nor more than eighty thousand square miles, except in case of islands, which may contain less than that amount.

SEC. 4. The second and third clauses of the second section of the fourth article of the Constitution, which provides for delivering up fugitives from justice and fugitives from service or labor, shall have the same power in the Territories and new States as in the States of the Union; and the said clause, in respect to fugitives from justice, shall be construed to include all crimes committed within and against the laws of the State from which the fugitive fled, whether the acts charged be criminal or not in the State where the fugitive was found.

SEC. 5. The second section of the third article of the Constitution, in respect to the judicial power of the United States, shall be deemed applicable to the Territories and new States, as well as to the States of the Union.

ARTICLE 14.

SEC. 1. The elective franchise and the right to hold office, whether federal, State, territorial, or municipal, shall not be exercised by persons of the African race, in whole or in part.

SEC. 2. The United States shall have power to acquire, from time to time, districts of country in Africa and South America for the colonization, at expense of the federal Treasury, of such free negroes and mulattoes as the several States may wish to have removed from their limits, and from the District of Columbia, and such other places as may be under the jurisdiction of Congress.

SEC. 3. Congress shall have no power to abolish slavery in the places under its exclusive jurisdiction and situate within the limits of States that permit the holding of slaves.

SEC. 4. Congress shall have no power to abolish slavery within the District of Columbia so long as it exists in the adjoining States of Virginia and Maryland, or either, nor without the consent of the inhabitants, nor without just compensation first made to such owners of slaves as do not consent to such abolishment. Nor shall Congress at any time prohibit officers of the federal government, or members of Congress, whose duties require them to be in said District from bringing with them their slaves and holding them as such during the time their duties may require them to remain there, and afterwards taking them from the District.

SEC. 5. Congress shall have no power to prohibit or hinder the transportation of slaves from one State to another, or to a Territory in which slaves are permitted by law to be held, whether such transportation be by land, navigable rivers, or by sea; but the African slave trade shall be forever suppressed, and it shall be the duty of Congress to make such laws as shall be necessary and effectual to prevent the migration or importation of slaves or persons owing service or labor into the United States from any foreign country, place, or jurisdiction whatever.

SEC. 6. In addition to the provision of the third paragraph of the second section of the fourth article of the Constitution, Congress shall have power to provide by law, and it shall be its duty so to provide, that the United States shall pay to the owner who shall apply for it the full value of his fugitive slave, in all cases when the marshal, or other officer whose duty it was to arrest said fugitive, was prevented from so doing by violence or intimidation; or when, after arrest, said fugitive was rescued by force, and the owner thereby prevented and obstructed in the pursuit of his remedy for the recovery of his fugitive slave, under the said clause of the Constitution, and the laws made in pursuance thereof; and in all such cases, when the United States shall pay for such fugitives, they shall have the right, in their own name, to sue the county in which said violence, intimidation, or rescue was committed, and to recover from it, with interest and damages, the amount paid by them for said fugitive slave. And the said county, after it has paid the said amount to the United States, may, for its indemnity, sue and recover from the wrongdoers or rescuers by whom the owner was prevented from the recovery of his fugitive slave, in like manner as the owner himself might have sued and recovered.

SEC. 7. No future amendment of the Constitution shall effect this and the preceding article; nor the third paragraph of the second section of the first article of the Constitution; nor the third paragraph of the second section of the fourth article of said Constitution; and no amendment shall be made to the Constitution which will authorize or give to Congress any power to abolish or interfere with slavery in any of the States by whose laws it is or may be allowed or sanctioned.

Source: *Congressional Globe,* 36th Cong., 2nd sess., Senate Report 288, 8–10.
(Report of the Senate Committee of Thirteen; also Joint Resolution, S.R. 52)

NEW YORK SENATOR WILLIAM HENRY SEWARD (REPUBLICAN)

December 24, 1860

Mr. Seward submitted the following resolutions, which were considered:

Resolved, That the following article be, and the same is hereby proposed and submitted as an amendment to the Constitution of the United States, to be valid, to all intents and purposes, as a part of said Constitution, when ratified by the legislatures of three fourths of the several States:

1st. No amendment shall be made to the Constitution which will authorize or give to Congress the power to abolish or interfere, within any State, with the domestic institutions thereof, including that of persons held to labor or service by the laws of said State.

2d. The fugitive slave act of 1850 shall be so amended as to give to the alleged fugitive a jury trial.

3d. The legislatures of the several States shall be respectfully requested to review all of their legislation affecting the right of persons recently resident in other States, and to repeal or modify all such acts as may contravene the provisions of the Constitution of the United States, or any laws made in pursuance thereof.

Source: *Congressional Globe,* 36th Cong., 2nd sess., Senate Report 288, 10–11.
(Report of the Senate Committee of Thirteen)

TENNESSEE REPRESENTATIVE THOMAS AMOS ROGERS NELSON
(OPPOSITION PARTY)

December 27, 1860

Mr. Nelson withdrew his joint resolution to amend the Constitution of the United States, and in place thereof submitted the following, which he stated was identically the same as that submitted by Mr. Crittenden to the special committee of the Senate.

JOINT RESOLUTION proposing certain amendments to the Constitution of the United States

Whereas serious and alarming dissensions have arisen between the northern and southern States, concerning the rights and security of the rights of the slaveholding States, and especially their rights in the common territory of the United States; and whereas it is eminently desirable and proper that those dissensions which now threaten the very existence of this Union, should be permanently quieted and settled by constitutional provisions which shall do equal justice to all sections, and thereby restore to the people that peace and good will which ought to prevail between all the citizens of the United States: Therefore—

Resolved by the Senate and House of Representatives of the United States of America in Congress assembled, two thirds of both Houses concurring, That the following articles be, and are hereby, proposed and submitted as amendments to the Constitution of the United States, which shall be valid to all intents and purposes as part of said Constitution when ratified by conventions of threefourths of the several States:

Article 1. In all the territory of the United States now held or hereafter acquired, situate north of latitude thirty-six degrees and thirty minutes, slavery or involuntary servitude, except as a punishment for crime, is prohibited while such territory shall remain under territorial government. In all the territory south of said line of latitude slavery of the African race is hereby recognized as existing, and shall not be interfered with by Congress, but shall be protected as property by all the departments of the territorial government during its continuance; and when any territory, north or south of said line, within such boundaries as Congress may prescribe, shall contain the population requisite for a member of Congress, according to the then Federal ratio of representation of the people of the United States, it shall, if its form of government be republican, be admitted into the Union, on an equal footing with the original States, with or without slavery, as the constitution of such new State may provide.

Article 2. Congress shall have no power to abolish slavery in places under its exclusive jurisdiction, and situate within the limits of States that permit the holding of slaves.

Article 3. Congress shall have no power to abolish slavery within the District of Columbia so long as it exists in the adjoining States of Virginia and Maryland, or either, nor without the consent of the inhabitants, nor without just compensation first made to such owners of slaves as do not consent to such abolishment. Nor shall Congress at any time prohibit officers of the federal government or members of Congress, whose duties require them to be in said District, from bringing with them their slaves, and holding them as such during the time their duties may require them to remain there, and afterwards taking them from the District.

Article 4. Congress shall have no power to prohibit or hinder the transportation of slaves from one State to another, or to a Territory in which slaves are by law permitted to be held, whether that transportation be by land, navigable river, or by the sea.

Article 5. That in addition to the provisions of the third paragraph of the second section of the fourth article of the Constitution of the United States, Congress shall have power to provide by law, and it shall be its duty so to provide, that the United States shall pay to the owner who shall apply for it, the full value of his fugitive slave, in all cases, when the marshal, or other officer, whose duty it was to arrest said fugitive, was prevented from so doing by violence or intimidation, or when, after arrest, said fugitive was rescued by force, and the owner thereby prevented and obstructed in the pursuit of his remedy for the recovery of his fugitive slave, under the said clause of the Constitution and the laws made in pursuance thereof. And in all such cases, when the United States shall pay for such fugitive, they shall have the right, in their own name, to sue the county in which said violence, intimidation, or rescue was committed, and to recover from it, with interest and damages, the amount paid by them for said fugitive slave. And the said county, after it has paid said amount to the United States, may, for its indemnity, sue and recover from the wrongdoers, or rescuers, by whom the owner was prevented from the recovery of his fugitive slave, in like manner as the owner himself might have sued and recovered.

Article 6. No future amendment of the Constitution shall affect the five preceding articles, nor the third paragraph of the second section of the first article of the Constitution, nor the third paragraph of the second section of the fourth article of said Constitution; and no amendment shall be made to the Constitution which shall authorize or give to Congress any power to abolish or interfere with slavery in any of the States by whose laws it is or may be allowed or permitted.

And whereas, also, besides those causes of dissension embraced in the foregoing amendments proposed to the Constitution of the United States, there are others which come within the jurisdiction of Congress, and may be remedied by its legislative power; and whereas it is the desire of Congress, as far as its power will extend, to remove all just cause for the popular discontent and agitation which now disturb the peace of the country and threaten the stability of its institutions: Therefore—

1. *Resolved by the Senate and House of Representatives of the United States of America in Congress assembled,* That the laws now in force for the recovery of fugitive slaves are in strict pursuance of the plain and mandatory provisions of the Constitution, and have been sanctioned as valid and constitutional by the judgement of the Supreme Court of the United States; that the slaveholding States are entitled to the faithful observance and execution of those laws, and that they ought not to be repealed or so modified or changed as to impair their efficiency; and that laws ought to be made for the punishment of those who attempt by rescue of the slave or other illegal means, to hinder or defeat the due execution of said laws.

2. That all State laws which conflict with the fugitive slave acts, or any other constitutional acts of Congress, or which in their operation impede, hinder, or delay the free course and due execution of any of said acts, are null and void by the plain provisions of the Constitution of the United States. Yet those State laws, void as they are, have given color to practices and led to consequences which have obstructed the due administration and execution of acts of Congress, and especially the acts for the delivery of fugitive slaves, and have thereby contributed much to the discord and commotion now prevailing. Congress, therefore, in the present perilous juncture, does not deem it improper, respectfully and earnestly, to recommend the repeal of those laws to the several States which have enacted them, or such legislative corrections or explanations of them as may prevent their being used or perverted to such mischievous purposes.

3. That the act of the eighteenth of September, eighteen hundred and fifty, commonly called the fugitive slave law, ought to be so amended as to make the fee of the commissioner, mentioned in the eighth section of the act, equal in amount in the cases decided by him, whether his decision be in favor of or against the claimant. And to avoid misconstruction, the last

clause of the fifth section of said act, which authorizes the person holding a warrant for the arrest or detention of a fugitive slave to summon to his aid the *posse comitatus,* and which declares it to be the duty of all good citizens to assist him in its execution, ought to be so amended as to expressly limit the authority and duty to cases in which there shall be resistance or danger of resistance or rescue.

4. That the laws for the suppression of the African slave trade, and especially those prohibiting the importation of slaves in the United States, ought to be made effectual, and ought to be thoroughly executed, and all further enactments to those ends ought to be properly made.

[NOTE: The four attached resolutions were a part of Crittenden's submission to the Senate on December 18, but were not a part of his submission to the Special Committee of Thirteen on December 22.]

Source: *Congressional Globe,* 36th Cong., 2nd sess., House of Representatives Report No. 31, 16–19.
(Journal of the Committee of Thirty-Three)

PENNSYLVANIA SENATOR WILLIAM BIGLER (DEMOCRAT)

December 28, 1860

That amendments to the Constitution be submitted, embracing the following propositions, to wit:

First. That the territory now owned by the United States shall be divided by a line from east to west on the parallel of 36° 30'.

Second. That the territory south of said line, with the view to the formation of States, shall be divided into four Territories, of as near equal size as Congress may deem best, considering the formation of the country, and having due regard to the convenience of the inhabitants of the Territories now organized; that the territory north of said line shall in like manner be divided into eight Territories.

Third. That when the inhabitants of such Territories, or either of them, shall become sufficiently numerous, Congress shall provide governments for the same; and when the *bona fide* inhabitants in any Territory shall be equal to the then ratio of representation in Congress, the fact to be ascertained by a census taken under the direction of Congress, it shall be the duty of the President of the United States, by proclamation, to announce the admission of such State into the Union.

Fourth. That in all the Territories south of said line of 36° 30', involuntary servitude, as it now exists in the States south of Mason and Dixon's line, shall be recognized and protected by all the departments of the territorial governments; and in all the Territories north of said line, involuntary servitude, except as a punishment for crime, shall be prohibited.

Fifth. That Congress shall be denied the power to abolish slavery in places now under its jurisdiction situate within the limits of slaveholding States, as also within the District of Columbia, so long as slavery may exist in either of the States of Virginia or Maryland.

Sixth. That in addition to the present provision for the rendition of fugitives from labor, it shall be made the duty of the non-slaveholding States to provide efficient laws for the delivery of fugitives from labor to the persons to whom such service or labor may be due.

Seventh. That neither these proposed amendments nor the third paragraph of the second section of the first article of the Constitution, nor the third paragraph of the second section of the fourth article of the Constitution, shall be liable to future amendment.

Source: *Congressional Globe*, 36th Cong., 2nd sess., Senate Report 288, 15.

(Report of the Senate Committee of Thirteen)

MASSACHUSETTS REPRESENTATIVE CHARLES FRANCIS ADAMS (REPUBLICAN)

December 28, 1860

On motion of Mr. Nelson, the committee proceeded to consider the following resolution submitted by Mr. Adams:

Resolved, That it is expedient to propose an amendment to the Constitution of the United States providing that no amendment having for its object any interference within the States with the relation between their citizens and those described in the second section of the first article of the Constitution as "all other persons" shall originate with any state that does not recognize that relation within its own limits, or shall be valid without the assent of every one of the States composing the Union.

Source: *Congressional Globe,* 36th Cong., 2nd sess., House of Representatives Report No. 31, 19.

(Journal of the Committee of Thirty-Three)

VIRGINIA REPRESENTATIVE JOHN SINGLETON MILLSON (DEMOCRAT)

December 31, 1860

On motion of Mr. Nelson, the committee agreed to lay aside the joint resolution to amend the Constitution of the United States, in order to consider the following proposition presented by Mr. Millson to amend the Constitution, to wit:

The Congress may provide for the government of the territory now belonging to the United States, or which may hereafter be acquired by them, and may establish inferior legislatures therein, with such powers of legislation, consistent with the Constitution, as Congress may limit and prescribe; but neither Congress nor such inferior legislature shall prohibit the migration or introduction of such persons as may be held to service or labor under the laws of any State into any part of the territory which may lie south of thirty-six degrees thirty minutes north latitude, nor by any law or regulation therein discharge such persons from such service or labor. But the claim of the party to whom such service or labor may be due shall be recognized by all departments of the territorial government, and protected by apt and proper regulations therein. But into all other territory not included within the limits of any State the migration of such persons shall be prohibited.

Source: *Congressional Globe,* 36th Cong., 2nd sess., House of Representatives Report No. 31, 22.

(Journal of the Committee of Thirty-Three)

Maryland Representative Henry Winter Davis (American Party)

December 31, 1860

Mr. H. Winter Davis proposed to amend the foregoing by striking it all out and inserting the following:

No territory shall be acquired by the United States by conquest, discovery, treaty, or otherwise, nor shall any State not formed of territory of the United States be admitted into the Union, unless upon the votes of two-thirds of the States in the Senate, and of two-thirds of the votes of all the members of the House of Representatives, and approved by the President.

If slavery or involuntary servitude exist by the law of any territory hereafter acquired by the United States at the time of acquisition, it shall not be abolished so long as it shall remain a Territory; and if slavery do not exist by law in any territory hereafter acquired at the time of acquisition, it shall not be established so long as it shall remain a Territory. But in either case the people in their State constitution of government may permit or forbid slavery, as to them may seem good.

Source: *Congressional Globe,* 36th Cong., 2nd sess., House of Representatives Report No. 31, 22–23.

(Journal of the Committee of Thirty-Three)

Ohio Representative Thomas Corwin (Republican)

December 31, 1860

Mr. Corwin proposed, as a substitute for the propositions of Mr. Millson and Mr. Davis, the following:

First. That all the territory hereafter acquired, and not admitted into the Union as States when acquired, shall be organized as Territories, and shall have full power to elect all officers, executive, legislative, and judicial, at such times and for such terms as the people of said Territory shall ordain and establish by law.

Second. That the legislative power of the Territories, when organized, shall extend to all subjects which may be embraced by the legislative power of the States; and each Territory shall send one delegate to Congress, who shall be entitled to a seat in the House of Representatives, with all the privileges of a member from any State except the right to vote.

Third. That whenever any Territory shall have a population of free white inhabitants equal to the number required to give one member of Congress by the apportionment of representation at the time, she shall be entitled to admission into the Union on an equal footing with all the States; and whether her constitution shall establish or prohibit slavery, neither shall be a ground of objection to her admission.

Source: *Congressional Globe,* 36th Cong., 2nd sess., House of Representatives Report No. 31, 23.

(Journal of the Committee of Thirty-Three)

Tennessee Representative Emerson Etheridge (Opposition Party)

January 7, 1861

The Clerk read Mr. ETHERIDGE's resolution, as follows:

A joint resolution providing for amendments to the Constitution of the United States

Be it resolved by the Senate and House of Representatives of the United States of America in Congress assembled, That the following amendments to the Constitution of the United States be proposed to the several States for their adoption or ratification:

ARTICLE 1. Congress shall have no power to interfere with slavery in any of the States of the Union.

ART. 2. Congress shall have no power to interfere with or abolish slavery in any of the navy-yards, dock-yards, arsenals, forts, or other places ceded to the United States, within the limits of any States where slavery exists.

ART. 3. Congress shall have no power to interfere with or abolish slavery in the District of Columbia, without the consent of the States of Maryland and Virginia; nor without the consent of the inhabitants of said District; nor without making just compensation to the owners.

ART. 4. Congress shall have no power to prohibit the removal or transportation of slaves from one slave State to another slave State.

ART. 5. The migration or importation of persons held to service or labor for life, or a term of years, into any of the States, or the Territories belonging to the United States, is perpetually prohibited; and Congress shall pass all laws necessary to make said prohibition effective.

ART. 6. In all that part of the territory of the United States, not included within the limits of any State, which lies north of the parallel of 36° 30' of north latitude, slavery, or involuntary servitude, except for crime, whereof the party shall have been duly convicted, shall be prohibited; and in all that territory of the United States, not included within the limits of any State, which lies south of said parallel of 36° 30' of north latitude, neither Congress nor any Territorial Legislature shall have power to pass any law abolishing, prohibiting, or in any manner interfering with the right to hold slaves; and wherever, in any portion of the territory owned by the United States north or south of the said parallel of 36° 30', there shall be, within an area of not less than sixty thousand square miles, a population equal to the ratio of representation for a member of Congress, the same shall be admitted by Congress into the Union as a State, upon the same footing with the original States in all respects whatever, with or without slavery, as its constitution may determine.

ART. 7. No territory beyond the present limits of the United States and the Territories thereof shall be hereafter acquired by, or annexed to, the United States, unless the same be done by a concurrent vote of two-thirds of both Houses of Congress, or, if the same be acquired by treaty, by a vote of two-thirds of the Senate.

ART. 8. Article four and section two of the Constitution of the United States shall be so amended as to read as follows: A person charged in any State with treason, felony, or other crime, *(against the laws of said State,)* who shall flee from justice and be found in another State, shall, on demand of the executive authority of the State from which he fled, be delivered up, to be removed to the State having jurisdiction of the crime.

Source: *Congressional Globe,* 36th Cong., 2nd sess., 279.

Tennessee Governor Isham Green Harris (Democrat)

January 7, 1861

GENTLEMEN OF THE SENATE, AND HOUSE OF REPRESENTATIVES:

The ninth section of the third article of the Constitution provides that, on extraordinary occasions, the Governor may convene the General Assembly. Believing the emergency contemplated, to exist at this time, I have called you together. In welcoming you to the capitol of the State, I can but regret the gloomy auspices under which we meet. Grave and momentous issues have arisen, which, to an unprecedented degree, agitate the public mind and imperil the perpetuity of the Government.

The systematic, wanton, and long continued agitation of the slavery question, with the actual and threatened aggressions of the Northern States and a portion of their people, upon the well-defined constitutional rights of the Southern citizen; the rapid growth and increase, in all the elements of power, of a purely sectional party, whose bond of union is uncompromising hostility to the rights and institutions of the fifteen Southern States, have produced a crisis in the affairs of the country, unparalleled in the history of the past, resulting already in the withdrawal from the Confederacy of one of the sovereignties which compose it, while others are rapidly preparing to move in the same direction. Fully appreciating the importance of the duties which devolve upon you, fraught, as your action must be, with consequences of the highest possible importance to the people of Tennessee; knowing that, as a great Commonwealth, our own beloved State is alike interested with her sisters, who have resorted, and are preparing to resort, to this fearful alternative, I have called you together for the purpose of calm and dispassionate deliberation, earnestly trusting, as the chosen representatives of a free and enlightened people, that you will, at this critical juncture of our affairs, prove yourselves equal to the occasion which has called for the exercise of your talent and patriotism.

A brief review of the history of the past is necessary to a proper understanding of the issues presented for your consideration. . . .

{Here Governor Harris presented his case that the "Constitution distinctly recognizes property in *slaves*," and that the current political crisis was brought on by the organization of an anti-slavery party which was attempting to circumscribe the rights of the Southern slaveholder. He then listed the abuses the South had suffered at the hands of this "anti-slavery cloud."}

These evils can be obviated to a great extent, if not entirely, by the following amendments to the Constitution:

1st. Establish a line upon the Northern boundary of the present Slave States, and extend it through the Territories to the Pacific Ocean, upon such parallel of latitude as will divide them equitably between the North and South, expressly providing that all the territory now owned or that may be hereafter acquired North of that line, shall be forever free, and all South of it, *forever* slave. This will remove the question of existence or non-existence of slavery in our States and Territories entirely and forever from the arena of politics. The question being settled by the Constitution, is no longer open for the politician to ride into position by appealing to fanatical prejudices, or assailing the rights of his neighbors.

2d. In addition to the fugitive slave clause provide, that when a slave has been demanded of the Executive authority of the State to which he has fled, if he is not delivered, and the owner permitted to carry him out of the State in peace, that the State so failing to deliver, shall pay to the owner double the value of such slave, and secure his right of action in the Supreme Court of the United States. This will secure the return of the slave to his owner, or his value, with a sufficient sum to indemnify him for the expenses necessarily incident to the recovery.

3d. Provide for the protection of the owner in the peaceable possession of his slave while in transit, or temporarily sojourning in any of the States of the Confederacy; and in the event of the slave's escape or being taken from the owner, require the State to return, or account for him as in case of the fugitive.

4th. Expressly prohibit Congress from abolishing slavery in the District of Columbia, in any dock yard, navy yard, arsenal, or district of any character whatever, within the limits of any slave State.

5th. That these provisions shall never be changed, except by the consent of all the slave States.

With these amendments to the Constitution, I should feel that our rights were reasonably secure, not only in theory, but in fact, and should indulge the hope of living in the Union in peace. Without these, or some other amendments, which promise an equal amount and certainty of security, there is no hope of peace or security in the government. . . .

{Harris concluded his address by offering the opinion that Tennessee must either see its constitutional rights "*respected,* and *fully* and *perfectly* secured in the present Government," or the state must align itself with a "Confederacy of Southern States."}

Source: Robert H. White, *Messages of the Governors of Tennessee, 1857–1869* (Nashville: Tennessee Historical Commission, 1959), 255–264.

Virginia Governor John Letcher (Democrat)

January 7, 1861

EXECUTIVE DEPARTMENT,
RICHMOND, Jan. 7, 1861.

Gentlemen of the Senate and House of Delegates:

My proclamation, issued on the 15th day of November last, states succinctly the consideration which induced me to convene you in extraordinary session.

Duty, however, requires of me a more detailed exposition of my views upon the subjects therein referred to, as well as the presentation of such recommendations as are demanded by a proper regard for the public interests, and the faithful, prompt and efficient execution of the laws of this great and growing commonwealth. These views and recommendations will be presented with as much brevity as the extraordinary circumstances of the times will justify. . . .

{Governor Letcher then recommended, as he had a year earlier, that the legislature call a convention of all the states to consider the adoption of constitutional amendments that would address the Southern states' grievances.}

In the present condition of public affairs, why cannot such additional amendments as the circumstances now existing require be proposed for ratification and adoption? The necessity is manifest, and the duty to adopt all constitutional measures before we resort to the ultimate remedy of secession is imperative. Is it not monstrous to see a government like ours destroyed, merely because men cannot agree about a domestic institution, which existed at the formation of the government, and which is now recognized by fifteen out of the thirty-three states composing the Union?. . .

{Letcher here devoted several pages highlighting the South's grievances stemming from "systematic and persistent warfare upon the institution of domestic slavery."}

The controversy now has reached a point when *it must be settled* on some fair, just and permanent basis, if we are to be reunited, and peace, quiet and order restored to the country. The excitement now existing is ruinous to the financial and commercial business, and to the agricultural, planting, mechanical, mercantile and manufacturing interests of all sections. Unless a settlement of the controversy shall be speedily effected, every species of property must fall to merely nominal prices, and a scene of general and ruinous bankruptcy, far exceeding, in extent and severity, any that has preceded it, must be the inevitable result. Even now, hundreds and thousands have been thrown out of employment, and at this inclement season poverty, want and misery must be the portion of them and their dependent families. It is time the conservative spirit of the country was aroused and stimulated to energetic action. No time is to be lost in putting into immediate requisition all fair, honorable and constitutional means that promise to secure a satisfactory and permanent adjustment.

What, then, is necessary to be done? The northern states must strike from their statute books their personal liberty bills, and fulfill their constitutional obligations in regard to fugitive slaves and fugitives from justice. If our slaves escape into non-slaveholding states, they must be delivered up; if abandoned, depraved and desperately wicked men come into slave states to excite insurrections, or to commit other crimes against our laws, and escape into free states, they must be given up for trial and punishment, when lawfully demanded by the constituted authorities of those states whose laws have been violated.

Second—We must have proper and effective guarantees for the protection of slavery in the district of Columbia. We can never consent to the abolition of slavery in the district, until Maryland shall emancipate her slaves; and not then, unless it shall be demanded by the citizens of the district.

Third—Our equality in the states and territories must be fully recognized, and our rights of person and property adequately protected and secured. We must have guarantees that slavery shall not be interdicted in any territory now belonging to, or which may hereafter be acquired by the general government; either by the congress of the United States or a territorial legislature: that we shall be permitted to pass through the free states and territories without molestation; and if a slave shall be abducted, that the state in which he or she shall be lost, shall pay the full value of such slave to the owner.

Fourth—Like guarantees must be given, that the transmission of slaves between the slaveholding states, either by land or water, shall not be interfered with.

Fifth—The passage and enforcement of rigid laws for the punishment of such persons in the free states as shall organize, or aid and abet in organizing, either by the contribution of money, arms, munitions of war, or in any other mode whatsoever, companies of men, with a view to assail the slaveholding states, and to excite slaves to insurrection.

Sixth—That the general government shall be deprived of the power of appointing to local offices in the slaveholding states, persons who are hostile to their institutions, or inimical to their rights—the object being to prevent the appointing power from using patronage to sow the seeds of strife and dissension between the slaveholding and non-slaveholding classes in the southern states.

These guarantees can be given without prejudice to the honor or rights, and without a sacrifice of the interests, of either of the non-slaveholding states. We ask nothing, therefore, which is not clearly right and necessary to our protection: And surely, when so much is at stake, it will be freely, cheerfully and promptly assented to. It is in the interest of the north and the south to preserve the government from destruction; and they should omit the use of no proper or honorable means to avert so great a calamity. The public safety and welfare demand instant action. . . .

{Governor Letcher concluded by stating that it would be a "serious mistake" to presume that non-slaveholders would not fight to defend slavery and with the hope that a settlement of the crisis could be attained. He declared, however, that any attempt on the part of the federal government to "interfere with the rights and institutions of Virginia" would be resisted.}

Source: State of Virginia, *Journal of the House of Delegates of the State of Virginia, for the Extra Session, 1861* (Richmond: William F. Ritchie, Public Printer, 1861), Doc. 1, iii–xxvii.

ALABAMA SECESSION CONVENTION

January 10, 1861

MINORITY REPORT.

Mr. CLEMENS, from the minority of the same Committee, made a report with resolutions as follows:

The undersigned, a minority of the Committee of Thirteen, to whom was referred all matters touching the proper mode of resistance to be adopted by the State of Alabama, in the present emergency, beg leave to present the following

REPORT:

Looking to harmony of action among our own people as desirable above all other things, we have been earnestly desirous of concurring with the majority in the line of policy marked out by them, but, after the most careful consideration, we have been unable to see in Separate State Secession the most effectual mode of guarding our honor and securing our rights. Without entering into any argument upon the nature and amount of our grievances, or any speculations as to the probability of our obtaining redress and security in the Union, but looking alone to the most effectual mode of resistance, it seems to us that this great object is best to be attained by the concurrent and concerted action of all the States interested, and that it becomes us to make the effort to obtain that concurrence, before deciding finally and conclusively upon our own policy.

We are further of opinion that, in a matter of this importance, vitally affecting the property, the lives and the liberties of the whole people, sound policy dictates that an ordinance of secession should be submitted for their ratification and approval. To that end, the resolutions which accompany this report have been prepared and are now submitted to the Convention.

The undersigned purposely refrain from a detailed statement of the reasons which have brought them to the conclusions at which they have arrived. The action proposed by the majority of the Committee is, in its nature, final and conclusive—there is no chance for rehearing or revision; and we feel no disposition to submit an argument, whose only effect will be to create discontent, and throw difficulties in the way of a policy, the adoption of which we are powerless to prevent. In submitting our own plan, and using all fair and honorable means to secure its acceptance, our duty is fully discharged; to insist upon objections when they can have no effect but to excite dissatisfaction among the people is alike foreign to our feelings and our conceptions of patriotic duty.

The resolutions herein before referred to, are prayed to be taken as part of this Report, and the whole is herewith respectfully submitted.

JERE. CLEMENS,
DAVID P. LEWIS,
WM. O. WINSTON,

A. KIMBAL,

R. S. WATKINS,

R. JEMISON JR.

WHEREAS, repeated infractions of the Constitution of the United States by the people and States of the Northern section of the Confederacy have been followed by the election of sectional candidates, by a strictly sectional vote, to the Presidency and Vice Presidency of the United States, upon a platform of principles insulting and menacing to the Southern States; and WHEREAS, it becomes a free people to watch with jealous vigilance, and resist with manly firmness every attempt to subvert the free and equal principles upon which our Government was originally founded, and ought alone to be maintained; therefore,

Be it resolved by the people of Alabama in Convention assembled, That the States of Delaware, Maryland, Virginia, North Carolina, South Carolina, Georgia, Florida, Mississippi, Louisiana, Texas, Arkansas, Tennessee, Kentucky and Missouri, be and they are hereby requested to meet us in general Convention in the city of Nashville, in the State of Tennessee, on the 22d day of February, 1861, for the purpose of taking into consideration the wrongs of which we have cause to complain; the appropriate remedy therefor, and the time and manner of its application.

Be it further resolved, That the State of Alabama shall be represented in said Convention by nine delegates, one to be selected from each Congressional district, and two from the State at large, in such manner as shall hereafter be directed and provided for by this Convention.

Be it further resolved, That our delegates selected shall be instructed to submit to the general Convention the following basis of a settlement of the existing difficulties between the Northern and the Southern States, to wit:

1. A faithful execution of the Fugitive Slave Law, and a repeal of all State laws calculated to impair its efficacy.
2. A more stringent and explicit provision for the surrender of criminals charged with offences against the laws of one State and escaping into another.
3. A guarantee that slavery shall not be abolished in the District of Columbia, or in any other place over which Congress has exclusive jurisdiction.
4. A guarantee that the inter-State slave trade shall not be interferred with.

5. A protection to slavery in the Territories, while they are Territories, and a guarantee that when they ask for admission as States they shall be admitted into the Union with or without slavery as their Constitutions may prescribe.
6. The right of transit through free States with slave property.
7. The foregoing clauses to be irrepealable by amendments to the Constitution.

Be it further resolved, That the basis of settlement prescribed in the foregoing resolution shall not be regarded by our delegates as absolute and unalterable, but as an indication of the opinion of this Convention, to which they are expected to conform as nearly as may be, holding themselves, however, at liberty to accept any better plan of adjustment which may be insisted upon by a majority of the slaveholding States.

Be it further resolved, That if the foregoing proposition for a conference is refused, or rejected, by any of all of the States to which it is addressed, Alabama, in that event, will hold herself at liberty, alone, or in conjunction with such States, as may agree to unite with her, to adopt such plan of resistance, and mature such measures, as in her judgement may seem best calculated to maintain the honor and secure the rights of her citizens; and in the meantime we will resist, by all means at our command, any attempt on the part of the General Government to coerce a seceding State.

Be it further resolved, That the President of this Convention be instructed to transmit copies of the foregoing preamble and resolutions to the Governors of each of the States therein named.

And also the following resolution from the same:

Be it resolved by the people of Alabama in Convention assembled, That an ordinance of secession from the United States is an act of such great importance, involving consequences so vitally affecting the lives, liberty and property of the citizens of the seceding State, as well as of the States by which it is surrounded, and with which it has heretofore been united, that in our opinion it should never be attempted until after the most thorough investigation, and discussion, and then only after a full and free ratification at the polls by a direct vote of the people, at an election held under the forms and safeguards of the law in which that single issue, untrammeled and undisguised in any manner whatever, should alone be submitted.

Mr. CLEMENS moved that the preamble and first series of resolutions be taken up and substituted for the ordinance.

The ayes and noes was demanded.

The ayes and nays were then called on the motion of Mr. Clemens, and it was lost. Ayes, 45, nays, 54.

Source: William R. Smith, ed., *The History and Debates of the Convention of the People of Alabama, Begun and Held in the City of Montgomery, on the Seventh Day of January, 1861, in Which Is Preserved the Speeches of the Secret Sessions and Many Valuable State Papers* (Montgomery: White, Pfister, 1861), 77–80.

Virginia Senator Robert Mercer Taliaferro Hunter (Democrat)

January 11, 1861

I say, therefore, sir, that the South is bound to take this course unless it can get some guarantees which will protect it in the Union, some constitutional guarantees which will serve that end; and I now ask, what should be the nature of the guarantees that would effectually prevent the social system from such assaults as these? I say, they must be guarantees of a kind that will stop up all the avenues through which they have threatened to assail the social system of the South. There must be constitutional amendments which shall provide: first, that Congress shall have no power to abolish slavery in the States, in the District of Columbia, in the dock-yards, forts, and arsenals of the United States; second, that it shall not abolish, tax, or obstruct the slave trade between the States; third, that it shall be the duty of each of the States to suppress combinations within their jurisdiction for armed invasions of another; fourth, that States shall be admitted with or without slavery, according to the election of the people; fifth, that it shall be the duty of the States to restore fugitive slaves when within their borders, or to pay the value of the same; sixth, that fugitives from justice shall be deemed all those who have offended against the laws of a State within its jurisdiction, and who have escaped therefrom; seventh, that Congress shall recognize and protect as property whatever is held to be such by the laws or prescriptions of any State within the Territories, dock-yards, forts, and arsenals of the United States, and wherever the United States has exclusive jurisdiction; with the following exceptions: First, it may leave the subject of slavery or involuntary servitude to the people of the Territories when a law shall be passed to that effect with the usual sanction, and also with the assent of a majority of the Senators from the slaveholding States, and a majority of the Senators from the non-slaveholding States. That exception is designed to provide for the case where we might annex a Territory almost fully peopled, and whose people ought to have the right of self-government, and yet might not be ready to be admitted as a State into the Union.

The next exception is, that "Congress may divide the Territories, to the effect that slavery or involuntary servitude shall be prohibited in one portion of the territory, and recognized and protected in another; provided the law has the sanction of a majority from each of the sections as aforesaid," and that exception is designed to provide for the case where an unpeopled Territory is annexed and it is a fair subject of division between the two sections.

Such, Mr. President, are the guarantees of principle, which, it seems to me, ought to be established by amendments to the Constitution; but I do not believe that these guarantees alone would protect the social system of the South against attack, and perhaps overthrow, from the superior power of the North.

Source: *Congressional Globe,* 36th Cong., 2nd sess., 328–329.

TENNESSEE STATE REPRESENTATIVE GEORGE GANTT {MAURY COUNTY}

January 11, 1861

The success of the Black Republican party, and the secession of the Cotton States may be treated as accomplished facts. These events press upon Tennessee questions of the gravest and highest moment. She cannot waive them—her safety and her honor demand that she must meet them.

She is vitally interested in slavery as a political institution, and in slaves as property. Her slaves are entitled to the status of all other property, both under the Federal Constitution and the local law; but whilst every other species of property is permitted to spread freely throughout the States and Territories, at the will of the owner, this alone is marked out of destruction, by the sentiment which called the Black Republican party into being. The basis of its organization is hatred to slavery; and so exclusively is the case, that if the sentiment of hate were withdrawn it would perish in an hour. It denies that the Constitution recognizes and protects slaves as property; it holds that it has the power to exclude slave property from the common Territories, in the face of an express decision of the Supreme Court of the United States; its avowed policy is that slavery is a wrong and to be dealt with as such—a sin for which not only the slave-holding States are responsible, but which rests also upon the non-slaveholding States; that it is to be confined in perpetual siege in the States where it now exists, and placed in a course of ultimate extinction. Its President elect champions the sentiment that it is and must continue to be the subject of a perpetual struggle, until it prevails everywhere, or is abolished everywhere in the broad borders of the Republic. . . .

Tennessee desires the co-operation of her sister Slave States in the effort she proposes to make, and earnestly invites them to join her in the same. Therefore,

Be it resolved by the General Assembly of Tennessee:

1. That the Governor appoint a commission of not less than ten of our ablest and wisest citizens, to meet in convention a similar commission on behalf of the other Slave States, in the city of Louisville, Kentucky, between the 20th and 25th of January, 1861.
2. That said Convention adopt a basis of settlement, upon which, if possible, the Union may be reconstructed, and by which the rights of property and honor of the slave States may be rendered secure from injury or attack.
3. That the delegates composing said Convention, repair with the ultimatum adopted by them, to the city of Washington, and lay the same before the Congress of the United States, and urge that body to submit it, in the form of an amendment or amendments to the Federal Constitution, on or before the 20th day of February, 1861.
4. That while Tennessee will abide by the ultimatum agreed upon by the Convention, she deems it proper to express her own view of what it should embrace, and which is as follows:
   1. A declaratory amendment to the Federal Constitution, to the effect that, under it, African slavery, as it exists in the slave States, is property, and entitled by it, as well as the local law to the status, of every other species of property.
   2. An amendment which will compel the States to surrender on demand, slaves escaped from their owners, or on refusal, to pay double their value, by suit in the Federal Court, at the instance of the owner.

3. An amendment whereby this property shall be rendered secure in transit through the non-slaveholding States, and whilst in such States temporarily sojourning with the owner.

4. An amendment running a line on the northern borders of the slave States, until it touches our territories, and then west, on the parallel of thirty-six degrees and thirty minutes, until it touches the boundary of the State of California, and then with her boundary to the Pacific Ocean; and declaring that in all the States and Territories south of said line, slavery shall exist, and in all north of it shall be forever prohibited.

Source: *House Journal of the Extra Session of the Thirty-Third General Assembly of the State of Tennessee, Which Convened at Nashville, on the First Monday in January, A.D. 1861* (Nashville: J. O. Griffith, Public Printers, 1861), 43–45.

Pennsylvania Senator William Bigler (Democrat)

January 14, 1861

A BILL to provide for taking the sense of the people of the several States on certain proposed amendments to the Constitution of the United States.

Whereas the Union is in imminent danger of final dissolution, the consequence of a protracted strife and agitation about the institution of African slavery; and whereas it is believed that legislative remedies are insufficient to meet and remove the cause of this impending disaster; and as amendments to the Constitutions can only be submitted by a vote of two thirds of both Houses of Congress, and owing to the unhappy divisions existing in those houses at present, it is not believed that the assent of two thirds of the members of either can be had to such amendments to the Constitution as would reconcile the differences between the North and the South; . . .

That the following articles be, and they are hereby, proposed and submitted as amendments to the Constitution of the United States, which shall be valid, to all intents and purposes, as part of said Constitution, when ratified by the conventions of three fourths of the States held for that purpose.

Article 1. That the territory now held, or that may hereafter be acquired, by the United States shall be divided by a line from east to west on the parallel of thirty-six degrees thirty minutes north latitude.

PART FOUR

Article 2. That in all of the territory north of said line of latitude, involuntary servitude, except as a punishment for crime, is prohibited, and in all the territory south of said line involuntary servitude, as it now exists in the States south of Mason and Dixon's line, is hereby recognized, and shall be sustained and protected by all the departments of the territorial governments; and when any Territory north or south of said line, within such boundaries as Congress may prescribe, shall contain the population requisite for a member of Congress, according to the then federal ratio of representation of the people of the United States, it shall then be the duty of Congress to admit such Territory into the Union on terms of equality with the original States.

Article 3. Congress shall not have power to abolish slavery in the places under its exclusive jurisdiction and situate within the limits of States that permit the holding of slaves, nor shall Congress have the power to abolish slavery in the District of Columbia so long as it exists in the States of Maryland and Virginia, or either of them, nor without just compensation being first made to the owners of such slaves.

Article 4. That, in addition to the provisions of the third paragraph of the second section of the fourth article of the Constitution of the United States, Congress shall have the power to provide by law, and it shall be its duty so to provide, that the United States shall pay to the owner who shall apply for it, the full value of his fugitive slave, in all cases, when the marshal, or other officer, whose duty it was to arrest said fugitive, was prevented from so doing by violence or intimidation, or when, after arrest, said fugitive was rescued by force, and the owner thereby prevented and obstructed in the pursuit of his remedy for the recovery of his fugitive slave, under the said clause of the Constitution and the laws made in pursuance thereof; and in all such cases, when the United States shall pay for such fugitive, they shall have the right, in their own name, to sue the county in which said violence, intimidation, or rescue was committed, and to recover from it, with interest and damages, the amount paid by them for said fugitive slave; and the said county, after it has paid said amount to the United States, may, for its indemnity, sue and recover from the wrong-doers, or rescuers, by whom the owner was prevented from the recovery of his fugitive slave, in like manner as the owner himself might have sued and recovered.

Article 5. Congress shall have no power to prohibit or hinder the transportation of slaves from one State to another, or to a Territory in which slaves are by law permitted to be held, whether transportation be by land, navigable rivers, or by sea; but the African slave trade shall never be revived, except by the unanimous consent of both branches of Congress.

Article 6. Hereafter the President of the United States shall hold his office during the term of six years, and shall not be eligible to re-election.

Article 7. The Constitution shall not be hereafter amended so as to destroy the effect of the third paragraph of the second section of the first article of the Constitution, nor the third paragraph of the second section of the fourth article of the Constitution, nor so as to authorize Congress to interfere with or destroy any of the domestic institutions of the States, without the consent of all the States.

Source: *Congressional Globe*, 36th Cong., 2nd sess., 351; Senate Bill 537, 1, 5–8.

MISSOURI SENATOR TRUSTEN POLK (DEMOCRAT)

January 14, 1861

{Senator Polk began his address by articulating the causes of the sectional crisis, generalizing that "the action of the Government affecting the institution of slavery has been prejudicial to the South, and violative of its constitutional rights."}

Mr. President, has the South no cause for alarm for the safety of her institutions and the security of her rights? Is not her very existence at stake? How long could she retain the institution of slavery after the whole power of the Federal Government shall have been brought to bear upon her for its destruction? Think what could be effected by the Federal legislation. Abolition of slavery in the District of Columbia; abolition in the arsenals, dock-yards, and forts; outlawry of it on the high seas, and wherever the flag of the Union floats; exclusion of it from the common Territories belonging equally to all the States; circumscribing it as with a wall of fire within the States. . . .

{Senator Polk here presented the value of slavery throughout the South, and expressed the concern that a "real and profound alarm" was spreading throughout the slaveholding states.}

This very alarm is one of the most intolerable of the grievances inflicted on the South by the ceaseless and systematic aggressions of Northern abolitionism and negroism. No people can consent to live in the midst of alarms by day, and terror by night. Last of all others will the American people in the slaveholding States of this Confederacy consent to it.

Sir, the "terror by night" is ranked by the sacred penman in the same category with "the arrow that flieth by day, and the pestilence that walketh in darkness, and the destruction that wasteth at noon-day."

I am also satisfied, sir, that there is a settled purpose on the part of the people of the southern States to have the difficulties now brought upon them settled fully and forever, and settled at once. Nothing short of this will meet the exigencies of the present crisis. And in order to such settlement, irrepealable amendments of the Constitution ought to be made, covering the following points:

1. Express and unequivocal recognition of the right of property in slaves.

2. A similar recognition of the right of the owner to take his slaves into the common territory of the United States, and to have his right of property in them protected by the Federal Government there, and wherever else its jurisdiction extends.

3. That Congress shall have no power to abolish slavery in places under its immediate jurisdiction situated within the limits of the States that permit the holding of slaves.

4. Nor within the District of Columbia, so long as slavery shall exist in either of the States of Virginia or Maryland, nor without the consent of the inhabitants, nor without just compensation first made to such owners as do not consent to such abolishment.

5. Nor shall Congress have power to prohibit or hinder the transportation of slaves from one State to another, nor to the District of Columbia, nor to a Territory of the United States.

6. That, when the owner shall be prevented from retaking his fugitive slave, or when such fugitive shall be rescued from him by force, he shall receive compensation for the value of his slave.

All this the slaveholding States ought to have, and all of this the non-slaveholding ought to be willing to concede. They ought to be willing to make these concessions, first, for the sufficient and commanding reason that they would relieve the common country.

Secondly. They are fully warranted by the Constitution as it now stands, and are in perfect concord with both its provisions and spirit. According to the opinion of the Supreme Court of the United States—the appropriate and the appointed tribunal for the arbitrament of such questions—the tribunal of last resort—they are guaranteed by the Constitution, as it was made by our fathers.

{Polk continued, arguing that the Republican Party was the cause of the national unrest, the Crittenden resolutions would be satisfactory to him although the prohibition of slavery north of the 36° 30' parallel was unjust to the South, and that Missouri had suffered greatly at the hands of the anti-slavery movement. He concluded by hoping that "if dissolution must come, let it be peaceful."}

Source: *Congressional Globe,* 36th Cong., 2nd sess., 357–358.

Pennsylvania Representative Thomas Birch Florence (Democrat)

January 14, 1861

Whereas alarming dissensions having arisen between the northern and southern States, as to the rights to the common territory of the United States, it is eminently desirable and proper that such dissensions should be settled by the constitutional provisions which give equal justice to all sections, whereby to restore peace: Therefore,

Resolved by the Senate and House of Representatives, That the following articles be proposed and submitted as an amendment to the Constitution, which shall be valid as a part of the Constitution, when ratified by conventions of three fourths of the people of the States.

First. In all the territories, now or hereafter acquired, north of latitude 36° 40', slavery or involuntary servitude, except punishment for crime, shall be prohibited; while south of that latitude it shall remain; and in all territory south of that latitude, slavery is hereby recognized as existing, and not to be interfered with by Congress, but be protected as property by all departments of the territorial government during its continuance as a Territory. When territory north or south of such line, within such boundaries as Congress may prescribe, shall contain the population necessary for a member of Congress, with a republican form of government, it shall be admitted into the Union on an equality with the original States, with or without slavery, as the constitution of the State may prescribe.

Second. Congress shall have no power to abolish slavery in places under its jurisdiction, or in States permitting slavery.

Third. Congress shall have no power to abolish slavery in the District of Columbia, while it exists in Virginia or Maryland, or either. Congress shall never, at any time, prohibit the officers of the Government, or members of

Congress, whose duties require them to live in the District of Columbia, from bringing slaves and holding them as such.

Fourth. Congress shall have no power to hinder the transportation of slaves from one State to another, whether by land, navigable rivers, or sea.

Fifth. Congress shall have power by law to pay the owner who shall apply the full value of the fugitive slave in all cases where the marshal is prevented from discharging his duty, by force or rescue, made after the arrest. In all such cases the United States shall have power to sue the county in which such violence or rescue is made, and the county shall have the right to sue the individuals who committed the wrong in the same manner as the owner could sue.

Sixth. No future amendments shall affect the preceding articles, and Congress shall never have power to interfere with slavery in the States where it is now permitted.

Source: *Congressional Globe*, 36th Cong., 2nd sess., 378.

TENNESSEE JOINT SELECT COMMITTEE ON FEDERAL RELATIONS

January 14, 1861

Mr. Barksdale {William H. Barksdale; Smith, Sumner, and Macon Counties}, from the Joint Select Committee on Federal Relations, reported that they had had under consideration House Resolutions, Nos. 24 and 25; and also Senate Resolution, No. 5, and recommend resolutions in lieu, which are herewith submitted.

BARKSDALE, *Chairman.*

Which resolutions in lieu, are as follows:

The success of the Black Republican party, and the secession of the Cotton States, may be treated as accomplished facts.[2] These events press upon Tennessee questions of the gravest and highest moment. She cannot waive them—her safety and her honor demand that she must meet them.

---

2. The "Black Republican Party" was a derogatory term used by secessionists in order to define the northern party as the party of the black man.

She is vitally interested in slavery as a political institution, and in slaves as property. Her slaves, of right, are entitled to the status of all other property, both under the Federal Constitution and the local law; but whilst every other species of property is permitted to spread freely throughout the States and Territories, at the will of the owner, this alone is marked out for destruction, by the sentiment which called the Black Republican party into being. The basis of its organization is hatred to slavery; and so exclusively is this the case, that if the sentiment of hate were withdrawn, it would perish in an hour. It denies that the Constitution recognizes and protects slavery as property; it holds that it has the power to exclude slave property from the common Territories, in the face of an express decision of the Supreme Court of the United States; its avowed policy is, that slavery is a wrong, and to be dealt with as such; a sin for which not only the slaveholding States are responsible, but which rests also upon the non-slaveholding States; that it is to be confined in perpetual siege in the States where it now exists, and placed in a course of ultimate extinction. Its President-elect champions the sentiment that it is and must continue to be the subject of a perpetual struggle, until it prevails everywhere, or is abolished everywhere in the broad borders of the Republic.

This sentiment has taken possession of all the State Governments in the north; and, finally, in the recent Presidential election, by a purely sectional vote, has elected its candidate to the office of President. On the 4th of March next, it will be duly installed into all the chief seats of power in the Federal Union. The purse, the sword, the army, the navy, then pass into its hands. It cannot be doubted for a moment that this power will be used to the prejudice of slave property—which will then be exposed to its attacks. As property, it will not receive the fostering care of the General Government, but it will be outlawed—treated as a sin—dealt with as a wrong.

Already in a minority on this question, the secession of the cotton States leaves us in a hopeless minority. It takes not the prescience of prophecy to foretell, that in a few years, under these circumstances, if we tamely submit to the dominion of this anti-slavery spirit, that in all the boundaries of Tennessee, "the sun will not rise upon a slave, or set upon a master." Our slave property is interwoven with the whole frame work of our society, and identified with all our industrial pursuits; its destruction involves degradation and ruin. It is vain to think of protecting it under the present forms of the Constitution. Tennessee has loved the Federal Union, and fondly cherished the hope that it was destined to be perpetual; and now, surrounded by the great and impressive facts of the hour, she feels it her solemn duty to make a last effort for the reconstruction of that Union, and the protection of her honor and property therein; failing in this, she will be driven to resume her delegated powers, and unite her destiny with her sister slave States in a Southern Union.

Therefore be it resolved by the General Assembly of Tennessee,

1. That a Convention of all the slave-holding States shall assemble as early as practicable, to define and adopt a basis upon which, if possible, the Union may be reconstructed, and that in the opinion of the General Assembly of the State of Tennessee, said basis of adjustment should embrace the following propositions, as amendments to the Federal Constitution, to-wit:

1. A declaratory amendment to the Federal Constitution, to the effect that, under it African slavery as it exists in the slave States, is property, and entitled by it, as well as the local law to the States of every other species of property.
2. In all the territory of the United States now held, or hereafter acquired, situated north of latitude thirty-six degrees and thirty minutes, slavery or involuntary servitude, except as a punishment for crime, is prohibited, while such territory shall remain under territorial government. In all the territory south of said line of latitude, slavery of the African race is hereby recognized as existing, and shall not be interfered with by Congress, nor by the territorial Legislature; but shall be protected as property by all the departments of the government during its continuance; and when any territory, north or south of said line, within such boundaries as Congress may prescribe, shall contain the population requisite for a member of Congress, according to the then federal ratio of representation of the people of the United States, it shall, if its form of government be republican, be admitted into the Union on an equal footing with the original States, with or without slavery, as the Constitution of such new State may provide.
3. Congress shall have {no} power to abolish slavery in places under its exclusive jurisdiction, and situate within the limits of States that permit the holding of slaves.
4. Congress shall have no power to abolish slavery within the District of Columbia, so long as it exists in the adjoining States of Virginia and Maryland, or either, nor without the consent of the inhabitants, nor without just compensation made to such owners of slaves as do not consent to such abolishment. Nor shall Congress at any time

prohibit officers of the Federal Government or members of Congress, whose duties require them to be in said District, from bringing with them, their slaves, and holding them as such, during the time their duties may require them to remain there, and afterwards taking them from the District.

5. Congress shall have no power to prohibit or hinder the transportation of slaves from one State to another, or to a territory in which slaves are by law permitted to be held, whether that transportation be by land, navigable rivers, or by the sea.

6. That, in addition to the provisions of the third paragraph of the second section of the fourth article of the Constitution of the United States, Congress shall have power to provide by law, and it shall be its duty to so provide, that the United States shall pay to the owner who shall apply for it, the full value of his fugitive slave, in all cases, when the marshal or other officer, whose duty it was to arrest said fugitive, was prevented from so doing by violence or intimidation, or when, after arrest, said fugitive was rescued by force, and the owner thereby prevented and obstructed in the pursuit of his remedy for the recovery of his fugitive slave, under the said clause of the Constitution and the laws made in pursuance thereof. And in all such cases when the United States shall pay for such fugitive, they shall have the right, in their own name, to sue the county in which said violence, intimidation, or rescue was committed, and to recover from it, with interest and damages, the amount paid by them for said fugitive slave. And the said county, after it has paid said amount to the United States, may, for its indemnity, sue and recover from the wrong-doers, or rescuers, by whom the owner was prevented from the recovery of his fugitive slave, in like manner as the owner himself might have sued and recovered.

7. No future amendment of the Constitution shall affect the five preceding articles, nor the third paragraph of the second section of the first article of the Constitution, nor the third paragraph of the second section of the fourth article of said Constitution, and no amendment shall be made to the Constitution which will authorize or give to Congress any power to abolish or interfere with slavery in any of the States by whose laws it is or may be allowed or permitted.

8. An amendment whereby this property shall be rendered secure in transit through the non-slaveholding States, and whilst in such States temporarily sojourning with the owner.

9. For amendment to the effect, that all fugitives are to be deemed those offending the laws within the jurisdiction of the State, and who escape therefrom to other States, and that it is the duty of each State to suppress armed invasion of another State.

Source: *House Journal of the Extra Session of the Thirty-Third General Assembly of the State of Tennessee, Which Convened at Nashville, on the First Monday in January, A.D. 1861* (Nashville: J. O. Griffith, Public Printers, 1861), 63–66.

GEORGIA DELEGATE HERSCHEL VESPASIAN JOHNSON (DEMOCRAT)

January 18, 1861

The State of Georgia is attached to the Union, and desires to preserve it, if it can be done consistent with her rights and safety; but existing circumstances admonish her of danger: that danger arises from the assaults that are made upon the institution of domestic slavery, and is common to all the Southern States. . . . The Executive Department of the government is about to pass into the hands of a sectional, political party, pledged to principles and a policy which we regard as repugnant to the Constitution. . . . Therefore, whilst the State of Georgia will not and cannot, compatibly with her safety, abide permanently in the Union, without new and ample security for future safety, still she is not disposed to sever her connection with it precipitously, nor without respectful consultation with her Southern confederates. . . . Therefore,

First. *Be it ordained by the State of Georgia in sovereign Convention assembled,* That Delaware, Maryland, Virginia, Kentucky, North Carolina, Louisiana, Texas, Arkansas, Tennessee, and Missouri be and they are hereby respectfully invited to meet with this State by delegates in a Congress, at Atlanta, Georgia, on the 16th of February, 1861, to take into consideration the whole subject of their relations to the Federal Government, and to devise such a course of action as their interest, equality, and safety may require.

Section second. *Be it further ordained, &c.,* That the independent Republics of South Carolina, Florida, Alabama, and Mississippi be and they are hereby cordially invited to send Commissioners to said Congress.

Section third. *Be it further ordained,* That inasmuch as Georgia is resolved not to abide permanently in this Union without satisfactory guarantees of future security, the following propositions are respectfully suggested for the consideration of her Southern Confederates as the substance of what she regards indispensable amendments to the Constitution of the United States, to-wit:

1. That Congress shall have no power to abolish or prohibit slavery in the territories or any place under their exclusive jurisdiction.

2. Each State shall be bound to surrender fugitive slaves, and if any fugitive slave shall be forcibly taken or enticed from the possession of any officer legally charged therewith for the purpose of rendition, the United States shall pay the owner the value of such slave, and the county in which such rescue or enticement may occur, shall be liable to the United States for the amount so paid to be recovered by suit in the Federal Courts.

3. It shall be a penal offence definable by Congress and punishable in the Federal Courts for any person to rescue or entice, or to encourage, aid or assist others to rescue or entice any fugitive slave from any officer legally charged with the custody thereof, for the purpose of rendition.

4. Whatever is recognized as property by the Constitution of the United States shall be held to be property in the Territories of the United States, and in all places over which Congress has exclusive jurisdiction, and all kinds of property shall be entitled to like and equal protection therein by the several departments of the general government.

5. New States formed out of territory now belonging to the United States, or which may be hereafter acquired, shall be admitted into the Union with or without slavery as the people thereof may determine at the time of admission.

6. Congress shall have no power to prohibit or interfere with the slave trade between the States, nor to prohibit citizens of the United States passing through, or temporarily sojourning in the District of Columbia from having with them their slaves, and carrying them away, but it shall be the duty of Congress to provide by law for the punishment of all persons who may interfere with this right in the same way as is provided for in the foregoing third proposition.

7. No State shall pass any law to prohibit the citizens of any other State travelling, or temporarily sojourning therein, from carrying their slaves and returning with them; and it shall be a penal offence, definable by Congress, and punishable by the Federal Courts, for any person to entice away, or harbor, or attempt to entice away or harbor, the slave or slaves of such citizen so travelling, or temporarily sojourning.

8. The obligation to surrender fugitives from justice as provided for under the Constitution of the United States extends, and shall be held to extend as well to fugitives charged with offences connected with or committed against slavery or slave property as to any other class of offences, and for the purposes of this proposition, whatever is defined to be a criminal offence in one State shall be deemed and held a criminal offence in every other State.

9. The Supreme Court having decided that negroes are not citizens of the United States, no person of African descent shall be permitted to vote for Federal Officers, nor to hold any office or appointment under the government of the United States.

Source: *Journal of the Public and Secret Proceedings of the Convention of the People of Georgia, Held in Milledgeville and Savannah in 1861. Together with the Ordinances Adopted* (Milledgeville, Ga.: Boughton, Nisbet & Barnes, State Printers, 1861), 15–18.

PENNSYLVANIA REPRESENTATIVE THOMAS BIRCH FLORENCE (DEMOCRAT)

January 19, 1861

Mr. FLORENCE. I ask the unanimous consent of the House to have printed certain amendments which I intend to propose to the proposition made by the committee of thirty-three. I do it with the view that gentlemen may have an opportunity of reading them.

There being no objection, it was so ordered.

The amendments are as follows:

ARTICLE I. Persons held to service or labor for life in any State, under the laws thereof, may be taken into any territory of the United States south of latitude 36° 30', and the right to such service or labor shall not be impaired thereby. And any Territorial Legislature shall have the exclusive right to make all needful rules and regulations for the protection of such right, and of such persons, and for the maintenance and treatment of such persons and their descendants, in their domestic relations. But Congress or any Territorial Legislature shall not have the power to impair or abolish such right of service in the said Territory; nor in any other place within the jurisdiction of the United States, without the consent of all the States which maintain such service.

ART. II. When any Territory of the United States shall have a population equal to the ratio of representation for one member of Congress, and the people shall have formed a constitution for a republican form of government, it shall be admitted as a sovereign State into the Union, on an equal footing with the other States, by the proclamation of the President of the United States; and the people may, in the constitution for such State, either prohibit or regulate the right to labor or service, and alter and amend the constitution at their will. And if the President refuses to admit such Territory as a State, this article shall not deprive Congress of the power to admit such State.

ART. III. The present right of representation in section two, article one, of the Constitution of the United States, shall never be altered, without the consent of all the States maintaining the right to service or labor for life. And the regulation of the right to labor or service in any of the States, is hereby recognized to be exclusively the right of each State within its own limits; and this Constitution shall never be altered or amended to impair this right of each State without its consent: *Provided,* That this article shall not be construed to absolve the United States Government from rendering assistance to suppress insurrections or domestic violence, as provided in section four, article four, of this Constitution.

ART. IV. The exclusive power to regulate or abolish the right to labor or service for life in the District of Columbia, is hereby ceded to the State of Maryland, to be exercised in common with such right in that State, subject, nevertheless, to the judicial jurisdiction of the District of Columbia.

ART. V. No State shall pass any law in any way interfering with, or obstructing the recovery of fugitives from justice, or from labor or service; or any law of Congress made under article four, section two, of this Constitution; and all laws in violation of this article may be declared void by the Supreme Court of the United States, at the suit of any State.

ART. VI. As a right of comity between the citizens of the several States, the right of transit with persons held to labor or service for life, or for years, from one State to another, shall not be interfered with without the consent of all the States maintaining such service.

ART. VII. Whenever any State shall grant by law to citizens of other States the right of sojourn for a limited period with persons held to service or labor, if such persons escape, they shall be subject to recovery as fugitives under the provisions of this Constitution, and shall be returned to the State from which they were brought.

ART. VIII. The traffic in slaves with Africa is hereby forever prohibited; and the descendants of Africans shall not be made citizens.

ART. IX. All acts of any inhabitant of the United States tending to incite persons held to service or labor to insurrection or acts of domestic violence, or to abscond, shall be considered and prohibited as contrary to law and a penal offense.

ART. X. The county of any State wherein a person owing service or labor is rescued from the custody of the owner, agent, or officer, shall be bound to pay the full value of such person, for the use of the owner, at the suit of the United States.

ART. XI. Persons held to service or labor for life, under the laws of any State or Territory, shall not be taken into any Territory of the United States while in a territorial condition north of latitude 36° 30'.

ART. XII. Alleged fugitives from labor or service, on request, shall have a trial by jury at the place to which they may be returned.

ART. XIII. All alleged fugitives charged with crime committed in violation of the laws of the State from which they fled, shall, on demand, be returned to such State, and shall have the right of trial by jury; and, if such person claims to be a citizen of another State, shall have a right of appeal, or of writ of error, to the Supreme Court of the United States.

ART. XIV. Citizens of any State sojourning in another State shall not be subject to violence or punishment, nor injured in their persons or property, without trial by jury and due process of law.

ART. XV. No State, or the people thereof, shall retire from this Union without the consent of three fourths of all the States.

ART. XVI. The reserved power of the people in three fourths of the States to call and form a national convention to alter, amend, or abolish this Constitution, according to its provisions, shall never be questioned, notwithstanding the directions in article five of the Constitution.

ART. XVII. The articles eight, nine, and ten, of these amendments, shall not be altered without the consent of all the States maintaining service or labor for life.

[NOTE: Florence reiterated these resolutions on January 28, 1861 (*Congressional Globe,* 36th Cong., 2nd sess., 598; and again on February 27, 1861, appendix, 302) as a substitute to the propositions of the Committee of Thirty-Three.]

Source: *Congressional Globe,* 36th Cong., 2nd sess., 479.

Tennessee State Senate

January 22, 1861

Resolutions proposing amendments to the Constitution of the United States

1. Resolved by the General Assembly of the State of Tennessee, That a Convention of delegates from all the slaveholding States should assemble at Nashville, Tennessee, or such other place as a majority of the States co-operating may designate, on the fourth day of February, 1861, to digest and define a basis upon which, if possible, the Federal Union and the Constitutional rights of the slave States may be perpetuated and preserved.

2. Resolved, That the General Assembly of the State of Tennessee appoint a number of delegates to said Convention, of our ablest and wisest men, equal to our whole delegation in Congress; and that the Governor of Tennessee immediately furnish copies of these resolutions to the Governors of the slaveholding States and urge the participation of such States in said Convention.

3. Resolved, That in the opinion of this General Assembly, such plan of adjustment should embrace the following propositions as amendments to the Constitution of the United States:

1. A declaratory amendment that African slaves, as held under the institutions of the slaveholding States, shall be recognized as property, and entitled to the *status* of other property, in the States where slavery exists, in all places within the exclusive jurisdiction of Congress in the slave States, in all the Territories south of 36 deg. 30 min., in the District of Columbia, in transit and whilst temporarily sojourning with the owner in the nonslaveholding States, and Territories north of 36 deg. 30 min., and when fugitives from the owner, in the several places above named, as well as in all places in the exclusive jurisdiction of Congress in the nonslaveholding States.

2. That in all the territory now owned, or which may be hereafter acquired by the United States south of the parallel of 36 deg. 30 min., African slavery shall be recognized as existing, and be protected by all the departments of the Federal and Territorial Governments; and in all north of that line, now owned or to be acquired, it shall not be recognized as existing; and whenever States formed out of any of said territory south of said line, having a population equal to that of a Congressional District, shall apply for admission into the Union, the same shall be admitted as slave States;

whilst States north of the line, formed out of said territory, and having a population equal to a Congressional District, shall be admitted without slavery; but the States formed out of said territory north and south having been admitted as members of the Union, shall have all the powers over the institution of slavery possessed by the other States of the Union.

3. Congress shall have no power to abolish slavery in places under its exclusive jurisdiction, and situate within the limits of States that permit the holding of slaves.

4. Congress shall have no power to abolish slavery within the District of Columbia, as long as it exists in the adjoining States of Virginia and Maryland, or either, nor without the consent of the inhabitants, nor without just compensation made to such owners of slaves as do not consent to such abolishment. Nor shall Congress at any time prohibit the officers of the Federal Government or members of Congress whose duties require them to be in said District, from bringing with them their slaves, and holding them as such during the time their duties may require them to remain there, and afterwards taking them from the District.

5. Congress shall have no power to prohibit or hinder the transportation of slaves from one State to another, or the Territory in which slaves are by law permitted to be held, whether that transportation be by land, navigable rivers, or by sea.

6. In addition to the fugitive slave clause, provide that when a slave has been demanded of the Executive authority of the State to which he has fled, if he is not delivered, and the owner permitted to carry him out of the State in peace, that the State so failing to deliver, shall pay to the owner the value of such slave, and such damages as he may have sustained in attempting to reclaim his slave, and secure his right of action in the Supreme Court of the United States, with execution against the property of such State, and of the individuals thereof.

7. No future amendment of the Constitution shall affect the six preceding articles, nor the third paragraph of the second section of the first article of the Constitution, nor the third paragraph of the second section of the fourth article of said Constitution; and no amendment shall be made to the Constitution which will authorize or give to Congress any power to abolish or interfere with slavery in any of the States by whose laws it is, or may be allowed or permitted.

8. That slave property shall be rendered secure in transit through, or whilst temporarily sojourning in nonslaveholding States, or Territories, or in the District of Columbia.

9. An amendment to the effect, that all fugitives are to be deemed those offending the laws within the jurisdiction of the State, and who escape therefrom to other States; and that it is the duty of each State to suppress armed invasions of another State.

[Note: Resolutions passed the Tennessee legislature on January 22, 1861.]

Source: *Senate Journal of the Extra Session of the Thirty-Third General Assembly of the State of Tennessee, Which Convened at Nashville, on the First Monday in January, A.D. 1861* (Nashville: J. O. Griffith, Public Printers, 1861), 75–77. See also Lucius E. Chittenden, ed., *A Report of the Debates and Proceedings in the Secret Sessions of the Conference Convention, for Proposing Amendments to the Constitution of the United States, Held at Washington, D.C., in February, A.D. 1861* (New York: D. Appleton, 1864), 454–455. Resolutions were read to the U.S. House of Representatives on January 28, 1861; *Congressional Globe*, 36th Cong., 2nd sess., 599; House Misc. Doc. No. 27.

Tennessee State Senator John Watkins Richardson (Whig)

January 22, 1861

Mr. Richardson offered the following in lieu of the terms of adjustment as proposed in the third resolution:

Article 1. In all the territory of the United States now held, or hereafter acquired, situated North of latitude thirty-six degrees and thirty minutes, slavery or involuntary servitude, except as a punishment for crime, is prohibited, while such territory shall remain under territorial government. In all the territory South of said line of latitude slavery of the African race is hereby recognized as existing, and shall not be interfered with by Congress; but shall be protected as property by all the departments of the territorial government during its continuance; and when any territory, north or South of said line, within such boundaries as Congress may prescribe, shall contain the population requisite for a member of Congress, according to the then Federal ratio of representation of the people of the United States, it shall, if its form of government be republican, be admitted into the Union on an equal footing with the original States, with or without slavery, as the Constitution of such new State may provide.

Art. 2. Congress shall have no power to abolish slavery in places under its exclusive jurisdiction, and situate within the limits of States that permit the holding of slaves.

Art. 3. Congress shall have no power to abolish slavery within the District of Columbia, so long as it exists in the adjoining States of Virginia and Maryland, or either, nor without the consent of the inhabitants, nor without just compensation first made to such owners of slaves as do not consent to such abolishment. Nor shall Congress at any time prohibit officers of the Federal Government or members of Congress, whose duties require them to be in said District, from bringing with them their slaves, and holding them as such, during the time their duties may require them to remain there, and afterwards taking them from the District.

Art. 4. Congress shall have no power to prohibit or hinder the transportation of slaves from one State to another, or to a territory in which slaves are by law permitted to be held, whether that transportation be by land, navigable rivers, or by the sea.

Art. 5. That in addition to the provisions of the third paragraph of the second section of the fourth article of the Constitution of the United States, Congress shall have power to provide by law, and it shall be its duty to so provide, that the United States shall pay to the owner who shall apply for it the full value of his fugitive slave, in all cases, when the marshal or other officer, whose duty it was to arrest said fugitive, was prevented from so doing by violence or intimidation, or when, after arrest, said fugitive was rescued by force, and the owner thereby prevented and obstructed in the pursuit of his remedy for the recovery of his fugitive slave, under the said clause of the Constitution and the laws made in pursuance thereof. And in all such cases, when the United States shall pay for such fugitives, they shall have the right, in their own name, to sue the county in which said violence, intimidation or rescue was committed, and to recover from it, with interest and damages, the amount paid by them for said fugitive slave. And the said county, after it has paid said amount to the United States, may, for its indemnity, sue and recover from the wrongdoers, or rescuers, by whom the owner was prevented from the recovery of his fugitive slave, in like manner as the owner himself might have sued and recovered.

Art. 6. No future amendment of the Constitution shall affect the five preceding articles, nor the third paragraph of the second section of the first article of the Constitution, nor the third paragraph of the second section of the fourth article of said Constitution, and no amendment shall be made to the Constitution which shall authorize or give to Congress any power to abolish or interfere with slavery in any of the States by whose laws it is or may be allowed or permitted.

[Note: Richardson's amendment is identical to Crittenden's of December 18th. The Tennessee Senate declined Senator Richardson's substitute proposal by a vote of 16–8.]

Source: *Senate Journal of the Extra Session of the Thirty-Third General Assembly of the State of Tennessee, Which Convened at Nashville, on the First Monday in January, A.D. 1861* (Nashville: J. O. Griffith, Public Printers, 1861), 77–79.

KENTUCKY STATE SENATOR BENJAMIN P. CISSELL

January 25, 1861

Resolved by the General Assembly of the Commonwealth of Kentucky, That a convention of delegates from all the slaveholding States should assemble at Nashville, Tennessee, or such other place as a majority of the States co-operating may designate, on the 4th day of February, 1861, to digest and define the basis upon which, if possible, the Federal Union and the constitutional rights of the slave States may be perpetuated and preserved.

Resolved, That the General Assembly of Kentucky appoint a number of delegates to said convention of our ablest and wisest men, equal to our whole delegation in Congress, to be appointed in the following manner, to-wit: one from each of the Congressional districts in the State, by the joint vote of the Senators and Representatives from said districts, and the other two by the Governor, all of whom shall be by him commissioned to represent the State of Kentucky in said convention; and that the Governor of Kentucky immediately furnish copies of these resolutions to the Governors of the slaveholding States, and urge the participation of such States in said convention.

Resolved, That in the opinion of this General Assembly, such plan of adjustment should embrace the following propositions as amendments to the constitution of the United States:

First. A declaratory amendment that African slaves, as held under the institutions of the slaveholding States, shall be recognized as property, and entitled to the *status* of other property in the States where slavery exists; in all places within the exclusive jurisdiction of Congress within the slave States; in all the territories south of 36 degrees 30 minutes; in the District of Columbia; in transit and whilst temporarily sojourning with the owner in the non-slaveholding States and territories north of 36 degrees 30 minutes; and when fugitives from the owner in the several places above named, as well as in all places in the exclusive jurisdiction of Congress in the non-slaveholding States.

Second. That in all the territory now owned, or which may be hereafter acquired by the United States, south of the parallel of 36 degrees 30 minutes, African slavery shall be recognized as existing, and be protected by all the departments of the Federal and Territorial Governments; and in all north of that line, now owned or to be acquired, it shall not be recognized as existing; and whenever States formed out of any of said territory south of said line, having a population equal to that of a Congressional district, shall apply for admission into the Union, the same shall be admitted as slave States; whilst States north of the line, formed out of said territory, and having a population equal to a Congressional district, shall be admitted without slavery; but the States formed out of said territory, North and South, having been admitted as members of the Union, shall have all the powers over the institution of slavery possessed by the other States of the Union.

Third. Congress shall have no power to abolish slavery in places under its exclusive jurisdiction, and situate within the limits of States that permit the holding of slaves.

Fourth. Congress shall have no power to abolish slavery within the District of Columbia, as long as it exists in the adjoining States of Virginia and Maryland, or either, nor without the consent of the inhabitants, nor without just compensation made to such owners of slaves as do not consent to such abolishment. Nor shall Congress, at any time, prohibit officers of the Federal Government, or members of Congress whose duties require them to be in said District, from bringing with them their slaves, and holding them as such, during the time their duties may require them to remain there, and afterwards take them from the District.

Fifth. Congress shall have no power to prohibit or hinder the transportation of slaves from one State to another, or to a territory in which slaves are by law permitted to be held, whether that transportation be by land, navigable rivers, or by the sea.

Sixth. In addition to the fugitive slave clause, provide that when a slave has been demanded of the executive authority of the State to which he has fled, if he is not delivered, and the owner permitted to carry him out of the State in peace, that the State so failing, shall pay to the owner the value of such slave, and such damages as he may have sustained in attempting to reclaim his slave, and secure his right of action in the Supreme Court of the United States, with execution against the property of such State and of the individuals thereof.

Seventh. No future amendment of the constitution shall affect the six preceding articles, nor the third paragraph of the second section of the first article of the constitution, nor the third paragraph of the second section of the fourth article of said constitution, and no amendments shall be made to the constitution which will authorize or give to Congress any power to abolish or interfere with slavery in any of the States by whose laws it is or may be allowed or permitted.

Eighth. That slave property shall be rendered secure in transit through, or whilst temporarily sojourning, in non-slaveholding States or Territories, or in the District of Columbia.

Ninth. An amendment to the effect that all fugitives are to be deemed those offending the laws within the jurisdiction of the State, and who escape therefrom to other States; and that it is the duty of each State to suppress armed invasions of another State.

Source: *Journal of the Called Session of the Senate of the Commonwealth of Kentucky Begun and Held in the Town of Frankfort, on Thursday the Seventeenth Day of January, in the Year of Our Lord 1861, and of the Commonwealth the Sixty-Ninth* (Frankfort: Kentucky Yeoman Office, 1861), 83–85.

Pennsylvania Representative Edward Joy Morris (Republican)

January 30, 1861

Mr. MORRIS, of Pennsylvania, said:

Mr. SPEAKER: Great as are the perils by which the Union is surrounded, I cannot permit myself to believe that they are insurmountable, unless we are destitute of the virtues to which it owes its origin. I trust that we are not so much estranged by sectional animosities, as to be unable to agree on some plan of conciliation for the preservation of the Union. Convinced, as I am, that there is no just cause for the present troubles, and least of all in the election of Abraham Lincoln to the Presidency, I am, nevertheless, disposed to assent to any honorable plan of settlement which shall secure permanent peace between the two great sections of the country. . . .

{Representative Morris here argued that slavery would be more secure under the federal constitution than through disunion. He emphasized that the slave states had no more reason to fear interference with the institution "than they have to fear an invasion of Mongolian Tartars from the steppes of Asia."}

As I said, sir, in the outset of my remarks, I am willing to vote for any honorable plan of settlement. I do not think the Crittenden propositions, as they now stand, have any chance of adoption by Congress; but I will cheer-fully vote to refer them to the people, and abide their decision. The border State plan is less objectionable, and, if I understand it aright, I can vote for it without any compromise of principle. For the propositions of the commit-tee of thirty-three, I shall vote with great pleasure, and it seems to me they ought to satisfy every reasonable man. The admission of New Mexico as a State, as proposed, will introduce into the Union all the territory south of 36° 30', and which is at all adapted to slave labor. That slavery will be es-tablished there I doubt, as the climate and products of that Territory do not require slave labor for the development of its scanty resources. When New Mexico is admitted as a State, we shall be rid of the slavery question so far as it depends on the present territory of the United States, and there will be, I trust, a lasting peace on that troublesome question.

Should all other propositions fail, I will bring forward the following, as an amendment to the Constitution:

"Neither Congress nor a Territorial Legislature shall make any law re-specting involuntary servitude except as a punishment for crime; but Con-gress may pass laws for the suppression of the African slave trade, and for the rendition of fugitives from labor or service in the States."

The object of this amendment would be to forever banish the question of slavery from congressional or territorial legislation.

{Representative Morris concluded by arguing that he had faith in the people of the territories to decide for themselves whether or not to tolerate slavery.}

Source: *Congressional Globe*, 36th Cong., 2nd sess., January 30, 1861 (appendix), 214, 218.

ILLINOIS REPRESENTATIVE WILLIAM KELLOGG (REPUBLICAN)

February 1, 1861

Mr. KELLOGG, of Illinois. I design, at the proper time and before the final vote is taken upon the resolutions reported by the select committee of thirty-three in relation to the disturbed state of the country, to offer a resolution as a substitute for those reported from that committee. I desire, sir, now to present it to the House, that it may be printed, to enable me to offer it at the proper time.

No objection being made, the resolution was received, and ordered to be printed.

Mr. MCCLERNAND {John Alexander McClernand, Illinois}. I ask that the joint resolution may be read.

The resolution was read, as follows:

Resolved by the Senate and House of Representatives of the United States of America in Congress assembled, (two thirds of both Houses concurring,) That the following articles be, and are hereby, proposed and submitted as amendments to the Constitution of the United States, which shall be valid to all intents and purposes, as part of said Constitution, when ratified by conventions of three fourths of the several States:

ART. 13. That in all the Territory now held by the United States, situated north of latitude 36° 30', involuntary servitude, except in the punishment of crime, is prohibited, while such Territory shall remain under a territorial government. That in all the Territory now held south of said line, neither Congress nor any Territorial Legislature shall hinder or prevent the migration to said Territory of persons held to service from any States of this Union where that relation exists by virtue of any law or usage of such State, while it shall remain in a territorial condition; and when any Territory north or south of said line, within such boundaries as Congress may prescribe, shall contain the population requisite for a member of Congress, according to the then Federal ratio of representation of the people of the United States, it may, if its form of government be republican, be admitted into the Union on an equal footing with the original States, with or without the relation of persons held to service and labor, as the constitution of such new State may provide.

ART. 14. That nothing in the Constitution of the United States, or any amendment thereto, shall be so construed as to authorize any department of the Government to, in any manner, interfere with the relation of persons held to service in any State where that relation exists, nor in any manner to establish or sustain that relation in any State where it is prohibited by the laws or constitution of such State; and that this article shall not be altered or amended without the consent of every State in the Union.

ART. 15. The third paragraph of the second section of the fourth article of the Constitution shall be taken and construed to authorize and empower Congress to pass laws necessary to secure the return of persons held to service or labor under the laws of any State who may have escaped therefrom, to the party to whom such service or labor may be due.

ART. 16. The migration or importation of persons held to service or involuntary servitude into any State, Territory, or place within the United States, from any place or country beyond the limits of the United States or Territories thereof, is forever prohibited.

Source: *Congressional Globe,* 36th Cong., 2nd sess., 690.

OHIO REPRESENTATIVE CLEMENT LAIRD VALLANDIGHAM (DEMOCRAT)

February 7, 1861

Mr. VALLANDIGHAM. With the consent of the gentlemen from Maryland [Mr. DAVIS] who holds the floor, I desire to ask unanimous consent to submit the following proposed amendments to the Constitution, differing materially from any yet offered. I ask that they may be printed, and that gentlemen will be kind enough to read and consider them with candor. As soon next week as I can obtain the floor, I propose to speak in their support.

No objection being made, the joint resolution was received and ordered to be printed. It is as follows:

Joint resolution proposing amendments to the Constitution.

Whereas the Constitution of the United States is a grant of specific powers delegated to the Federal Government by the people of the several States, all powers not delegated to it nor prohibited to the States being reserved to the States respectively, or to the people; and whereas it is the tendency of stronger governments to enlarge their powers and jurisdiction at the expense of weaker governments, and of majorities to usurp and abuse power and oppress minorities, to arrest and hold in check which tendency compacts and constitutions are made; and whereas the only effectual constitutional security for the rights of minorities, whether as people or as States, is the power expressly reserved in constitutions of protecting those rights by their own action; and whereas this mode of protection by checks and guarantees is recognized in the Federal Constitution, as well as in the case of the equality of the States, in representation and in suffrage in the Senate, as in the provision for overruling the veto of the President, and for amending the Constitution, not to enumerate other examples; and whereas, unhappily, because of the vast extent and diversified interests and institutions of the several States of the Union, sectional divisions can no longer be suppressed; and whereas it concerns the peace and stability of the Federal Union and Government that a division of the States into mere slaveholding and non-slaveholding sections, causing hitherto, and from the nature and necessity of the case, inflammatory and disastrous controversies upon the subject of slavery, ending already in present disruption of the Union, should be forever hereafter ignored; and whereas this important end is best to be attained by the recognition of other sections without regard to slavery, neither of which sections shall alone be strong enough to oppress or control the others, and each be vested with the power to protect itself from aggressions: Therefore,

Be it resolved by the Senate and House of Representatives of the United States of America in Congress assembled, (two thirds of both Houses concurring,) That the following articles be, and are hereby, proposed as amendments to the Constitution of the United States, which shall be valid to all intents and purposes as part of said Constitution when ratified by conventions in three fourths of the several States:

ARTICLE XIII.

SEC. 1. The United States are divided into four sections, as follows:

The States of Maine, New Hampshire, Vermont, Massachusetts, Rhode Island, Connecticut, New York, New Jersey, and Pennsylvania, and all new States annexed and admitted into the Union, or formed or erected within the jurisdiction of any of said States, or by the junction of two or more of the same or of parts thereof, or out of territory acquired north of said States, shall constitute one section, to be known as the NORTH.

The States of Ohio, Indiana, Illinois, Michigan, Wisconsin, Minnesota, Iowa, and Kansas, and all new States annexed and admitted into the Union, or erected within the jurisdiction of any of said States, or by the junction of two or more of the same or of parts thereof, or out of territory now held or hereafter acquired north of latitude 36° 30' and east of the crest of the Rocky Mountains, shall constitute another section, to be known as the WEST.

The States of Oregon and California, and all new States annexed and admitted into the Union, or formed or erected within the jurisdiction of any of said States, or by the junction of two or more of the same or of parts thereof, or out of territory now held or hereafter acquired west of the crest of the Rocky Mountains and of the Rio Grande, shall constitute another section, to be known as the PACIFIC.

The States of Delaware, Maryland, Virginia, North Carolina, South Carolina, Georgia, Florida, Alabama, Mississippi, Louisiana, Texas, Arkansas, Tennessee, Kentucky, and Missouri, and all new States annexed and admitted into the Union, or formed or erected within the jurisdiction of any of said States, or by the junction of two or more of the same or of parts thereof, or out of territory acquired east of the Rio Grande and south of latitude 36° 30', shall constitute another section, to be known as the SOUTH.

SEC. 2. On demand of one third of the Senators of any one of the sections on any bill, order, resolution, or vote, to which the concurrence of the House of Representatives may be necessary, except on a question of adjournment, a vote shall be had by sections, and a majority of the Senators from each section voting shall be necessary to the passage of such bill, order, or resolution, and to the validity of every such vote.

SEC. 3. Two of the electors for President and Vice President shall be appointed by each State in such manner as the Legislature thereof may direct for the State at large. The other electors to which each State may be entitled shall be chosen in the respective congressional districts into which the State may at the regular decennial period have been divided, by the electors of each district having the qualifications requisite for electors of the most numerous branch of the State Legislature. A majority of all the electors in each of the four sections in this article established shall be necessary to the choice of President and Vice President; and the concurrence of a majority of the States of each section shall be necessary to the choice of President by the House of Representatives, and of the Senators from each section to the choice of Vice President by the Senate, whenever the right of choice shall devolve upon them respectively.

SEC. 4. The President and Vice President shall hold their offices each during the term of six years; and neither shall be eligible to more than one term except by the votes of two thirds of all the electors of each section, or of the States of each section, whenever the right of choice of President shall devolve upon the House of Representatives, or of the Senators from each section, whenever the right of choice of Vice President shall devolve upon the Senate.

SEC. 5. The Congress shall by law provide for the case of a failure by the House of Representatives to choose a President, and of the Senate to choose a Vice President, whenever the right of choice shall devolve upon them respectively, declaring what officer shall then act as President; and such officer shall act accordingly until a President shall be elected. The Congress shall also provide by law for a special election for President and Vice President in such case, to be held and completed within six months from the expiration of the term of office of the last preceding President, and to be conducted in all respects as provided for in the Constitution for regular elections of the same officers, except that if the House of Representatives shall not choose a President, should the right of choice devolve upon them, within twenty days from the opening of the certificates and counting of the electoral votes, then the Vice President shall act as President, as in the case of the death or other constitutional disability of the President. The term of office of the President chosen under such special election shall continue six years from the 4th day of March preceding such election.

ARTICLE XIV.

No State shall secede without the consent of the Legislatures of all the States of the section to which the State proposing to secede belongs. The President shall have power to adjust with seceding States all questions arising by reason of their secession; but the terms of adjustment shall be submitted to the Congress for their approval before the same shall be valid.

ARTICLE XV.

Neither the Congress nor a Territorial Legislature shall have power to interfere with the right of the citizens of any of the States within either of the sections to migrate upon equal terms with the citizens of the States within either of the other sections, to the Territories of the United States; nor shall either have power to destroy or impair any rights of either person or property in the Territories. New States annexed for admission into the Union, or formed or erected within the jurisdiction of other States, or by the junction of two or more States, or parts of States, and States formed with the consent of the Congress, out of any territory of the United States, shall be entitled to admission upon an equal footing with the original States, under any constitution establishing a government republican in form, which the people thereof may ordain, whenever such States shall contain, within an area of not less than thirty thousand square miles, a population equal to the then existing ratio of representation for one member of the House of Representatives.

Source: *Congressional Globe,* 36th Cong., 2nd sess., 794–795.

Connecticut Representative Orris Sanford Ferry (Republican)

February 11, 1861

Mr. FERRY asked the unanimous consent of the House to offer the following resolution:

Resolved, That the Committee on the Judiciary be instructed to inquire into the expediency of so amending the Constitution of the United States as expressly to forbid the withdrawal of any State from the Union without the consent of two thirds of both Houses of Congress, the approval of the President, and the consent of all the States; to report by joint resolution proposing such amendment, or otherwise.

Mr. WINSLOW {Warren Winslow, North Carolina} objected; and the resolution was not received.

Source: *Congressional Globe,* 36th Cong., 2nd sess., 854.

WASHINGTON PEACE CONFERENCE

February 15, 1861

{The Washington Peace Conference met at the Willard Hotel in Washington from February 4 through February 27, 1861. The conference was convened at the request of the Virginia legislature; twenty-one states sent 131 representatives. Former president John Tyler of Virginia was the presiding officer. The conference debated each article in turn. Other than the proposed articles and final votes, the material between the sections is not included.}

Mr. Guthrie {James Guthrie, Louisville, Kentucky}: That committee {General Committee upon Proposals} has given earnest and careful consideration to the subjects and propositions which have from time to time been presented to it. It has held numerous and protracted sessions, and the differences of opinion naturally existing between the members have been discussed in a spirit of candor and conciliation. The committee have not been so fortunate as to arrive at an unanimous conclusion. A majority of its members, however, have agreed upon a report which we think ought to be satisfactory to all sections of the Union, one which if adopted will, we believe, accomplish the purpose so much desired by every patriotic citizen. We think it will give peace to the country. In their behalf I have now the honor to submit, for the consideration of the Conference, the following:

Proposals of Amendment to the Constitution of the United States

Article 1. In all the territory of the United States not embraced within the limits of the Cherokee treaty grant, north of a line from east to west on the parallel of 36 degrees 30 minutes north latitude, involuntary servitude, except in punishment of crime, is prohibited whilst it shall be under a Territorial government; and in all the territory south of said line, the status of persons owing service or labor, as it now exists, shall not be changed by law while such territory shall be under a Territorial government; and neither Congress nor the Territorial government shall have power to hinder or prevent the taking to said territory of persons held to labor or involuntary service, within the United States, according to the laws or usages of the State from which such persons may be taken, nor to impair the rights arising out of said relations, which shall be subject to judicial cognizance in the federal courts, according to the common law; and when any territory north or south of said line, within such boundary as Congress may prescribe, shall contain a population required for a member of Congress, according to the then federal ratio of representation, it shall, if its form of government be republican, be admitted into the Union on an equal footing with the original States, with or without involuntary service or labor, as the Constitution of such new State may provide.

Article 2. Territory shall not be acquired by the United States, unless by treaty; nor, except for naval and commercial stations and depots, unless such treaty shall be ratified by four-fifths of all members of the Senate.

Article 3. Neither the Constitution, nor any amendment thereof, shall be construed to give Congress power to regulate, abolish, or control within any State or Territory of the United States, the relation established or recognized by the laws thereof touching persons bound to labor or involuntary service therein, nor to interfere with or abolish involuntary service in the District of Columbia without the consent of Maryland and without the consent of the owners, or making the owners who do not consent just compensation; nor the power to interfere with or prohibit representatives and others from bringing with them to the City of Washington, retaining, and taking away, persons so bound to labor; nor the power to interfere with or abolish involuntary service in places under the exclusive jurisdiction of the United States within those States and Territories where the same is established or recognized; nor the power to prohibit the removal or transportation, by land, sea, or river, of persons held to labor or involuntary service in any State or Territory of the United States to any other State or Territory thereof where it is established or recognized by law or usage; and the right during transportation of touching at ports, shores, and landings, and of landing in case of distress, shall exist. Nor shall Congress have power to authorize any higher rate of taxation on persons bound to labor than on land.

Article 4. The third paragraph of the second section of the fourth article of the Constitution shall not be construed to prevent any of the States, by appropriate legislation, and through the action of their judicial and ministerial officers, from enforcing the delivery of fugitives from labor to the person to whom such service or labor is due.

Article 5. The foreign slave-trade and the importation of slaves into the United States and their Territories, from places beyond the present limits thereof, are forever prohibited.

Article 6. The first, second, third, and fifth articles, together with this article of these amendments, and the third paragraph of the second section of the first article of the Constitution, and the third paragraph of the second section of the fourth article thereof, shall not be amended or abolished without the consent of all the States.

Article 7. Congress shall provide by law that the United States shall pay to the owner the full value of his fugitive from labor, in all cases where the marshal or other officer, whose duty it was to arrest such fugitive, was prevented from so doing by violence or intimidation, or when, after arrest, such fugitive was rescued by force, and the owner thereby prevented and obstructed in the pursuit of his remedy for the recovery of such fugitive.

Source: Lucius E. Chittenden, ed., *A Report of the Debates and Proceedings in the Secret Sessions of the Conference Convention, for Proposing Amendments to the Constitution of the United States, Held at Washington, D.C., in February,* A.D. *1861* (New York: D. Appleton, 1864), 43–45.

Virginia Delegate James Alexander Seddon (Democrat)

February 15, 1861

The report by the majority, I think, is a wide departure from the course we should have adopted. Virginia has prepared and presented a plan, and has invited this Conference to consider it. I think we ought to take up her proposal, amend and perfect them if need be, and then adopt or reject them. To avoid all misconstruction as to my individual opinions or position, I have reduced by views to writing, which, with the leave of the Conference, I will now read.

No objection being made, Mr. Seddon proceeded to read the following: Report of Mr. Seddon.

The undersigned, acting on the recommendation of the Commissioners from the State of Virginia, as a member of the committee appointed by this Convention to consider and recommend propositions of adjustment, has not been so happy as to accord with the report submitted by the majority; and as he more widely dissents from the opinions entertained by the other dissenting members, he feels constrained, in vindication of his position and opinions, to present on his part this brief report, recommending, as a substitute for the report of the majority, a proposition subjoined. To this course he feels the more impelled, by deference to the resolutions of the General Assembly of his State, inviting the assemblage of this Convention, and suggesting a basis of adjustment.

These resolutions declare, that "in the opinion of the General Assembly of Virginia the propositions embraced in the resolutions presented to the Senate of the United States by the Hon. John J. Crittenden, so modified as that the first article proposed as an amendment to the Constitution of the United States shall apply to all territory of the United States now held or hereafter acquired south of latitude 36° 30', and provided that slavery of the African race shall be effectively protected as property therein during the continuance of the territorial government, and the fourth article shall secure to the owners of slaves the right of transit with their slaves between and through the non-slaveholding States or Territories, constitute the basis of such an adjustment of the unhappy controversy which now divides the States of this Confederacy, as would be accepted by the people of the Commonwealth."

Joint Resolutions proposing certain amendments to the Constitution of the United States.

Whereas, serious and alarming dissensions have arisen between the Northern and Southern States, concerning the rights and security of the rights of the slaveholding States, and especially their rights in the common territory of the United States; and *whereas,* it is eminently desirable and proper that those dissensions, which now threaten the very existence of this Union, should be permanently quieted and settled by constitutional provisions, which shall do equal justice to all sections, and thereby restore to the people that peace and good will which ought to prevail between all the citizens of the United States: Therefore,

Resolved, by this Convention, the following articles are hereby approved and submitted to the Congress of the United States, with the request that they may, by the requisite constitutional majority of two-thirds, be recommended to the respective States of the Union, to be, when ratified by Conventions of three-fourths of the States, valid and operative as amendments of the Constitution of the Union.

Article 1. In all the territory of the United States, now held or hereafter acquired, situate north of latitude thirty-six degrees and thirty minutes, slavery or involuntary servitude, except as a punishment for crime, is prohibited, while such territory shall remain under territorial government. In all the territory south of said line of latitude, slavery of the African race is hereby recognized as existing, and shall not be interfered with by Congress, but shall be protected as property by all the departments of the territorial government during its continuance; and when any territory, north or south of said line, within such boundaries as Congress may prescribe, shall contain the population requisite for a member of Congress, according to the then federal ratio of representation of the people of the United States, it shall, if its form of government be republican, be admitted into the Union on an equal footing with the original States, with or without slavery, as the Constitution of such new State may provide.

Article 2. Congress shall have no power to abolish slavery in places under its exclusive jurisdiction, and situate within the limits of States that permit the holding of slaves.

Article 3. Congress shall have no power to abolish slavery within the District of Columbia, so long as it exists in the adjoining States of Virginia and Maryland, or either, nor without the consent of the free white inhabitants, nor without just compensation first made to such owners of slaves as do not consent to such abolishment. Nor shall Congress at any time prohibit officers of the Federal Government, or members of Congress, whose duties require them to be in said District, from bringing with them their slaves, and holding them as such during the time their duties may require them to remain there, and afterwards taking them from the District.

Article 4. Congress shall have no power to prohibit or hinder the transportation of slaves from one State to another, or to a Territory in which slaves are by law permitted to be held, whether that transportation be by land, navigable rivers, or by sea. And if such transportation be by sea, the slaves shall be protected as property by the Federal Government. And the right of transit by the owners with their slaves, in passing to or from one slaveholding State or Territory to another, between and through the non-slaveholding States and Territories, shall be protected. And in imposing direct taxes pursuant to the Constitution, Congress shall have no power to impose on slaves a higher rate of tax than on land, according to their just value.

Article 5. That, in addition to the provisions of the third paragraph of the second section of the fourth article of the Constitution of the United States, Congress shall provide by law, that the United States shall pay to the owner who shall apply for it, the full value of his fugitive slave, in all cases, when the marshal, or other officer, whose duty it was to arrest said fugitive, was prevented from so doing by violence or intimidation, or when, after arrest, said fugitive was rescued by force, and the owner thereby prevented and obstructed in the pursuit of his remedy for the recovery of his fugitive slave, under said clause of the Constitution and the laws made in pursuance thereof. And in all such cases, when the United States shall pay for such fugitive, they shall reimburse themselves by imposing and collecting a tax on the county or city in which said violence, intimidation, or rescue was committed, equal in amount to the sum paid by them, with the addition of interest and the costs of collection; and the said county or city, after it has paid said amount to the United States, may, for its indemnity, sue and recover from the wrong-doers, or rescuers, by whom the owner was prevented from the recovery of his fugitive slave, in like manner as the owner himself might have sued and recovered.

Article 6. No future amendment of the Constitution shall affect the five preceding articles, nor the third paragraph of the second section of the first article of the Constitution, nor the third paragraph of the second section of the fourth article of said Constitution, and no amendment shall be made to the Constitution which will authorize or give to Congress any power to abolish or interfere with slavery in any of the States, by whose laws it is or may be allowed or permitted.

Article 7, Sec. 1. The elective franchise and the right to hold office, whether federal, State, territorial, or municipal, shall not be exercised by persons who are, in whole or in part, of the African race.

[Note: Seddon also included herein the four resolutions Crittenden included in his proposal of December 18. Crittenden added Article 7 to his original amendment on January 3, having borrowed it from Senator Stephen Douglas's proposal of December 24, 1861. See *Congressional Globe*, 36th Cong., 2nd sess., 237 and S.R. 54.]

Source: Lucius E. Chittenden, ed., *A Report of the Debates and Proceedings in the Secret Sessions of the Conference Convention, for Proposing Amendments to the Constitution of the United States, Held at Washington, D.C., in February,* A.D. *1861* (New York: D. Appleton, 1864), 47–50.

Ohio Delegate Reuben Hitchcock (Republican)

February 22, 1861

I have an amendment in three sections which I shall offer to the report of the committee. I ask that it may be read, laid on the table, and printed.

The motion was agreed to, and the amendment read as follows:

Strike out Section 3, and insert the three following.

Sec. 3. Congress shall have no power to regulate, abolish, or control within any State the relations established or recognized by the laws thereof, touching persons held to service or labor therein.

Sec. 4. Congress shall have no power to discharge any person held to service or labor in the District of Columbia, under the laws thereof, from such service or labor, or to impair any rights, pertaining to that relation under the laws now in force within the said District, while such relation shall exist in the State of Maryland, without the consent of said State, and of those to whom the service or labor is due, or making to them just compensation therefor; nor the power to interfere with or prohibit members of Congress, and officers of the Federal Government whose duties require them to be in said District, from bringing with them, retaining, and taking away persons so held to service or labor; nor the power to impair or abolish the relations of persons owing service or labor in places under the exclusive jurisdiction of the United States, within those States and Territories where such relations are established or recognized by law.

Sec. 5. Congress shall have no power to prohibit the removal or transportation of persons held to labor or service in any State or Territory of the United States, to any State or Territory thereof, where the same obligation or liability to labor or service is established or recognized by law; and the right during such transportation, by sea or river, of touching at ports, shores, and landings, and of landing in case of distress, shall exist; nor shall Congress have power to authorize any higher rate of taxation on persons held to service or labor than on land.

Strike out Section 7, and insert:

Sec. 9. Congress shall provide by law, that in all cases where the marshal, or other officer whose duty it shall be to arrest any fugitive from service or labor, shall be prevented from so doing by violence of a mob or riotous assemblage, or where, after arrest, such fugitive shall be rescued by like violence, and the party to whom such service or labor is due shall thereby be deprived of the same, the United States shall pay to such party the full value of such service or labor.

Source: Lucius E. Chittenden, ed., *A Report of the Debates and Proceedings in the Secret Sessions of the Conference Convention, for Proposing Amendments to the Constitution of the United States, Held at Washington, D.C., in February*, A.D. *1861* (New York: D. Appleton, 1864), 270–271.

Virginia Delegate James Alexander Seddon
(Democrat)

February 23, 1861

I move to amend the substitute offered by the gentleman from Pennsylvania, by the insertion after the clause providing for the division of the territory, of the following:

All appointments to office in the Territories lying north of the line 36° 30', as well before as after the establishment of Territorial governments in and over the same, or any part thereof, shall be made upon the recommendation of a majority of the Senators representing, at the time, the non-slave-holding States. And, in like manner, all appointments to office in the Territories which may lie south of said line of 36° 30' shall be made upon the recommendation of a majority of the Senators representing, at the time, the slaveholding States. But nothing in this article shall be construed to restrain the President of the United States from removing, for actual incompetency or misdemeanor in office, any person thus appointed, and appointing a temporary agent, to be continued in office until the majority of Senators as aforesaid may present a new recommendation; or from filling any vacancy which may occur during the recess of the Senate; such appointments to continue *ad interim*. And to insure, on the part of the Senators, the selection of the most trustworthy agents, it is hereby directed that all the net proceeds arising from the sales of the public lands, shall be distributed annually among the several States, according to the combined ratio of representation and taxation; but the distribution aforesaid may be suspended by Congress, in case of actual war with a foreign nation, or imminent peril thereof.

[Note: Seddon's amendment was offered as additional language to an amendment proposed by Thomas E. Franklin, Lancaster, Pennsylvania; see page 291.]

Source: Lucius E. Chittenden, ed., *A Report of the Debates and Proceedings in the Secret Sessions of the Conference Convention, for Proposing Amendments to the Constitution of the United States, Held at Washington, D.C., in February,* A.D. *1861* (New York: D. Appleton, 1864), 328–329.

Illinois Representative William Kellogg (Republican)

February 26, 1861

I now offer, as an amendment to the amendment known as the Crittenden amendment, the following:

Strike out all after the word "that," and insert:

The following articles be, and are hereby, proposed and submitted as amendments to the Constitution of the United States, which shall be valid, to all intents and purposes, as part of said Constitution, when ratified by conventions of three fourths of the several States.

Art. 13. That in all the territory now held by the United States, situate north of latitude 36° 30', involuntary servitude, except in the punishment for crime, is prohibited while such territory shall remain under a territorial government; that in all the territory now held south of said line, neither Congress nor any Territorial Legislature shall hinder or prevent the migration to said territory of persons held to service from any State of this Union, when that relation exists by virtue of any law or usage of such State, while it shall remain in a territorial condition; and when any territory north or south of said line, within such boundaries as Congress may prescribe, shall contain the population requisite for a member of Congress, according to the then Federal ratio of representation of the people of the United States, it may, if its form of government be republican, be admitted into the Union on an equal footing with the original States, with or without the relation of persons held to service and labor, as the constitution of such new State may provide.

Art. 14. That nothing in the Constitution of the United States, or any amendment thereto, shall be so construed as to authorize any department of the Government to, in any manner, interfere with the relation of persons held to service in any State where that relation exists, nor in any manner to establish or sustain that relation in any State where it is prohibited by the laws or constitution of such State. And that this article shall not be altered or amended without the consent of every State in the Union.

Art. 15. The third paragraph of the second section of the fourth article of the Constitution shall be taken and construed to authorize and empower Congress to pass laws necessary to secure the return of persons held to service or labor under the laws of any State who may have escaped therefrom, to the party to whom such service or labor may be due.

Art. 16. The migration or importation of persons held to service or involuntary servitude into any State, Territory, or place within the United States, from any place or country beyond the limits of the United States or Territories thereof, is forever prohibited.

Art. 17. No Territory beyond the present limits of the United States and the Territories thereof, shall be annexed to or be acquired by the United States, unless by treaty, which treaty shall be ratified by a vote of two thirds of the Senate.

[Note: This is the same amendment as proposed by Kellogg on February 1 except for the addition of Article 17.]

Source: *Congressional Globe,* 36th Cong., 2nd sess., 1243.

Virginia Delegate James Alexander Seddon (Democrat)

February 26, 1861

The substitute which I propose embodies the Crittenden resolutions, with the modifications suggested by Virginia. These are principally confined to the first section, which is made to apply to our future as well as our present territory. I have modified the form of the substitute in several particulars, and now offer it without farther introduction. These are the amendments which I understand the delegation from Virginia is instructed to insist upon:

Joint Resolutions: Proposing Certain Amendments to the Constitution of the United States.

WHEREAS, serious and alarming dissensions have arisen between the Northern and Southern States, concerning the rights and security of the rights of the slaveholding States, and especially their rights in the common territory of the United States; and whereas, it is eminently desirable and proper that those dissensions, which now threaten the very existence of this Union, should be permanently quieted and settled by constitutional provisions, which shall do equal justice to all sections, and thereby restore to the people that peace and good will which ought to prevail between all the citizens of the United States: therefore,

Resolved, by this Convention, that the following articles are hereby approved and submitted to the Congress of the United States, with the request that they may, by the requisite constitutional majority of two-thirds, be recommended to the respective States of the Union, to be, when ratified by conventions of three-fourths of the States, valid and operative as amendments of the Constitution of the Union.

Article 1. In all the territory of the United States now held or hereafter acquired, situate north of latitude 36° 30', slavery or involuntary servitude, except as a punishment for crime, is prohibited, while such territory shall remain under territorial government. In all the territory now or hereafter acquired south of said line of latitude, slavery of the African race is hereby recognized as existing, and shall not be interfered with by Congress; but shall be protected as property by all the departments of the territorial government during its continuance; and when any territory, north or south of said line, within such boundaries as Congress may prescribe, shall contain the population requisite for a member of Congress, according to the then federal ratio of representation of the people of the United States, it shall, if its form of government be republican, be admitted into the Union on an equal footing with the original States, with or without slavery, as the constitution of such new State may provide.

Article 2. Congress shall have no power to abolish slavery in places under its exclusive jurisdiction, and situate within the limits of States that permit the holding of slaves.

Article 3. Congress shall have no power to abolish slavery within the District of Columbia, so long as it exists in the adjoining States of Virginia and Maryland, or either, nor without the consent of the free white inhabitants, nor without just compensation first made to such owners of slaves as do not consent to such abolishment. Nor shall Congress at any time prohibit officers of the Federal Government or members of Congress, whose duties require them to be in said District, from bringing with them their slaves and holding them, as such, during the time their duties may require them to remain there, and afterwards taking them from the District.

Article 4. Congress shall have no power to prohibit or hinder the transportation of slaves from one State to another, or to a Territory in which slaves are by law permitted to be held, whether that transportation be by land, navigable rivers, or by the sea. And if such transportation be by sea, the slaves shall be protected as property by the Federal Government. And the right of transit by the owners with their slaves in passing to or from one slaveholding State or Territory to another, between and through the non-slaveholding States and Territories shall be protected. And in imposing direct taxes pursuant to the Constitution, Congress shall have no power to impose on slaves a higher rate of tax than on land, according to their just value.

Article 5. That in addition to the provisions of the third paragraph of the second section of the fourth article of the Constitution of the United States, Congress shall provide by law, that the United States shall pay to the owner who shall apply for it, the full value of his fugitive slave, in all cases, when the marshal, or other officer, whose duty it was to arrest said fugitive, was prevented from so doing by violence or intimidation, or when, after arrest, said fugitive was rescued by force, and the owner thereby prevented and obstructed in the pursuit of his remedy for the recovery of his fugitive slave, under the said clause of the Constitution and the laws made in pursuance thereof. And in all such cases, when the United States shall pay for such fugitive, they shall reimburse themselves by imposing and collecting a tax on the county or city in which said violence, intimidation, or rescue was committed, equal in amount to the sum paid by them, with the addition of interest and the costs of collection; and the said county or city, after it has paid said amount to the United States, may, for its indemnity, sue and re-cover from the wrong-doers, or rescuers, by whom the owner was prevented from the recovery of his fugitive slave, in like manner as the owner himself might have sued and recovered.

Article 6. No future amendment of the Constitution shall affect the five preceding articles, nor the third paragraph of the second section of the first article of the Constitution, nor the third paragraph of the second section of the fourth article of said Constitution, and no amendment shall be made to the Constitution which will authorize or give to Congress any power to abolish or interfere with slavery in any of the States by whose laws it is or may be allowed or permitted.

Article 7. Sec. 1. The elective franchise and the right to hold office, whether Federal, State, territorial, or municipal, shall not be exercised by persons who are, in whole or in part, of the African race.

And whereas, also, besides those causes of dissension embraced in the foregoing amendments proposed to the Constitution of the United States, there are others which come within the jurisdiction of Congress, and may be remedied by its legislative power: and whereas it is the desire of this Convention, as far as its influence may extend, to remove all just cause for the popular discontent and agitation which now disturb the peace of the country, and threaten the stability of its institutions: Therefore,

[Note: Seddon included the four resolutions that John Crittenden attached to the end of his December 18 proposal to amend the Constitution. This amendment is almost identical to the proposal Seddon made on February 15. Crittenden added Article 7 to his original amendment on January 3, having borrowed it from Senator Stephen Douglas's proposal of December 24, 1861. See *Congressional Globe*, 36th Cong., 2nd sess., 237 and S.R. 54.]

Source: Lucius E. Chittenden, ed., *A Report of the Debates and Proceedings in the Secret Sessions of the Conference Convention, for Proposing Amendments to the Constitution of the United States, Held at Washington, D.C., in February,* A.D. *1861* (New York: D. Appleton, 1864), 418–420.

KENTUCKY DELEGATE JAMES BROWN CLAY (DEMOCRAT)

February 26, 1861

I gave notice some days ago that I should offer as a substitute the Critten-den resolutions—pure and undefiled—without the crossing of a "t" or the dotting of an "i." I now offer them as follows, and demand a vote by States:

Whereas, the Union is in danger; and owing to the unhappy divisions existing in Congress, it would be difficult, if not impossible, for that body to concur, in both its branches, by the requisite majority, so as to enable it either to adopt such measures of legislation, or to recommend to the State such amendments to the Constitution as are deemed necessary and proper to avert that danger; and whereas, in so great an emergency, the opinion and judgement of the people ought to be heard, and would be the best and surest guide to their representatives: Therefore,

Resolved, That provision ought to be made by law, without delay, for taking the sense of the people, and submitting to their vote the following resolutions as the basis for the final and permanent settlement of those dis-putes that now disturb the peace of the country and threaten the existence of the Union.

And that whereas serious and alarming dissensions have arisen between the Northern and Southern States, concerning the rights and security of the rights of the slaveholding States, and especially their rights in the common territory of the United States; and whereas, it is eminently desirable and proper that those dissensions, which now threaten the very existence of this

Union, should be permanently quieted and settled by constitutional provisions, which shall do equal justice to all sections, and thereby restore to the people that peace and good will which ought to prevail between all the citizens of the United States: Therefore,

Resolved, That the following articles be, and hereby are, proposed and submitted as amendments to the Constitution of the United States, which shall be valid to all intents and purposes as part of said Constitution, when ratified by conventions of three-fourths of the several States:

Article 1. In all the territory of the United States now held or hereafter acquired, situate north of latitude 36° 30', slavery or involuntary servitude except as a punishment for crime, is prohibited, while such territory shall remain under territorial government. In all the territory south of said line of latitude, slavery of the African race is hereby recognized as existing, and shall not be interfered with by Congress; but shall be protected as property by all the departments of the territorial government during its continuance; and when any Territory, north or south of said line, within such boundaries as Congress may prescribe, shall contain the population requisite for a member of Congress, according to the then Federal ratio of representation of the people of the United States, it shall, if its form of government be republican, be admitted into the Union on an equal footing with the original States, with or without slavery, as the constitution of such new States may provide.

Article 2. Congress shall have no power to abolish slavery in places under its exclusive jurisdiction, and situate within the limits of States that permit the holding of slaves.

Article 3. Congress shall have no power to abolish slavery within the District of Columbia, so long as it exists in the adjoining States of Virginia and Maryland, or either, nor without the consent of the inhabitants, nor without just compensation first made to such owners of slaves as do not consent to such abolishment. Nor shall Congress at any time prohibit officers of the Federal Government or members of Congress, whose duties require them to be in said District, from bringing with them their slaves, and holding them, as such, during the time their duties may require them to remain there, and afterwards taking them from the District.

Article 4. Congress shall have no power to prohibit or hinder the transportation of slaves from one State to another, or to a Territory in which slaves are by law permitted to be held, whether that transportation be by land, navigable rivers, or by the sea; and the right of transit by the owners with their slaves in passing to or from one slaveholding State or Territory to another, between and through the non-slaving States and Territories, shall be protected.

Article 5. That, in addition to the provisions of the third paragraph of the second section of the fourth article of the Constitution of the United States, Congress shall have power to provide by law, and it shall be its duty so to provide, that the United States shall pay to the owner who shall apply for it, the full value of his fugitive slave in all cases, when the marshal or other officer whose duty it was to arrest said fugitive was prevented from so doing by violence or intimidation, or when, after arrest, said fugitive was rescued by force, and the owner thereby prevented and obstructed in the pursuit of his remedy for the recovery of his fugitive slave, under the said clause of the Constitution and the laws made in pursuance thereof. And in all such cases, when the United States shall pay for such fugitive, they shall have the power to reimburse themselves by imposing and collecting a tax on the county or city in which said violence, intimidation, or rescue was committed, equal in amount to the sum paid by them, with the addition of interest and the costs of collection; and the said county or city, after it has paid said amount to the United States, may, for its indemnity, sue and recover from the wrong-doers, or rescuers, by whom the owner was prevented from the recovery of his fugitive slave, in like manner as the owner himself might have sued and recovered.

Article 6. No future amendment of the Constitution shall affect the five preceding articles, nor the third paragraph of the second section of the first article of the Constitution, nor the third paragraph of the second section of the fourth article of said Constitution; and no amendment shall be made to the Constitution which will authorize or give to Congress any power to abolish or interfere with slavery in any of the States by whose laws it is or may be allowed or permitted.

Article 7. Sec. 1. The elective franchise, and the right to hold office, whether federal, State, territorial, or municipal, shall not be exercised by persons who are, in whole or in part, of the African race.

Sec. 2. The United States shall have the power to acquire, from time to time, districts of country in Africa and South America, for the colonization, at expense of the Federal Treasury, of such free negroes and mulattoes as the several States may wish to have removed from their limits and from the District of Columbia, and such other places as may be under the jurisdiction of Congress.

And whereas, also, besides those causes of dissension embraced in the foregoing amendments proposed to the Constitution of the United States, there are others which come within the jurisdiction of Congress, and may be remedied by its legitimate power: and whereas it is the desire of this Convention, as far as its influence may extend, to remove all just cause for the popular discontent and agitation which now disturb the peace of the country, and threaten the stability of its institutions: Therefore,

[Note: Clay included the four resolutions that John Crittenden attached to the end of his December 18 proposal to amend the Constitution. Crittenden added sections 1 and 2 of Article 7 on January 3 to his original amendment after acknowledging that both were borrowed from Stephen Douglas's amendment of December 24, 1861. See *Congressional Globe*, 36th Cong., 2nd sess., January 3, 1861, 237 and S.R. 54.]

Source: Lucius E. Chittenden, ed., *A Report of the Debates and Proceedings in the Secret Sessions of the Conference Convention, for Proposing Amendments to the Constitution of the United States, Held at Washington, D.C., in February,* A.D. *1861* (New York: D. Appleton, 1864), 421–424.

VIRGINIA REPRESENTATIVE SHERRARD CLEMENS (DEMOCRAT)

February 27, 1861

Joint resolution

Whereas the Union is in danger; and owing to the unhappy divisions existing in Congress, it would be difficult, if not impossible, for that body to concur, in both its branches, by the requisite majority, so as to enable it either to adopt such measures of legislation, or to recommend to the States such amendments to the Constitution, as are deemed necessary and proper to avert that danger; and whereas, in so great an emergency, the opinion and judgement of the people ought to be heard, and would be the best and surest guide to their Representatives; Therefore,

Resolved by the Senate and House of Representatives of the United States of America in Congress assembled, That provision ought to be made by law, without delay, for taking the sense of the people, and submitting to their vote the following resolutions as the basis for the final and permanent settlement of those disputes that now disturb the peace of the country and threaten the existence of the Union.

Joint Resolutions proposing certain amendments to the Constitution of the United States.

Whereas serious and alarming dissensions have arisen between the northern and southern States, concerning the rights and security of the rights of the slaveholding States, and especially their rights in the common territory of the United States; and whereas it is eminently desirable and proper that those dissensions, which now threaten the very existence of this Union, should be permanently quieted and settled by constitutional provisions which shall do equal justice to all sections, and thereby restore to the people that peace and good will which ought to prevail between all the citizens of the United States: Therefore,

Resolved by the Senate and House of Representatives of the United States of America in Congress assembled, (two thirds of both Houses concurring,) That the following articles be, and are hereby, proposed and submitted as amendments to the Constitution of the United States, which shall be valid to all intents and purposes as part of said Constitution, when ratified by conventions of three fourths of the several States.

Art. 1. In all the territory of the United States now held or hereafter acquired, situate north of the southern boundary of Kansas and the northern boundary of New Mexico, slavery or involuntary servitude, except as a punishment for crime, is prohibited, while such territory shall remain under territorial government. In all the territory south of said line now held or hereafter acquired, slavery of the African race is hereby recognized as existing, and shall not be interfered with by Congress; but shall be protected as property by all the departments of the territorial government during its continuance; and when any Territory, north or south of said line, within such boundaries as Congress may prescribe, shall contain the population requisite for a member of Congress, according to the then Federal ratio of representation of the people of the United States, it shall, if its form of government be republican, be admitted into the Union on an equal footing with the original States, with or without slavery, as the constitution of such new State may provide.

Art. 2. Congress shall have no power to abolish slavery in places under its exclusive jurisdiction, and situate within the limits of States that permit the holding of slaves.

Art. 3. Congress shall have no power to abolish slavery within the District of Columbia so long as it exists in the adjoining States of Virginia and Maryland, or either, nor without the consent of the inhabitants, nor without just compensation first made to such owners of slaves as do not consent to such abolishment. Nor shall Congress at any time prohibit officers of the Federal Government, or members of Congress, whose duties require them to be in said District, from bringing with them their slaves, and holding them as such, during the time their duties may require them to remain there, and afterwards taking them from the District.

Art. 4. Congress shall have no power to prohibit, or hinder the transportation of slaves from one State to another, or to a Territory in which slaves are by law permitted to be held, whether that transportation be by land, navigable rivers, or by the sea.

Art. 5. That, in addition to the provisions of the third paragraph of the second section of the fourth article of the Constitution of the United States, Congress shall have power to provide by law, and it shall be its duty so to provide, that the United States shall pay to the owner who shall apply for it, the full value of his fugitive slave, in all cases, when the marshal, or other officer, whose duty it was to arrest said fugitive, was prevented from so doing by violence or intimidation, or when, after arrest, said fugitive was rescued by force, and the owner thereby prevented and obstructed in the pursuit of his remedy for the recovery of his fugitive slave, under the said clause of the Constitution and the laws made in pursuance thereof. And in all cases, when the United States shall pay for such fugitive, they shall have the power to reimburse themselves by imposing and collecting a tax on the county or city in which said violence, intimidation, or rescue was committed, equal in amount to the sum paid by them, with the addition of interest and the costs of collection; and the said county or city, after it has paid said amount to the United States, may, for its indemnity, sue and recover from the wrong-doers or rescuers, by whom the owner was prevented from the recovery of his fugitive slave, in like manner as the owner himself might have sued and recovered.

Art. 6. No future amendment of the Constitution shall affect the five preceding articles, nor the third paragraph of the second section of the first article of the Constitution, nor the third paragraph of the second section of the fourth article of said Constitution; and no amendment shall be made to the Constitution which will authorize or give to Congress any power to abolish or interfere with slavery in any of the States by whose laws it is or may be allowed or permitted.

Art. 7. Sec. 1. The elective franchise and the right to hold office, whether Federal, State, territorial, or municipal, shall not be exercised by persons who are, in whole or in part, of the African race.

Sec. 2. The United States shall have the power to acquire, from time to time, districts of country in Africa and South America, for the colonization, at the expense of the Federal Treasury, of such free negroes and mulattoes as the several States may wish to have removed from their limits, and from the District of Columbia, and such other places as may be under the jurisdiction of Congress.

And whereas also, besides those causes of dissension embraced in the foregoing amendments proposed to the Constitution of the United States, there are others which come within the jurisdiction of Congress, and may be remedied by its legislative power; and whereas it is the desire of Congress, as far as its power will extend, to remove all just cause for the popular discontent and agitation which now disturb the peace of the country and threaten the stability of its institutions: Therefore,

[Note: Clemens proposed here a duplicate of John J. Crittenden's amendment of December 18 including the four resolutions that Crittenden attached to the end of his amendment. Crittenden added sections 1 and 2 of Article 7 on January 3 to his original amendment after acknowledging that both were borrowed from Stephen Douglas's amendment of December 24, 1861. See *Congressional Globe,* 36th Cong., 2nd sess., January 3, 1861, 237. The House defeated these resolutions by a vote of 113–80.]

Source: *Congressional Globe,* 36th Cong., 2nd sess., 1260–1261.

OHIO REPRESENTATIVE THOMAS CORWIN (REPUBLICAN)

February 27, 1861

Mr. CORWIN. Before the previous question is called upon the engrossment and third reading of the joint resolution, I propose to submit the amendment which I proposed the other day.

Mr. TAPPAN {Mason Weare Tappan, New Hampshire}. I wish to make an inquiry of the Chair, with the permission of the gentleman from Ohio. [Cries of "Object!"]

The amendment was read as follows:

Strike out the amendment proposed in the joint resolution, and insert, in lieu thereof, as follows:

ART. 12. No Amendment shall be made to the Constitution which will authorize or give to Congress the power to abolish or interfere, within any

State, with the domestic institutions thereof, including that of persons held to labor or service by the laws of said State.

[Note: Corwin's amendment was approved by the U.S. House of Representatives on February 28, 1861, by a vote of 133 to 65; 1285; and by the U.S. Senate on March 4, 1861, by a vote of 24–12; 1403.]

Source: *Congressional Globe*, 36th Cong., 2nd sess., 1263.

Washington Peace Conference

February 27, 1861

The PRESIDENT:—The Conference will now proceed to the consideration of the order of the day, the proposals of amendment to the Constitution reported by the majority of the committee.

Mr. GUTHRIE {James Guthrie, Kentucky}:—I suppose, under the rules which the Conference has adopted, discussion of these proposals is no longer in order. I hope now the Conference will proceed to the vote. The opinions of each delegation are undoubtedly fixed, and cannot be changed by farther argument.

I move you, sir, the adoption of the first section of the report as amended, which I ask to have read by the Secretary.

The section was read by the Secretary, as follows:

SECTION 1. In all the present territory of the United States, north of the parallel of 36° 30' of north latitude, involuntary servitude, except in punishment of crime, is prohibited. In all the present territory south of that line, the status of persons held to involuntary service or labor, as it now exists, shall not be changed; nor shall any law be passed by Congress or the Territorial Legislature to hinder or prevent the taking of such persons from any of the States of this Union to said territory, nor to impair the rights arising from said relation; but the same shall be subject to judicial cognizance in the Federal courts, according to the course of the common law. When any Territory north or south of said line, within such boundary as Congress may prescribe, shall contain a population equal to that required for a member of Congress, it shall, if its form of government be republican, be admitted into the Union on an equal footing with the original States, with or without involuntary servitude, as the Constitution of such State may provide. (Approved by a vote of 9 to 8.)

SECTION 2. No territory shall be acquired by the United States, except by discovery, and for naval and commercial stations, depots, and transit routes, without the concurrence of a majority of all the Senators from States which allow involuntary servitude, and a majority of all the Senators from States which prohibit that relation; nor shall territory be acquired by treaty, unless the votes of a majority of the Senators from States from each class of States hereinbefore mentioned be cast as a part of the twothirds majority necessary to the ratification of such treaty. (Approved by a vote of 11 to 8.)

SECTION 3. Neither the Constitution nor any amendment thereof shall be construed to give Congress power to regulate, abolish, or control, within any State, the relation established or recognized by the laws thereof touching persons held to labor or involuntary service therein, nor to interfere with or abolish involuntary service in the District of Columbia without the consent of Maryland and without the consent of the owners, or making the owners who do not consent just compensation; nor the power to interfere with or prohibit representatives and others from bringing with them to the District of Columbia, retaining and taking away, persons so held to labor or service; nor the power to interfere with or abolish involuntary service in places under the exclusive jurisdiction of the United States within those States and Territories where the same is established or recognized; nor the power to prohibit the removal or transportation of persons held to labor or involuntary service in any State or Territory of the United States to any other State or Territory thereof, where it is established or recognized by law or usage; and the right during transportation, by sea or river, of touching at ports, shores, and landings, and of landing in case of distress, shall exist; but not the right of transit in or through any State or Territory, or of sale or traffic, against the laws thereof. Nor shall Congress have power to authorize any higher rate of taxation on persons held to labor or service than on land.

The bringing into the District of Columbia of persons held to labor or service for sale, or placing them in depots to be afterwards transferred to other places for sale as merchandise, is prohibited. (Approved by a vote of 12 to 7.)

SECTION 4. The third paragraph of the second section of the fourth article of the Constitution shall not be construed to prevent any of the States, by appropriate legislation, and through the action of their judicial and ministerial officers from enforcing the delivery of fugitives from labor to the person to whom such service or labor is due. (Approved by a vote of 15 to 4.)

SECTION 5. The foreign slave trade is hereby forever prohibited; and it shall be the duty of Congress to pass laws to prevent the importation of slaves, coolies, or persons held to service or labor, into the United States and the Territories from places beyond the limits thereof. (Approved by a vote of 16 to 5.)

SECTION 6. The first, third, and fifth sections, together with this section of these amendments, and the third paragraph of the second section of the first article of the Constitution, and the third paragraph of the second section of the fourth article thereof, shall not be amended or abolished without the consent of all the States. (Approved by a vote of 11 to 9.)

SECTION 7. Congress shall provide by law that the United States shall pay to the owner the full value of his fugitive from labor, in all cases where the marshal, or other officer, whose duty it was to arrest such fugitive, was prevented from so doing by violence or intimidation from mobs or riotous assemblages, or when, after arrest, such fugitive was rescued by like violence and intimidation, and the owner thereby deprived of the same; and the acceptance of such payment shall preclude the owner from further claim to such fugitive. Congress shall provide by law for securing to the citizens of each State the privileges and immunities of citizens in the several States. (Approved by a vote of 12 to 7.)

[Note: This amendment was first proposed on February 15, 1861 (see Chittenden, 43–45) in a different form. Also see *Congressional Globe,* 36th Cong., 2nd sess., Senate Resolution No. 70, February 28, 1861, 1269–1270. The House of Representatives declined to receive the Washington Peace Conference amendment by a vote of 93–67 on March 1, 1861; *Congressional Globe,* 36th Cong., 2nd sess., 1333. The Senate rejected the Washington Peace Conference amendment by a vote of 28–7 on March 4, 1861; *Congressional Globe,* 36th Cong., 2nd sess., 1405.]

Source: Lucius E. Chittenden, ed., *A Report of the Debates and Proceedings in the Secret Sessions of the Conference Convention, for Proposing Amendments to the Constitution of the United States, Held at Washington, D.C., in February,* A.D. *1861* (New York: D. Appleton, 1864), 440–445.

February 28, 1861

Mr. DOOLITTLE. The Senator from California will allow me to say a single word. I observe that, in his report, the State of Wisconsin is mentioned as having sent delegates to this convention, commonly denominated the peace convention {the Washington Peace Conference}. That is a mistake. I desire, also, to give notice that when this subject shall come up for consideration, I shall offer as an amendment to the first section of article thirteen, as proposed, the following proviso:

Provided, however, and this section shall take effect upon the express condition, That no State, or any part thereof, heretofore admitted, or hereafter to be admitted, into the Union, shall have power to withdraw from the jurisdiction of the United States; and that this Constitution, and all laws passed in pursuance thereof, shall be the supreme law of the land therein, anything contained in any Constitution, act, or ordinance of any State Legislature or convention to the contrary notwithstanding.

The section will then read as follows:

SEC. I. In all the present territory of the United States north of the parallel of 36° 30' of north latitude, involuntary servitude, except in punishment of crime, is prohibited. In all the present territory south of that line, the *status* of persons held to involuntary service or labor, as it now exists, shall not be changed; nor shall any law be passed by Congress or the Territorial Legislature to hinder or prevent the taking of such persons from any of the States of this Union to said territory, nor to impair the rights arising from said relation; but the same shall be subject to judicial cognizance in the Federal courts, according to the course of the common law. When any Territory north or south of said line, within such boundary as Congress may prescribe, shall contain a population equal to that required for a member of Congress, it shall, if its form of government be republican, be admitted into the Union on an equal footing with the original States, with or without involuntary servitude, as the constitution of such State may provide: *Provided, however* (and this section shall take effect upon the express condition), That no State, nor any part thereof, heretofore admitted, or hereafter to be admitted, into the Union, shall have power to withdraw from the jurisdiction of the United States; and that the Constitution, and all laws passed in pursuance thereof, shall be the supreme law of the land therein, anything contained in any constitution, act, or ordinance, of any State Legislature or convention, to the contrary notwithstanding.

Source: *Congressional Globe,* 36th Cong., 2nd sess., 1270.

OHIO SENATOR GEORGE ELLIS PUGH (DEMOCRAT)

March 2, 1861

Now, sir, I was greatly in hopes that the Senate would have allowed me, by unanimous consent, to withdraw the demand for the yeas and nays, for I should then have withdrawn the amendment, and come to something practical. As it will be necessary under the rules of the Senate, despite my wishes, that we shall come to a vote upon this verbal amendment, I shall now propose another amendment, which will be next in order, which is to strike out all after the caption, "Article thirteen," and insert what I send to the Chair. It is the Crittenden proposition. . . .

That the following articles be, and are hereafter, proposed and submitted as amendments to the Constitution of the United States, which shall be valid to all intents and purposes as part of said Constitution, when ratified by conventions of three fourths of the several States:

Article I. In all the territory of the United States now held or hereafter acquired, situate north of latitude of 36° 30', slavery or involuntary servitude, except as a punishment for crime, is prohibited while such territory shall remain under territorial government. In all the territory now held or hereafter acquired south of said line of latitude, slavery of the African race is hereby recognized as existing, and shall not be interfered with by Congress; but shall be protected as property by all the departments of the territorial government during its continuance; and when any Territory, north or south of said line, within such boundaries as Congress may prescribe, shall contain the population requisite for a member of Congress, according to the then federal ratio of representation of the people of the United States, it shall, if its form of government be republican, be admitted into the Union on an equal footing with the original States, with or without slavery, as the constitution of such new State may provide.

Article II. Congress shall have no power to abolish slavery in places under its exclusive jurisdiction and situate within the limits of States that permit the holding of slaves.

Article III. Congress shall have no power to abolish slavery within the District of Columbia so long as it exists in the adjoining States of Virginia and Maryland, or either, nor without the consent of the inhabitants, nor without just compensation first made to such owners of slaves as do not consent to such abolishment. Nor shall Congress at any time prohibit officers of the federal government or members of Congress, whose duties require them to be in said District, from bringing with them their slaves and holding them as such during the time their duties may require them to remain there, and afterwards taking them from the District.

Article IV. Congress shall have no power to prohibit, or hinder the transportation of slaves from one State to another, or to a Territory in which slaves are by law permitted to be held, whether that transportation be by land, navigable rivers, or by the sea. But the African slave trade shall be forever suppressed, and it shall be the duty of Congress to make such laws as shall be necessary and effectual to prevent the migration or importation of slaves, or persons owing service or labor, into the United States from any foreign country, place, or jurisdiction whatever.

Sec. 2. That persons committing crimes against the rights of those who hold persons to service or labor in one State, and fleeing to another, shall be delivered up in the same manner as persons committing other crimes; and that the laws of the States from which such persons flee shall be the test of criminality.

Sec. 3. Congress shall pass efficient laws for the punishment of all persons in any of the States, who shall in any manner aid and abet invasion or insurrection in any other State, or commit any other act tending to disturb the tranquility of its people, or government of any other State.

Article V. That, in addition to the provisions of the third paragraph of the second section of the fourth article of the Constitution of the United States, Congress shall have power to provide by law, and it shall be its duty so to provide, that the United States shall pay to the owner who shall apply for it, the full value of his fugitive slave in all cases when the marshal, or other officer, whose duty it was to arrest said fugitive, was prevented from so doing by violence or intimidation, or when, after arrest, said fugitive was rescued by force, and the owner thereby prevented and obstructed in the pursuit of his remedy for the recovery of his fugitive slave, under the said clause of the Constitution and the laws made in pursuance thereof. And in all such cases, when the United States shall pay for such fugitive, they shall have the power to reimburse themselves by imposing and collecting a tax on the county or city in which said violence, intimidation, or rescue was committed, equal in amount to the sum paid by them, with the addition of interest and the costs of collection; and the said county or city, after it has paid said amount to the United States, may, for its indemnity, sue and recover from the wrong-doers or rescuers, by whom the owner was prevented from the recovery of his fugitive slave, in like manner as the owner himself might have sued and recovered.

Article VI. No future amendment of the Constitution shall affect the five preceding articles, nor the third paragraph of the second section of the first article of the Constitution, nor the third paragraph of the second section of the fourth article of said Constitution; and no amendment shall be made to the Constitution which will authorize or give to Congress any power to abolish or interfere with slavery in any of the States by whose laws it is or may be allowed or permitted.

Article VII. Sec. 1. The elective franchise and the right to hold office, whether Federal, State, Territorial, or municipal, shall not be exercised by persons who are, in whole or in part, of the African race.

[Note: Crittenden's original proposal on December 18 did not contain either article IV or VII; Crittenden added article VII on January 3, 1861 (Congressional Globe, 36th Cong., 2nd sess., 237) having borrowed it from Senator Stephen Douglas's proposal of December 24. The first section of article IV also came from the Douglas amendment. Sections 2 and 3 of article IV were borrowed by Pugh from Senator Robert Toombs's proposal of December 22. The Senate rejected the amendment by a vote of 25 to 14 on March 4, 1861. *Congressional Globe*, 36th Cong., 2nd sess., 1400.]

Source: *Congressional Globe*, 36th Cong., 2nd sess., 1367–1368.

Virginia Delegate Henry Alexander Wise (Democrat)

March 9, 1861

Mr. WISE—With the assent of the gentleman from Louisa [Mr. {William M.} AMBLER], I rise to a privileged question, that of making a report from the Committee on Federal Relations, or rather a minority report. I ask leave to present my dissenting report in the form of a minority report, and which I now beg leave to read.

{Alexander Wise here listed the "wrongs" perpetrated upon the South by the non-slaveholding states and generally by the people of the North. Included among his grievances was the charge "that the Constitution of the United States has been broken."}

Thus, under the pretext of enforcing laws of the Federal Government, the jurisdiction of which is now denied and abjured by the seceding States, the nation is imminently threatened by an unnatural and unnecessary civil war; equally unnecessary, whether the Union is to be finally dissolved or restored.

These indications are made but too plainly manifest by the failure of the Conference, inaugurated by the Legislature of this Commonwealth herself, to agree on any terms of adjustment; by the disclaimer of all power on the part of the federal authorities to negotiate for peace with the commissioners of the seceded States; by the inaugural address of the incumbent President of the United States, declaring the policy, powers and purposes of his administration of the Federal Government, and supposed to represent the sentiments of large majorities of the States constituting the major section of the United States; by his failure to suggest any mode, whilst disclaiming all powers of adjustment; by the failure of Congress to recognize the results of the Peace Conference, or to recommend any other plan of peace; and by the concentration of Federal troops at various points, and the reinforcing and holding of certain forts and arsenals, with the obvious intent and purpose of overcoming any resistance to the execution of federal laws by the seceded States, and to overawe the further secession and free action of the slaveholding States.

Under these circumstances of peril to every thing precious to a State, this Commonwealth feels compelled to appeal to her confederates still remaining in the Union, and to ask for their determinate conclusions on the following points of difference and dissension, as to which she is bound to demand, and seeks to obtain satisfactory guarantees and assurances for the future:

1. As to a full recognition of the rights of property in African slaves.

2. As to slavery in the District of Columbia

3. As to the powers of the Federal Government over African slavery, and the employment of slave labor in the forts, arsenals, dock yards, and all places ceded by the States for federal uses.

4. As to protection against the pretension to lay and collect excessive *direct taxes* on slaves.

5. As to the rendition of fugitive slaves.

6. As to protection of the right and comity of transit with slaves through the limits of the States, by land or water; and of the right of transportation of slaves on the high seas.

7. The protection of the right of citizens of the United States, owning slaves to sojourn temporarily with their slaves in waiting, in the limits of non-slaveholding States.

8. The protection of equality of settlement by owners of slaves, with their slave property, in the common territories of the United States.

9. As to the rights of negroes or free persons of the African race to all the privileges and immunities of citizens of the several States.

10. As to the equality of the African race with the white race in the States where it may reside, and the protection of that equality by State laws, and by the laws of the United States.

11. As to the better security of the independence of the Judicial Department of the Government of the United States, by changing the mode of appointing the Federal Judges.

12. As to the protection of the slaveholding States against the abduction of their slaves, by repealing such State or Federal laws as may countenance the wrong, or by passing such laws by the States and by the Federal Government as may be necessary and proper to suppress it.

13. As to the protection of the domestic tranquility of the people of the United States, by suppressing the incendiary assemblages, associations and publications which have engendered the sectional wrongs and hatred which have rent the Union asunder and now threaten a civil war.

14. The protection of the public peace by suppressing societies and individual efforts for the collection of money and other means to invade the States or territories of the United States.

15. And by suppressing all organizations seeking and introducing foreign aid and influence, to incite domestic violence in any of the States or Territories of the United States.

Upon these points, and any others which may arise requiring them, this Commonwealth needs and ought to demand additional assurances and guarantees to those now existing; and those assurances and guarantees can, on the main points of dissension and severance, only be made sure by obtaining, not merely Constitutional amendments, or the pledges of States by resolves or otherwise, but by grants of power to check abuses or wrongs by a majority of the States.

Source: George H. Reese, ed., *Proceedings of the Virginia State Convention of 1861: February 13–May 1* (Richmond: Virginia State Library, 1965), 1:534, 536–537.

ARKANSAS DELEGATE HUGH FRENCH THOMASON (UNIONIST DEMOCRAT)

March 11, 1861

Mr. Thomason presented the following preamble and

RESOLUTIONS:

We, the people of the State of Arkansas, in convention assembled, in view of the unfortunate and distracted condition of our once happy and prosperous country, and of the alarming dissentions existing between the northern and southern sections thereof; and desiring that a fair and equitable adjustment of the same may be made; do hereby declare the following to be just causes of complaint on the part of the people of the southern states, against their brethren of the northern, or non-slaveholding states:

1. People of the northern states have organized a political party, purely sectional in its character, the central and controlling idea of which is hostility to the institution of African slavery, as it exists in the southern states, and that party has elected a President and Vice President of the United States, pledged to administer the government upon principles inconsistent with the rights, and subversive of the interests of the people of the southern states.

2. They have denied to the people of the southern states the right to an equal participation in the benefits of the common territories of the Union, by refusing them the same protection to their slave property therein that is afforded to other property, and by declaring that no more slave states shall be admitted into the Union.

3. They have declared that Congress possesses, under the constitution, and ought to exercise, the power to abolish slavery in the territories, in the District of Columbia, and in the forts, arsenals and dock yards of the United States, within the limits of the slaveholding states.

4. They have, in disregard of their constitutional obligations, obstructed the faithful execution of the fugitive slave laws by enactments of their state legislatures.

5. They have denied the citizens of southern states the right of transit through non-slaveholding states with their slaves, and the right to hold them while temporarily sojourning therein.

6. They have degraded American citizens by placing them upon an equality with negroes at the ballot-box.

To redress the grievances hereinbefore complained of, and as a means of restoring harmony and fraternal good will between the people of all the states, the following amendments to the constitution of the United States are proposed:

1. The President and Vice President of the United States shall each be chosen alternately from a slaveholding and non-slaveholding state—but, in no case, shall both be chosen from slaveholding or non-slaveholding states.

2. In all the territory of the United States now held, or which may hereafter be acquired, situate north of latitude 36 deg. 30 min., slavery or involuntary servitude, except as a punishment for crime is prohibited while such territory shall remain under territorial government. In all the territory now held, or which may hereafter be acquired, south of said line of latitude, slavery of the African race is hereby recognized as existing, and shall not be interfered with by Congress, but shall be protected as property by all the departments of the territorial government, during its continuance. And when any territory, north or south of said line, within such boundaries as Congress may prescribe, shall contain the population requisite for a member of Congress, according to the then federal ratio of representation of the people of the United States, it shall, if its form of government be republican, be admitted into the Union on an equal footing with the original states, with or without slavery, as the constitution of such new state may provide.

3. Congress shall have no power to legislate upon the subject of slavery, except to protect the citizen in his right of property in slaves.

4. That in addition to the provisions of the third paragraph of the second section of the fourth article of the constitution of the United States, Congress shall have power to provide, by law, and it shall be its duty so to provide, that the United States shall pay to the owner, who shall apply for it, the full value of his fugitive slave, in all cases, when the marshal, or other officer, whose duty it was to arrest said fugitive, was prevented from so doing by violence; or when, after arrest, said fugitive was rescued by force, and the owner thereby prevented and obstructed in the pursuit of his remedy for the recovery of his fugitive slave under the said clause of the constitution and the laws made in pursuance thereof. And in all such cases, when the United States shall pay for such fugitive, they shall have the right, in their own

name, to sue the county in which said violence, intimidation or rescue was committed, and to recover from it, with interest and damages, the amount paid by them for said fugitive slave. And the said county, after it has paid said amount to the United States, may, for its indemnity, sue and recover from the wrongdoers or rescuers, by whom the owner was prevented from the recovery of his fugitive slave, in like manner as the owner himself might have sued and recovered.

5. The third paragraph, of the second section of the fourth article of the constitution, shall not be construed to prevent any of the states from having concurrent jurisdiction with the United States, by appropriate legislation, and through the action of their judicial and ministerial officers, from enforcing the delivery of fugitives from labor to the person to whom such service or labor is due.

6. Citizens of slaveholding states when traveling through, or temporarily sojourning with their slaves in non-slaveholding states, shall be protected in their right of property in such slaves.

7. The elective franchise, and the right to hold office, whether federal, state, territorial or municipal, shall not be exercised by persons of the African race, in whole or in part.

8. These amendments, and the third paragraph of the second section of the first article of the constitution, and the third paragraph of the second section of the fourth article thereof, shall not be amended or abolished, without the consent of all the states.

Source: *Journal of the Convention of the State of Arkansas, Which Was Begun and Held in the Capitol, in the City of Little Rock, on Monday, the Fourth Day of March, One Thousand, Eight Hundred and Sixty-One* (Little Rock: Johnson & Yerkes, State Printers, 1861), 51–54.

Virginia Secession Convention

March 19, 1861

Mr. R. Y. CONRAD {Robert Y. Conrad, Frederick County}—The Committee on Federal Relations have had under further consideration the reports referred to them, and have directed me to make a report upon the subject of the proposed amendments to the Constitution of the United States, which

I will send to the Clerk's desk. These amendments, I may state, in general, are neither of the schemes precisely which have been submitted for the consideration of the Convention, to the extent of being properly termed either the one or the other. They are Virginia's propositions of amendments to the Constitution, combining, in view of the Committee, all the advantageous features of both of Virginia's schemes that have hitherto been before the public mind.

I move that the report be printed and referred to the Committee of the Whole.

The report was then read by the Secretary as follows:

The Committee on Federal Relations have, according to order, had under consideration sundry resolutions to them referred, and amendments proposed to the Federal Constitution, and beg leave to report the following amendments to be proposed to the Constitution of the United States, to be appended to their former report:

ARTICLE XIII

SECTION 1. In all the present territory of the United States, North of the parallel of thirty-six degrees and thirty minutes of North latitude, involuntary servitude, except in punishment of crime, is prohibited. In all the present territory South of that line, involuntary servitude, as it now exists, shall remain and shall not be changed; nor shall any law be passed by Congress or the Territorial Legislature to hinder or prevent the taking of persons held to service or labor from any of the States of this Union to said territory, nor to impair the rights arising from said relation; nor shall said rights be in any manner affected by any pre-existing law of Mexico; but the same shall be subject to judicial cognizance in the federal courts, according to the remedies and the practice of the common law. When any territory North or South of said line, within such boundary as Congress may prescribe, shall contain a population equal to that required for a member of Congress, it shall, if its form of government be republican, be admitted into the Union on an equal footing with the original States, with or without involuntary servitude, as such Constitution of the State may provide. In all territory which may hereafter be acquired by the United States involuntary servitude is prohibited, except for crime, North of the latitude of 36 deg. and 30 min., but shall not be prohibited by Congress or any Territorial Legislature South of said line.

SECTION 2. No territory shall be acquired by the United States, except by discovery and for naval and commercial stations, depots and transit routes, without the concurrence of a majority of all the Senators from States which allow involuntary servitude, and a majority of all the Senators of States which prohibit that relation; nor shall territory be acquired by treaty, unless the votes of a majority of the Senators from each class of States herein before mentioned be cast as a part of the two-thirds majority necessary to the ratification of such treaty.

SECTION 3. Neither the Constitution, nor any amendment thereof, shall be construed to give Congress power to legislate concerning involuntary servitude in any State or Territory wherein the same is acknowledged or may exist by the laws thereof, nor to interfere with or abolish the same in the District of Columbia without the consent of Maryland and Virginia, and without the consent of the owners, or making the owners who do not consent just compensation; nor the power to interfere with or prohibit representatives and others from bringing with them to the District of Columbia, retaining and taking away, persons so held to labor or service, nor the power to interfere with or abolish involuntary service in places under the exclusive jurisdiction of the United States within those States and Territories where the same is established or recognized; nor the power to prohibit the removal or transportation by land or water of persons held to labor, or involuntary service in any State or Territory of the United States to any other State or Territory thereof where it is established or recognized by law or usage; and the right during transportation, by sea or river, of touching at ports, shores and landings, and landing in case of need, shall exist, but not the right of sojourn or sale in any State or Territory, against the laws thereof. Nor shall Congress have power to authorize any higher rate of taxation on persons held to labor or service than on land.

The bringing into the District of Columbia persons held to labor or service for sale, or placing them in depots to be afterwards transferred to other places for sale as merchandise, is prohibited.

SECTION 4. The third paragraph of the second section of the fourth article of the Constitution shall not be construed to prevent any of the States, by appropriate legislation, and through the action of their judicial and ministerial officers, from enforcing the delivery of fugitives from labor to the person to whom such service or labor is due.

SECTION 5. The importation of slaves, coolies or persons held to service or labor in the United States and the Territories, from places beyond the limits thereof, is hereby forever prohibited.

SECTION 6. Congress shall provide by law that the United States shall pay to the owner the full value of his fugitive slave from labor, in all cases where the marshal, or other officer, whose duty it was to arrest such fugitive, was prevented from so doing by violence or intimidation from mobs, or riotous assemblages, or by violence, or when, after arrest, such fugitive was rescued by like intimidation or violence, and the owner thereby deprived of the same.

SECTION 7. The elective franchise and the right to hold office, whether Federal or Territorial, shall not be exercised by persons who are of the African race.

SECTION 8. No one of these amendments nor the third paragraph of the second section of the first article of the Constitution, nor the third paragraph of the second section of the fourth article thereof, shall be amended or abolished without the consent of all the States.

Source: George H. Reese, ed., *Proceedings of the Virginia State Convention of 1861: February 13–May 1* (Richmond: Virginia State Library, 1965), 2:35–37.

VIRGINIA DELEGATE ROBERT HENRY TURNER (DEMOCRAT)

March 26, 1861

The preamble I desire shall be as follows:

"Seven States having withdrawn from the Federal Union and formed a new and distinct Government, it has become necessary for Virginia, if she remains in the present Federal Union, to obtain guarantees by way of amendments to the Constitution of the United States, upon the following points."

The fact of the withdrawal, I desire to be stated as the cause of the necessity for the guarantees. That is all I wish to be stated in the preamble; that the position of Virginia, in the Northern Confederacy or the Union as it now exists, compels her to demand guarantees for her future safety. In arriving at those guarantees, I wish that they shall be such that she can remain in this Union alone; that if every other sister slave State shall withdraw, she may retain self-protecting power. I propose to show the manner in which that self-protecting power may be secured. The first point I propose is:

1st. A recognition, that by virtue of the Constitution, African slavery does exist in all the territory of the United States, and must be protected by the Federal Government.

That by virtue of the Constitution of the United States, African slavery, sir, not "involuntary servitude," not "persons held to labor," or anything else, but that "African slavery does exist in all the territory of the United States, and must be protected by the Federal Government."

The second proposition is:

2d. Upon all questions relating to the acquisition of territory a concurrent majority of the Senators in Congress from the slaveholding and non-slaveholding States shall be required. . . .

3d. With a view to settle the vexed question of the territories it is agreed that in all the territory of the United States, now held or hereafter acquired, situate North of 36 degrees 30 minutes north latitude, slavery is prohibited, and in all the territory of the United States now held or hereafter acquired South of said line, African slavery is recognized as existing, and shall receive its necessary protection as property from the various departments of the Government. . . .

4th. On all questions relating to laying taxes, duties, imposts and excises, or any other means necessary to raise revenue for the support of the General Government, a concurrent vote of a majority of the Senators in Congress, from the slaveholding and non-slaveholding States, shall be required. . . .

5th. The right of transit by the citizens of the several States with their property, slaves included, through the States and Territories.

6th. The rendition of fugitive slaves, and in case of their loss by violence or intimidation, remuneration by the General Government to the owner; and Congress shall provide for its reimbursement by laying and collecting a tax upon the State, city, or county in which said loss occurred.

7th. That Congress shall not abolish or interfere with slavery, as it now exists, in the District of Columbia; nor shall it abolish or interfere with slavery in any of the States, by whose laws it is or may be allowed or permitted.

8th. The withholding from persons who are in whole or in part of the African race, the elective franchise and the right to hold office whether Federal, State, Territorial or Municipal.

9th. Congress shall have no power to abolish slavery in places under the exclusive jurisdiction of the Federal Government, and situate within the limits of States that permit the holding of slaves.

10th. That the importation of slaves from foreign countries into the United States shall be forever prohibited.

11th. That Congress shall have no power to interfere with the slave trade between the States.

12th. That the foregoing amendments shall not be subject to repeal or modification except with the consent of all the States of the Union.

Source: George H. Reese, ed., *Proceedings of the Virginia State Convention of 1861: February 13–May 1* (Richmond: Virginia State Library, 1965), 2:389–391.

VIRGINIA DELEGATE HENRY ALEXANDER WISE (DEMOCRAT)

March 29, 1861

My impression was that they could not, and desiring to offer a series of amendments for the second part of the report of the Committee of Twenty-One, and to have these amendments, consisting of some nine or ten sections, in lieu of their eight or nine sections, I ask that the House will receive the amendments, order them to be printed for their information, and have them referred to the Committee of the Whole with the report, to be offered by me at the proper time. I ask this as a courtesy from the House for their own benefit as well as mine, that they may have an opportunity of seeing the competing propositions before they come before the Committee for consideration. I move, sir, that these amendments be received by the House, referred to the Committee of the Whole, and ordered to be printed.

The motion was agreed to.

Amendments were proposed by Mr. Wise, to propositions of the second part of the report of the Committee of Twenty-One on Federal Relations, so as to make the same read as follows:

Amendment 1st—Amend by striking out the first and second sections of the report and inserting:

Section 1. In all the present territory of the United States, involuntary servitude, as it now exists, shall remain and shall not be changed; nor shall any law be passed by Congress or the territorial legislatures to hinder or prevent the taking of persons held to service or labor, from any of the States of this Union to said territory; nor to impair the rights arising from said relation; nor shall said rights be in any manner affected by any pre-existing law of Mexico in the part acquired from her; but the same shall be protected as other rights, and be subject to judicial cognizance in the Federal Courts, according to the existing laws, and to the remedies and practice of the common law, so far as they may be consistent with each other. And when any territory, within such boundary as Congress may prescribe, shall contain a population equal to that required for a member of Congress, it shall, if its form of government be republican, be admitted into the Union on an equal footing with the original States, with or without involuntary servitude, as such Constitution of the State may provide. In all territory which may hereafter be acquired by the United States, involuntary servitude is prohibited, except for crime, north of thirty-six degrees thirty minutes, but shall not be prohibited by Congress or any territorial legislature south of that line.

Amendment 2.—Amend by striking out the 3rd section of the report and inserting:

Section 2. Neither the Constitution, nor any amendment thereof, shall be construed to give Congress power to abolish involuntary servitude in any territory; nor in the District of Columbia; nor in the sites of forts, magazines, arsenals, or other places ceded by the States to the Federal Government, within the limits of those States where involuntary servitude is established or recognized; nor within any forts, magazines, arsenals, or other places reserved within the limits of any territory for the uses of the Government of the United States; but Congress shall pass all laws necessary and proper to protect the property in persons held to service or labor, in said territory, District, or other places ceded or reserved to the United States. Nor shall any law be passed by Congress to hinder or prevent the taking of persons held to service or labor to or from the District of Columbia, or to hinder or prevent the retaining of the same within the limits thereof. Nor shall Congress have the power to prohibit the removal or transportation, by land or water, of persons held to service or labor in any State or Territory of the United States to any other State or Territory thereof, where it is established or recognized by law or usage; and the owner of property in persons held to service or labor, or his agent, shall have the right of transit through any State or Territory of the United States with such property and persons, to and from any State or territory recognizing said property by law or usage, and the right during transportation, by sea or river, of touching at ports, shores and landings, and of landing and sojourning with said property, in cases of need, temporarily, any law of any State or Territory to the contrary notwithstanding. And Congress shall not have the power to lay on persons held to service or labor in any of the States or territories of the United States any other tax than a capitation tax, to be apportioned as capitation or other direct taxes are directed to be apportioned throughout the United States according to the fourth clause of section nine of article first of the Constitution of the United States.

Amendment 3.—Amend by inserting:

Section 3. In all cases where the property in persons held to service or labor in any State or Territory of the United States, or in the District of Columbia, has been or hereafter may be taken for public use, as in cases of impressment in war or otherwise, the owner thereof shall be justly compensated as in cases of other property so taken; and in all cases involving questions of property in said persons, the rights of property in them shall be recognized and protected by the United States and their authorities as the rights of other property are recognised and protected.

Amendment 4.—Amend section 4th of the report, by adding, after the word "due," the words "and it shall be the duty," *et seq.*—so that the 4th section, as amended, shall read:

Section 4. The third paragraph of the second section of the fourth article of the Constitution shall not be construed to prevent any of the States, by appropriate legislation and through the action of their judicial and ministerial officers, from enforcing the delivery of fugitives from labor to the person to whom such service or labor is due.

And it shall be the duty of all the States to pass all laws necessary and proper to aid by their authorities, judicial and ministerial, in the execution of the laws passed by Congress for the delivery of fugitives from service or labor to the person to whom such service or labor is due. And in case the owner, or his agent, of the person held to service or labor, shall be unlawfully deprived of his property in such person by force or violence by mobs or riotous assemblages or by secret associations or conspiracies, in the limits of any State, such States shall make just compensation therefor, and it shall be the duty of Congress to provide by law for the enforcement of such compensation.

Amendment 5. Amend the 5th section of the report, by adding, after the word "prohibited," the words "Provided that" *et seq.*—so that the 5th section, as amended, shall read:

Section 5. The importation of slaves, coolies or persons held to service or labor, into the United States, and the territories from places beyond the limits thereof is hereby forever prohibited. Provided, that nothing herein contained shall be deemed to apply to the Southern States which have declared, or may hereafter declare, their separation from the Confederacy, in case their separate independence shall be acknowledged and continued.

Amendment 6. Amend by striking out the 6th section of the report.

Amendment 7. Amend by changing section 7th of the report to section 6th; and by adding, after the word "race," the words "and no person" et seq.—so that the section, as amended, shall read:

Section 6. The elective franchise and the right to hold office, whether federal or territorial, shall not be exercised by persons who are of the African race.

And no person of the African race shall be deemed and held entitled, under the Constitution of the United States, to the privileges and immunities of citizens in the several States. And the several States are prohibited from passing any laws establishing equality of the African with the white race within their limits.

Amendment 8th. Amend by inserting:

Section 7. The second clause of the second section of the second article of the Constitution of the United States shall be so amended as to take from the President of the United States the power of nominating and appointing the judges of the Supreme and other Federal Courts of the United States, and their nomination and appointment shall be vested in the Senate of the United States alone; and three-fourths of the whole number of Senators shall be required to confirm the appointments.

Amendment 9th. Amend by inserting:

Section 8. It shall be the duty of the several States, and of the Congress of the United States, within their respective jurisdictions, to pass all laws necessary and proper, to protect and preserve the domestic tranquility of the people of the several States, by suppressing all attempts of individual persons, or of assemblages, or associations to excite any portion of the people of the States to acts which will cause, or tend to cause, animosity or hostility between the various sections, or any invasions of any of the States or territories of the United States, of which will introduce or invite foreign influence to divide the Union, or which may tend to destroy the same.

Amendment 10. Amend by changing section 8th of the report to section 9th, viz:

Section 9. No one of these amendments, nor the third paragraph of the second section of the first article of the Constitution, nor the third paragraph of the second section of the fourth article thereof, shall be amended or abolished without the consent of all the States.

Source: George H. Reese, ed., *Proceedings of the Virginia State Convention of 1861: February 13–May 1* (Richmond: Virginia State Library, 1965), 2:575–579.

Virginia Delegate William Leftwich Goggin

April 4, 1861

Mr. GOGGIN's amendment was then read, as follows:

AN ORDINANCE OF THE STATE OF VIRGINIA

Whereas, the State of Virginia has made every honorable effort to restore the friendly relations which should exist between the General Government and the several States of the Union—upon terms perfectly just to all, but deeming it unnecessary to refer to the causes of complaint which have existed for a series of years, still more aggravated as those causes now are by the declared purposes of a mere sectional majority—and as all the efforts so made have proved unavailing—without reciting the differences of opinion which exist in regard to the powers of the State Government, or those of the Government of the United States, as derived from the reserved rights of the one, the constitutional authority of the other, or the inherent rights of the people, constituting a Government which seeks to protect the persons and property of those who compose and who have ordained and established it, against the abuses of such Government itself, or which arise from its connection with the Government of other States, or that of an association of States, the people of Virginia, in Convention assembled, deem it proper now to declare that the time has arrived when it becomes them to assume, as they do, their position as the people of a *sovereign independent State*.

1. Be it, therefore, ordained by the people of Virginia, and they do hereby declare, That the said State is no longer one of the Union of States known as the United States of America, and that the people of the said State owe no allegiance or duty to any Government whatever. . . .

5. Be it further declared, That the people of Virginia have ever cherished an ardent attachment for the Union and the Constitution of the United States while it was the bond of peace and fraternity; and that it can now only be restored upon the original basis by an amendment of the Constitution through the primary agency of the non-slaveholding States themselves proposing suitable and sure guarantees, and by a full and unconditional, plain and positive recognition of the rights of property in slaves, as held under the laws of any of the States; so as also to obtain satisfactory assurances and guarantees, for the future, as to slavery in the District of Columbia;

as to the powers of the Federal Government over African slavery, and the employment of slave labor in the forts, arsenals, dock yards, and all places ceded by the States for Federal uses; as to protection against excessive direct taxes on slaves; as to the rendition of fugitive slaves; as to the transit with slaves through any of the States by land or water, and of the right of transportation on the high seas of slaves from one State to another State or Territory; as to the protection of slave property in the common territories of the United States; as to the better security of the independence of the judiciary, and for protection against unjust taxation in the form of excessive imposts laid upon foreign importations.

Source: George H. Reese, ed., *Proceedings of the Virginia State Convention of 1861: February 13–May 1* (Richmond: Virginia State Library, 1965), 3:155–158.

Amendments as approved by Virginia's Secession Convention

April 13, 1861

AMENDMENTS TO THE CONSTITUTION

The first division of the report of the Committee on Federal Relations having been completed, the Committee then proceeded to consider the amendments to the Constitution of the United States, constituting the second branch of the report of the Committee on Federal Relations.

The first section was reported as follows:

"ART. XIII—SECTION 1. In all the present territory of the United States, north of the parallel of thirty-six degrees and thirty minutes of north latitude, involuntary servitude, except in punishment of crime, is prohibited. In all the present territory south of that line, involuntary servitude, as it now exists, shall remain, and shall not be changed; nor shall any law be passed by Congress or the Territorial Legislature to hinder or prevent the taking of persons held to service or labor, from any of the States of this Union to said territory, nor to impair the rights arising from said relation; nor shall said rights be in any manner affected by any pre-existing law of Mexico; but the same shall be subject to judicial cognizance in the Federal courts, according to the remedies and practice of the common law. When any Territory north or south of said line, within such boundary as Congress may prescribe, shall contain a population equal to that required for a member of Congress, it shall, if its form of government be republican, be admitted into the Union on an equal footing with the original States, with or without involuntary servitude, as such Constitution of the State may provide. In all territory which may hereafter be acquired by the United States, involuntary servitude is prohibited, except for crime, north of the latitude of thirty-six degrees and thirty minutes; but shall not be prohibited by Congress, or any Territorial Legislature south of said line."

{Approved April 13, 1861, 3:692.}

"SECTION 2. No territory shall be acquired by the United States, except by discovery and for naval and commercial stations, depots and transit routes, without the concurrence of a majority of all the Senators from States which allow involuntary servitude, and a majority of all the Senators of States which prohibit that relation; nor shall territory be acquired by treaty, unless the votes of a majority of the Senators from each class of States hereinbefore mentioned be cast as a part of the two-third majority necessary to the ratification of such treaty."

{Approved April 13, 1861, 3:710.}

"SEC. 3. Neither the Constitution, nor any amendment thereof, shall be construed to give Congress power to legislate concerning involuntary servitude in any State or Territory wherein the same is acknowledged or may exist by the laws thereof, nor to interfere with or abolish the same in the District of Columbia without the consent of Maryland and Virginia, and without the consent of the owners, or making the owners, who do not consent, just compensation; nor the power to interfere with or prohibit representatives and others from bringing with them to the District of Columbia, retaining and taking away, persons so held to labor or service, nor the power to interfere with or abolish involuntary service in places under the exclusive jurisdiction of the United States within those States and Territories where the same is established or recognized; nor the power to prohibit the removal or transportation by land or water, of persons held to labor, or involuntary service in any State or Territory of the United States to any other State or Territory thereof, where it is established or recognized by law or usage; and the right during transportation, by sea or river, of touching at ports, shores and landings, and landing in case of need shall exist, but not the right of sojourn or sale in any State or territory against the laws thereof. Nor shall Congress have power to authorize any higher rate of taxation on persons held to labor or service than on land.

"The bringing into the District of Columbia persons held to labor or service for sale, or placing them in depots to be afterwards transferred to other places for sale as merchandise, is prohibited."

{Approved April 13, 1861, 3:711.}

"[SEC. 4.] In all cases where property in persons held to service or labor in any State or Territory of the States or in the District of Columbia has been or hereafter may be taken for public use as in the case of impressment in war or otherwise, the owner thereof shall be justly compensated as in the case of other property taken; and in all cases involving the question of property in said persons, the rights of property in them shall be recognized and protected by the United States and other authorities, as rights to any other property are recognized and protected."

{Approved April 13, 1861, 3:713.}

EVENING SESSION

"SECTION 4. The third paragraph of the second section of the fourth article of the Constitution shall not be construed to prevent any of the States, by appropriate legislation, and through the action of their judicial and ministerial officers, from enforcing the delivery of fugitives from labor to the person to whom such service or labor is due."

{Approved April 13, 1861, 3:714.}

"SECTION 5. The importation of slaves, coolies or persons held to service or labor, into the United States, and the territories, from places beyond the limits thereof, is hereby forever prohibited."

{The subsequent and lengthy debate considered whether this section would allow slaves from the seceded states to be imported into the United States. To clarify the intent of the article, Henry Wise introduced the following amendment: "Provided that nothing herein contained shall be deemed to apply to the Southern States which have declared, or may hereafter declare their separation from this Confederacy, in case their separate independence shall be acknowledged and continued." After a rather heated discussion on the nature of the seceded states and whether there existed any possibility for reconciliation between the northern and southern states, the convention accepted the Wise amendment by a vote of 63–58. At this point in Virginia's deliberations, Governor John Letcher interrupted the proceedings by delivering a dispatch from Governor Francis W. Pickens of South Carolina announcing that Fort Sumter was under bombardment. Four days later the convention voted (88–55) to secede and the citizens of the state concurred on May 23 with a vote of 86 to 14 percent.}

{Approved April 13, 1861, 3:714–729.}

Source: George H. Reese, ed., *Proceedings of the Virginia State Convention of 1861: February 13–May 1* (Richmond: Virginia State Library, 1965), 3:659–660, 692, 710–711, 711, 713, 714–729.

Three Congressional Speeches

The Congressional Globe *over Secession Winter is a rich source for tak-*
ing the pulse of the nation on the brink of disunion. Republicans were
largely unwilling to compromise on the territorial issue because they had
just won a presidential election on that very subject. Democrats from the
lower southern states were unwilling to compromise because they did not
believe Northerners would abide by the terms of any adjustment. General
characterizations of the "other" reveal how far apart the two sections were
by November 1860. Political discourse furthered predetermined notions of
"fanatics" North and South, but did little to reach any common understand-
ing on the state of the nation. In that environment, no one was surprised
that substantial compromise proved elusive. Representatives from the bor-
der states demonstrated the most willingness to reach a common accord, but
found little support. The following three speeches represent the spectrum of
political sentiment on the eve of Lincoln's inauguration and provide insights
into the impasse that consumed Congress over that fateful winter.

ILLINOIS REPRESENTATIVE OWEN LOVEJOY (REPUBLICAN)

U.S. House of Representatives
January 23, 1861

Even before an antiabolitionist mob killed his brother in Alton, Illinois, Owen Lovejoy (1811–1864) had become an avowed abolitionist. Trained for the ministry, he served a Congregationalist church in Princeton, Illinois, for seventeen years before becoming a political activist. He favored the 1846 Wilmot Proviso, opposed Stephen Douglas's Kansas-Nebraska Act, and became a supporter of the nascent Republican Party. From 1856 until 1864, he agitated against slavery in the U.S. House of Representatives. He lobbied for the recruitment of black men in the U.S. Army, and after the Emancipation Proclamation he fought for equal pay for black troops. Lovejoy supported the passage of both the Homestead Act and the transcontinental railroad bill in 1862. Upon Lovejoy's death, President Lincoln eulogized him as the "best friend I had in Congress."

When Lovejoy rose to make this speech, five states had already seceded and the House Committee of Thirty-Three had concluded its deliberations. The representative from Illinois spoke against secession and compromise. The unity and permanency of the Constitution, he asserted, must be upheld or other states would threaten to leave to advance their special interests. Slavery was temporary and local, not permanent and national, he lectured. Confirming his stance as a moderate abolitionist, as were most Republicans, Lovejoy restated his opposition to abolishing slavery in the states where it already existed.

STATE OF THE UNION.

—

SPEECH OF HON. OWEN LOVEJOY,
OF ILLINOIS,
IN THE HOUSE OF REPRESENTATIVES,
January 23, 1861.

The House having under consideration the report from the select committee of thirty-three—

Mr. LOVEJOY said:

Mr. SPEAKER: I acknowledge the appropriateness and am impressed with the truth of the remark made a day or two since by the gentleman from

Virginia, [Mr. {John Singleton} MILLSON,] when he said he was embarrassed by the solemnity of uttering words under circumstances like those in which the country now finds itself. I, sir, feel that embarrassment, and I pray for that "wisdom which is from above, which is first pure and then peaceable" {James 3:17}, to direct my thoughts into right channels, and to enable me to clothe those thoughts in such language as befits the occasion and this presence—I might say, sir, without any empty compliment, this august presence; for placed as we are, with the question before us whether the glorious fabric of our Government shall be dissolved, every Representative before me is multiplied into the thousands whom he represents, till I seem to stand in the awful and august presence of thirty-two million people.

Sir, the present aspect of public affairs not only naturally suggests, but compels us to the consideration and discussion of the primary principles of our Government—a frequent recurrence to which (I think it is Jefferson who has declared) is essential to the preservation and perpetuation of public liberty. What then, Mr. Speaker, is our theory of government? It is with admirable and philosophical precision, though with extreme brevity, set forth in the declaration which our fathers made when they resorted to an appeal to arms and to the God of battles to settle the controversy which then existed between the colonies and the mother country. After laying down axiomatic principles in reference to the natural rights of man, the author of that declaration proceeds to say, that to protect these natural rights, (previously enumerated,) governments are instituted among men, deriving all their just powers from the consent of the governed, and that when a Government becomes subversive of those rights, it is the privilege and the duty of the people to alter, amend, or abolish such Government, and to reconstruct it on such principles as seem to them best adapted to promote the great purposes for which Governments are instituted—to wit, to protect the natural rights of man.

Mr. Speaker, I have heard at the other end of the Capitol, and also in this Hall, an allusion made to this subject; and as I believe there is an error very generally obtaining in regard to the purposes of government, I wish here to state what I believe is substantially true, that men entering the social or governmental state, do not surrender a portion of their rights for the purpose of securing protection to those which remain. That is not our theory of government. Our theory is this: that men enter into social or political state to secure protection for those rights, and all of those rights, unabated, undiminished, with which God, the Creator, has clothed them.

Now we come to the consideration of the question: who made this Government? By what power does it exist? Who poured into it the tide of vitality, which gave it energy and life and power? Who? Shall I answer it in accordance with the miserable dogma of secession, under the protection of which it is now sought to subvert and destroy the Government? Is it "we, the States," enter into a compact? Is it "we, the States," form a league? Is that the language? No, sir. "We, the people of the United States," for purposes enumerated, do establish and ordain the following Constitution. It is the wildest dogma of secession and treason and rebellion, by which these criminals against God and man seek to shelter themselves, that this Government is a mere rope of sand, a league, a compact, a partnership, to be dissolved at the will of any one single member of the firm. It is, "we, the people," not "we, the people of the State of South Carolina," not "we, the people of New York, Massachusetts, and Pennsylvania;" but "we, the people of the United States," one, indivisible, in our original sovereign power—subject to no one this side of the Throne of Omnipotence—we ordain and establish the following Constitution.

Now, Mr. Speaker, I do not deny—I concede readily, fully, that the people of South Carolina and the people of Georgia, a communication from whose recent Representatives we have just listened to—I concede that they have a right to alter, amend, or abolish their own State governments. They may protect slavery or abolish slavery. They may abolish all laws against murder and polygamy if they please, or they may punish these crimes by imprisonment or by hanging. They may establish a form of religion if they choose. They may declare by law that no citizen shall be eligible to office who does not belong to the established Church around which they have thrown their legal sanction. All this they can do. But, Mr. Speaker, there is one thing which the people of South Carolina cannot do: they cannot abolish the Government of the United States. They cannot dissolve the Union, for the very reason that they did not make it. They were a part of it, I grant you; they were a part of the "people of the United States"; and the citizens of a school district and of a county are a part of the people of a State; but can they meet together in school districts or town halls and abolish the State Government, by having somebody to go through the derisive mockery of absolving them from their allegiance to the laws of the State, simply because they are a part of the people who helped to make the State Government? Nobody believes that. No more can the people of South Carolina or of Georgia abolish the United States Government, or absolve their citizens from their oath of fealty and from the obligation of obedience which every one of them owes to that Government. And I insist that every citizen of those States who abjures the

Constitution, who refuses to recognize its obligations and to obey it, stands perjured before God and the civilized world.

Mr. Speaker, I now come to this question of coercion. I desire that what I have stated in regard to allegiance shall be kept in mind. It is folly, jesuitical wickedness[1] for a State to suppose it can absolve its individual citizens from their oath of fealty to the Government of the United States. The citizens of South Carolina owe a certain baron fealty {obligatory oath of loyalty} to the State; but their ultimate and highest fealty is due to the sovereign to which baron and liegeman are bound alike to bend the knee. That sovereignty is one and indivisible; and within its chartered limits ultimate and absolute; and no State has a right to absolve its citizens from their obligation.

I do not hold that the Government of the United States has any power to punish citizens of South Carolina, or Georgia, as citizens of those States; but I insist that it has very much to do with them as American citizens, living in Georgia and South Carolina, and we mean to enforce upon them their obligation to the Constitution, obedience to the laws; for the law of the United States is supreme, as the Constitution is, over the citizens of the United States, whether living in Georgia or Massachusetts.

As to this coercion, sir, it is a forcible illustration of the fable of the wolf and the lamb.[2] This cry of coercion is simply a pretext under color of which the citizens of Georgia and of South Carolina come and steal our property without even the poor excuse of having made a formal declaration of war. The title to this property vests in the Government of the United States as really, as sacredly, as the title to private property can vest in an individual. The title-deeds are in the archives of the Government. They are recorded. We own the land on which these forts stand. We built the forts. We paid for them; and they are ours. These citizens of the United States living in South Carolina and Georgia, fancying themselves absolved from their oath of allegiance by this Jesuitical process of State convention and State action, come and take possession of our forts, seize our guns, take our munitions of war; and when we propose to go and take them back, they cry, "Coercion! Coercion!" They say we are going to coerce a sovereign State of this Union; going to invade their homes, violate the sanctities of the domestic circle; and then declare—and it sounds very formidable—that they will pour out their

---

1. A form of finely tuned logical argumentation purposefully intending to mislead.

2. An Aesop fable which demonstrates that a tyrant can always find an excuse for his tyranny.

blood, every drop of it—intrench themselves behind every blade of grass and defend their wives and daughters and firesides to the very last extremity, rather than be coerced. That is, rather than let those robbers, and pirates, and traitors be taken and hung. That is the simple English of it. Coercion is simply this: When a man who has committed a crime and takes refuge in a private house, and the officers of justice come to arrest him, it will not do for the inmates of that household to interpose the sanctities of home between the law and its victim. "But what if the whole family sympathize with and justify the offender?" Then I would burn the house and hang every rebel, though a traitor dangled from every tree of an unbroken forest.

And so I say with regard to the State of South Carolina, which interposed itself between the Federal Government and the constitutional administration and execution of the Federal laws. It cannot avail itself of this cry of coercion. If they thrust themselves between the United States and the execution of its laws, and bid us defiance, and say we shall not enforce obedience to the constitutional enactments of the Federal Government, then I say that the mighty wheels of this huge Government must roll over any man, or number of men, who stand between this Government and the arrest of those who have violated its laws.

Sir, the 7th day of January, 1861, is a day long to be remembered in the annals of the American people. On that day a steamboat, called the Star of the West, was gliding over the waters of the Atlantic into one of the ports of the United States {Charleston Harbor}. A cannon-ball came hissing and skimming across its prow; the stars and stripes sprang out to the breeze—as if startled by an event so unusual—to tell the persons, whoever they might be, that fired that shot, that the vessel aimed at was under the protection of the stars and stripes. In a moment, another ball comes hissing and plunging into its sides—another, and another—and that flag, for the first time since its folds were unfurled to the breeze, turned and flapped ingloriously by the sides of the mast, and the vessel that bore it returned to the place of its departure. Never before, on the American continent, was that flag insulted. The almanacs that our children will read among the memorabilia of 1861, opposite the 7th day of January, 1861, will have written, "The American flag, for the first time, fired upon by American citizens." I do not know how others may feel, but I confess I cannot keep it out of my mind—these balls booming, hissing, disgracing, and defying the flag of the United States, burn and sting to the very quick continually.

Mr. Speaker, it is under these circumstances, with the flag of our country disgraced and insulted—never before disgraced or insulted—that we meet here to-day; and it is proposed to compromise, to concede, to conciliate. Compromise with whom? With traitors who have fired on our flag! Conciliate whom? Rebels who have bid your Government defiance! Sir, whatever I might yield under other circumstances, whatever arrangements I might make, whatever compromises I might give my vote to support, never, as God lives, will I vote for one particle of compromise until that insult is atoned, apologized for, or avenged; never!

And what are the compromises suggested? In the first place, however, who are the high contracting parties to this proposed peace arrangement and settlement of this whole question? The South and the North—slavery and freedom. Now, Mr. Speaker, it does seem to me that our experience in making compromises and settling difficulties in that mode does not afford any great encouragement to enter into any new arrangement of that nature for similar purposes; and I wish to state distinctly that, for one, I want to see this farce, comedy, or tragedy, whichever it may be, of disunion played out to the very last act. I want to know just what it is, and all that it is. The first act has been played a good many times, but we have never yet come to the fifth. We began it in 1820, when southern gentlemen rose in this Hall, left the floor, and declared they would dissolve the Union if they could not get Missouri in as a slave State. And they played a comedy again in 1832, which, if General {Andrew} Jackson had had his way, would have been a tragedy; then they played another in 1840, and again in 1850.[3] Now I say, without compromise, without conciliation, without concession, let us understand what this disunion means; and let us know in future whether South Carolina or Mississippi, or any other State, can peril the prosperity, send a thrill of mental anguish all over this country, and bring upon the thousands pecuniary ruin, just by saying, "We will dissolve the Union if you will not do so and so." It is not consistent with the honor and safety of the national Government to adopt any measures whatever for the redress of any wrong, real or imaginary, until the threat of disunion and rebellion is removed. I want to know that before I will yield any terms of compromise, concession, or conciliation. Until then my vote will be a calm, firm, decided negative. There are no wrongs to redress; and if there were, I would do nothing for their removal until this game of secession has been played out.

---

3. He is referring to Democratic aggressiveness during the 1820 Missouri Compromise, the nullification crisis of 1832, the imposition of a stringent gag rule in 1840 that prohibited even the reception of antislavery petitions by the House of Representatives, and the threat of secession in 1850.

But what are the compromises proposed? First, the {Southern Democratic candidate John C.} Breckinridge platform is to be incorporated into the Constitution; and I am to swear, when I take the oath to support the Constitution, that I will protect slavery in the Territories, and allow it unlimited expansion and perpetuity. The very proposition is an outrage to the Christian civilization of the age.

What next? Before commenting, sir, on the propositions distinctly recommended by the committee of thirty-three, I desire to allude to some remarks of the chairman, made on Monday last, when submitting their report.

That gentleman informed us that thirty years ago his career in this House began with a compromise; and he seems not unwilling that it should close in a similar manner. As the men of that period sowed the seed of future compromise, so he—unwittingly, I presume—scatters the seminal germ of a future harvest. In less than thirty years, should we now yield to the clamor of the slaveholding interest, menacing disunion, we shall have a demand for a constitutional amendment prohibiting the publication of anything from the press, or the utterance of anything from the lips, "intended" to excite servile insurrection. I know that the gentleman placed a good deal of emphasis on the word "intent." Why, sir, who has any such intent? And could they carry out such an intention? Do the slaves take papers, or listen to sermons, or hear lectures printed or uttered in the free States? Is it not forbidden in most of, if not all, the slaveholding States, to teach a slave to read even the oracles of God? Sir, this innuendo is aimed, if it have any meaning or purpose at all, at the anti-slavery literature of the free States, to the suppression of free speech, and the putting down of fanatical men like Lovejoy. [Laughter.] Criminal intent is inferred from the natural tendency of the act, and will be apparent to compromisers frightened at the cry of disunion. And we shall have United States commissioners as censors of the press, as we now have to aid in the capture of fugitive slaves.

Mr. DUNN {William McKee Dunn, Indiana}. I wish to say to the gentleman from Illinois that there is nothing in the report of the committee of thirty-three which can be construed into any proposed interference with the freedom of speech or of the press.

Mr. LOVEJOY. I did not mean to say that anything of this kind was in the report of the committee. I referred to the remarks of the gentleman from Ohio, [Mr. {Thomas} CORWIN,] and am predicting the future aggressions of the slave power if we yield to its demands now. And the disguised assault of the chairman on the anti-slavery, or even abolition press, seems to suggest and invite such aggressions. I cannot forbear, sir, turning aside a moment from the report proper, to utter my feeble voice of protest and reprobation against a suggestion even remotely looking in this direction.

I now come to the proposition as to New Mexico. What is said in defense of this? That it is not much of a compromise. The South tells us that if we subjugate them, we shall have to fight for it. But we, more amiable, subjugate ourselves and, like the servile ox, bow our necks and put on the collar they proffer, with the initials "C. C.," (compromise collar,) and bless God and "Massa" that it is no larger. We reach out our wrists for handcuffs, and console ourselves by saying, "It is not as bad as it might be; we can move our fingers a little." We voluntarily place our foot on the anvil to have the smith rivet our fetters, and chuckle over the fact that it is a trace, and not a log-chain. And, passing from the august presence of our subjugators, with collar, cuff, and chain, we rattle a *Te Deum* {Christian hymn of praise} that the collar is so narrow, the cuff so light, and the chain so small.

Sir, the whole history of these compromises should teach us that this slave power will leap over all barriers in its clamorous and insatiable demands. When anything is wanted to sustain, defend, or perpetuate its dominion, or which threatens its supremacy, nothing is necessary except to raise the cry of disunion, secession. Compromise, or we will dissolve the Union; and there will be found a Judas to betray, a Peter to deny, and a hired soldiery to drive the nails, and the form of freedom is fastened, bleeding and quivering, to the sacred wood of compromise.[4] I will {have} none of it. I demand to know— without compromise, without conciliation, and without concession—I demand to know whether I have a country; whether I have a Government; or whether thirty-two million people are to be turned out homeless and orphans upon the world, floating like waifs upon the ocean, without any government, and without any protection, unless they hold it at the mercy of some single State of this Union, or worse still, at the nod of the slave power.

We were reminded, sir, of an ancestral name by the speech of the gentleman from Virginia [Mr. {Sherrard} CLEMENS] yesterday—a very excellent speech, by the way. It was intimated in that speech that it would be worthy of a certain gentleman on this floor to lead off in this compromise. I would be glad—if it be not improper, and I know it is not, for nothing that I say is prompted by any other feelings than those of kindness, respect, and esteem—I would be glad to say that there was an old revolutionary hero who declared: "Live or die, sink or swim, survive or perish, I am for this

---

4. Stark comparison to *The Last Supper* and Crucifixion of Christ during which Judas betrayed Jesus for a handful of coins and Peter denied knowing him.

resolution."[5] Sir, it was in this spirit that the nation was born, and it is in this spirit that it must be born again, or saved, and not by your temporizing policy, not by concessions, not by conciliation. Gentlemen of the North, of the South, and of the whole Union, it is your interest, as it is mine, to know whether you have a Government that has any stability or not.

Mr. Speaker, I want to say a word to my Republican brethren. [Laughter.] Gentlemen, Representatives, you are asked to desert the party and the principles which you were proud to uphold before the people, and when you entered this House at the opening of the session; and the question is, shall we abandon the cardinal article of our faith—prohibition of slavery in the Territories of the United States, and the Federal Government released from its dictation and control? Perhaps this drift towards a compromise foreshadows a purpose to organize a new party, "sloughing off," as the phrase is, the extremes, both North and South. In this new arrangement all the radicals like myself are to be left out. I wish you a merry time of it, my masters. A very interesting play, Hamlet with Hamlet left out! There never was a party that had such a golden opportunity since the organization of the Government, as we had at the beginning of the session. What we needed was unity, firmness, decision. If we had stood still, we should ere this have seen the salvation of God. We ought to have imitated Rarey[6] as he stands in the center of the inclosure with an untamed and infuriated horse, sweeping around in still narrowing circles; anon, with ears laid back, nostrils distended, and open mouth, he rushes toward that immovable man; the spectators tremble, and a wave of fearful anxiety sweeps over the multitude; but the horse-tamer, without the twinge of a muscle, keeps his eye fixed on that of the infuriated animal; and the latter, though he comes close to his master, does not touch him, but turns again to dart around the enclosure, again to rush toward his master, but not to touch him; and this process is repeated till this noble animal comes and bows his neck to the hand of his subduer, overcome by the magic power of calmness, self-possession, and a firm will.

So with this disunion Mazeppa.[7] It was very furious, and covered itself with foam, and threatened to devour us. Its very fury and precipitancy proved its conscious weakness and fear. If we had been cool, calm, self-pos-

---

5. Quote ascribed to John Adams in a speech by Daniel Webster given a month after Adams's death on July 4, 1826.

6. John Solomon Rarey (1827–1866) was a renowned horse whisperer from Ohio.

7. A narrative poem written by Lord Bryon (1788–1824) in 1819 in which Mazeppa is punished for having an affair with a countess by being strapped naked to a wild horse.

sessed, doing nothing to conciliate on the one hand, and nothing to irritate on the other, we should have had, ere now, a strap around the leg of this disunion courser. But no; like the old Whigs, having achieved a victory, we were affrighted at our own success, even as the witch of Endor[8] fell aghast before the venerable form she had conjured up. We appointed a committee of compromise—a grave mistake for us, a carnival for the Democracy, affording them a possible opportunity of reconstructing, what was, but for our folly, an irrecoverably lost party. If we had only known in that our day the things which belonged to our peace. [Laughter.] Solomon {son of David, king of Israel} says, "In vain is the snare set in the sight of any bird" {Proverbs 1:17}; but I doubt, though his researches seem to have been extensive, if he ever fell in with that species of the feathered tribe described by modern naturalists as the gull.

But the premier, as he is called, is for a compromise, I am told. I do not know, and will not believe that, until I am obliged to; although I confess, instead of philosophical and polished essays, sailing like a beautiful barge around Point-no-point, I wish the Cicero of the American Senate had turned his eye on the Catiline of Georgia, and said, in the abrupt and vehement invective of the Roman consul, "*Quousque tandem abutere, Catilina, patientia nostra!*"[9]

It is said that our President elect is for compromise. This I do not, cannot, and never will believe, until I have it from his own lips or his own acts. I know he has too much regard for the common appellation by which he is familiarly known, of "Honest Old Abe," ever to believe that he will betray the principles of the Republican party, which were made distinctly and squarely in the last campaign, of inflexible, unalterable opposition to the extension of human slavery. But, sir, even if it were true that the President elect and future Cabinet advise compromise, I will not follow their lead one step. If they or an angel from Heaven preach any other Republican gospel than that which was proclaimed at Chicago, let them be *anathema maranatha* {1 Corinthians 16:22}—accursed till the people come to curse them. For all the

---

8. The Witch of Endor was an eleventh-century medium who summoned the spirit of the prophet Samuel at the demand of King Saul of Israel.

9. The quote translates as "When, O Catiline, do you mean to cease abusing our patience?" In 63 BC, the Roman senator Marcus Tullius Cicero accused Lucius Sergius Catiline of plotting to overthrow the Roman government. In this case, it is unclear to whom Lovejoy was referring. Georgia's senators over Secession Winter were Robert Toombs and Alfred Iverson Sr. Both withdrew from Congress after Georgia seceded on January 19, 1861.

batons of earth, and all the diadems of Heaven, I would not, in their place, betray or disappoint the hopes of the people whose confidence and suffrages have placed them in power.

Under the leadership of no man or angel, by the entreaties of no friends, by the threats of no enemies, by no hope of reward or fear of proscription, will I ever yield the millionth part of a hair more guarantee to this slave power, at any time; and, were it otherwise, I would not until we settle the question whether we have a Government or not. The spider's most attenuated thread is cord, is cable, to that gossamer line that I will yield in the way of compromise or concession to the claims of slavery. [Laughter.] I wanted to say a good many kind things in this speech. [Renewed laughter.]

Mr. JOHN COCHRANE {New York}. I move that the gentleman's time be extended.

Mr. WINSLOW {Warren Winslow, North Carolina}. I object.

Mr. LOVEJOY. I must pass over some things. I was paying my regards to the Republican party. I repeat, that we made the issue squarely, distinctly, without hypocrisy or disguise, before the people, and they decided that a President should be elected who was opposed to the extension of human slavery. They elected him in a constitutional mode; and all that we ask is, that he shall be inaugurated. And let me tell you, gentlemen, who are friends of compromise, who want these differences settled, let me tell you that one twelve months of the administration of Abraham Lincoln will do more to disabuse the public mind than all the compromises and peace measures that can be patched up in Congress. Let him have a trial, and fair trial. We will abate not one jot of our principle, or add anything to our creed.

I think I know something of the anti-slavery feeling of the people. It is earnest, religious, ineradicable; it may be deceived, but cannot be annihilated; it will spring up from discomfiture with irrepressible elasticity and strength; it is law-abiding and loyal to the Constitution; but it has resolved that this Government shall not be administered under the control of the slaveholding power. If disappointed as to the ultimate results of the recent election, God has raised up the man who will lead it to substantial success. His home overlooks the river called Beautiful. One who, to the sagacity of New York, and the honesty of Illinois, adds the firmness of Jackson, the statesmanship of Pitt, the religious sentiment of Wilberforce, and the administrative ability of William of Orange.[10] The people, by their suffrages,

---

10. William Pitt, the 1st Earl of Chatham (1708–1778), was a British statesman who supported the position of the colonies in the run up to the American Revolution. William

will bear him to the Executive chair, when freedom's hopes will not be disappointed, nor her purposes thwarted by the timidity of the fearful nor the treachery of the corrupt.

Sir, it is said that this Republican party is in favor of the abolition of slavery in the States. The Republican party are in favor of no such thing. "Well, but LOVEJOY is," as I have heard it whispered around here. I merely wish to repeat—and I am willing to do so for the thousandth time, if it is necessary to disabuse the public mind—that I am not in favor of abolishing slavery in the States where it exists by any act of Congress. I never held to that doctrine, and never advocated it. If a bill were brought in here for that purpose to-day, I would not vote for it; because I do not think that the Constitution gives us the power to abolish it; and not because I do not wish to see it abolished, for God knows that I do. I want to see despotism abolished everywhere. I want to see slavery abolished in South Carolina; but it does not follow, therefore, that I would vote to have the Army and Navy go down there and abolish it. I want to see it abolished in the slave States; and if I were a native of Maryland, Virginia, Kentucky, Tennessee, or any of the slave States, I would vote to abolish it. Washington has said as much; and I hope there is nothing criminal in my now saying it.

But the Republican party do not believe, there is not a man who voted for Lincoln who believes, that we have the constitutional power to abolish slavery in the States where it now exists; and I do not suppose there is one who desires that that power should be exercised unconstitutionally, as we hold it is. I am willing, if it will not be thought tedious, to go over this question of equality which my Democratic friends in Illinois and I have gone over so often. "You are in favor of negro equality." No, we are not; not in the sense which you mean. I believe this: that all men are created equal, and that every human being has an equal title to life, liberty, and the fruits of an honest toil. That I do believe. But we do not hold that they are socially equal, or that they are necessarily politically equal, or intellectually equal. We claim that the poorest and the lowest human being who bears God's image, and was redeemed by the blood of Christ, has a right to liberty, life, and the fruits of his labor. This we do believe; at least I do. The chairman of the

---

Wilberforce (1759–1833) was an English abolitionist who led the fight for ending the British slave trade and supported the campaign to abolish slavery throughout the British Empire. William of Orange (1650–1702) became king of England in 1689 and began moving the country from the personal rule of his predecessors to a more Parliament-centered government.

committee, the other day, speaking of the distinction which was insisted on between *persons* and *property,* said mirthfully that we might, if we chose, call it divinity or theology. This, though not so intended, I know, seemed to be in mockery of four million human beings that were lying prostrate around him, crushed, bleeding, and hopeless. There is one glorious being {Jesus Christ} who never derides the sufferings of the poor and lowly. On His thigh and on His vesture is written the blessed and only Potentate, King of Kings and Lord of Lords. This exalted personage humbled Himself and came down, till He nestled beside the lowest form, the most degraded type of humanity, and whispered in accents of divine love, "my brother." We might as well mock at the bloody agony of Christ, as to jeer at the miseries of the poor slave.

The Union men of the border States, it is said, want something to stand upon. I am willing to disabuse the minds of the people of the southern States; and more than that, I am willing to go and canvass those States, if you will guaranty my personal safety. [Laughter.] This remark excites a smile; but I insist upon it, Mr. Speaker, that had I been permitted to go into either of those States, Maryland, Virginia, Tennessee, Kentucky, and especially Kentucky—for I have many constituents from that State who came to me after hearing me speak during the last campaign, with a warm greeting of hand and tongue, saying they were as strong and as ultra Abolitionists as myself—I would have given them all the vantage ground they desired. If the Union men of the slave States want something to stand upon, I will give them the Constitution of the United States. It seems to me, if I were known there, or had the advantage of being a native-born citizen of one of those States, I could take those stars and stripes, and waving them before the multitude, tell them it was the flag that {George} Washington followed; the flag which led on the soldiers of the Revolution, while tracking their pathway in blood; that it was the flag which floated over Yorktown {Virginia} and Saratoga {New York}; the flag beneath which {Thomas} Sumter and {Francis} Marion fought {during the American Revolution}; the flag that was bathed in a flood of glory on the lakes, and guided the hero of the Hermitage {Andrew Jackson} in 1812 and 1815 {during the War of 1812} and still later, coming to that gorge of the mountain at Buena Vista {during the war with Mexico}, where armed foes poured down in almost countless hosts; I would tell them that northern soldiers and southern soldiers, side by side, followed that flag and snatched victory from the very jaws of defeat. I know I could turn back this insane mania of disunion.

Mr. HINDMAN {Thomas C. Hindman, Arkansas}. Will the gentleman allow me a question?

Mr. LOVEJOY. Certainly.

Mr. HINDMAN. Would the gentleman, at the same time, tell those people, that while they and his fellow-citizens won those territories by the joint expenditure of blood and treasure, he and his party would not permit them to remove with their slave property into the domain of the United States so acquired?

Mr. LOVEJOY. Certainly I would. I might thank the gentleman for that question. Yes, sir; I would say to the citizens of the slave States that I believe in the equality of the States; that I believe in the equality of the citizens of the States; that I believe that the citizens of South Carolina, Tennessee, and Arkansas have the same right to go into the Territories as the citizens of New York, Pennsylvania, or Massachusetts. I would say that neither one of them could carry their slaves there; and, therefore, they are still upon an equality. They can go there without their slaves and we can go there without slaves, and we are upon a perfect equality in regard to that matter. But let me say that the Territories are for your free non-slaveholding population, who want them free States, as we do. Southern Illinois was settled by that class of people. Southern Indiana was settled by that class of people. If I recollect aright, only about two million are interested in slave property, while the other six million, and all the millions of the free States, are interested in having free States.

Besides that, I want to ask the gentleman another question. Would he like to carry anything into the Territories that would keep the citizens of the free States from going there? If slavery goes into the Territories, the citizens of the free States will not go there.

Mr. HINDMAN. The ancestors of the gentleman, I believe, lived under the jurisdiction of States which recognized the institution of slavery; and I am not aware that any of them emigrated because of the existence of slavery in any of the thirteen States.

But the gentleman says he desires to know whether I wish to take into the Territories any property or institution which would exclude northern men from going there. I desire to take into the Territories of the Union the property recognized by the constitution of my State. I feel that I am entitled to go with it there with my fellow-citizens; and I am not content to yield up that right, under any circumstances whatever, in reference to any portion of the Territories of this Government. If northern men will allow that to prevent them from emigrating there, it is an indulgence upon their part, and an idle fantasm, in behalf of which I am not bound to sacrifice my rights.

Mr. LOVEJOY. I need not go into a discussion of that point. I might argue it from the single stand-point of property. It certainly is not competent for a State to enact any laws in regard to property which are going to operate and be enforced in any territory outside of that State where the laws are enacted. If a man is prohibited, as he is in Indian territory, from taking there many things which are recognized as property in New York, he still might go there, but could not expect to carry with him the local laws of the State from which he went. A State might abolish all laws against a plurality of wives. Could a citizen of such State take a harem to the Territories?

Mr. HINDMAN. Will the gentleman allow me a moment?

Mr. LOVEJOY. I have but little time. Shall I have an extension?

Mr. WINSLOW {Warren Winslow, North Carolina}. I object.

Mr. LOVEJOY. I hope the gentleman will not take up my time.

Mr. HINDMAN. I acknowledge that I have consumed a portion of the gentleman's time, and I trust the House will allow him as much time as I have consumed.

Mr. LOVEJOY. But I must pass on from this point. I desire to get it distinctly before the House, if I can, that whether compromises are, in the nature of things, desirable and necessary or not, still, at the present time, it is wholly improper and utterly perilous to the country, to enter into any compromise whatever. Every nation has some nucleus thought, some central idea, which they enshrine, and around which they cluster and fasten. The old Roman citizen had his Capitol and his Pantheon; France has her Napoleon and military glory; England has her constitutional monarchy; and the old Jews had their temple and shekinah. The American people, sir, have this one central idea or thought, embalmed and enshrined as a nucleus thought, around which they all cluster, and to which they all adhere with a spirit of superstitious idolatry: the Union, the Constitution, the flag of their country, are a sort of trinity, to which the American people pay political homage and worship.

And now, I insist, in this time of peril, of agitation, and rebellion, it is no time to tamper with that holy instrument around which all American hearts cluster, and to which they cling with the tenacity of a semi-religious attachment. Do this, and by and by Pennsylvania, if she cannot have protection of her coal and iron, which is her negro, will dissolve the Union. If New York is denied free trade, she will encircle the brow of her mayor with the diadem and place the scepter in his hand. If Massachusetts fails to obtain her fishing bounties, she will secede. If Maine cannot have protection to her lumber and fishing interests, she will dissolve the Union. Michigan, I believe, wants the St. Clair flats cleared; and if you do not comply with her wishes in this regard, she will throw herself upon her sovereignty, dissolve the Union, and shed so much blood that the ensanguined tide shall pour over Niagara's rocks, and the fishermen at the mouth of the St. Lawrence will be startled with the reddened ripple around the prow of their boats, as was the mariner on the Mediterranean when the waters of Egypt were turned into blood. Illinois wants protection of her beef; or, what is more likely, she will not consent to pay tribute to Pennsylvania every time she shoes a horse or sharpens a plow. Oregon demands the payment of her war debt, or she will throw off her allegiance. California demands the building of a Pacific railroad, or she will erect a Pacific republic. And so, sir, this grand fabric of our Government, baptized in our fathers' blood, and handed down to us to be in turn bequeathed to our children, is at the beck and mercy of any State that is disaffected or displeased in regard to some Federal legislation, or, more preposterous still, in reference to some State enactments. We are like sea-weed, waifs on the ocean, without anchorage, with no common rallying point around which to cluster, where our hearts can center, and where we can say: "In life or death, in weal or woe, sunshine or storm, we are for the flag of our country, our Constitution, and our Union." In this the hour of our peril, whatever may be our dissensions, it is unpatriotic and unstatesmanlike to place all the glories of the past, all the immense and varied interests of the present, and all the glorious hopes of the future, at the mercy and caprice of any one State in this Union. I think it is the highest statesmanship now, here, in this very year of our Lord 1861, to settle this question, without compromise, without concession, without conciliation: have we a Government that is permanent and fixed, and that will protect and shelter us?

Mr. Speaker, {Napolean} Bonaparte said, while standing on the sands of Egypt, near the Pyramids, "forty centuries are looking down upon us."[11] Representatives, more than forty centuries are looking down upon us. The past, the present, the future—thirty million, forty million, fifty million, rising up to one hundred million, who are to come and live and pass away upon American soil—all these are looking upon us; and standing in the presence of that cloud of witnesses, and speaking for them all, I say, "Maintain

11. From a speech to his troops in Egypt on July 21, 1798.

your Government pure and simple, without compromise, and establish the fact that it is permanent, stable, potent—a Government that must be obeyed at home, that thus it may be respected abroad."

Mr. Speaker, the American Congress has a higher and nobler mission than to be engaged in the sacrilegious work of sacrificing the rights of freedom to the interests of slavery. Slavery is temporary; slavery is local; by the action of the slave States it will pass away, as it has passed away in New York and Pennsylvania. It is proposed that we shall declare, by a constitutional amendment, that we will never touch slavery in the States; and you have heard what I have to say about that. But suppose that Maryland, or Virginia, or Kentucky, or Tennessee, want to touch it; suppose they want us to pay them something, and they will emancipate their slaves: by this proposed amendment you bind the Federal Government, and tie the hands of the States, and say that they shall not do anything of the sort, unless every single slave State consents to it. Virginia, Maryland, Kentucky, and Tennessee are all to be placed in the power of the Gulf States, who want to perpetuate this practice forever. It will not do, gentlemen. The interests now trembling on your decision are too momentous, too valuable, too far-reaching, for us to tamper or trifle with them, or to alter or amend in one single iota that great charter of American liberty, the Constitution of the United States.

Sir, it is a crime to make shipwreck of this Government. Let the American people who made this Government preserve it consecrated to freedom. Let the great principles which underlie it travel in the greatness of their strength and the fullness of their beneficence round the globe; and when the earth is encircled with an ocean of republics fashioned after our own, and freedom's temple is complete, and the topstone is brought in with shoutings of "freedom and glory unto it," high, in letters of light, on the living stones of which that temple is built, shall be written: THE AMERICAN REPUBLIC—*The American Constitution,* as having taught the people of the earth that man's inalienable birthright was FREEDOM.

Source: *Congressional Globe,* 36th Cong., 2nd sess., appendix, 84–87.

Missouri Representative John Richard Barret
(Democrat)

U.S. House of Representatives
February 21, 1861

A graduate of St. Louis University, John Richard Barret (1825–1903) represented St. Louis County in the Missouri House of Representatives before being elected to Congress as a Democrat in 1858. In this exceptional and revealing speech, Barret chastises Republicans as "red-mouthed Abolitionists" and "small demagogues and pitiful pettifoggers" who are unnecessarily endangering the "very existence of the Union," while at the same time presenting a logical case against secession. Secession, he argues, "cannot render slave property more secure." Representing a slave state and a border state, Barret makes a compelling case for compromise.

STATE OF THE UNION.

—

SPEECH OF HON. J. R. BARRET,

OF MISSOURI,

IN THE HOUSE OF REPRESENTATIVES,

February 21, 1861.

The House having under consideration the report from the select committee of thirty-three—

Mr. BARRET said:

Mr. SPEAKER: In 1783, George Washington, in a letter to the Governors of the several States, used the following language:

"There are four things which I humbly conceive are essential to the well-being, I may even venture to say to the existence, of the United States as an independent power: 1. An indissoluble Union under our Federal head. 2. A sacred regard for public justice. 3. The adoption of a proper peace regulation. 4. The prevalence of that pacific and friendly disposition among the people of the United States which will induce them to forget their local politics and prejudices."

In 1787, acting upon this advice from the Father of his Country, whom to love was the delight of the whole nation, the people of the United States, in order to form a more perfect Union, establish justice, insure domestic tranquility, provide for the common defense, promote the general welfare, and secure the blessings of liberty to themselves and their posterity, did ordain and establish our blessed Constitution. To say that those who formed that sacred instrument were good and great is not enough. They seemed inspired from above—special messengers from the very throne of the Eternal; bearers of the high and holy mission of teaching to all the earth the true doctrines of self-government.

The Constitution, as a peace regulation, would, in all things, be complete; and the Union thus formed, under one Federal head, would be indissoluble, if there existed a sacred regard for public justice and such a friendly and pacific feeling among the people as to induce them to forget their local politics and prejudices.

George Washington seemed impressed with this idea when, in 1796, he, in the most affectionate, solemn, and earnest manner, warned his countrymen against every attempt to alienate one portion of the people from the rest, and enjoined upon all the constant love of liberty, and especially the preservation of the unity of the Government, as the palladium of our political safety and prosperity.[12]

In utter disregard of the warnings and injunctions, in direct conflict with the spirit of the Constitution and the principles of public justice, a party was formed in the North, founded entirely upon local politics and prejudices, and with the avowed object of making war upon southern institutions. And in 1820, upon the application of Missouri for admission as a State, an issue, based upon geographical discriminations, was directly made, which endangered, even at that early day, the very existence of the Union. It may be well to call attention to the views of Mr. Jefferson, upon this proposition and the party making it, as he is one of the *fathers of the Republic,* to whom this anti-slavery party now delight to refer.

In a letter to Mr. Monroe {President James Monroe}, of March 3, 1820, he says:

"The Missouri question is the most portentous one which ever threatened our Union. In the gloomiest moment of the revolutionary war, I never had an apprehension equal to that I felt from this source."

---

12. Washington's Farewell Address (September 17, 1796) prophetically warned against political parties and geographical divisions among the people. Barret may well have had this sentence in mind when he gave his speech: "I have already intimated to you the danger of parties in the State, with particular reference to the founding of them on geographical discriminations. Let me now take a more comprehensive view, and warn you in the most solemn manner against the baneful effects of the spirit of party generally."

PART FIVE

In his writings, volume seven, he says:

"The question is a mere party trick; the leaders of Federalism, defeated in their schemes of obtaining power, by rallying partisans to the principle of monarchism—a principle of personal, not of local division—have changed their tact and thrown out another barrel to the whale. They are taking advantage of the virtuous feeling of the people to effect a division of parties by geographical lines; they expect this will insure them, on local principles, the majority they could never obtain on principles of Federalism."

In a letter to Mr. {John} Adams, January 22, 1821, he says:

"What does the holy alliance, in and out of Congress, mean to do with us on the Missouri question? And this, by the way, is but the name of the case: it is only the John Doe and Richard Roe of the ejectment. {Ejectment is a legal term.} The real question, as seen in the States afflicted with this unfortunate population is 'are our slaves to be presented with freedom and a dagger?' For if Congress has the power to regulate the conditions of the inhabitants of the States within the States, it will be but the exercise of that power to declare that all shall be free."

In a letter to La Fayette {Marquis de Lafayette, French supporter of the American Revolution}, November 4, 1823, he says:

"On the eclipse of Federalism with us, although not its extinction, its leaders got up the Missouri question under the false front of lessening the measure of slavery, but with the real view of producing a geographical division of parties which might insure them the next President."

To Mr. Holmes {Congressman John Holmes of Massachusetts}, April 22, 1820:

"I have been among the most sanguine in believing that our Union would be of long duration. I now doubt it much, and see the event at no great distance, and the direct consequence of this question. My only comfort and consolation is that I shall not live to see it; and I envy not the present generation the glory of throwing away the fruits of their fathers' sacrifices of life and fortune, and of rendering desperate the experiment which was to decide, ultimately, whether man is capable of self-government. This treason against human hope will signalize their epoch in future history as the counterpart of the model of their predecessors.

"This momentous question, like a fire-bell in the night, awakened me and filled me with horror. I considered it, at once, as the knell of the Union. It is hushed, indeed, for the moment; but this is a reprieve only, not a final sentence. A geographical line, coinciding with a marked principle, moral and political, once conceived and held up to the angry passions of men, will never be obliterated; and every new irritation will mark it deeper and deeper."

For peace and for the Union, the South upon this question made a compromise of their rights which even the Constitution would not justify.

But this compromise did not secure peace. It was a "reprieve only," and not a "final sentence." It was but a temporary success of sectionalism, which encouraged more thorough organization. On the 30th January, 1832, the Anti-slavery Society of New England was formed. This was an association, not professedly political, having for its object the abolition of slavery by moral means. The delightful amusement of witch-burning had been played out, and so industrious and puritanical a people could not remain idle. In 1848, these humanitarians, assisted by politicians, succeeded in getting up another national agitation, which once more threatened the Union, until peace was restored by the compromise of 1850. Afterwards, a union of politicians, with the various anti-slavery societies, formed the Republican party, an organization wholly sectional in its character, determined upon effecting the ultimate extinction of slavery, regardless of plighted faith and national obligations.

This party is now under the management of two distinct classes. The first is composed of the out-and-out, red-mouthed Abolitionists, who believe that it is the right and duty of every slave to cut his master's throat. These are the bold and desperate men who attempt to carry out practically the great leading ideas and moving principles of the Republican party. They are men who would have rejoiced to see John Brown President, Hinton Rowan Helper Vice President, and Dred Scott Chief Justice of the Supreme Court of the United States.[13]

Mr. KILGORE {David Kilgore, Indiana}. I desire to ask the gentleman a question.

Mr. BARRET. I am unwilling to be interrupted. After concluding my remarks, I will answer any questions the gentleman may desire to ask.

---

13. John Brown famously attacked Harpers Ferry, Virginia, in October 1859. Hinton Rowan Helper (1829–1909) was a southern critic of slavery. In 1857 he published *The Impending Crisis of the South: How to Meet It*, in which he argued that slavery hampered the economic prospects of non–slave owners and encouraged them to overthrow the slave oligarchy. A smaller version was published in 1859 that contained the endorsement of sixty-eight Republicans. As a result, Helper was reviled throughout the South, with his books being burned and banned. Dred Scott was the subject of Chief Justice Roger B. Taney's 1857 Supreme Court decision, which declared that the Missouri Compromise of 1820 was unconstitutional and that Dred Scott remained a slave.

Mr. KILGORE. I wanted to ask if the gentleman includes all the members of the Republican party in that category?

Mr. BARRET. I decline yielding the floor. I say most prominent among this Abolition class are preachers of the Gospel, men making pretense of much true piety and Christian charity.

> "When devils will their blackest sins put on,
> They do suggest at first with heavenly shows,"
> "How smooth and even they do bear themselves!
> As if allegiance in their bosoms sat,
> Crowned with faith and constant loyalty."
> "They are meek, and humble mouth'd;
> They sign their place and calling, in full seeming,
> With meekness and humility."[14]

They carry the Bible in their hands, religion on their tongues, and hell in their wicked hearts. The second class is made up of cunning and ambitious politicians. Believing it necessary to their success, they have succeeded in forming sectional parties—parties distinctly northern and southern, slavery and anti-slavery; and to this end they have employed with marked effect, the wicked, reckless, and lawless fanaticism of the Abolitionist; and while they appropriate the *service* to their own purposes, they would have us believe that they condemn the *servants*. From this second class of managers proceed all the artful platforms, so cunningly devised as to reveal just enough to hold the Abolitionist, and to conceal just enough to catch the more moderate, and the good men who are sometimes found in the Republican party.

I shall say nothing of the small demagogues and pitiful pettifoggers who make themselves so prominent now in the hour of party success. They are but the light, surface material, drawn by the Republican current from every eddy. They are without size and substance, and float upon the tide; because its influx may raise, while its reflex can never lower them.

Under this management, the Republican party has combined States against States, and arrayed section against section, until, by the power of numbers, by a sectional plurality, led on by party drill, and by the stimulus of pay and rations, and under the inducement of coveted honors, fat salaries, and the sweets of patronage, place, and power, and at the same time

---

14. William Shakespeare, *Othello*, act 2, scene 3; *Henry V*, act 2, scene 2; *Henry VIII*, act 2, scene 4.

penetrated and fired with the delicious idea that they were moving in the cause of human rights, and of the equality of man, have succeeded in getting possession of the General Government.

The South, the defeated section, believing that this geographical party, in its very nature, is inimical to them, and that their main object in taking possession of the Government is to use all its powers and patronage in carrying out their leading idea—which must result in the complete subjugation of the South, and the destruction of their institution of slavery—have become alarmed, and they ask for further guarantees of their safety. They ask only their rights under the Constitution, but they want such explanatory amendments as will prevent the perversion of that instrument into the means of their own destruction.

Now, what is that leading idea, and have the southern people any cause for fear? In 1859, Mr. SEWARD {William H. Seward, New York} said of the Republican party, of which he is the acknowledged leader and originator:

"The secret of its assured success lies in the fact that it is a party of one idea—the idea of equality; equality of all men, before human tribunals and human laws, as they are equal before divine tribunals and divine laws."[15]

On previous occasions he had used similar language. At Buffalo, in 1856, he said:

"If all men are created equal, no one can rightfully acquire or hold dominion over, or property in, another man, without his consent. If all men are created equal, one man cannot rightfully exact the service or the labor of another man, without his consent. The subjugation of one man to another by force, so as to compel involuntary labor or service, subverts that equality between the parties which the Creator established."

In the Senate, on the 11th of March, 1850, he said:

"All this is just and sound; but assuming the same premises—to wit, that all men are equal by the law of nature and of nations—the right of property in slaves falls to the ground; for one who is equal to the other cannot be the owner of property of that other. But you answer that the Constitution recognizes property in slaves. It would be sufficient, then, to reply, that the constitutional obligation must be void, because it is repugnant to the law of nature and nations."

---

15. From William Seward's "On the Irrepressible Conflict" speech delivered in Rochester, New York, on October 25, 1858.

These sentiments had been proclaimed by the Anti-Slavery party in every convention, and they were not only not disclaimed by the party at Chicago, but emphatically reasserted in the following resolution:

"That the maintenance of the principles promulgated in the Declaration of Independence, and embodied in the Federal Constitution, 'that all men are created equal; that they are endowed by their Creator with certain inalienable rights; that among them are life, liberty, and the pursuit of happiness; that to secure these rights, Governments are instituted among men, deriving their just powers from the consent of the governed,' is essential to the preservation of republican institutions."[16]

To this bold enunciation of the real Abolition doctrine of the party some timid man made objection; but this objection was soon dispelled by that great leader of the party, Mr. {Joshua Reed} Giddings, of Ohio. He would not allow any dodging, and advocated the resolution with feeling. He said, and truthfully:

"The Republican party was founded on this doctrine of negro equality; that it grew upon it, and existed upon it. When you leave this truth out, you leave out the party."

Mr. Curtis, of New York,[17] in advocating the resolution, declared:

"That the words were truths by which the Republican party lives, and upon which alone the future of this country in the hands of the Republican party is passing."

In the nomination and election of Mr. Lincoln, the future of this country did pass into the hands of the Republican party upon the doctrine of negro equality. Judging from his speeches, we must regard Mr. Lincoln as the very embodiment of the sentiments of Mr. Giddings and Mr. Curtis, and of the Abolition party generally. Listen to his words at Chicago, in 1858:

"My friends, I have detained you about as long as I desired to do, and I have only to say, let us discard all quibbling about this man or the other man, this race, that race, and the other race being inferior, and therefore must be placed in an inferior position, discarding our standard which we have left us; let us discard all these things, and unite as one people throughout the land, until we shall once more stand up declaring that all men are created equal."

---

16. The 1860 Republican Party platform adopted in Chicago.

17. Probably George William Curtis, writer and speaker, and one of the founders of the Republican Party.

He makes it still stronger in the same speech:

"My friends, I could not, without launching off upon some new topic, which would detain you too long, continue to-night. I thank you for this most extensive audience you have furnished me to-night. I leave you, hoping that the lamp of liberty will burn in your bosoms until there shall be no longer a doubt that all men are created free and equal."[18]

Afterwards, at Galesburg, Mr. Lincoln said:

"I believe that the entire records of the world, from the date of the Declaration of Independence up to within three years ago, may be searched in vain for a single affirmation, from one single man, that the negro was not included in the Declaration of Independence."[19]

Mr. Lincoln will not be content with an admission of the abstract equality of men, but wishes to reduce it to practice. The Illinois Journal, of September 16, 1856, contains the following, which is prefaced: "We are indebted to Mr. Lincoln for a verbatim report of the speech":

"That central idea, in our political opinion, at the beginning was, and until recently continued to be, the equality of men. And although it was always submitted patiently to whatever inequality there seemed to be as a matter of actual necessity, its constant working has been a steady progress towards the practical equality of all men.

"Let past differences as nothing be; and with steady eye on the real issue, let us reinaugurate the good old central ideas of the Republic. We can do it. The human heart is with us; God is with us. We shall again be able, not to declare that all the States, as States, are equal, nor yet that all citizens, as citizens, are equal; but renew the broader, better declaration, including both these and much more, that all men are created equal."—*Speech at banquet in Chicago.*

On the 10th of October, 1854, at Peoria, Illinois, he used the following language:

"What I do say is, that no man is good enough to govern another man without the other's consent. I say this is the leading principle, the sheet anchor, of American republicanism. Our Declaration of Independence says:

"'We hold these truths to be self-evident: that all men are created equal; that they are endowed by their Creator with certain inalienable rights; that among these are life, liberty, and the pursuit of happiness. That to secure

---

18. From speech in Chicago, July 10, 1858.
19. From the Lincoln-Douglas debate in Galesburg, Illinois, October 7, 1858.

these rights Governments are instituted among men, deriving their just powers from the consent of the governed.'

"I have quoted so much at this time merely to show that, according to our ancient faith, the just powers of Governments are derived from the consent of the governed. Now, the relation of master and slave is *pro tanto* {to that extent} a total violation of this principle. The master not only governs his slave without his consent, but he governs him by a set of rules altogether different from those which he prescribes for himself. Allow all the governed an equal voice in the Government; and that, and that only, is self-government."—*Howell's Life of Lincoln,* p. 279.[20]

The stump orators in slave and free States all advocated the claims of Mr. Lincoln upon this doctrine of negro equality; and prominent among these was a Dutch upstart, who went from city to city, insulting the people of this country by explaining to them their Declaration of Independence.[21] If that Declaration did not mean to place the negro upon an equality with the white man, this is his opinion of that sacred instrument. I quote his own words:

"There is your Declaration of Independence, a diplomatic dodge, adopted merely for the purpose of excusing the rebellious colonies in the eyes of civilized mankind. There is your Declaration of Independence, no longer the sacred code of the rights of man, but a hypocritical piece of special pleading, drawn up by a batch of pettifoggers, who, when speaking of the rights of men, meant but the privileges of a set of aristocratic slaveholders, but styled it 'the rights of man' in order to throw dust in the eyes of the world, and to inveigle noble-hearted fools into lending them aid and assistance. There are your boasted revolutionary sires, no longer heroes and sages, but accomplished humbuggers and hypocrites, who said one thing and meant another; who passed counterfeit sentiments as genuine, and obtained arms, and money, and assistance, and sympathy, on false pretenses! There is your great American Revolution, no longer the great champion of universal principles, but a mean Yankee trick—a wooden nutmeg—the most impudent imposition ever practiced upon the whole world."[22]

---

20. From Lincoln's "Sheet Anchor" speech in Peoria, Illinois, on October 16, 1854, against the passage earlier in the year of the Kansas-Nebraska Act.

21. Barret's "Dutch upstart" was Carl Schurz (1829–1906), a German American political leader, journalist, orator, dedicated reformer, and, under President Rutherford B. Hayes, secretary of the interior. (Thanks to Nick Sacco for this identification.)

22. From a speech Schurz delivered in Springfield, Massachusetts, January 4, 1860, four months before Republicans in Chicago nominated Lincoln as their presidential candidate.

Mr. Speaker, there are in the Declaration of Independence many self-evident truths. Why should the Chicago platform contain that one concerning equality? Was it the expression of a sentiment honestly entertained, or was it a mere pretense to draw the honest elector into the support of the party by false pretenses?

But they say these principles, promulgated in the Declaration, are embodied in the Constitution. The Declaration announces the fact that all men are created equal, and entitled to life, liberty, &c. The Constitution returns the fugitive slave to his master. Is this a case of principle, promulgated in the one and embodied in the other? Then, for which are the Republican party: for the promulgation or the embodiment?

Sir, I do not believe in that interpretation of our bill of rights. Our forefathers, in the promulgation of a great international principle of human freedom, never intended to establish a law paramount to the Constitution itself, declaring their own slaves entitled to their freedom, and themselves law-breakers in holding them in bondage. That there should be a prejudice against slavery in the minds of northern men is but natural; and for it I make due allowance. But that prejudice has grown into a sickly sentimentality; into a wild, wicked, and dangerous fanaticism; into a social and political disease; a great national curse. And now, the cardinal doctrine, the great leading central idea, the fundamental principle of Republicanism, has become the equality of the negro with the white man. Hence the persistent denunciation of slavery in the States; hence the establishment and encouragement of underground railroads; hence the personal liberty bills; hence the bloody strife in Kansas; hence the devilish raids upon our border; hence the incitement to civil war, and the excitement of servile insurrection.

The Republicans believe that whether promulgated by the Declaration, or embodied in the Constitution, the negro is the equal of the white man, and entitled by the higher law to his freedom; that slavery is the sum of all villainies; that thieves are less amenable to the moral code than slaveholders; "that slavery is a sin against God and a crime against man, which no human enactment or usage can make right; and that Christianity and patriotism alike demand its abolition." They believe, with Mr. SUMNER {Charles Sumner, Massachusetts}, that—

"Slavery is a wrong so grievous and unquestionable, that it should not be allowed to continue; nay, that it should cease at once; nay, that a wrong so transcendent, so loathsome, so direful, must be encountered wherever it can be reached; and the battle must be continued without truce or compromise, until the field is entirely won."[23]

That it is the object of the Republican party to abolish slavery in the States, I need only read from the organs and leaders of the party, and from Mr. Lincoln himself.

The Chicago Democrat, of the 11th of August, 1860, is suggestive:

Blair {Francis P. Blair Jr., Missouri} is a Republican of the radical school. He is a Republican of the Seward, the Sumner, and the Lincoln school. He believes in making the States all free. He believes slavery to be an evil and a curse, and that the duty of the Federal Government is to prevent its extension.

"While the great doctrine of the duty of the Federal Government to make 'the States all free' thus receives indorsement in a slaveholding State, shall the Republicans of the free States lower their standard of principle?

"The day of compromising, half-way measures, has gone by. The people are determined to force the politicians up to the point of making the States all free. If the politicians are not prepared for this, they must get out of the road. Unless they do, they will be run over."

"The year of jubilee {year of liberation} has come! Already is the child born who shall live to see the last shackle fall from the limbs of the slave on this continent. Universal emancipation is near at hand.

"The only class of people who are standing in the way of the accomplishment of this great work are the office-hunters—the fossils and the flunkeys of the North. They cannot, or will not, see that the path of duty is the path of safety; and they prefer party to principle. Such men would have the Republican party in the free States lower its standard, and pretend not to be devoted to the extinction of slavery everywhere, while our gallant Republicans in the slave States are winning victories upon this very principle, in the face of the slave power.

"But the great heart of the Republican masses revolts against such hypocrisy and such truckling. They throw their banner to the breeze, inscribed with Lincoln's glorious words, 'The States must be made all free'; and under it will march on to victory after victory, conquering and to conquer."

In October, 1855, Mr. SEWARD said:

---

23. From Sumner's speech, "The Anti-Slavery Enterprise," delivered in New York on May 9, 1855.

"Slavery is not and never can be perpetual. It will be overthrown either peacefully and lawfully under this Constitution, or it will work the subversion of the Constitution together with its own overthrow."[24]

{Hinton Rowan} Helper, in a work indorsed by sixty-eight members of this Congress, has fully exposed the intentions of his party. He says:

"But we are wedded to one purpose, from which no power can divorce us. We are determined to *abolish slavery at all hazards,* in defiance of all opposition, of whatever nature, which it is possible for the slaveocrats to bring against us. Of this they may take due notice, and govern themselves, accordingly."—Page 149.

"Abolition is but another name for patriotism, magnanimity, reason, prudence, wisdom, religion, progress, justice, and humanity."—Page 118.

"The oligarchs say we cannot abolish slavery without infringing on the right of property. Again we tell them we do not *recognize property in man.*

"Impelled by a sense of duty to others, we would be fully warranted in emancipating all the slaves *at once,* without any compensation whatever to those who claim to be their absolute owners."—Page 123.

"Of you, the introducers, aiders, and abettors of slavery, we demand indemnification for the damage our lands have sustained on account thereof: the amount of damage is $7,544,118,825; and now, sirs, we are ready to receive the money, and if it is perfectly convenient to you, we would be glad to have you pay it in specie. It will not avail you, sirs, to parley or prevaricate. We must have a settlement. Our claim is just, and overdue."

"It is for you to decide whether we are to have justice peaceably, or by violence; for, whatever consequences may follow, we are determined to have it, one way or the other. Do you aspire to become the victims of white non-slaveholding vengeance by day, and of barbarous massacres by the negroes at night?

"Would you be instrumental in bringing upon yourselves, your wives, and your children, a fate too horrible to contemplate? Shall history cease to cite as an instance of unexampled cruelty the massacre of St. Bartholomew, because the South shall have furnished a more direful scene of atrocity and carnage?[25]

---

24. From Seward's "The Advent of the Republican Party" speech delivered in Albany, New York, on October 12, 1855.

25. The 1572 Massacre of St. Bartholomew in Paris was directed against French Calvinist Protestants during the French Wars of Religion. Lasting several weeks, the massacre resulted in the killing of between 5,000 and 30,000 Protestants.

PART FIVE

Now, sirs, you must emancipate them, {slaves,} speedily emancipate them, or we will emancipate them for you."—Pages 126, 128.

"The great revolutionary movement which was set on foot in Charlotte, Mecklenburg County, North Carolina, May 20, 1775, has not yet terminated, nor will it be, until every slave in the United States is freed from the tyranny of his master."—Page 95.[26]

"But we are wedded to one purpose, from which no earthly power can divorce us. We are determined to abolish slavery, at all hazards, in defiance of all opposition, of whatever nature which it is possible for the slaveocrats to bring against us. Of this they may take due notice, and govern themselves accordingly."—Page 149.

"The pro-slavery slaveholders deserve to be at once reduced to a parallel with the basest criminals that lie fettered within the cells of our public prisons."—Page 158.

"No opportunity for inflicting a mortal wound in the side of slavery shall be permitted to pass us unimproved. Thus, terror-engenderers of the South, have we fully and frankly defined our position. We have no modifications to propose; no compromises to offer; nothing to retract. Frown, fret, foam, prepare your weapons, threat, strike, shoot, stab, bring on civil war, dissolve the Union. Sirs, you can neither foil nor intimidate us; our purpose is as firmly fixed as the eternal pillars of heaven; we have determined to abolish slavery, and, so help us God, abolish it we will."—Page 187.[27]

As early as 1837, Mr. Lincoln seemed as sound on some of these propositions as Helper. He was then a member of the Illinois Legislature; and on the 12th of January Mr. Ralston introduced the following resolutions:

"*Resolved by the General Assembly of the State of Illinois,* That we highly disapprove of the formation of abolition societies, and of the doctrines promulgated by them.

"*Resolved,* That the right of property in slaves is sacred to the slaveholding States by the Federal Constitution, and that they cannot be deprived of that right without their consent."

---

26. The Mecklenburg Declaration of Independence allegedly was signed on May 20, 1775, by citizens in Charlotte declaring their independence from Great Britain. No conclusive evidence exists to confirm the original document's existence.

27. All quotes are from Helper's *The Impending Crisis of the South: How to Meet It* (1857) and not the 1860 version titled *Compendium of the Impending Crisis of the South* (1860). It was the 1860 edition that was endorsed by members of Congress and other antislavery individuals (including Harriet Beecher Stowe, Horace Greeley, and Frederick Law Olmsted). See chapter 8, "Testimony of Living Witnesses," 141–170.

Mr. Lincoln voted against them. (See House Journal, p. 243.) In 1839, still a member of the Legislature, he voted against the following resolution:

"That the General Government cannot do indirectly, what it is clearly prohibited from doing directly; that it is the openly declared design of the Abolitionists of this nation to abolish slavery in the District of Columbia, with a view to its ultimate abolishment in the States";

"and that, therefore, Congress ought not to abolish slavery in the District of Columbia."—*House Journal,* p. 126.

Such votes, such expressions, by the President elect and his party, leave us no longer in doubt as to their intentions; and what Mr. Clay {Henry Clay, Kentucky} said of the anti-slavery party in 1838 is true of the Republican party in 1861. We have only to insert New Mexico, in place of Florida, to make the application complete:

"With the Abolitionists, the rights of property are nothing; the deficiency of the powers of the General Government are nothing; the acknowledged and incontestable powers of the States are nothing; civil war, a dissolution of the Union, and the overthrow of the Government in which are concentrated the fondest hopes of the civilized world, are nothing. A single idea has taken possession of their minds, and onward they pursue it, overlooking all barriers, reckless and regardless of consequences. With this class the immediate abolition of slavery in the District of Columbia, and in the Territory of Florida, the prohibition of the removal of slaves from State to State, and the refusal to admit any new States comprising within their limits the institution of domestic slavery, are but so many means conducing to the accomplishment of the ultimate but perilous end at which they avowedly and boldly aim, are but so many short stages in the long and bloody road to the distant goal at which they would finally arrive. Their purpose is abolition, universal abolition—peaceably, if they can; forcibly, if they must."—*Appendix Globe,* vol. 7, p. 355.

I know that many of the Republican party shrewdly disavow any intention to interfere directly with slavery in the States. It would be too great a strain of the higher law, even, to justify so flagrant an outrage. But the same object can be accomplished indirectly. Admit no more slave States. Then, according to Mr. SUMNER, "slavery will die, like the poisoned rat, of rage, in his hole." Create dissatisfaction among the slaves in the border States; induce them to seek refuge in the free States; prevent their recapture and return, by personal liberty bills; and slave property will be thus rendered so insecure, unprofitable, and even dangerous, in the border States, that they will rid themselves of it; and once free, it is expected that those States will cooperate in making an amendment to the Constitution, providing for the ultimate extinction of slavery throughout the land.

Abolition of slavery, directly or indirectly, is demanded by the people of the North. Men high in authority, leaders of party, preachers, teachers, editors, judges, lawyers, law-makers, State and national, openly avow it; and no scheme has yet been suggested, however unconstitutional; no plan has yet been attempted, however wicked and infernal, which looked towards the freedom of a negro, which has not met with approval in the ranks of the Republican party. Many of that party believe that the design of John Brown was founded in the deepest wisdom and benevolence, and executed in unrivaled heroism, integrity, and self-forgetfulness; that his life was a complete success, his death an unparalleled and most honorable triumph; that the blood of John Brown appeals to God and humanity against slaveholders; that the heart of this nation, and of the civilized world, will respond to that appeal in one defiant shout: "resistance to slaveholders is obedience to God."

John Brown was a true, practical Republican. He considered the negro an equal of the white man. He believed slavery a sin against God, and a crime against man. He believed in the insurrectionary and bloody schemes promulgated by the distinguished Republican Hinton Rowan Helper, and cordially indorsed by sixty-eight Republican members of this Congress. He believed with the Republicans of Natick, "that it was the right and the duty of slaves to resist their masters, and the right and duty of the people of the North to incite them to resistance, and to aid them in it." Theodore Parker says:

"John Brown sought by force what the Republican party works for with other weapons; the two agree in the end, and differ only in the means."[28]

I know that there are many members of the Republican party who blame John Brown. Of such I may say:

"They know the right, and they approve it, too;
Condemn the wrong, and yet the wrong pursue."[29]

The Republican party has one million eight hundred and fifty-eight thousand two hundred voters in the North, and only twenty-seven thousand

---

28. Theodore Parker (1810–1860) was a Massachusetts-based Unitarian minister. A dedicated abolitionist, he supported, philosophically and financially, the efforts of John Brown.

29. From *Metamorphoses, Book the Seventh, The Story of Medea and Jason* by the Roman poet Ovid (Publius Ovidius Naso).

and thirty-two voters in the South. It could hardly be more sectional. They have gained possession of the Government. As to what will be their policy, we can judge only from the sentiments expressed by their leaders and their party organs.

On the 13th day of August last, Mr. SEWARD used the following language, which, from him, and under the circumstances, is full of meaning:

"What a commentary upon the wisdom of man is given in this single fact that, fifteen years only after the death of John Quincy Adams, the people of the United States, who hurled him from power and from place, are calling to the head of the nation, to the very seat from which he was expelled, Abraham Lincoln, whose claim to that seat is that he confesses the obligation of that higher law which the sage of Quincy proclaimed, and that he avows himself, for weal or woe, for life or death, a soldier on the side of freedom in the irrepressible conflict between freedom and slavery."

He afterwards said:

"I tell you, fellow-citizens, that with this victory comes the end of the slave power in the United States."

Helper, on page 183 of his book, reduces this sentiment of his distinguished leader into a more practical shape. He says:

"Once for all, within a reasonably short period, let us make the slaveholders do something like justice to their negroes, by giving each and every one of them his freedom and sixty dollars in current money."[30]

The wheels of Government are to be moved with a high hand. For years have we been warned of this intention. Mr. SEWARD said, in the Senate, March 3, 1858:

"Let the Supreme Court recede. Whether it recede or not, we shall reorganize that court, and thus reform its political sentiments and practices, and bring them into harmony with the Constitution and the laws of nature."

Massachusetts, through one of her distinguished Senators, [Mr. {Henry} WILSON,] sustained this doctrine:

"We shall change the Supreme Court of the United States, and place men in that court who believe, with its immortal Chief Justice, John Jay, that our prayers will be impious to Heaven while we support and sustain human slavery."

Through one of her Representatives, [Mr. {Anson} BURLINGAME,] she has gone even further:

---

30. *The Impending Crisis of the South: How to Meet It* (1857).

"When we shall have elected a President, as we will, who will not be the President of a party, but the tribune of the people, and after we have exterminated a few doughfaces {Northerners with Southern sympathies} from the North, then, if the slave Senate will not give way, we will grind it between the upper and nether millstones of our power."

From these and many like expressions of the leaders of the Republican party, the southern people have concluded that the administration of Mr. Lincoln will abolish slavery in the District of Columbia; that they will prevent inter-State slave trade, restrict slavery in all the Territories, reorganize the Supreme Court, and put the Government actually and perpetually on the side of freedom.

I know that it is claimed that the only object of the Republican party is to prohibit slavery in the Territories. And, according to the gentleman from Ohio, [Mr. {John} SHERMAN,] no sane man would for a moment suppose that slavery could ever go north of the 36° 30', and hence the only practical issue was as to the existence of slavery in New Mexico. This, then, is a statement of the case. Two different forms of labor exist in this country, bond and free. The Constitution does not prescribe, or proscribe, either, for the Territory of New Mexico. The people of the South claim the right to take their bondmen into New Mexico. The people of the North deny the existence of any such right. Upon a fair submission of this question to the voters of the whole country at the election in November last, there were, in the free States, 1,574,091, and in the slave States, 1,257,195—total, 2,831,286 voters, who were of opinion that a citizen of the United States had a right to take his bondman into New Mexico, or any other Territory of the United States; while there were in the free States 1,858,200, and in the slave, 27,032, voters—total, 1,885,232, who were of a different opinion. This opinion of the South had already been sustained by a decision of that august tribunal, the Supreme Court of the United States {in the Dred Scott decision}, which, by the very Constitution, is a coordinate branch of this Government, and its decisions are final, and the supreme law of the land. There are not more than seven slaves now in New Mexico, and such are in its climate and soil that it cannot possibly be a free State; and yet, the gentleman from Ohio considers the question of slavery in New Mexico the all-important one upon which, as he says, the Union is being disrupted, and State after State is going out.

Was it the whole end aim of the Republican party to make this Territory free? Was it for this that nearly three million people placed themselves upon sectional ground, and arrayed North against South? Was it for this that they went through with a protracted, expensive, and laborious canvas? Was it for this that they brought about a sectional agitation, a hostile feeling, which threatens the very existence of the Union? Was it for this that they sought the possession of the General Government, and the reorganization of the Supreme Court? I deny that such a respectable number of Republicans even, however excited, however prejudiced, could be so greatly moved by so pitiful an object. If the position of the gentleman from Ohio be correct, the existence of the Republican party is dependent upon the *status* of New Mexico on the slavery question, and the determination of that would, as a matter of course, put an end to the politics of that party, and to the party itself.

The gentleman from Ohio is not the only distinguished Republican who believes that the sole object of his party is the prohibition of slavery in the Territories; nor do I stand alone in the opinion that, if that be true, the party must soon cease to exist. Mr. {Edward} Bates, of Missouri, a prominent candidate before the Chicago convention for President, thus spoke in the rotunda at St. Louis,[31] August 10, 1856:

"The Republican party is not a mere array of men. It is a hasty agglomeration made up of the odds and ends of every other party that ever existed at the North. Mr. SEWARD, ever an eminent Whig and unquestionably a man of ability, is one of its leaders. He was that distinguished Whig, he is that distinguished Republican. At the North, whole slabs of the American party have united with the new organization, and it is now animated by an ardent enthusiasm which furnishes proof of its transitory nature. In proportion to its ardor will be the shortness of its life. Its only aim is the prohibition of slavery in the Territories; and even if it should succeed in accomplishing its object by a congressional enactment, its whole force and vitality would be exhausted in the effort, and it would decline."

Of this party, Mr. H. WINTER DAVIS, the distinguished member from Maryland, and a candidate for the Vice Presidency in the Chicago convention, spoke as follows, in this House, January 6, 1857:

"The Republican party was a hasty levy *en masse* of the northern people to repel or revenge an intrusion by northern votes alone. With its occasion it must pass away. Within two years, Kansas must be a State of the Union. She must be admitted with or without slavery, as her people prefer. Beyond Kansas, there is no question that is practically open. I speak to practical men.

---

31. Undoubtedly a reference to the Old St. Louis County Courthouse. The initial Dred Scott trial was conducted in the west wing of the building, which is now administered by the National Park Service.

Slavery does not exist in any other Territory; it is excluded by law from several, and not likely to exist anywhere; and the Republican party has nothing to do, and can do nothing. It has no future. Why cumbers it the ground?"

No, Mr. Speaker, a party organized under such circumstances, composed of such materials, announcing such sentiments, fighting such battles, must have an object far beyond the prevention of slavery in a Territory where it can never exist.

Sir, the restriction of slavery in the Territories is but one of the means. The great end to be accomplished is, as Mr. Lincoln says, the ultimate extinction of slavery. At any rate, the South fears that this is the object, and that the whole power and patronage of the Government will be used in its accomplishment; and moved by this fear, and by actual wrongs, the cotton States, exercising the right claimed by Massachusetts in 1814, and afterwards upon the annexation of Texas, have thrown off their allegiance to this Government and declared their independence.[32]

It is not to be denied that the seceding States, yea, the whole South, have been subjected to a long train of abuses by the anti-slavery party. An incessant war has been made upon them, because {they are} slaveholders; their constitutional rights have been denied them; their slaves constantly interfered with; and laws made for their protection have been purposely obstructed; and now, it would seem to be the purpose of this anti-slavery Republican party, not only to destroy the value of $4,000,000,000 worth of their property, but to convert it into the means of their own destruction. In vain they have warned the northern people against this unholy crusade; in vain have they remonstrated against the obstruction of the laws; in vain have they appealed to the generous sympathies of their brethren, asking only for the peaceful enjoyment of rights guaranteed by the Constitution. Their warnings, remonstrances, and appeals have been answered only with repeated injuries. Wrongs like these, if inflicted by the Government, would be just cause for revolution. Such grievances could only be redressed by a resort to arms. But this Government has done no wrong. There is no complaint against the Government. On the contrary, all unite in the opinion that

---

32. In protest of federal demands imposed on Massachusetts during the War of 1812, the Massachusetts legislature called for a secret convention to convene in Hartford, Connecticut. The delegates issued a set of resolutions designed to protect citizens from the wartime expansion of congressional authority at the presumed expense of state sovereignty. Andrew Jackson's victory in New Orleans and news of the signing of the Treaty of Ghent (December 24, 1814) ended the convention's deliberations and purpose.

it is the best form of government ever instituted among men. The southern confederacy have adopted it; and now, after our dismemberment, it is the only plan of government upon which there is the slightest hope for a reconstruction.

But besides, the Government has provided a mode of redressing the grievances which this sectional minority has imposed upon the South. The very election which raised a sectional President into power manifested the existence of a national conservative element which insured a constitutional check upon his administration, and its certain termination at the end of four years. An opposition which, if united, could have defeated that election, could surely have protected themselves, under the Constitution and in the Union, against the aggressions of any sectional minority.

Under these circumstances, I now enter my solemn protest against the action of the seceding States. It was, in my opinion, unwise and selfish, an irreparable injury to themselves, an act of cruel injustice to the middle and border slave States, and to the General Government, and of gross ingratitude to a million and a half of gallant men of the North, who have made every sacrifice and dared every danger in support of the Constitution and in defense of southern rights. Has it ever recurred to our precipitate brethren of the South that those northern friends, like themselves, owe allegiance to their respective States, and that, by secession, they leave a noble army of northern conservatives, with all their valor and devotion, to be swept down by the assaults of resistless numbers, to rise no more forever? By this hasty act, they have forced upon the border States the fearful alternative of submission, on the one hand, to a power which could at any moment override all their rights; or rebellion, secession, and civil war, on the other, which, in their exposed position, would be their utter ruin. In my judgement, such a respectable number of States, so vast in extent, with a population so large, and an interest so great, were entitled to some consideration at the hands of those States for which, in all their struggles against northern aggression, they had been a cloud by day and a pillar of fire by night {Exodus 13:21}.

But this disunion, while it may bring upon the country the direst of all calamities, is a remedy for no evil, real or imaginary. It cannot render slave property more secure, or in any manner perpetuate it. It yields up forever the equal participation in the Territories by the slave States, while it furnishes no greater protection for slavery where it exists. In the Union, the South, with a minority North, were stronger than even a united South could possibly be out of the Union, with or without arms. The cotton States should, therefore, have remained in the Union. Then, if this northern party—formerly Abolition, now Republican—should attempt to reorganize the Supreme Court, and make of it a machine to sustain their bad morals and worse politics; if they should fasten upon the Government the doctrine of the higher law, and employ all its patronage and power in an organized and direct attack upon slavery, then would we make war, not against the Government, but against its enemies; then might we fight, under the Constitution, against those who would subvert it; fight for this beautiful capital, hallowed in its very name, location, and in all its associations; fight for the archives, the flag, the honor of this great nation.

But, whether secession, disunion, revolution—call it what you will—be right or wrong, is not now the question. It exists; it is all around and about us. It has shocked and unsettled every department of the Government, and paralyzed business in all its branches. Its baleful influence has spread sorrow and gloom, disaster, and destitution, over the whole land.

The question now is: what shall be done to restore peace, happiness, and prosperity? Who can, who will save the country from the threatened doom?

The gentleman from Ohio [Mr. {John} SHERMAN] appealed to the border States to "arrest the tide, which, but for them, would in a few days place us in hostile array against each other." Believing that the border States, free and slave, understood practically this question of slavery, about which the pestiferous States of South Carolina and Massachusetts only theorize, I took upon myself the responsibility of calling those States together, that they might counsel with each other.

The committee appointed by those States agreed almost unanimously upon a plan of adjustment; but when that plan was in substance proposed in the House of Representatives, the gentleman and his party voted unanimously against its consideration. At that time the border slave States occupied a position for effective interference; but the rejection of a proposition so reasonable, so just, weakened their confidence in their northern brethren. And that confidence was not in the slightest restored by the gentleman from Ohio, when, in a speech "alternately gentle as the dews and as boisterous as the thunder," he accompanies his pleas for peace with a recommendation of war, and meets all propositions of conciliation with promised adherence to the Chicago platform.

It is difficult to tell what these border States will do. The elections lately held are no proper indices of their intentions. Having large interests involved, they take time for consideration. Although not consulted by the cotton States, they choose to consult one another. But let the North be assured of one thing: that those border States are unanimous in the opinion that this is a proper occasion for the settlement of this pest question of slavery, *now and forever.*

But, sir, while I can speak for no other, I can say but little even for my own State. Missouri occupies the geographical center of this nation; she lies in the very highway of civilization, and in the march of empire. She now contains a white population equal to that of Florida, South Carolina, Alabama, and Mississippi, combined; and for her future greatness she looks to the North, to the South, to the East, and to the West. Sir, Missouri was born of the Union; she was rocked in the cradle of the Union; she has grown up, lived, and prospered in the Union, and she loves the Union with unceasing devotion; but not a Union of the North with a fragment of the South, but the Union as our fathers made it—a Union of all the States in one grand and glorious Republic. Thus situated, thus interested, Missouri claims the right to criticise the conduct of her sister States, North and South. But, if the doctrine of coercion obtain, and the attempt be made to whip the cotton States into *self*-government, then Missouri will be found side by side with the other border slave States in armed resistance. And I now say to our northern friends, beware. And I say this not in a spirit of menace, but of solemn warning.

Long before the 6th of November, South Carolina declared that she would not submit to the election of a sectional President. This was treated as an idle threat; and the taunting reply was, that South Carolina could not be kicked out of the Union. When Congress assembled, and it became evident that she would secede, and would, most likely, be followed by all the other cotton States, the country was suddenly awakened to the real danger, and was at once convulsed with fear. In the Senate, and in this House, committees were constituted, of able men, and the many propositions looking to the safety of the country were laid before them, but nothing of a practical nature was accomplished. In the emergency, all eyes are turned to the distinguished Senator from New York, believing that he who had raised could easily rule the storm. After many long weeks of painful anxiety, that Senator comes forward and coolly tells us that all this is nothing more than might be expected; that in two or three years, when the lightening-flash and the thunder-clap have subsided into a perfect calm, he may recommend something in the shape of a small Franklin rod for the protection of the people.[33] Like a physician called to see a patient, writhing, almost, with the agonies of death, he furnishes no remedy for relief, but delivers a very learned lec-

---

33. This is a reference to a lightning rod first developed by Benjamin Franklin in 1749.

ture on the subject of pathology in the sick room. The danger increases; State after State goes out; "The Union must and shall be preserved," is the borrowed eloquence of every Republican orator. The Government is disrupted, and civil war threatens the destruction of thirty million people and to cover the whole land with desolation. Our rulers tell us that they wish to test the strength of the Government; that they wish to see whether we have any Government at all. Commerce is destroyed, manufactures ruined, and business of all kinds prostrated; until the people, the rightful sovereigns of the nation, the makers of Government, and its rulers, are reduced by desperation to the humble position of petitioners, and, by thousands and by tens of thousands, they earnestly ask their own *servants* for concession, for compromise, for peace; to all which, they receive the slighting reply that *it is very likely that Mr. Lincoln will adhere to the Chicago platform.* And now, when the dreadful issue is forced upon us, and the question is: "Union or no Union; Constitution or no Constitution; Government or no Government; country or no country;" the President elect says that "there is nothing wrong;" that "nobody is hurt;" "keep cool;" "there's no crisis; and if there is, it is all artificial"; while his Premier amuses himself and entertains the Senate by spinning cunning rhetoric into pointless platitudes and useless generalities.

Republicans, I once more give you warning. You have complete control of this Congress, and in your hands rests the destiny of this nation. Your Chicago platform is not a panacea for all the ills which now afflict us. It was made in time of peace and prosperity, and not in time of revolution and adversity. It was intended only as a basis of party action, and admirably adapted to party ends. What if it should now be abandoned, utterly destroyed? Your Greeleys, your Sewards, your Giddingses, could easily make for you another, and far better suited to the times. And now let me remind you that the election of your candidate for President was not the adoption of your platform.[34] The disruption of the Democratic party, the dissatisfaction with the present Administration, and that restless spirit which always desires change, contributed to your success in procuring a plurality of the votes for your candidate, while there was a majority of nearly a million against your platform.

---

34. Horace Greeley was founder and editor of the *New York Tribune* and a strong supporter of the Republican Party and of Abraham Lincoln. William Seward was a Republican senator from New York, and Joshua Reed Giddings was a former Republican representative from Ohio.

But you say the flag has been dishonored, the Constitution violated, the Union endangered, the Government defied; and you cry for war, and invoke the potential arm of Federal power to avenge all wrongs and enforce obedience. You forget that this is not a Government of force. The Union, so necessary to the establishment of the Government, was founded in the affections, which are stronger to bind a people together than any written Constitution or confederated authority. While this Government thus formed is all-powerful for good, it is impotent for evil. It was made for common defense and general welfare; but the Constitution does not provide for making war upon the very power that gave the Government existence. What if the misguided people of Charleston, in a moment of precipitation and excitement, did open a fire upon *their portion* of a common flag? What if they had blotted out the star which represents their own State—South Carolina? You now tolerate in your ranks hundreds of men who, but a few years ago, marched under a flag with only sixteen stars. Your Vice President elect has made speeches under such a flag. Your respect for the Constitution has greatly increased of late. It was a distinguished Republican who, but a short time ago, pronounced that Constitution the fountain of all our evils. And for years your party has taught obedience to a higher law, and not to the Constitution of the United States.

But, all at once, you have become great lovers of union. You abuse disunion in others, while you tolerate men in your ranks who were willing to let the Union slide; men who have declared that they considered the Union a lie, an imposture, a covenant with death and an agreement with hell. If you so love the Union, why will you not do something to save it. Since there is no longer a question in regard to slavery in the Territories, the Republican party would have to fall back upon its abolitionism but for this Union question. And now, while they regard disunion as the best move ever made towards abolition, they find it necessary, for political effect, to pretend much devotion to the Union. But the other day, one of the Republican leaders said, "we can win on Union, but we cannot win on compromise." Have we come to this? Our difficulties are not to be adjusted, the Union is not to be saved, because the party in power wishes to convert the very distresses of the country into political capital.

Sir, we have indeed fallen upon strange times. But yesterday we were told that Governments were instituted among men, deriving all their just powers from the consent of the governed. That, inasmuch as the negro had not given his assent to this Government, his enslavement is a sin against God, and a crime against man. Now, this is a Government of force, of supreme power, of which even the consent of the white man forms no constituent element. But a short time ago we were told by the Senator from New York that, between free and slave labor, there was an irrepressible conflict; now he says, "that the different forms of labor, if slavery was not perverted to purposes of political ambition, need not constitute any element of strife in the Confederacy." But a short time ago we were told that it was necessary to protect the Territories from slavery, and to drive back the slave power which was threatening the invasion even of the free States. Now, says the great leader of the Republican party, "there is no fear of slavery anywhere; and the protection of the Territories from slavery has ceased to be a practical question."

Gentlemen of the Republican party, this is no time for trifling; no time for diplomacy; no time for promoting political dogmas and advancing partisan interests; no time for trying to preserve doubtful political consistency. Questions of grave moment force themselves upon you. Shall a sacrifice be made of our house, race, lineage, and blood, for those of a strange clime? Shall every seven white men cut each other's throats for the sake of one negro? Will you disregard all ties of consanguinity, and use all your endeavors to ruin ten million of the noblest race on earth, under the pretext of benefiting about one third that number of the most degraded? Shall this free, glorious, happy America throw away all her grand achievements, and tear from her brow the wreath of science, commerce, politics, and war, and no longer stand forth the loveliest of all the nations? Shall this model Republic, having no model on earth, cease forever to be an example worthy of study and imitation? These are important questions, and you alone can decide them. As I have before said, you hold in your hands the destiny of this great nation.

The formation of the Union by the adoption of the Constitution was celebrated with deep, passionate enthusiasm throughout the original colonies. "'Tis done, we have become a nation," was the exultant boast of the whole people. And that was but the dawn of the day which promised glory and happiness to all our America. A few months ago that day was at noontide, and we in the full realization of all its blessed promises. If now, in our calamity, the same spirit of concession, compromise, and patriotism, which formed the Union, should secure its preservation and its establishment for all time as the palladium of our political safety and prosperity, and if that proud bird of liberty should once more take his flight, bearing the sacred motto of "*E Pluribus Unum*" in letters of ever-living light, the whole earth would be illuminated with joy and gladness. The loud shout of a freeman's exultation would break from the deep forests of Maine, and mingle with the harmonious strains of gratitude wafted over the golden plains of California. Thirteen infant colonies rejoiced over the birth of this nation; thirty-four grown up States, empires within themselves, with their thirty million people, will rise up in one grand, national jubilee over its preservation. But if, in spite of all appeals, and regardless of all obligations, partisan feeling and small politics shall overrule concession, compromise, patriotism, be assured that whole columns of curses, rising from the bosoms of an agonized and outraged people, will ascend to Heaven against those would not save, as against those who would destroy, a nation's happiness, a nation's prosperity.

Mr. Speaker, there are many propositions in the hands of the committee of thirty-three which would restore peace to this country, and I have done all in my humble power to secure their adoption. I have had the honor of being taunted by men from the North, and men from the South, as a Union-saver. Would that it were in my power, by a word, by a vote, by any act, by any sacrifice, to save this beautiful and holy house of our fathers; and that I could thus win this proud title, which, though bestowed in derision, is a title worth dying for; worth having lived for.

Source: *Congressional Globe*, 36th Cong., 2nd sess., appendix, 246–250.

Texas Senator Louis Trezevant Wigfall (Democrat)

United States Senate
March 4, 1861

Born in South Carolina, educated in South Carolina and Virginia, Louis Trezevant Wigfall (1816–1874) established a law practice in Marshall, Texas, in 1848 and immediately became involved in politics. He was elected to the Texas House of Representatives and later the Texas Senate. He then represented Texas in the U.S. Senate from December 1859 until March 1861. Wigfall was a member of the Provisional Congress of the Confederacy and commander of the Texas Brigade of the Army of Northern Virginia. In early 1862 he resigned his commission to become a member of the First and Second Confederate Congresses. After the war, he fled to England for eight years, but returned in 1873, the year before his death.

As this speech during the early morning hours of March 4, Inauguration Day, demonstrates, Wigfall was a fire-breathing secessionist who saw no place for the "free white States" in the Union as long as Northerners "insist upon negro equality . . . excite our slaves to insurrection against their masters . . . and array one class of citizens against the other." As Wigfall warmed to the issue of secession and its necessity, he clearly pointed his accusations at the "Black Republicans," at Northerners in general, and at abolitionists, all of whom had conspired to "deny the right of self-government to the free white man of the South." Although Texas formally seceded on February 23, Wigfall remained at his seat in the Senate for another month, daring his colleagues to remove him. The Senate obliged on July 11, 1861, by formally expelling Wigfall for engaging in a "conspiracy for the destruction of the Union and Government."

STATE OF THE UNION

The PRESIDING OFFICER. The joint session (H.R. No. 80) proposing an amendment to the Constitution of the United States is before the Senate as in Committee of the Whole; and the Senator from Texas is entitled to the floor.

Mr. WIGFALL. Mr. President, I think I can say with truth, that this is positively my last appearance on these boards. I would have made that pledge last night, but it is said that a certain place not mentionable to ears polite is filled with good intentions. I trust that the Senator from Ohio [Mr. {Benjamin Franklin} WADE] will have this sin placed on his shoulders, not on mine. I was utterly astonished to see the Senator rise here and charge upon the Democratic party the offense, and he seemed so to regard it, of containing all the elements of secession, disruption of the Union, rebellion, resistance to the Government, &c. Why, sir, the Senator from Ohio himself, in the State of Maine, in the year 1855, is reported to have used this language:

"There was no freedom at the South for either white or black. He would strive to protect the free soil of the North from the same blighting curse. There was really no union now between the North and the South. He believed that no two nations upon the earth entertained feelings of more bitter rancor towards each other than these two sections of the Republic. The only salvation of the Union, therefore, was to be found in divesting it entirely from all taint of slavery. There was no union with the South. Let us have a Union, said he, or let us sweep away this remnant which we call a Union. I go for a Union where all men are equal, or for no Union at all. I go for right."

If that is not tolerably strong secession and disunion sentiment, I am suffering under the inability to understand the meaning of the English language.

Mr. WADE. I ask the Senator if he does not believe that every word of it is true?

Mr. WIGFALL. I answer with all frankness that I do, so far as the irrepressible conflict between the two sections is to be considered; and hence it is that I am now, and have for a long time past, been utterly opposed to quack medicines.

Mr. WADE. If the Senator will let me, I propose to say here, what I have frequently said, that I believe that speech of mine was not reported by a regular reporter; and I never supposed that the person who did report it took it down right at the time. The language was modified from what it is there, I think. I have always held so. I think it is a little different from what I spoke.

Mr. WIGFALL. I never have seen any denial of the Senator. I recollect, in the canvass {election} of 1856, having used it very frequently in speeches in my own State, and supposing that Cluskey's text-book had everything in it which anybody wanted to have, I sent for the text-book; and looking under the title of "Abolitionists and Republicans," I found the very sentence which I was looking for.[35] That is all I know about it.

Mr. WADE. It was so reported; but the first time I ever knew it was so reported, I stated what I have said now, that I did not think it was correctly reported. I do not think so now; and I stated so to Mr. CLAY {Clement Claiborne Clay Jr.}, of Alabama, here, on one occasion.

Mr. WIGFALL. The Senator was certainly so understood in Maine, and he was so reported in the Boston Atlas. That is the paper from which this extract is taken. From 1855 to 1861, the Senator has been so understood throughout the entire limits of the southern country. Under these circumstances, it did strike me as a little singular that the Senator should have risen here and denounced, with some degree of acrimony and bitterness, disunion sentiments, and complained that we had produced the whole difficulty. Now, sir, a gross injustice has been done that Senator by the party which he so ably, and I will add so faithfully, represents upon this floor. He is, in fact, the real author of the irrepressible conflict doctrine. The Senator from New York {William H. Seward}, in 1858, dressed the idea in that phraseology, and got the credit for it. In 1860, it was understood that one Abraham

---

35. In 1856, Michael Walsh Cluskey, Confederate major and delegate to the Confederate Second Congress, published a Democratic treatise titled *The Political Text-book, or Encyclopedia.* By 1860, it had gone through fourteen editions.

Lincoln was the author; and persons in the northern States and in the Republican party not being so well informed, nor having so closely scrutinized their writings and speakings as we further south have done, were ignorant of the fact that there was a double plagiarism—first by the distinguished Senator from New York, who copied it from the Senator from Illinois; but the Senator from Illinois had stolen the thunder of the Senator from Ohio. He is the real irrepressible conflict man; the genuine *bona fide* sarsaparilla Dr. Townsend.[36] [Laughter.]

Mr. {Stephen A.} DOUGLAS. You do not mean "the Senator from Illinois," but Mr. Lincoln.

Mr. WIGFALL. The President elect; he was not the Senator; no, he was not elected to the Senate.

Mr. DOUGLAS. That is the only correction I want made. [Laughter.]

Mr. WIGFALL. Certainly, I am glad to have made it. I did not allude to you, of course; I was speaking of Abraham. [Laughter.] Now, sir, the Senator from Ohio has paid me the compliment of saying that I am the only physician who has discovered the disease under which the body-politic is suffering. I feel flattered by the compliment, and will not deny the soft impeachment. [Laughter.] I have been for some time laboring under that impression. I think that bread pills will not cure; and that in this case, after death has literally come, the doctor and some of those who are now officiating are the very individuals who have produced death. That I believe further to be true. If there is, Mr. President, any class of men in this country who are more responsible for the present disruption of this Union than another class, it is that class of men who are called "Union-savers." They have been dealing with people as though the people had no sense; they have been getting up their quack medicines; they have been compromising, and couching their compromises in language which was not intended to be understood. They have made compromise and platforms which may be construed one way at the North and another way at the South; and while they have kept the word of promise to the ear, they have invariably broken it to the hope. There ought to have been no irrepressible conflict in our Government between slave labor and hireling labor, between the free white States and the free negro States. Senators have a cant, a short way of talking of the slave States. There are no slave States; there are some States in which negroes are held as slaves, and in which white men are held as freemen; some States in

36. Dr. Samuel P. Townsend (1813–1870) held the patent for the restorative compound "extract of sarsaparilla."

which negroes black boots and white men do not drive carriages. There are other States in which white men black boots and wear liveries, not the entire class, not the respectable class, not the farming class of the country, not the bone and sinew of the country; but those States may, with propriety, be called the hireling States of the Union; the others, the slave States if you please; or, as in some of the States, negroes are slaves and white men are free, and in others negroes are free and white men perform menial services, I suppose the better application would be "the free white States" and the "free negro States." So much for that.

I desire to pour oil on the waters, to produce harmony, peace, and quiet here. It is early in the morning {March 4, 1861}, and I hope I shall not say anything that may be construed as offensive. I rise merely that we may have an understanding of this question. It is not slavery in the Territories, it is not expansion, which is the difficulty. If the resolution which the Senator from Wisconsin introduced here, denying the right of secession, had been adopted by two thirds of each branch of this department of the Government, and had been ratified by three fourths of the States, I have no hesitation in saying that, so far as the State in which I live and to which I owe my allegiance is concerned, if she had no other cause for a disruption of the Union taking place, she would undoubtedly have gone out. The moment you deny the right of self-government to the free white men of the South, they will leave the Government. They believe in the Declaration of Independence. They believe that—

"Governments are instituted among men, deriving their just powers from the consent of the governed; that, whenever any form of government becomes destructive of these ends, it is the right of the people to alter or to abolish it, and to institute a new Government, laying its foundation on such principles and organizing its powers in such form as to them shall seem most likely to effect their safety and happiness."

That principle of the Declaration of Independence is the one upon which the free white men of the South predicated their devotion to the present Constitution of the United States; and it was the denial of that, as much as anything else, that has created the dissatisfaction in that section of the country. There is no instrument of writing that has ever been written that has been more misapprehended and misunderstood and misrepresented than this same unfortunate Declaration of Independence, and no set of gentlemen have ever been so slandered as the fathers who drew and signed that declaration. If there was a thing on earth that they did not intend to assert, it was that a negro was a white man. As I said here a short time ago, one of the greatest charges they made against the British Government was, that old King George was attempting to establish the fact practically that all men were created free and equal. They charged him in the Declaration of Independence with exciting their slaves to insurrection. That is one of the grounds upon which they threw off their allegiance to the British Parliament. Another great misapprehension is, that the men who drafted that Declaration of Independence had any peculiar fancy for one form of government rather than another. They were not fighting to establish a democracy in this country; they were not fighting to establish a republican form of government in this country. Nothing was further from their intention. Alexander Hamilton, after he had fought for seven years, declared that the British form of government was the best that the ingenuity of man had ever devised; and when John Adams said to him, "without its corruptions"; "why," said he, "its corruptions are its greatest excellence; without the corruptions, it would be nothing." In the Declaration of Independence, they speak of George III after this fashion. They say:

"A prince whose character is thus marked by every act which may define a tyrant, is unfit to be the ruler of a free people."

Now, I ask any plain common sense man what was the meaning of that? Was it that they were opposed to a monarchical form of government? Was it that they believed a monarchical form of government was incompatible with civil liberty? No, sir; they entertained no such absurd idea. Not one of them entertained it; but they say that George III was a prince whose character was "marked by every act which may define a tyrant," and that therefore he was "unfit to be the ruler of a free people." Had his character not been so marked by every quality which would define a tyrant, he might have been the fit ruler of a free people; *ergo,* a monarchical form of government was not incompatible with civil liberty. That was clearly the opinion of those men. I do not advocate it now; for I have said frequently that we are wiser than our fathers, and our children will be wiser than we are. One hundred years hence, men will understand their own affairs much better than we do. We understand our affairs better than those who preceded us one hundred years. But what I assert is, that the men of the Revolution did not believe that a monarchial form of government was incompatible with civil liberty. What I assert is, that when they spoke of "all men being created equal," they were speaking of the white men who then had unsheathed their swords—for what purpose? To establish the right of self-government in themselves; and when they had achieved that, they established, not democracies, but republican forms of government in the thirteen sovereign, separate, and independent colonies. Yet the Declaration of Independence is constantly quoted to prove negro equality. It proves no such thing; it was intended to prove no such thing. The "glittering generalities" which a distinguished former Senator from Massachusetts (Mr. Choate) spoke of as contained in the Declaration of Independence, one of them at least—about all men being created equal—was not original with Mr. Jefferson. I recollect seeing a pamphlet called the Principles of the Whigs and Jacobites, published about the year 1745, when the last of the Stuarts, called "the Pretender," {James Francis Edward, Prince of Wales (1688–1766)} was striking a blow that was fatal to himself, but a blow for his crown, in which pamphlet the very phraseology is used word for word and letter for letter. I have not got it here to-night. I sent the other day to the library to try and find it, but could not find it; it was burnt, I believe, with the pamphlets that were burnt some time ago. That Mr. Jefferson copied it or plagiarized it is not true, I suppose, any more than the charge that the distinguished Senator from New York plagiarized from the Federalist in preparing his celebrated compromising speech which was made here a short time ago. It was the cant phrase of the day in 1745, which was only about thirty years previous to the Declaration of Independence. This particular pamphlet, which I have read, was published; others were published at the same time. That sort of phraseology was used. There was a war of classes in England; there were men who were contending for legitimacy; who were contending for the right of the Crown being inherent, and depending on the will of God, "the divine right of kings," for maintaining a hereditary landed aristocracy; there was another party who were contending against this doctrine of legitimacy, and the right of primogeniture. These were called the Whigs; they established this general phraseology in denouncing the divine right and the doctrine of legitimacy, and it became the common phraseology of the country; so that in the obscure county of Mecklenburg, in North Carolina, a declaration containing the same assertions was found as in this celebrated Declaration of Independence, written by the immortal Jefferson. Which of us, I ask, is there upon this floor who has not read and reread whatever was written within the last twenty-five or thirty years by the distinguished men of this country? But enough of that.

The Senator from Ohio says, very justly, that these matters cannot be compromised in this way. The Senator from New York, twelve years ago, declared that it was the duty of the people of the North to abolish slavery; he then said they must teach hatred of it in their schools, and preach it in their pulpits; they must teach their people to hate slavery. He has accomplished that; and they now not only hate slavery, but they hate slaveholders.

As I said before, there ought not to have been, and there did not necessarily result from our form of government, any irrepressible conflict between the slaveholding and the non-slaveholding States. Nothing of the sort was necessary. Strike out a single clause in the Constitution of the United States, that which secures to each State a republican form of government, and there is no reason why, under precisely such a Constitution as we have, States that are monarchical and States that are republican, could not live in peace and quiet. They confederate together for common defense and general welfare, each State regulating its domestic concerns in its own way; those which preferred a republican form of government maintaining it, and those which preferred a monarchical form of government maintaining it. But how long could small States, with different forms of government, live together, confederated for common defense and general welfare, if the people of one section were to come to the conclusion that their institutions were better than those of the other, and thereupon straightway set about subverting the institutions of the other?

That the people of the North shall consider themselves as more blessed than we, more civilized, and happier, is not a matter at which we would complain at all, if they would only content themselves with believing that to be the fact; but when they come and attempt to propagandize, and insist that we shall be as perfect as they imagine themselves to be, then it is that their good opinion of themselves becomes offensive to us. Let my neighbor believe that his wife is an angel and his children cherubs, I care not, though I may know he is mistaken; but when he comes impertinently poking his nose into my door every morning, and telling me that my wife is a shrew and my children brats, then the neighborhood becomes uncomfortable, and if I cannot remove him, I will remove myself; and if he says to me, "you shall not move, but you shall stay here, and you shall, day after day, hear the demerits of your wife and children discussed," then I begin to feel a little restive, and possibly might assert that great original right of pursuing whatever may conduce to my happiness, though it might be kicking him out of my door. If New England would only be content with the blessings which she imagines she has, we would not disturb her in her happiness; but she insists, with that puritanical—

Mr. FOSTER {Lafayette Sabine Foster, Connecticut}. Will the Senator allow me to ask a question? When he has said that the Senator from Ohio was responsible for all this doctrine, I ask why charge New England? I ask whether it is kind to give the Senator from Ohio all the credit for this matter, and then charge it on New England? [Laughter.]

Mr. WIGFALL. Certainly; I will explain it easily enough. You know the leader of your party, the Senator {William H. Seward} from New York, said a short time ago, and it is true, I believe, that the "Massachusetts school of politics" has spread; and so far as Ohio is concerned, I believe that the State from which the Senator who last interrupted me comes, Connecticut, is responsible for the politics of Ohio. I have heard something about "the Connecticut Reserve" in Ohio,[37] and that, I believe, has been a hot-bed of all the fanaticism of that country. The mere expression of "the irrepressible conflict" was credited first to Mr. LINCOLN, and then to Mr. SEWARD, and then to the Senator from Ohio; but this doctrine of perfectibility in the people of the free States is of New England origin. It began before your Revolution; long before that. It began when Charles {Charles Stuart, King Charles I (1600–1649)} lost his throne. I think it began before his time. Old John Knox[38] started it, and then it got down into England. They helped Cromwell to cut off their King's head. After that, better than even the Puritans, they were called Independents; then they were called fifth-monarchy men; and then Cromwell had to run them out of England; and then they went over into Holland, and the Dutch let them alone, but would not let them persecute anybody else; and then they got on that ill-fated ship called the Mayflower, and landed on Plymouth Rock {in 1620}.[39] [Laughter.] And from that time to this they have been kicking up dust generally, and making a muss whenever they could put their fingers in the pie. [Laughter.] They confederated with the other States in order to save themselves from the power of the old King George III; and no sooner had they got rid of him than they turned in to persecuting their neighbors. Having got rid of the Indians, and witches, and Baptists, and Quakers in their country; after selling us our negroes for the love of gold, they began stealing them back for the love of God. [Laughter.] That is the history as well as I understand it.

There was properly no irrepressible conflict between the slaveholding States and the non-slaveholding States. They could have lived long in perfect peace and amity. We could have had slaves; they could have had none; we never attempted to thrust them upon them. We never wished to carry our

---

37. In the years after the American Revolution, many people from New England settled in the Connecticut Western Reserve, the northeast corner of the Northwest Territory (later Ohio).

38. John Knox (1513–1572) was a Scottish minister, theologian, and leader of the Protestant Church in Scotland.

39. Wigfall here carefully shared his understanding of the English Civil War, 1640–1660.

institutions among them. But when we acquired common territory, we said, "that territory belongs to us in common with you." When the Mexican war broke out, we had to settle the question by the sword; and the slaveholding States, with about one third of the population of the Union, furnished two thirds of the army; with double our population, you furnished about twenty thousand men; with half your population, we furnished forty thousand. The territory was acquired. You told us we should not go there; that the air was too pure in Utah to be breathed by slaves, but polygamists might live there. That did not offend the northern sentiment or morality. So this thing has gone on.

The Senator from Ohio to-night spoke of the Constitution as expounded by "that eminent jurist, Judge Story."[40] Judge Story was an eminent man in the way of making books. He made a great many of them. I am not going to detract from him, nor discuss his character here at this hour of the morning; but I will say, that if there was a man next to the Union-savers who is more responsible for a dissolution of the Union than every other man who ever lived, that man is Joseph Story; and if I were going to propose a compromise by which this Union would be saved, I would just provide an amendment to the Constitution vesting in Congress the power to make an appropriation to buy up all the commentaries on the Constitution written by Joseph Story, and have them publicly burned, [laughter;] and then, if you could eradicate from the minds of the American people the false doctrine, as to the form of Government under which they are living, that has been created by those miscalled commentaries on the Constitution,[41] and eradicate from their minds the prejudices which have been taught under the teachings and advice of the Senator from New York, [Mr. SEWARD,] in which the northern people have been taught to hate slavery, in their schools and in their pulpits; if these things could be accomplished, and the American people could, all of them, north of Mason and Dixon's line, be made Democrats, in the just acceptation of the term, not *sans culottes*,[42] but States-rights men, who believe

---

40. Joseph Story (1779–1845) sat on the U.S. Supreme Court from 1811 until 1845.

41. Associate Justice Story published his three-volume *Commentaries on the Constitution of the United States* in 1833 and *Commentaries of the Conflict of Laws* the following year. In these works, Story defended the power of the national government at the expense of state governments. His writings were interpreted by the white South as being antisouthern and antislavery.

42. During the French Revolutions (1792–1802), the bulk of the revolutionary army consisted of people of the lower economic classes who wore "long" pants instead of the abbreviated pantaloons (or culottes) favored by the wealthy.

that the Constitution is a compact between States, and that the Federal Government derives its authority from the written instrument, and can exercise no power that is not expressly delegated, or both necessary and proper for carrying out the delegated power—could all these things be done, I would then consider the question as to whether, under existing circumstances, a reconstruction would be practicable.

But as things are, it is useless, I am satisfied, to talk about a reconstruction. This Federal Government is dead. The only question is, whether we will give it a decent, peaceable, Protestant burial, or whether we shall have an Irish wake at the grave.[43] [Laughter.] Now, I am opposed to fighting, and would prefer a peaceable burial; but if the Republican Senators insist upon fighting, and they can get the backbone again put into their President elect, and can get Mr. Chase {Salmon P. Chase} reinstated in the Cabinet, from which he has been expelled, I do not know but that we shall have to fight.[44] If their President has recovered from that "artificial panic" under which he was laboring a short time ago, under the advice of the Lieutenant General {Winfield Scott} and the Secretary of War {Simon Cameron}—I believe they advised him to be frightened, so say the Republican papers in defense of him; it was done by the card; he goes by the platform—if they can recover him from that artificial fright under which he was laboring, and get him to take the Chicago platform fair and square, we shall have a fight; otherwise we shall not. I think myself it would be for the benefit of both sections that we should not have an Irish wake at our funeral; but that is for the North to decide, and not for us. Believing—no, sir, not believing, but knowing—that this Union is dissolved, never, never to be reconstructed upon any terms— not if you were to hand us blank paper, and ask us to write a constitution, would we ever again be confederated with you. Your people have been taught to hate us; your people have been taught to hate our institutions; your people have been taught to believe that you are Pharisees {in this case, hypocrites}; that your philacteries {a small box containing Hebrew texts} are full; that you are entitled to the high places in the synagogue; and you come and thrust yourselves into our presence, and thank God before our

43. Wigfall is making a distinction between a solemn and short burial and a longer, possibly rollicking sendoff for the deceased.

44. Salmon P. Chase served as governor and then senator from Ohio. President Lincoln appointed him secretary of the treasury (1861–1864) and later chief justice of the Supreme Court, where he presided from 1864 until 1873. Over Secession Winter, he served as a delegate to the Washington Peace Conference.

faces that you are not like us poor publicans, and your company has become distasteful to us; you tell us that ours is distasteful to you; we say, "grant it, then we will separate"; and you say we shall not. Then we are going to make the experiment, and we will trust in Providence. Napoleon Bonaparte, who was a wise man, once said he trusted Providence, but he said that he found that Providence always took sides with the artillery. We have taken the forts and guns, which you complain of, because we think Providence again will take sides with the artillery; and we have been securing a good deal of it. [Laughter.] Then, knowing that the Union is dissolved, that reconstruction is impossible, I would, myself, had I been consulted by the Union-savers, have told them that Union-saving was impracticable, but that peaceable separation was practicable. I would have advised that you should treat these sovereign States with the courtesy, at least, that you treated Brigham Young.[45] When he threatened to set up for himself, you sent commissioners there; but, when sovereign States assume the right of self-government, you send the bayonet and the broadsword. That is the difference in the manner in which you have treated these two questions. I suppose commissioners, in a few days, will be here from the confederate States. They were not sent by my advice. To be very candid with you, I do not think there is any Government here with which they could treat. [Laughter.] You have a sort of *de facto* {existing in fact}, certainly a revolutionary Government [laughter] that time and acquiescence on the part of the States may give the character of legitimacy to; but it surely has not that stamp now. One of the partners having withdrawn from a partnership dissolves the firm. It is true that, if the remaining partners go on, and still use the partnership name, by implication they are supposed to consent, acquiesce in the withdrawal, and to have reformed another. In the course of time, seven of your partners having withdrawn, if the rest shall acquiesce in the action of this revolutionary, irregular, wrongful, *de facto* Government that is about to inaugurate a President to-day, acquiescence may give legitimacy to it, and we may properly treat with you. [Laughter.] I judge that {Confederate} President {Jefferson} Davis, however, will waive these little irregularities, [laughter,] and probably send commissioners here, and then you will have the choice of peace or war; and that is a matter that you had better well consider. Turn your backs

---

45. Brigham Young (1801–1877) was the second president of the Church of Jesus Christ of Latterday Saints (Mormon Church) from 1847 until his death in 1877. He founded Salt Lake City, and in 1851 President Millard Fillmore appointed him the first governor of the Utah Territory.

upon these commissioners, attempt to reinforce the forts and retake those which we now have; attempt to collect the revenues, or do any other manner or matter of thing that denies to the free white men, living in those seven sovereign States, the right which they have asserted of self-government, and you will have war, and it will be war in all its stern realities. I say this not in bravado, but I say it because I know it and you know it.

The Senator from Illinois, [Mr. {Lyman} TRUMBULL,] to-night, supposed that if a little coercion had been used, instead of persuasion at first, all this thing would have been stopped; the treason would have been crushed in the egg. I think the Senator is mistaken. It was the unfortunate interference of the Lieutenant General {Winfield Scott} volunteering his advice, followed by the War Department, which has accelerated secession. Unfortunately for the country, the President seemed to have no well-defined opinions as to the form of government he was administering, or its character, or the powers of the States, or the powers of the Federal Government; and a provincial lawyer {Joseph Holt of Kentucky}, who, some way or other, got into a subordinate position in one of the offices—I believe the Interior—and remained there for some time, by a sad dispensation of Providence, became Postmaster General {in the James Buchanan administration}; and after that he got to be Secretary of War {also in the Buchanan administration}; and a Democratic President, having waited until twelve Democratic Senators had withdrawn, then sent in the name of this person to be confirmed by a Republican Senate—

Mr. DOOLITTLE {James Rood Doolittle, Wisconsin}. Will the honorable Senator allow me? Perhaps he can as well suspend at this point as any other; he will remember that he was talking about the recently appointed Secretary of War. If we are to take a recess at all, I suppose it is necessary we should take it now.

Mr. WIGFALL. I will finish in a few minutes. I do not wish to stop now, and commence again.

Mr. DOOLITTLE. You will remember where you left off.

Mr. DOUGLAS. There are objections to a recess.

Mr. WIGFALL. If you get up a discussion now, I will take much longer.

The PRESIDING OFFICER. The Senator from Texas has the floor.

Mr. WIGFALL. I will not detain the Senate much longer, it is near daylight now.

Mr. {Robert Ward} JOHNSON, of Arkansas. Give us the vote.

Mr. WIGFALL. You shall have one in a few minutes. I was saying, Mr. President, that the parenthesis that is now incumbent in the War Office, following, unfortunately, the advice of the Lieutenant General, attempted, in a very feeble way, coercion. The Senator from Illinois seemed to be shocked at my speaking with a feeling of gratification at the flag of what he chooses to call my country being insulted. It is not the flag of my country, I hope and believe; but I have not official information on that point. That flag was never insulted with impunity until it floated over a cargo of Black Republican hirelings, sent to one of the sovereign States of this Union to coerce them to obedience to a Government that was distasteful to them.

Mr. DOOLITTLE. I think I shall rise to a question of order. If the Senator from Texas does not know whether he belongs to this country or not, if he is really a foreigner in his own estimation, I desire to know whether he is in order in addressing the Senate of the United States. [Laughter.]

Mr. WIGFALL. I think the point is well taken; and if the Senator and those who act with him will acknowledge my State to be out of the Union, I will take my seat without a word further. [Laughter.] If they choose to call my name here, and to call not my name only, but the names of Senators who have filed here at your desk certified copies of the ordinances of secession of their States, and you treat them as blank paper, I shall treat them so too, for my purpose. I shall discuss your Government just as long as you choose to consider me a member of it; and as long as you please to call my name, I may stay here and vote; and if I find it convenient to defeat any of your nominations, I may see fit to do it; and when you get tired of that game, you will cease calling my name, and acknowledge my State out of the Union, and then you get rid of me. [Laughter.] That is a game two can play at.

Senators keep interrupting me until I shall make a very long speech, I am afraid. I was speaking of this parenthesis that is now incumbent in the War office. Without allowing even the President to know it, as it is said in the newspapers—I am not in the confidence of the last Cabinet, and I suspect will not be in the new one, [laughter,]—it is said that, without allowing even the President to know it, he surreptitiously, in the dead of night, sneaked a merchant vessel out of the harbor of New York, intending to sneak it into Charleston harbor; but they had put out the lights and blocked up the channel, and she was obliged to come up in broad daylight. A shot was thrown athwart the bow of this vessel containing armed men; they displayed a flag and it was fired at. I did say that that vessel had swaggered into Charleston harbor, had received a blow in the face, and had staggered out; and that this Secretary of War, who had brought the flag of this country in a condition to be fired at, had never dared, from that time to this, to resent the injury and insult; and in consequence of that, the State to which I owe my allegiance has withdrawn and cut loose from all connection with a Government that allows its flag to be so insulted. She has plucked her bright star from a bunting that can be fired at with impunity. If your President elect has recovered from that artificial fright, see if you cannot induce him to try and wipe out the insult; but I predicted last night that he would not; and I predict again that he will not. You fear to pass your force bills; you abandon them in both Houses. If you can get a Cabinet properly organized, with fire-eaters enough in it, the Cabinet may precipitate the country into a war, and then call upon what is denominated the conservative elements of your party to sustain the country in a war in which you have already involved it; but I know, and you know, that these men whom you represent are not in favor of war, and that their representatives here, a large number of them, fear it. What will be the result, I do not know; and to be very frank, I do not care.

Now, having explained why it was that I felt rejoiced at this insult to the flag of your country, I shall take up very little more time. The country is composed of States; and when that Government which was established by those States, and that flag which bears upon its broad folds the stars representing those States, is used for the purpose of making war upon some of those States, I say that it has already been degraded, and that it ought to be fired at, and it should be torn down and trampled upon. These are my feelings upon the subject; and "if this be treason, make the most of it."[46] I owe my allegiance—and Senators are not mistaken about that, for I have said it frequently—to the State which I here represent. I do not owe my allegiance to this Government. The Senator from Illinois spoke of the necessity of coercing these States, or not entertaining propositions from them, and likened it to the case of a Government in which there were revolted provinces. Your President elect, a short time ago, in a speech, asked the question gravely, what is the difference between a State and a country? And he seemed to be really in quest of information. Now, I was not astonished at that, for I did not expect anything better of him. From a man who is taken up because he is an ex-rail splitter, an ex-grocery keeper, an ex-flatboat captain, and an ex-Abolition lecturer, and is run upon that question, I would not expect any great information as to the Government which he was to administer. But I was surprised to hear a Senator—a Senator of education and ability, such as the Senator from Illinois is—compare the States of this Union, the States that formed this Government, the States without the consent of which this

46. From Patrick Henry's "Treason" speech in Virginia's House of Burgesses, May 30, 1765.

Government could not originally have had existence, and without the consent of which this Government cannot exist a day. To hear him talk about those States as revolted provinces did surprise and shock me.

Then, briefly, a party has come into power that represents the antagonism to my own section of the country. It represents two million men who hate us, and who, by their votes for such a man as they have elected, have committed an overt act of hostility. That they have done. You have won the Presidency, and you are now in the situation of the man who had won the elephant at a raffle. You do not know what to do with the beast now that you have it; and one half of you to-day would give your right arms if you had been defeated. But you succeeded, and you have to deal with facts. Our objection to living in this Union, and therefore the difficulty of reconstructing it, is not your personal liberty bill, not the territorial question, but that you utterly and wholly misapprehend the form of government. You deny the sovereignty of the States; you deny the right of self-government in the people; you insist upon negro equality; your people interfere impertinently with our institutions and attempt to subvert them; you publish newspapers; you deliver lectures; you print pamphlets, and you send them among us, first, to excite our slaves to insurrection against their masters, and next, to array one class of citizens against the other; and I say to you that we cannot live in peace, either in the Union or out of it, until you have abolished your Abolition societies; not, as I have been misquoted, abolish or destroy your school-houses; but until you have ceased in your school-houses teaching your children to hate us; until you have ceased to convert your pulpits into hustings; until you content yourselves with preaching Christ, and Him crucified, and not delivering political harangues on the Sabbath; until you have ceased inciting your own citizens to make raids and commit robberies; until you have done these things we cannot live in the same Union with you. Until you do these things, we cannot live out of the Union at peace.

Now, you have my views upon the subject. If the leaders of your party have any common sense left; if they have not become drunk upon fanaticism, and are not now suffering from delirium tremens, as I believe most of them are; if you have one particle of sense left, you will set about immediately seeing how this dissolution that has already taken place can be stopped from going further; how you can save some of these border States still to tax, and levy revenue and tribute from; how you may still find somebody that you can persecute with impunity; begin hatching up some sort of a compromise that will pay southern traitors for misrepresenting facts to their constituents. Do these things, and you may keep some of those border States still in; but above all things, try to have the dissolution that has already taken place a peaceable one. It may go very hard with us, and will certainly cost us a good deal of money; but you will not make much by the operation of war—not much. Your people will not thank you for reducing them to the dire necessity of direct taxes. Your ship-owners will not thank you for laying up their ships at their wharves to rot. Your manufacturers will not thank you for stopping the movements of their machinery; but that is your business, not mine.

Now, having made these few, little, conciliatory, peace-preserving remarks, I am not disposed to take up more time, and am willing that there should be a vote.

Source: *Congressional Globe,* 36th Cong., 2nd sess., 1397–1400.

Appendices

Secession Winter Time Line

1860

November 6   Abraham Lincoln elected president of the United States
December 3   2nd session of the 36th Congress convenes
December 17 South Carolina convenes secession convention
December 18 Senator John J. Crittenden introduces compromise amendment
December 20 South Carolina secedes
December 24 Senator Jefferson Davis introduces amendment to nationalize
             slavery

1861

January 3   Florida convenes secession convention
January 7   Mississippi convenes secession convention
January 7   Alabama convenes secession convention
January 9   Mississippi secedes
January 10   Florida secedes
January 11   Alabama secedes
January 16   Georgia convenes secession convention
January 19   Georgia secedes
January 23   Louisiana convenes secession convention
January 26   Louisiana secedes
January 28   Texas convenes secession convention

February 4	Secessionist convention convenes in Montgomery, Alabama
February 4	Washington Peace Conference convenes
February 8	Provisional Confederate States of America established
February 9	Jefferson Davis elected provisional president of the CSA
February 13	Virginia convenes secession convention
February 18	Jefferson Davis inaugurated president of the CSA
February 23	Texas secedes
February 27	Washington Peace Conference concludes
February 28	Missouri convenes secession convention
March 4	U.S. Senate approves Seward-Adams-Corwin amendment
March 4	U.S. Senate votes down Washington Peace Conference amendment
March 4	Abraham Lincoln inaugurated president of the United States
March 4	Arkansas convenes secession convention
March 11	Confederate Constitution created in Montgomery, Alabama
March 19	Missouri votes against secession
April 12	Bombardment of Fort Sumter begins
April 13	Fort Sumter surrenders
April 15	Lincoln calls for 75,000 troops
April 22	Florida is last state to ratify Confederate Constitution
May 6	Arkansas secedes
May 20	North Carolina convenes secession convention
May 20	North Carolina secedes
May 23	Virginia secedes
June 8	Tennessee secedes

Voting for Secession

South Carolina, December 20, 1860, secession convention, 169–0 (100%)

Mississippi, January 9, 1861, secession convention, 84–15 (85%–15%)

Florida, January 10, 1861, secession convention, 62–7 (90%–10%)

Alabama, January 11, 1861, secession convention, 61–39 (61%–39%)

Georgia, January 2, 1861–January 19, 1861, secession convention,
    208–89 (70%–30%)

Louisiana, January 26, 1861, secession convention, 113–17 (87%–13%)

Texas, February 1, 1861, secession convention, 166–8 (95%–5%)

    February 23, 1861, general ratification election, 46,129–14,697 (76%–24%)

Missouri, March 19, 1861, secession convention, 89–1 (against secession)

Arkansas, May 6, 1861, secession convention, 69–1 (99%–1%)

North Carolina, May 20, 1861, secession convention, 115–0 (100%)
Virginia, April 17, 1861, secession convention, 88–55 (62%–38%)
   May 23, 1861, general ratification election, 125,950–20,373 (86%–14%)
Tennessee, May 6, 1861, General Assembly
   House, 46–21 (69%–31%)   Senate, 21–4 (84%–16%)
   June 8, 1861, general ratification election, 104,913–47,238 (69%–31%)

Chronological Index of Proposed Constitutional Amendments

December 3, 1860	Cong.	President James Buchanan's Fourth Annual Message
December 6, 1860	Cong.	Senator Lazarus W. Powell, Kentucky (Democrat)
December 9, 1860	Kleg.	Governor Beriah Magoffin (Democrat)
December 12, 1860	Cong.	Representative John Cochrane, New York (Democrat)
December 12, 1860	Cong.	Representative Shelton F. Leake, Virginia (Independent Democrat)
December 12, 1860	Cong.	Representative Albert G. Jenkins, Virginia (Democrat)
December 12, 1860	Cong.	Representative Robert Mallory, Kentucky (Opposition Democrat)
December 12, 1860	Cong.	Representative William H. English, Indiana (Democrat)
December 12, 1860	Cong.	Representative John A. McClernand, Illinois (Democrat)
December 12, 1860	Cong.	Representative John W. Noell, Missouri (Democrat)
December 12, 1860	Cong.	Representative Thomas C. Hindman, Arkansas (Democrat)
December 12, 1860	Cong.	Representative Thomas A. R. Nelson, Tennessee (Opposition Party)
December 12, 1860	Cong.	Representative Miles Taylor, Louisiana (Democrat)
December 13, 1860	Cong.	Senator Andrew Johnson, Tennessee (Democrat)
December 17, 1860	Cong.	Representative Thomas B. Florence, Pennsylvania (Democrat)
December 17, 1860	Cong.	Representative John Cochrane, New York (Democrat)
December 17, 1860	Cong.	Representative Daniel E. Sickles, New York (Democrat)
December 18, 1860	Cong.	Senator John J. Crittenden, Kentucky (Whig/American–"Know Nothing"/Unionist)
December 22, 1860	Cong.	Senator Robert Toombs, Georgia (Democrat))
December 22, 1860	Cong.	Senator Jefferson Davis, Mississippi (Democrat)
December 24, 1860	Cong.	Senator Stephen A. Douglas, Illinois (Democrat)

December 24, 1860	Cong.	Senator William H. Seward, New York (Republican)
December 27, 1860	Cong.	Representative Thomas A. R. Nelson, Tennessee (Opposition Party)
December 28, 1860	Cong.	Senator William Bigler, Pennsylvania (Democrat)
December 28, 1860	Cong.	Representative Charles F. Adams, Massachusetts (Republican)
December 31, 1860	Cong.	Representative John S. Millson, Virginia (Democrat)
December 31, 1860	Cong.	Representative Henry W. Davis, Maryland (American Party)
December 31, 1860	Cong.	Representative Thomas Corwin, Ohio (Republican)
January 7, 1861	Cong.	Representative Emerson Etheridge, Tennessee (Opposition Party)
January 7, 1861	Tleg.	Governor Isham G. Harris (Democrat)
January 7, 1861	Vleg.	Governor John Letcher (Democrat)
January 10, 1861	ALSC	Alabama Minority Report from the Committee of Thirteen
January 11, 1861	Cong.	Senator Robert M. T. Hunter, Virginia (Democrat)
January 11, 1861	Cong.	House Special Committee of Thirty-Three
January 11, 1861	Tleg.	Representative George Gantt (Maury County)
January 14, 1861	Cong.	Senator William Bigler, Pennsylvania (Democrat)
January 14, 1861	Cong.	Senator Trusten Polk, Missouri (Democrat)
January 14, 1861	Cong.	Representative Thomas Birch Florence, Pennsylvania (Democrat)
January 14, 1861	Tleg.	Tennessee House of Representatives
January 18, 1861	GSC	Delegate Herschel Vespasian Johnson (Jefferson County) (Democrat)
January 19, 1861	Cong.	Representative Thomas B. Florence, Pennsylvania (Democrat)
January 22, 1861	Tleg.	Tennessee General Assembly
January 22, 1861	Tleg.	State Senator John W. Richardson (Rutherford and Williamson Counties) (Whig)
January 25, 1861	Kleg.	Senator Benjamin P. Cissell (Union County)
January 30, 1861	Cong.	Representative Edward J. Morris, Pennsylvania (Republican)
February 1, 1861	Cong.	Representative William Kellogg, Illinois (Republican)
February 7, 1861	Cong.	Representative Clement L. Vallandigham, Ohio (Democrat)
February 11, 1861	Cong.	Representative Orris S. Ferry, Connecticut (Republican)
February 15, 1861	WPC	Washington Peace Conference—Initial
February 15, 1861	WPC	James A. Seddon, Virginia (Democrat)

February 22, 1861	WPC	Delegate Reuben Hitchcock, Ohio
February 23, 1861	WPC	Delegate James A. Seddon, Virginia (Democrat)
February 26, 1861	Cong.	Representative William Kellogg, Illinois (Republican)
February 26, 1861	WPC	Delegate James A. Seddon, Virginia (Democrat)
February 26, 1861	WPC	Delegate James B. Clay, Kentucky (Democrat)
February 27, 1861	Cong.	Representative Sherrard Clemens, Virginia (Democrat)
February 27, 1861	Cong.	Representative Thomas Corwin, Ohio (Republican)
February 27, 1861	WPC	Washington Peace Conference—Final
February 28, 1861	Cong.	Senator James R. Doolittle, Wisconsin (Republican)
March 2, 1861	Cong.	Senator George E. Pugh, Ohio (Democrat)
March 9, 1861	VSC	Delegate Henry A. Wise (Princess Anne County) (Democrat)
March 11, 1861	ARSC	Delegate Hugh F. Thomason (Crawford County) (Unionist Democrat)
March 19, 1861	VSC	Committee on Federal Relations
March 26, 1861	VSC	Delegate Robert H. Turner (Warren County)
March 29, 1861	VSC	Delegate Henry A. Wise (Princess Anne County) (Democrat)
April 4, 1861	VSC	Delegate William L. Goggin (Bedford County) (Whig)
April 13, 1861	VSC	Amendments Approved by Virginia's Secession Convention

Key to Abbreviations

ALSC	Alabama Secession Convention
ARSC	Arkansas Secession Convention
Cong.	U.S. Congress
GSC	Georgia Secession Convention
Kleg.	Kentucky legislature
Tleg.	Tennessee legislature
Vleg.	Virginia legislature
VSC	Virginia Secession Convention
WPC	Washington Peace Conference

Glossary

Committee of Thirteen: The committee organized in the U.S. Senate in December 1860 to find a solution to the threatened secession of southern states.

Committee of Thirty-Three: The committee organized in the U.S. House of Representatives to find a solution to the threatened secession of southern states.

Confederate: Confederate (uppercase) generally refers to the Confederate States of America; confederate (lowercase) refers to being allied or united with others.

Fugitive Slave Law of 1850: Part of the Compromise of 1850 that placed fugitive slave cases under the exclusive jurisdiction of federal magistrates, allowed federal marshals to deputize bystanders to assist in the retention or capture of an alleged escaped slave, and provided a higher fee to justices if they agreed with the owner or slave catcher.

Mexican Cession: The present southwestern portion of the United States transferred from Mexico to the United States as a result of the 1848 Treaty of Guadalupe Hidalgo, which ended the war with Mexico. This area encompasses the present states of California, Arizona, Nevada, Utah, part of New Mexico, and part of Colorado.

Missouri Compromise of 1820: Under the terms of this agreement, Congress approved the admission of Maine into the Union as a non-slave state and of Missouri as a slave state. The law further provided that slavery would be prohibited in the remainder of the Louisiana Purchase north of 36° 30' north latitude, which is the southern border of Missouri.

Northwest Ordinance of 1787: In organizing the territory west of Pennsylvania and north of the Ohio River in 1787, Congress prohibited slavery with the language, "There shall be neither slavery nor involuntary servitude in the said territory otherwise than in the punishment of crimes, whereof the party shall have been duly convicted."

Posse comitatus: The authority by which law enforcement officials can temporarily deputize citizens to assist in keeping the peace or apprehending a criminal or fugitive.

Republican: Republican (uppercase) refers to the Republican Party; republican (lowercase) defines the nature of a republic in which ultimate power rests with the people who elect, directly or indirectly, representatives to carry out their will.

Secession Winter: A period generally defined as the months between Lincoln's election on November 6, 1860, and the bombardment of Fort Sumter on April 12–13, 1861.

Territorial Acquisitions: Following the American Revolution, the United States expanded its jurisdiction through the addition of lands held by other countries. These acquisitions included Louisiana (from France in 1803), Florida (from Spain in 1819), the Republic of Texas (which settlers there had wrested from Mexico in 1836), Oregon (from Great Britain in 1846), Mexican Cession (from Mexico in 1848), and Gadsden Purchase (from Mexico in 1853).

Territories: In 1860, the entire western portion of the present United States (with the exception of Oregon and California) was divided into territories. These included New Mexico, Utah, Washington, Nebraska, and Kansas. Congress organized the Dakota Territory on March 2, 1861; Oklahoma remained unorganized until 1890.

Wilmot Proviso: A resolution decreeing that if any land were acquired from Mexico as a result of the upcoming war, slavery would not be allowed there. Pennsylvania congressman David Wilmot proposed his dictum on August 8, 1846, as the U.S. House of Representatives debated an appropriation bill to fund negotiations with Mexico over conflicting land claims.

~

Bibliography

Selected Primary Sources

Alabama

Smith, William R., ed. *The History and Debates of the Convention of the People of Alabama, Begun and Held in the City of Montgomery, on the Seventh Day of January, 1861, in Which Is Preserved the Speeches of the Secret Sessions and Many Valuable State Papers.* Montgomery: White, Pfister, 1861.

Arkansas

Journal of Both Sessions of the Convention of the State of Arkansas, Which Was Begun and Held in the Capitol, in the City of Little Rock, on Monday. Little Rock: Johnson & Yerkes, State Printers, 1861.

Florida

Journal of the Proceedings of the Convention of the People of Florida, Begun and Held at the Capitol in the City of Tallahassee, on Thursday, January 3, A.D. 1861. Tallahassee: Office of the Floridian and Journal, 1861.

Georgia

Journal of the Public and Secret Proceedings of the Convention of the People of Georgia, Held in Milledgeville and Savannah in 1861. Together with the Ordinances Adopted. Milledgeville, Ga.: Boughton, Nisbet & Barnes, State Printers, 1861.

Kentucky

Journal of the Called Session of the House of Representatives of the Commonwealth of Kentucky, Begun and Held in the Town of Frankfort, on Thursday the Seventeenth Day of January, in the Year of Our Lord 1861, and of the Commonwealth the Sixty-Ninth. Frankfort: Printed at the Kentucky Yeoman Office, John B. Major, State Printer, 1861.

Journal of the Called Session of the Senate of the Commonwealth of Kentucky, Begun and Held in the Town of Frankfort, on Thursday the Seventeenth Day of January, in the Year of Our Lord 1861, and of the Commonwealth the Sixty-Ninth. Frankfort: Printed at the Kentucky Yeoman Office, John B. Major, State Printer, 1861.

Journal of the Called Session of the House of Representatives of the Commonwealth of Kentucky, Begun and Held in the Town of Frankfort, on Monday, the Sixth Day of May, in the Year of Our Lord 1861, and of the Commonwealth the Sixty-Ninth. Frankfort: Printed at the Kentucky Yeoman Office, John B. Major, State Printer, 1861.

Journal of the Called Session of the Senate of the Commonwealth of Kentucky, Begun and Held in the Town of Frankfort, on Monday, the Sixth Day of May, in the Year of Our Lord 1861, and of the Commonwealth the Sixty-Ninth. Frankfort: Printed at the Kentucky Yeoman Office, John B. Major, State Printer, 1861.

Report of the Kentucky Commissioners to the Late Peace Conference held in Washington City, Made to the Legislature of Kentucky. Frankfort: Printed at the Kentucky Yeoman Office, John B. Major, State Printer, 1861.

Louisiana

Official Journal of the Proceedings of the Convention of the State of Louisiana. New Orleans: J. O. Nixon, Printer to the State Convention, 1861.

Mississippi

Proceedings of the Mississippi State Convention, Held January 7th to 26th, A.D. 1861. Including the Ordinances, as Finally Adopted, Important Speeches, and a List of Members, Showing the Postoffice, Profession, Nativity, Politics, Age, Religious Preference, and Social Relations of Each. Jackson, Miss.: Power & Cadwallader, Book and Job Printers, 1861.

Missouri

Journal and Proceeding of the Missouri State Convention, Held at Jefferson City and St. Louis, March, 1861. St. Louis: George Knapp, Printers and Binders, 1861.

North Carolina

Journal of the Convention of the People of North Carolina Held on the 20th Day of May, A.D. 1861. Raleigh: Jno. W. Syme, Printer to the Convention, 1862.

South Carolina

Journal of the Convention of the People, South Carolina, Held in 1860-'61, Together with the Reports, Resolutions, Etc. Charleston: Evans & Cogswell, Printers to the Convention, 1861.

Tennessee

House Journal of the Extra Session of the Thirty-Third General Assembly of the State of Tennessee, Which Convened at Nashville, on the First Monday in January, A.D. 1861. Nashville: J. O. Griffith, Public Printers, 1861.

Senate Journal of the Extra Session of the Thirty-Third General Assembly of the State of Tennessee, Which Convened at Nashville, on the First Monday in January, A.D. 1861. Nashville: J. O. Griffith, Public Printers, 1861.

House Journal of the Second Extra Session of the Thirty-Third General Assembly of the State of Tennessee, Which Convened at Nashville on Thursday, the 25th Day of April, A.D. 1861. Nashville: J. O. Griffith, Public Printers, 1861.

Senate Journal of the Second Extra Session of the Thirty-Third General Assembly of the State of Tennessee, Which Convened at Nashville on Thursday, the 25th of April, A.D. 1861. Nashville: J. O. Griffith, Public Printers, 1861.

White, Robert H. *Messages of the Governors of Tennessee, 1857–1869.* Nashville: Tennessee Historical Commission, 1959.

Texas

Winkler, William. *Journal of the Secession Convention of Texas, 1861.* Austin: Austin Printing, 1912.

U.S. Congress

Congressional Globe, 36th Cong., 2nd sess., December 1860–March 1861. http://memory.loc.gov/ammem/amlaw/lwcglink.html#anchor36.

Virginia

Reese, George H., ed. *Proceedings of the Virginia State Convention of 1861: February 13–May 1.* 4 vols. 1861; Richmond: Virginia State Library, 1965.

Washington Peace Conference

Chittenden, L. E. *A Report of the Debates and Proceedings in the Secret Sessions of the Conference Convention, for Proposing Amendments to the Constitution of the United States, Held at Washington, D.C., in February, A.D. 1861.* New York: D. Appleton, 1864.

Selected Secondary Sources

Ayers, Edward L. *What Caused the Civil War? Reflections on the South and Southern History.* New York: W. W. Norton, 2005.

Bowman, Davis. *At the Precipice: Americans North and South during the Secession Crisis.* Chapel Hill: University of North Carolina Press, 2010.

Cook, Robert J., William L. Barney, and Elizabeth R. Varon. *Secession Winter: When the Union Fell Apart.* Baltimore: Johns Hopkins University Press, 2013.

Cooper, William J. *We Have the War upon Us: The Onset of the Civil War, November 1860–April 1861.* New York: Vintage Books, 2012.

Crofts, Daniel W. *Lincoln and the Politics of Slavery: The Other Thirteenth Amendment and the Struggle to Save the Union.* Chapel Hill: University of North Carolina Press, 2016.

———. *Reluctant Confederates: Upper South Unionists in the Secession Crisis.* Chapel Hill: University of North Carolina Press, 1989.

Daly, John Patrick. *When Slavery Was Called Freedom: Evangelicalism, Proslavery, and the Causes of the Civil War.* Lexington: University Press of Kentucky, 2002.

Davis, William C. *"A Government of Our Own": The Making of the Confederacy.* Baton Rouge: Louisiana State University Press, 1994.

Dew, Charles B. *Apostles of Disunion: Southern Secession Commissioners and the Causes of the Civil War.* Charlottesville: University Press of Virginia, 2001.

Fehrenbacher, Don E. *The Slaveholding Republic: An Account of the United States Government's Relations to Slavery.* New York: Oxford University Press, 2001.

Freehling, William W. *The Road to Disunion: Secessionists Triumphant.* Vol. 2. New York: Oxford University Press, 2007.

Holt, Michael F. *The Fate of the Country: Politicians, Slavery Extension, and the Coming of the Civil War.* New York: Hill and Wang, 2004.

Holzer, Harold. *Lincoln at Cooper Union: The Speech That Made Abraham Lincoln President.* New York: Simon & Schuster, 2004.

Huston, James L. *Calculating the Value of the Union: Slavery, Property Rights, and the Economic Origins of the Civil War.* Chapel Hill: University of North Carolina Press, 2003.

Karp, Matthew. *This Vast Southern Empire: Slaveholders at the Helm of American Foreign Policy.* Cambridge: Harvard University Press, 2016.

Lankford, Nelson D. *Cry Havoc! The Crooked Road to Civil War, 1861.* New York: Viking, 2007.

Lee, Charles Robert, Jr. *The Confederate Constitutions*. Chapel Hill: University of North Carolina Press, 1963.

May, Robert E. *The Southern Dream of a Caribbean Empire, 1854–1861*. 1973; Gainesville: University Press of Florida, 2002.

McClintock, Russell. *Lincoln and the Decision for War: The Northern Response to Secession*. Chapel Hill: University of North Carolina Press, 2008.

Potter, David M. *Lincoln and His Party in the Secession Crisis*. 1942; Baton Rouge: Louisiana State University Press, 1995.

Richards, Leonard L. *The California Gold Rush and the Coming of the Civil War*. New York: Knopf, 2007.

Simon, James F. *Lincoln and Chief Justice Taney: Slavery, Secession, and the President's War Powers*. New York: Simon & Schuster, 2006.

Sinha, Manisha. *The Slave's Cause: A History of Abolition*. New Haven: Yale University Press, 2016.

Smith, Timothy B. *The Mississippi Secession Convention: Delegates and Deliberations in Politics and War, 1861–1865*. Jackson: University Press of Mississippi, 2014.

Stegmaier, Mark J., ed. *Henry Adams in the Secession Crisis: Dispatches to the Boston Daily Advertiser, December 1860–March 1861*. Baton Rouge: Louisiana State University Press, 2012.

———. *Texas, New Mexico, and the Compromise of 1850: Boundary Dispute and Sectional Crisis*. Kent: Kent State University Press, 1996.

Varon, Elizabeth R. *Disunion: The Coming of the American Civil War, 1789–1859*. Chapel Hill: University of North Carolina Press, 2008.

Wakelyn, Jon L., ed. *Southern Pamphlets on Secession, November 1860–April 1861*. Chapel Hill: University of North Carolina Press, 1996.

Waugh, John C. *On the Brink of Civil War: The Compromise of 1850 and How It Changed the Course of American History*. Wilmington, Del.: SR Books, 2003.

Questions for Discussion

1. In considering James Buchanan's address to Congress, how might a Republican respond? A Southern Democrat? How do his comments reflect his pro-southern position?

2. Senator John J. Crittenden's proposal to divide the western territories at the 36° 30' parallel by continuing the Missouri Compromise to California seems like a reasonable solution. In accepting it, what would Northerners have given up? Southerners? How would either response have considered the *Dred Scott* decision?

3. If Congress had approved Crittenden's proposed amendment, which side would have conceded more—Northerners or Southerners?

4. South Carolina's Declaration of Secession specifically lists grievances the slave states have suffered. What were those grievances, and who was responsible for inflicting them on the South?

5. Considering all four declarations of secession, do they make a persuasive case for secession? Why or why not?

6. What are the similarities and differences between the Committee of Thirty-Three's minority report number two and the four declarations of secession?

7. Which of the two minority reports do you find more compelling? Why?

8. If the suggested amendments to the U.S. Constitution represent the solution to the problems facing the nation in 1860–1861, how would you characterize those problems?

9. What patterns can you identify that run through the proposed amendments?

10. James Buchanan was president of the United States when Owen Lovejoy, John Barret, and Louis T. Wigfall delivered their speeches. With which of the three would he have most agreed? Why?

11. Can you imagine Lovejoy, Barret, and Wigfall spending a social evening together? What commonalities in opinion might they have found? Do you think that they could have agreed on a compromise amendment? Why or why not?

12. If you were alive in 1861, would you have agreed more with Lovejoy, Barret, or Wigfall? Why?

13. Considering all the primary sources, what evidence exists that preserving white supremacy was a major factor in the South's need to secede?

Index

De Bow, James D. B., 32
De Bow's Review, 20, 22
  and *Lemmon v. The People*, 32, 34
Declaration of Independence, 42
  equality clause, 301–304, 324–326
  just powers clause, 71, 94–96, 279
declarations of secession, xviii, 93–113
  Georgia, 4, 24, 35, 93, 101–109
  Mississippi, 2, 24, 93, 99–101
  Texas, 4, 24, 93, 109–113
Delaware, xiv, 41, 95, 136, 160, 199,
  213, 229
Democratic Party, 22, 29, 317
  and election of 1860, 36–40, 51
  and Fugitive Slave Law, 39
  and secession, 321
  and slavery, 45
District of Columbia, 25, 39, 47, 116,
  232
  abolition of slavery in, 20, 58, 79,
  206, 308, 311
  slavery in, 44–45, 115
  slave trade in, xv, 146
Doolittle, James Rood, 332
  proposed amendment, 254–255
Douglas, Stephen, 30, 33, 37, 43,
  48–49, 162, 323, 334
  proposed amendment, 180–183
Dred Scott, 26, 30, 298
Dred Scott v. Sandford (1857), xi–xii,
  xiv, 25–33, 35, 37, 41, 58, 106,
  210, 311
Duell, Rodolphus Holland, 45
Dunn, W. McKee, 118, 284

Edward, Prince of Wales James Francis,
  326
election of 1852, 106
election of 1856, 106, 322
election of 1860, 28, 36–40, 56–57,
  106, 123, 288
  as constitutional crisis, 5–6
  as declaration of war, 50

results of, 59, 64, 199, 210, 260, 311
  and western territories, 36–38, 56
Emancipation Proclamation, 278
Emerson, John, 26
Emerson, Ralph Waldo, 15
Emory, William Hemsley, 131
Endor
  witch of, 287
England, 122, 292
English, William H., 46
  proposed amendment, 168–169
equality of the races, 100, 259, 321
  and Declaration of Independence,
  326
equality proclaimed by Republicans,
  106, 111–112, 261, 289, 300–
  304, 335
Etheridge, Emerson
  proposed amendment, 191–192

Fehrenbacher, Don E., xi, 19
Ferry, Orris, 53, 122
  proposed amendment, 231
Fifth Amendment. *See under*
  Constitution, U.S.
Fillmore, Millard, 21, 77
Finkelman, Paul, 52
Fitzpatrick, Benjamin, 87
Florence, Thomas Birch
  proposed amendments, 175–176,
  208–209, 215–217
Florida, 84, 199, 213, 229, 308, 316
  secession convention of, 41
  secession of, 41, 123, 135
  territory of, 84, 344
Fort Sumter, xii–xiii, xvii–xviii, 3, 9, 12,
  161, 275
Fort Yuma, 131
Foster, Lafayette Sabine, 327
Fourteenth Amendment. *See under*
  Constitution, U.S.
France, 100, 105, 152, 292
Franklin, Benjamin, 316n33